Organizing the Landscape

Organizing the Landscape

Geographical Perspectives on Labor Unionism

Andrew Herod, editor
Foreword by Richard A. Walker

University of Minnesota Press
Minneapolis
London

MINNESOTA

Photograph on title page and on cover of paperback edition courtesy of Southern Labor Archives, Special Collections Department, Pullen Library, Georgia State University.

Lyrics in chapter 6 from the *Local 34 Songbook* (1984) are reprinted by permission of Local 34, Federation of University Employees, Hotel Employees and Restaurant Employees International Union.

Published by the University of Minnesota Press
111 Third Avenue South, Suite 290
Minneapolis, MN 55401-2520
http://www.upress.umn.edu

Library of Congress Cataloging-in-Publication Data
Organizing the landscape : geographical perspectives on labor unionism /
    Andrew Herod, editor ; foreword by Richard A. Walker.
        p.   cm.
    Includes index.
    ISBN 0-8166-2970-6 (hbk. : alk. paper) — ISBN 0-8166-2971-4
(pbk. : alk. paper)
    1. Trade-unions.   2. Trade-unions — Organizing.   3. International
labor activities.   I. Herod, Andrew, 1964 –   .
    HD6483.075   1998
    331.88 — dc21   98-10856

10 09 08 07 06 05 04 03 02 01 00 99 98   10 9 8 7 6 5 4 3 2 1

For David Henry "Dai" Davies, who, through his life's work, first interested me in the labor movement and its possibilities.

Contents

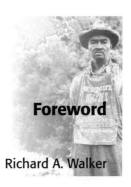

Foreword

Richard A. Walker

It is a propitious time for a revival of labor studies, now that there are signs of life in the labor movement after twenty or more years of steady decline. It has been a long, cold winter for workers in Europe and the Americas, after the triumphs of Thatcher, Reagan, and the neoliberals. Unionization has declined, real wages have fallen, overwork has increased, and benefits have been taken away. The poor and marginal workers have felt the sharp blade of welfare reform and government cuts on their necks, all the better to discipline the employed and the young to the necessity of wage labor under any and all circumstances. Now, at least, there is a changing of the guard at the head of the American Federation of Labor and Congress of Industrial Organizations (AFL–CIO) accompanied by a recommitment to organizing workers instead of the same internal politics of office holding and providing basic services in the face of dwindling numbers of aging members. In France, the public-sector workers pulled off an immensely successful general strike in 1995 in the face of austerity measures being implemented by the Chirac administration, and brought about the eventual fall of the prime minister. In Britain, the Tories were finally ushered out in disgrace and New Labour was given an overwhelming mandate in 1997. The ice has broken, at least, but whether Tony Blair is the sun who brings a new spring or, like Bill Clinton, the one who puts a happy face on the dark star of neoliberalism remains to be seen.

All the same, we are witnessing a revival of interest among academics in questions of labor and unionization, making this collection of essays by young geographers most timely. Some of the best minds of the generation just making its reputation are represented in the new labor geography. This group includes several of the authors in this book, among them Andrew Herod, Jane Wills, Brian Page, and Don Mitchell, as well as others such as Jamie Peck, Matt Sparke, and Melissa Wright. It bears watching what impact the new generation of labor-friendly scholars will have on labor studies generally, and on geography in particular, but they are moving things in the right direction. I would like to paint in broad strokes what I think ought to be the challenge for labor studies, and for political economy generally.

Twenty years ago, in the wake of the political upheavals and labor struggles of the 1960s, two of the hottest topics on the academic agenda were labor process studies in the vein of Harry Braverman's monumental *Labor and Monopoly Capital* (one thinks of the work of Michael Burawoy, Harley Shaiken, or Huw Beynon) and working-class history of the kind pioneered by E. P. Thompson in his *Making of the English Working Class* (in the United States it was Herbert Gutman and David Montgomery who led the charge of the New Left labor historians). By the late 1970s, a great volume of works had appeared on everything from the de-skilling of office workers to the traditions of working-class solidarity in New England mill towns. Both streams of research flowed from the great wellspring of Marxian thought then enjoying tremendous popularity in the English-speaking countries, but they represented separate currents separated by hidden shoals in the ideological bedrock of political economy. Labor process studies took to its logical extreme the classical laborist belief in the "point of production" as the key to all questions of work, exploitation, and organization. This was in stark opposition to Thompson's distanced stance to the mechanics of capitalist industry and close attention to the lived experience of the working class as a whole, and with proletarianization as a cultural construction as much as an iron law of capital accumulation. In more ways than one, Thompson was the English godfather to postmodernism and poststructuralism — whatever Parisian parentage they might claim.

Both lines of labor studies fell into disfavor during the 1980s. The initial cause was the disruption of everything solidly believed in by the Left for most of the twentieth century. The irony was that this occurred well *before* the collapse of communism in the Soviet bloc. Capitalism suddenly and unceremoniously revolutionized the whole landscape of industrial production, rendering obsolete any number of articles of faith about the course of mechanization, de-skilling, corporate concentration, and the nature of work, not to mention the location of industry. British industry, the English working class, and the Labour Party all collapsed together, to be fallen upon by the Thatcherite wolves. The manfacturing belt of the United States and the greatest corporate names in American industry were hollowed out, along with the old CIO unions and the liberal wing of the Democratic Party; in walked the terror squads of Reaganism to dispense with the old rules and regulations, standards of living, and ways of life in labor's strongholds.

Following this, studies of industry suddenly shifted out of the workplace and into the landscape. The spatial analysis of industry and work became all the

Richard A. Walker

rage. This was not the old calculus of optimal locations fostered by neoclassical economics and the writings of Alfred Weber, but a revived program of research into the development of major industrial sectors (especially high tech) and the fate of regions (both growing and collapsing), following the lead of Doreen Massey and Richard Meegan in England and Bennett Harrison and Barry Bluestone in the United States. The New Economic Geography was born, and a bright and eager generation of young scholars, many of them fired by Marxist ideas, leaped into the fray. They (I mean "we," for this was my cohort) were fired with the radical idea that capitalism was not so orderly and predictable as it had seemed in the postwar (or high Fordist) era, and that it had shed its old skin for a new one of many colors: flexible specialization, just-in-time production, new industrial spaces, and the like. The tired fields of industrial location and regional development were wholly made over by the end of the decade, with geographers marching arm in arm with political scientists, sociologists, and a few odd economists.

The New Economic Geography went down three tracks. The central one was rethinking the logic of organizational and technical change, with the recognition that there is a greater variety of forms or pathways than had previously been deemed possible. There was no single labor process to be mechanized and de-skilled, but complex bundles of work and work sites to be orchestrated in the immense social division of labor. Nor was there a single pattern of corporate concentration and spatial decentralization in the manner of product cycle theory, a legacy of late Fordism contradicted by the vibrancy of new industrial districts from central Italy to California and Japan. The key authors of this altered geography of industrialization were people such as Allen Scott, Michael Storper, Annalee Saxenian, Richard Florida, and Andrew Sayer (with a little help from yours truly). Their research gave new life to the idea of uneven development, and a lay of the land far less flattened than that generated by product cycle or less cost location models.

A second track pursued by economic geographers was the study of finance and capital. David Harvey's *Limits to Capital* set the tone for the decade, but it was left to younger researchers who experienced the financial explosion of the 1980s to try to get their arms around its ferocious dynamism and reconfigured landscapes of international money flows. Geographers such as Barney Warf, Nigel Thrift, Andrew Leyshon, Susan Roberts, and Ron Martin laid out the new currents of finance, excesses of speculative fever, and global capital flows for all to see. Plunging even deeper beneath the froth of globalization were the studies of profit rates, investment cycles, and uneven development by Michael Webber, David Rigby, and Meric Gertler. Although it might seem that the circuits of money would reveal the purest form of capitalism and make for a uniformitarian landscape of globalization — as many were predicting — it did nothing of the kind. Finance proved to have its own geography and its own (il)logic that was not only *not* the highest form of industrial capital but often at odds with it. Here again, uneven development and the variable topography of capitalism were revealed in a new light.

Third, economic geographers took up the question of business culture, or the resocialization of economics. Although many students think the idea of embeddedness sprang full-blown from the brow of sociologist Mark Granovetter, the social economy of capitalism is as plain as day in the operations of industrial districts regulated by local social conventions, international joint ventures in high tech requiring the stabilizing power of mutual trust, and the national economic institutions of Japan, the United States, or Germany. It even shows up in the oddities of financial operations in the City of London, consumer culture in Los Angeles, or managerial behavior in American boardrooms. Capitalism comes clad in a patchwork quilt of possible worlds, the understanding of which has been pursued by geographers such as Linda McDowell, Jane Jacobs, Susan Christopherson, and Erica Schoenberger, among others. Here, more than anywhere, rather than the mechanical unfolding of time in a uniform global economy, it is the peculiarities of place in a heterogeneous capitalism that are starkly revealed.

This last dimension of the New Economic Geography begins to shade off into cultural studies and social anthropology more than political economy in the traditional sense. But if economics no longer makes sense, whether neoclassical or Marxian, and if capitalism is not a thing but a heteroglossy, then what is left for economic geographers to do? And if all the attention is to be given to the brilliant organizational strategies of the new capitalism, the competitive advantage of the Japanese, or the financial wizardry of Wall Street (and hardly a crumb to labor studies or labor geography), then what is left of a Left in economics or geography? The sad answer is, not much. Even though the arenas of research just indicated carry on to this day, with some absolutely stunning intellectual achievements, the Young Turks who once entered the field are now middle-aged and the sense of discovery and adventure is gone. Meanwhile, insurgents in the discipline have moved on to greener pastures. In the 1990s, they moved out of political economy and into cultural studies in droves, both within geography and throughout the social sciences. (True, a good many of the best minds in geography and elsewhere went into environmental studies and political ecology, as well, but I do not believe that this undermined political economy, which suffered chiefly from its own internal contradictions.)

Culture studies quite simply stole the thunder from the Left and captured the young and rebellious because it spoke to the hot-button topics of difference, repression, power, and social change, while the economic geographers appeared to be in bed with business for the sake of a few good interviews and in chairs with the universities for a few secure jobs. Now, I do not say that the young are always fair in their judgment of their elders or aware of their own history, but they did have a point. The fire had gone out of economic geography and, along with it, Marxist theory. There really was not anything obviously radical — however insightful — about most of the work on industrial organization or finance capital, and the standard Marxist tropes did not seem to work very well in light of all that had been discovered about the discontinuities of capitalism.

In the meantime, the torch of radicalism passed to the radical feminists (who broke with the grand old men of the Left), the poststructuralists (followers of Michel Foucault and the bodily geometries of the oppressed), the postmodernists (adherents of Jacques Derrida, Jean-François Lyotard, and the purveyors of discourse theory), and the postcolonialists (in the manner of Homi Bhabha, Gayatri Spivak, and other critics of Eurocentric histories of the world). I have to admit that I have not been a great advocate of this form of inquiry, no doubt because of a certain pique incurred by youthful critics who blithely set up Marxist straw men (and I mean men) to shoot at instead of aiming to the Right; they have often seemed as absentminded about history as the rest of Americans (including the history of modern revolts preceding their own). But I am also disinclined to return the favor by selecting out the worst of PoMo foolishness for derision, in the manner of Alan Sokal's 1996 send-up of *Social Text*. Of course, it is absurd to act as if discourse were the nub of human action and power, and to strike heroic literary postures instead of actually doing something oppositional inside or outside the academy. But there is nothing wrong, and a great deal right, about shining some much overdue light on the dark domains of patriarchy, racism, homophobia, Eurocentrism, and the lot. That is the point, regardless of how it is dressed up in fancy neologisms.

Nevertheless, post-Marxist thinking, in its various guises, is also in many ways *less* radical than it seems because it establishes so tenuous a link to economic realities and the immense range of power granted to economic ruling classes. Class and political economy still matter more than any other single dimension of social power, in my view. This is not to say, with the fashionable critics of "political correctness" of the Right and the Left, that the one true line of oppression runs through class and all the rest is a diversion. This is patently wrong. This argument rests on an antiquated notion of the genuine working class or the honest poor, which is a labor romanticism at best and patronizing in the extreme. Moreover, it is blind to the makeup of the working class today. The workers of the world are now overwhelmingly women, people of color, and Third Worlders — even in the heartlands of Europe and North America.

Here is where the new wave of labor studies enters the scene, in geography and throughout the social sciences. It must begin from the standpoint of the new global working class, which in its great variety of peoples and backgrounds overturns many conventional suppositions from the outset. Equally must it build on the intellectual advances made in the study of capitalism over the past two decades. But it must get back to being political economy; that is, it must take the logic of capitalist economies and the force of class as essential premises. This does not abolish issues of difference, consciousness, or institutions — quite the contrary. Race, gender, nationality, and other social divides must be figured into the mix of how power is exercised and how classes are constituted — from the bottom up. But it does ground questions of difference in how the vectors of power bear on employment, work, and industry. The presumption still remains that for the great mass of the world's people work is the central fact of existence, and that the largest and most transformative system of working is that which is knit together by markets and operates under the rules of capitalism. We have not seen the "end of work" or the "end of capitalism" by a long shot. Nonetheless, if we are to steal back the thunder of the postmodernists and multicultural social critics, it is not enough to shout them down with slogans to the effect that "economics matters" but to show how the politics of power in all its facets matters to economics — to explain organization forms, capital–labor struggles, corporate success and failure, and the rise and fall of places.

What we need, in particular, is a political economy of place. Such a geographically informed study of labor and work would go beyond business organization, beyond business culture, and beyond strikes and unions. It would mean the study of the social relations of production in the classic sense of the exercise of control by the owning class and the extraction of surplus labor from the working class. But close attention would have to be paid to the influence of space and place: that economies and social relations exist in real locations bordered by other locales, but also tied to distant places by immensely complex lines of trade, ownership, investment, migration, and the rest. Thus, geographic inquiry must be telescopic, able to move up and down the scale of places — looking now at the small arena of the local and then at the scale of nations and continents, and finally at the global economy as a whole. There is no simple answer to the question of which scale is most important, whether in thought or in action. Globalism is as real as the persistence of localism, but when and where and how it matters is for us to puzzle out, not assume.

Political economy must never lose its connection to labor at the point of production, but it should also take in the larger systems of production at work today, extensive divisions of labor that embrace many workplaces, often many different

Richard A. Walker

firms linked up in coordinated networks, and many different sites often scattered across national borders and around the globe. It must recognize the divergent histories and trajectories of cities, regions, and countries, which cannot be reduced to a single logic of capital (even though that logic is at work as part of their historical development). This diversity of capitalisms across the earth has been noted by many scholars, but too often is reduced to a set of analytical boxes (as in Michael Porter) or some measure of associational life (as in Robert Putnam) in which a place either has the right stuff for competitiveness and further development or it does not. This is thin gruel indeed.

What is wanted, rather, is the study of the political history of production and economy, or the struggles, losses, and victories by which a ruling class gains power, holds on to it, and applies it for economic purposes, and the ways in which labor (and peasants, families, and so forth) have responded, survived, fought back, been divided to be conquered, or gained a measure of strength and autonomy. A term for this might be "political culture of place," but in a way that goes beyond a political scientist's notion of formal politics to the political economist's and geographer's sense of social and cultural context — and always with the question in mind, How, at the end of the day, were the conditions of labor and industry altered by events, and what did this mean for further capitalist investment, innovation, extraction of surplus, and growth?

The writers collected in this volume demonstrate the kind of serious attention to the geography of labor that is needed today and, along with it, an awareness of the historic impact of workers' actions on the course of capitalist development across a wide range of places. With this book, and others to follow, one can hope for a revivified radical geography and political economy of place. And that just might help make a difference in the struggles of working people for a better life in a hard world of hard work.

Foreword

Acknowledgments

This book arises out of a number of sessions on the geography of labor union-ism that I organized for the 1995 Chicago meeting of the Association of Amer-ican Geographers and all of the papers included (with the exception of that by Robert Hanham and Shawn Banasick) were first presented in Chicago. I would like to thank everyone who participated in these sessions, including those authors whose work appears in this volume, together with Dick Walker, Erica Schoen-berger, Ann Oberhauser, Rebecca Johns, Tod Rutherford, John Holmes, Sean Di-Giovanna, Alan Paul, Ray Baruffalo, Kevin Cox, and Neil Smith. I would also like to thank two anonymous reviewers for comments on the overall project, and the contributors for producing work on time (most of the time!) and for the quality of what they produced, all of which made my job as editor that much easier. Thanks must go also to the University of Minnesota Press, particularly Carrie Mullen, Jeff Moen, Laura Westlund, David Thorstad, Daniel Leary, Kath-ryn Grimes, Amy Unger, and Robin Moir for their interest in this project and their sterling work in bringing it to fruition, and to Peter Roberts, archivist at the Southern Labor Archives, Special Collections Department, Pullen Library, Georgia State University. I would also like to acknowledge financial support from the Department of Geography, University of Georgia. Last, but by no means least, I would like to thank Jennifer for her patience.

A.H.

The Spatiality of Labor Unionism:
A Review Essay

Andrew Herod

Social life is fundamentally spatial. Social actors, whether individuals, governments, corporations, environmental groups, or, indeed, labor unions, must operate within economic, political, and cultural landscapes that may either constrain or enable their actions. In the case of labor unions and their members, the operation of labor markets, the gender and racial makeup of the workforce, wage rates, working conditions, and labor laws can all vary geographically in quite significant ways, a geographic variation that presents both problems and opportunities to unions seeking to organize workers. If we consider just one example, that of creating national collective bargaining agreements (called "master contracts" in the U.S. context) designed to take certain conditions of work and wages out of competition (long a central objective of unions), we see that such political goals may require negotiators to address dramatic regional and local differences in work practices, wage rates, costs of living, unemployment rates, and a whole host of other social phenomena (see Herod 1997d for an example). Whatever else they may be, national agreements are, in fact, an explicit recognition on the part of unions that employers may use variations in conditions across the economic landscape as a source of economic and political power to whipsaw workers in different places against each other. Consequently, developing national agreements can be one way for unions to confront capital's (geographic) power.[1] Yet unions' abilities to develop just such national agreements are also conditioned by these very variabilities in the unevenly developed geography of capitalism. Whereas a union may be able to force recalcitrant employers in low unemployment regions to accept the conditions of a nationally negotiated pay raise because such employers face a tight labor market, in areas of higher unemployment local employers may have more political and economic space to resist such pressure. To be successful, then, such master contracts must negotiate the myriad geographical variations existing in the economic landscape to which they are applied. They are as much *geographical* agreements as political ones, and a union might attempt to pursue any one of a number of geographical solutions to address regional or

1

local variations in conditions, including taking a spatial average of conditions across an industry as a compromise basis for a national agreement, taking the best conditions available at one particular location and seeking to impose them in a geographically uniform fashion throughout the industry, developing a minimum floor around the worst conditions in the industry and ensuring that the rest of the industry does not sink below them, or a combination of these strategies.

If social life is fundamentally spatial, so too are social relations and identities constituted geographically. What it means to be a worker or a trade unionist varies both historically *and* geographically. Whether workers have grown up in Santiago or Soweto, Prague or Paris, Toledo, Ohio, or Toledo, Spain, Merthyr Tydfil or Miami, New York or New Delhi makes a difference to how they constitute themselves as social, political, and geographical actors. Hence, the development of particular cultures of work and political action in certain places may provide crucial social resources on which workers can draw in times of need (e.g., in regions known for their traditions of labor radicalism) or serve as an impediment to be overcome (as in the case when workers try to organize in regions known for their long history of antiunionism). Equally, understanding how the culture of those places was shaped may also require examining their historical and geographical links to other locations (e.g., is this a boomtown that has seen recent arrivals bringing with them ideas from elsewhere, or is it a physically isolated location with few cultural or economic links to other locations?). Likewise, workers may show great allegiance to particular places in ways that cut across class lines and throw into question aspatial understandings of class politics (cf. Hudson and Sadler 1986; Castells 1983; Herod 1991a, 1994; Martin, Sunley, and Wills 1994d).

Only by understanding how workers have certain feelings or a "sense of place" regarding their own communities, or perhaps feel spatially trapped and unable to follow the migration of work beyond the boundaries of their own localities, is it possible to understand why they often act in ways that aspatial class analyses cannot predict. For example, because they see the continued economic vitality of their own plant or community as vital to their own ability to reproduce themselves socially in situ on a daily or generational basis, locationally constrained workers may side with boosterist local capital and offer contract concessions to encourage investment in their own communities at the expense of developing alliances with other workers located elsewhere that challenge established class relations or the whipsawing activities of capital. In such cases, geographic loyalties and allegiances often seem more important than do those of class. Although it is easy to dismiss such instances and the formation of local cross-class alliances as merely bad cases of "false consciousness" on the part of workers, this is not

2

only intellectually dishonest in that it merely brushes away real-world situations that do not fit preexisting theoretical arguments, but also politically questionable, for it suggests that working-class people are too ignorant to recognize their "true" interests at particular historical moments in particular places. Indeed, by recognizing the geographical realities that workers face in particular locations it becomes possible to theorize how local class relations are spatially constituted and worked out, and thereby to explain (rather than to explain away) such activities by workers.

Despite the clearly geographical nature of social life, such spatial sensitivities have, at least until fairly recently, been neglected in the social sciences, which have historically tended instead to focus on the temporal aspects of society and everyday life — for instance, in considering how cities and regions change *over time*, how class or gender relations vary *historically*, or how profit rates and business cycles oscillate *temporally*. Ed Soja has suggested that, in fact, a definite antigeographical trend has run through much Western social theory and theorizing about society since the nineteenth century. He argues (1989, 10–11):

> So unbudgeably hegemonic has been this historicism of theoretical consciousness that it has tended to occlude a comparable critical sensibility to the spatiality of social life, a practical theoretical consciousness that sees the lifeworld of being creatively located not only in the making of history but also in the construction of human geographies, the social production of space and the restless formation and reformation of geographical landscapes.

Such historicism has been both intellectually foreshortening and politically paralyzing, for it has resulted in a blindness to the ways in which workers' lives are geographically situated and embedded, and how such spatial situatedness and embeddedness shapes the possibilities for their social action, both over time and in space.

By taking seriously the argument that "social being [is] actively emplaced in [both] space *and* time in an explicitly historical *and* geographical contextualization" (Soja 1989, 11; emphasis in original), the essays in this book are an effort to flesh out just such a critical sensibility to space and spatiality as it impacts and relates to labor unions. They show, among other things, how unions and workers have come to terms with geographic variations in wages and working conditions, how unions have developed spatial strategies and operated with distinct geostrategic goals and ambitions in mind, how they have shaped the geography of labor markets, how they have used geographic mobility as a subversive tool, how their activities have shaped the geography of capital itself, and how they have

3

created particular economic geographies in the social landscape as an integral part of their political praxis and exercise of power.

Geographers, of course, have long argued the importance of geography. In doing so, often they have either tended toward a simplistic justification of the need for a geographic perspective ("geography is important because everywhere is unique") in which geography as a discipline is reduced to the theoretically retarded pursuit of cataloging differences between places, or they have adopted a restrictive and conservative view of space, a view that owes much to the Kantian tradition out of which the modern discipline of geography emerged (cf. Smith 1989) and that has tended to portray space as an ontologically prior stage on which social relations are merely played out, rather than as a social construction whose active molding and manipulation are a fundamental source of power. As a result of such a narrow view, geographers have often failed to see the political content in the ways in which social actors organize their spatial relations and, consequently, the cultural, political, and economic landscape. This has been particularly so with regard to the geographic treatment of working-class people and their institutions, for geographers traditionally have paid scant attention to labor unions and their activities. With few exceptions (some of which are discussed in this book), geographers have overwhelmingly conceived of labor as little more than a locational factor in their explanations of the geography of industrial landscapes. This conception has its own roots in the Weberian locational analysis tradition on which much modern economic geography has been based, a tradition that principally examines the question of the location of economic activities from the explicit viewpoint of how industrialists (read: capitalists) make investment decisions with the goal of minimizing overall production costs and maximizing profits (Weber 1929; see Massey 1973 and Herod 1997b for critiques). By and large, geographers have not seen workers and unions as active geographical agents.

Historians, on the other hand, while paying much greater attention to various aspects of working-class life, have tended to assume that the key questions to be answered involve issues of social transformation over *time*. Certainly, several have been more sensitive than most to the geographical imagination. Shorter and Tilly's (1974) analysis of the geography of strikes in France, for example, analyzed territorial differences in strike activity at the level of France's *départements*. Fox (1971) argued for a geographical perspective to understanding patterns of historical development in France and the development of two essentially separate societies (conservative, peasant France and more radical, cosmopolitan, urban France) within one state. And Genovese and Hochberg's (1989) edited collection sought to examine a number of historical questions — the historical geography of a Puritan artisan's life, transport and the geography of capitalism, the decline of Spain as an imperial power, early social formation in the Mediterranean, the development of the European state system since 1500, and others—from a specifically geographical perspective. Some social and labor historians have also shown a growing interest concerning issues that involve key geographic concepts such as the spatial scale at which labor relations are conducted—as in debates over the spatial decentralization of industrial relations in the 1980s and 1990s and the abandonment in several countries of national systems of collective bargaining for those that are more locally oriented and constituted (see Katz 1993 for more on this debate). Even in such debates, however, which are at heart concerned with spatial issues, there is rarely much consideration of how workers actively mold and shape spatial relations and landscapes as an *integral* part of their political praxis and as a source of political power. Instead, it is assumed that the primary focus of interest is the *social* action that plays out on a preexisting, already-formed landscape that simply provides the setting for such action. In such a formulation, space is merely the container for social life and struggles. One gets little sense that the active process of making landscapes themselves is a fundamental part or outcome of this very social action, or that the spatiality of social life and the spatial organization of society are actively struggled over.

Although geographers and labor historians have frequently had little to say to each other, since the mid-1980s a growing interest has been paid by some geographers to the spatiality of labor unionism, its geographical context and constitution, and the ways in which unions and workers actively mold landscapes. Within geography, a number of issues have dominated this research, including how unions are organized spatially; how the geography of state regulation affects the geography of labor unionism; how unions have helped shape the economic geography of capitalism (both indirectly as capital has sought to avoid regions of high unionization and militancy, and directly as unions have struggled over the geography of work and capital investment); how new geographical relationships between work, home, and community are forcing unions to adopt new models of organizing with very different spatial assumptions than they have traditionally relied on; how unions have reorganized the spatial scale at which they operate as a means of addressing geographic variations in the economic or political conditions they confront; and how local cultural practices and contexts, including workers' "senses of place," have structured their activities and often led them to adopt political strategies that show greater allegiance to particular localities than to class. Implicit in this research is the acceptance that the manipulation of space by workers and unions is a potent form of social power and that power flows through spatial structures, just as it flows through social structures—indeed, that the social and the spatial are inseparable.

5

In the overview presented here, I examine four principal areas of research into the spatial context and constitution of labor unionism: (1) how the geography of labor law and state regulation of labor affects the spatial structure of unionism; (2) unions and the making of the economic geography of capitalism; (3) the political geography of union organizing; and (4) how the nature of unionization and unionism is affected by the particularities of place and local context. These are not mutually exclusive categories, and many of the works examined in this book could easily fit into several (if not all) of them. Nevertheless, by breaking down the subject matter in this way I not only want to make my summary more manageable, but also to focus on a number of geographic themes (spatial scale, mobility, spatial differentiation of the economic/political/cultural landscape, the regulation of space, place as context for, and shaper of, social action) as they play out in the landscape of union organization and life.

Geographies of Labor Union Regulation

Several researchers have sought to examine how the geography of labor regulation has affected the spatial patterning of unionism, whether there are particular spatial aspects of labor law and state regulation that underlie the current retrenchment of labor unions, and, if so, what these spatial issues might mean for understanding unions' contemporary problems. One of the earliest examinations along such lines was that contained in the work of Gordon Clark during the late 1980s, which looked at how the geography of labor regulation under U.S. labor law had placed certain structural constraints on unions' activities. Two goals shaped Clark's work. First, his intent was to reexamine critically traditional location theory based on Weberian principles and to argue that it had failed to incorporate any understanding of the ways in which regulatory structures — specifically the law — shaped economic geographies. Hence, he was primarily concerned with adding to economic geography a critical sensibility regarding the influence of systems of regulation and state action, a concern that drew on his earlier work (cf. Clark and Dear 1984; Clark 1985). Second, he argued that there were particular geographies of labor law that it was important to understand if the spatiality of labor unionism (in the United States) was to be comprehended.

In *Unions and Communities under Siege*, Clark (1989b) suggested that there was a spatial basis to U.S. unions' contemporary difficulties. Specifically, he argued that the classic liberal view of the state, as adopted by the New Dealers of Franklin Roosevelt's administration, saw the protection of *local* concerns and ways of doing things as paramount in any system of labor regulation (see also van Wezel Stone 1981). Consequently, the New Deal legislation that laid the basis for modern U.S. labor law as administered by the National Labor Relations Board (NLRB)

6

privileged local systems of labor-management relations and worker representation at the expense of implementing a more centralized, nationally oriented system of the type operating in many European nations (for a discussion of some European systems of labor law, see Fairweather and Shaw 1972; Ferner and Hyman, 1992; Department of Industrial Relations 1989; Thelen 1991; Undy et al. 1996; for a discussion of the geographical assumptions behind Japanese labor law, see the essay by Hanham and Banasick in this volume; for a discussion of the different geographical assumptions behind labor law and employment law in the United States, particularly concerning the tendencies of the former to reflect diverse local systems of bargaining whereas the latter usually provides uniform protections throughout a state or the nation, see Herod 1997a). Such localism is a recurrent theme in U.S. political and cultural life, as evidenced in the defense of local and states' rights within a federal system of government, a frequent distrust of "big government" and centralized political schemes, and a generalized belief among large segments of the population that, as former U.S. House of Representatives Speaker Thomas "Tip" O'Neill once put it, "all politics is local." Thus, Clark argues (1989b, xi):

> The current crisis of organized labor ought to be considered in terms of the local context of labor-management relations.... This argument... [is] premised upon two suppositions. First, whether by design or necessity, the structure of New Deal national labor legislation has sustained and maintained distinctive local labor-management practices. Second, as the economies of American communities (and the world) have become highly interdependent, reflecting the evolution of corporate structure and trade between economies, unions have found it difficult achieving a similar [geographic] scale of integration. Indeed, the crisis of the union movement can be traced, in part, to unions' dependence upon inter-community solidarity, a fragile democratic ideal which is often overwhelmed by economic imperatives operating at higher [spatial] scales in other places.

Much of Clark's work during the 1980s focused on examining how the activities of the NLRB influence the development of the economic landscape, what geographic assumptions lie behind these activities, and how the local geographical context within which they take place shapes them. For example, Clark showed (1986) how new "flexible" working arrangements in local labor markets are forcing the NLRB to adapt new models of labor relations (cf. Herod 1997a). Whereas traditionally the NLRB's role has been premised on the belief that industrial relations between workers and managers are by nature confrontational and that the

7

board should serve as umpire between the two—a belief conditioned by the conflicts of the 1930s when the board itself was established—the rise of team-work, codetermination, and "post-Fordist" modes of work organization (perhaps symbolized most clearly by the General Motors–United Auto Workers Saturn agreement) have forced a questioning of the board's role in industrial relations. More particularly, given that the introduction of "post-Fordist" labor-management relations across the space-economy of the United States has been highly spatially uneven, the board is having to become much more geographically flexible as it seeks simultaneously to accommodate in its rulings both "confrontational" and "cooperative" models of labor-management relations as they operate in dif-ferent parts of the industrial landscape. Clark (1989a) has similarly suggested that the board has faced a geographical dilemma in seeking to preserve *local* pre-rogatives regarding the use of propaganda in union representation elections while making *federal* declarations concerning what constitutes fair use of such propa-ganda. Hence, because union representation elections are spatially and organiza-tionally decentralized and local events regulated by centralized rules set nationally by the board in Washington, D.C., in developing rules concerning union repre-sentation elections and unfair labor practices the board has had to try "to be fair to local events [by] tak[ing] into account local customs and practices in adjudica-tion of disputes over the conduct of elections while at the same time accommo-dating geographical diversity within the logic of its [centrally determined] rules and regulations" (Clark 1989a, 60).

Elsewhere, Clark has argued (1988) that the NLRB can play a significant role in shaping the very geography of U.S. capitalism through its decisions. In his study of the NLRB's ruling regarding the Otis Elevator Company's decision to relocate work from its unionized New Jersey plant to a facility in Connecticut (*Otis Elevator* 255 NLRB 235 [1981]), for example, he showed how the board's reversal of its opinion that a company was obligated to negotiate over the impacts of work relocation could affect local economic geographies. Others too have examined how the board shapes the geography of production and union repre-sentation through its actions. Johnston (1986), for example, showed how two different decisions by the board relating to the same case crucially affected the geography of investment and hence of local labor markets. Whereas in 1982 the board found that an employer could not relocate union jobs to lower wage locations during the period of a union contract (*Milwaukee Spring I* [265 NLRB 28 (1982)]), in its subsequent ruling (*Milwaukee Spring II* [268 NLRB 87 (1984)]) the board reversed itself and determined that a firm could indeed relocate union jobs to nonunion facilities if this were not specifically prohibited by the contract, a reversal that Clark (1986, 293) has argued "laid the foundation for a radical

8

reorganization of American industry...across regions and across industries" because it allowed capital much greater freedom of movement as an option when faced by a successful union-organizing drive in a given locality.

Johnston argued further that the geography of legal frameworks was crucial to understanding organized labor's weak structural position within the U.S. economy. Although the Commerce Clause of the U.S. Constitution has sought to establish *nationally* uniform rules regarding commerce and commodity flows, the structure of U.S. labor law as spelled out under the National Labor Relations Act has emphasized decentralized and *local* solutions to labor-management disputes. Through the establishment by Congress under the Commerce Clause of uniform rules governing commodity flows, combined with the Uniform Commercial Code (which removed local identity from product-market exchange), commercial law has facilitated the creation of a national market for goods. On the other hand, law relating to labor relations, Johnston suggested, has promoted a spatially heterogeneous collection of labor laws and practices that have hampered unions' national activities and allowed capital great opportunity to play workers in different states or communities against each other on the basis of variations in local laws and conditions. Hence, Johnston (1986, 38) concluded, the geography of labor has been such a crucial shaper of investment patterns and the development of the industrial landscape that, given a national commodity market and a spatially heterogeneous labor market, "the location decision becomes one which weighs labor factors more heavily than access to the marketplace."

More recent work along such lines has shown how decisions by the NLRB and subsequently the law courts have affected the geography of dual unionism (Herod 1997e) and of work (Herod 1998a) in the East Coast longshoring industry in the United States. After expelling the International Longshoremen's Association (ILA) in 1953 for engaging in corrupt and undemocratic practices, the American Federation of Labor (AFL) sponsored a rival union to represent waterfront workers. The old ILA union, however, was determined to remain as the dockers' legally elected bargaining representative. Consequently, an NLRB election had to be called to determine which of the two unions would be the bargaining agent.[2] Given their differing political strengths and strategies — the old ILA represented dockers in ports from Maine to Texas, whereas the new union garnered most of its support in the Port of New York — the two unions pressured the board to allow two quite different representation and election units. The old ILA union argued that the appropriate representation unit for any election should be a single unit encompassing the entire East Coast, a unit that the union maintained would preserve the historical integrity of what it claimed were traditional coastwide bargaining systems. The new union argued for a port-by-port

9

system of local representation, which would allow only New York dockers to vote in any election. Clearly, the two unions' rival claims centered on the different geographies of their support. For the old ILA, a coastwide unit would allow it to swamp the new union in any election because the latter drew most of its support from New York; for the new union, on the other hand, a unit encompassing only New York would give it a better chance of defeating the old union in the nation's busiest port and subsequently of building a geographical base of support from which it could confront its rival in other ports along the coast. In the end, the NLRB ruled against a coastwide unit and in favor of a more geographically circumscribed and locally defined unit, thereby crucially shaping the geography of union representation in the industry by providing a representational structure within which dual unionism could potentially flourish, rather than one in which the new union would have been instantly outnumbered (Herod 1997e).

Within the longshoring industry, decisions by the NLRB and the courts also dramatically affected the evolving geography of work along the coast in response to technological innovation (Herod 1998a). With the introduction of containerization in the 1950s, much work traditionally confined to the piers potentially could be done at inland warehouses staffed by nondockers. This geographic reorganization of work spawned great jurisdictional conflicts between the dockers' union and the Teamsters union, which represented truckers and off-pier warehouse workers. In particular, the dockers' union attempted to manipulate the spatial extent of local labor markets by developing a series of union work rules to restrict certain types of container work to the piers, a move that truckers and off-pier workers challenged (for an account of how union rules in the Massachusetts textile industry shaped the geography of local labor markets, see Cope in this volume). Central to the two unions' competing claims to this work were their abilities to present to the board and the courts different representations of the historical geography of work in the industry. Dockers claimed that traditional pier work had moved inland and thus they had a right to claim it. Teamsters, on the other hand, maintained that they had historically done inland warehousing work and that the dockers were simply seeking to acquire work that they previously had not done. For both unions, claims to the contemporary work of packing and unpacking container cargo relied fundamentally on their abilities to present rival accounts of the past spatiality of work and labor markets in the industry. Only after several court decisions (including two by the U.S. Supreme Court in which the justices' interpretation of labor law turned on their understanding of the industry's precontainer *geography* of work) was the matter finally settled in favor of the dockers. The case study shows not only that decisions by the NLRB and the courts were important for shaping the geographic location of work and hence the spatial evolution of the industry, but also that both unions were engaged in struggles that were at heart spatial struggles over the geographic organization and representation of traditions of work on U.S. waterfronts and their hinterlands (for more on the spatiality of union traditions, see Wills in this volume).

Much of the work within U.S. geography examining the impact of state regulation of labor has focused on the activities of the NLRB, under whose aegis the vast majority of unionized workers fall. Baruffalo (1996), however, has shown how a different regulatory system can lead to quite different geographical strategies and practices of workers, unions, and employers. In particular, he shows how the geography of union practices in the U.S. railroad industry has been quite different from that of most other industries, a result of the fact, he suggests, that in the railroad industry unions are regulated not by the National Labor Relations Act (NLRA) but by the Railroad Labor Act (RLA). The RLA allows for congressional intervention in disputes that threaten "national security" and well-being. Consequently, whereas unions covered by the NLRA have often sought to build national master contracts as a way of taking certain conditions of work out of competition (cf. Moody 1988), the unions in the railroad industry have historically favored local agreements out of fear that national agreements (and hence, potentially, national stoppages) might cause undue interference from a Congress concerned about the impacts of any widespread rail strike on national security (however defined). Rail employers, on the other hand, have often pushed for national agreements precisely as a way of invoking congressional action to tame the unions. Hence, Baruffalo suggests, the regulatory structures under which unions labor — NLRA or RLA — have shaped the tendencies toward national or local actions in different industries. Finch and Nagel (1983) similarly show how changes in the regulatory environment in Connecticut in 1979 relating to binding arbitration in teacher contract disputes led to a greater standardization of contracts across the state and the concomitant loss of local "flavor" in the bargaining process.

A slightly different perspective on the use of the law as a regulator of unions' spatial activities is offered by Blomley's (1994) analysis of the British coal miners' strike of 1984–85. He examines the nexus between law, power, and space and shows how the National Union of Mineworkers adopted a strategy of spatially linking struggles in different parts of the country by dispatching hundreds of striking miners as "flying pickets" to support strike efforts in several coalfields. The Thatcher government, on the other hand, used the power of the state through the law to limit the geographic mobility of these flying pickets. The setting up and enforcement of police roadblocks at county lines to stop mobility among miners was a conscious *spatial* strategy by the government to contain the strike

11

and prevent the exercise of solidarity between workers across space (for more on the use of spatial mobility as a subversive strategy for linking disputes in different locations, see Mitchell in this volume; concerning the exercise of solidarity across space, see Wills in this volume). Through the use of such roadblocks to limit miners' mobility, the government hoped to protect the Nottinghamshire coalfields (where most miners had continued to work in defiance of the union's national strike call) from "infection" by outside forces coming from other coalfields, a spatial strategy that played into ideologies of localism, local rights (the "right" of Nottinghamshire miners to ignore the national union), and a biological metaphor of disease (in this case "radical, Trotskyite unionists," portrayed by the government as "the enemy within") infecting the supposedly healthy body politic.[3]

As we have seen, then, within the geographic literature one concern of much research has been to examine how the activities of state agencies responsible for administering labor law have shaped the spatiality of labor unionism and economic landscapes, and how the spatial context within which they find themselves has influenced their decision-making process. Much of this work has focused on the United States, a fact that may be explained as the result of happenstance or, alternatively, of the fact that U.S. labor relations are so legalistic that the mass of records from the accumulated decisions of the NLRB and the courts have provided plentiful empirical fodder for researchers interested in the geography of labor union regulation. As this work shows, regulation involves a spatial dimension and the ways in which the law is spatially constituted can dramatically shape the geographical possibilities for social action by workers and their unions.

Unions and the Economic Geography of Capitalism

A second area of research has sought to examine how the geography of labor unionism itself, rather than the geography of labor union regulation, has affected and reflected the geographic evolution of various economies. In his analysis of the spatiality of class struggle in the United States, Peet (1983), for example, highlighted how the geography of labor unionism and strikes shaped the spatial character of post–World War II economic development in the United States, as industry in the 1950s began a widespread relocation from the traditional industrial heartland of the Northeast and Midwest to the largely nonunion, right-to-work southern and southwestern states, a move referred to by some as the Snowbelt–Sunbelt shift.[4] As Peet suggests, the uneven geography of labor organization and power played a key role in the restructuring of the U.S. space-economy and continues to do so (see Cravey in this volume for an account of how the restructuring of the Mexican space-economy, in particular the new focus on industrial production in the border region, is auguring a new geography of unionism

Andrew Herod

in that country). Gordon (1978) points out that much of the historical geography of urbanization within the United States can be explained through an understanding of the geography of labor unionism. He suggests that part of the impetus toward manufacturing suburbanization, in the northern industrial core at least, can be explained as an effort by employers to escape geographically from the influence of organized urban labor, and he demonstrates how capital's use of mobility and its superior command of space allowed Chicago steel owners in the early twentieth century to relocate much production to Gary, Indiana, as a way to avoid the union. Page's essay in this volume takes a slightly different tack by suggesting that production in the meatpacking industry was decentralized out of Chicago not so much to avoid unions per se as to avoid more militant unions in large urban centers by relocating to smaller rural sites with more placid unions. Church and Stevens (1994) argue similarly that in Britain during the 1980s the flow of employment from urban to rural areas appears not to have been designed to escape unions per se in urban manufacturing centers (both urban and rural areas had similar levels of union density), but may partly have been to escape more militant labor. Whereas these authors have suggested that production suburbanization and decentralization were shaped at least in part either to avoid unions altogether or at least to avoid militant unions, Kane and Bell (1985) show how workers themselves were actively involved in shaping the urban geography of some parts of the United States by creating their own new suburban communities and thus, they argue, traditional portraits of the process of suburbanization as being led by the middle class seeking refuge from the trauma of urban living are too narrow. Parson (1982, 1984), too, recounts how organized labor played a central role in the process of postwar suburbanization and the remaking of the United States' urban geography. Through struggles over public housing, urban renewal, construction jobs, and access to suburban housing for members, U.S. unions actively encouraged and molded the process of suburbanization as a solution to the housing problems faced by many of their members.

Work by Earle (1992b) has examined the geography of strike action in the northern industrial core during the 1880s and 1890s to throw light on the spatiality of labor power during this time and to undermine some long-held misconceptions based on historicist theorizations. Although the process of industrialization destroyed many traditional shared values that had historically bound workers together in smaller preindustrial communities and thereby undercut labor's power at the lower end of the urban hierarchy, Earle found that in larger cities the bringing together of workers to share new common experiences facilitated an increase in workers' political and economic power. In other words, at the end of the nineteenth century the geography of labor power (as measured through

13

strike action) was increasingly remade as a phenomenon of the larger industrial cities in the United States. This finding is important not only because it highlights the fact that workers had different experiences of industrialization and modernization depending on their geographic location, but also because it contradicts historian Herbert Gutman (1963), who argued that the breakdown of long-standing preindustrial community social structures during the Gilded Age had caused an *absolute* loss of workers' power. By adding a spatial perspective to the analysis of late-nineteenth-century capitalism, Earle reveals the limitation of Gutman's more narrowly focused historical argument.

Whereas Earle illuminated how a spatial perspective can provide insights into the world of labor that a purely historical approach cannot, Hudson and Sadler (1983, 1985, 1986) show that an understanding of workers' "sense of place" is crucial to comprehending their responses to the closure of mills in the European steel industry during the 1980s. As restructuring of the industry proceeded, class-based actions were increasingly foreshadowed by territorially based campaigns in many steel communities, that is, space became a more important social dimension than class around which to organize. This led steelworkers in some communities to identify their interests as place-specific and therefore set them in competition with steelworkers in other locations. In contrast, a more class-oriented strategy, Hudson and Sadler suggest, one directed at the actions of the central state (in the British case, the decision to close particular mills as a way to cut capacity in readiness for privatization, and, in the French case, the government's policy of allocating different levels of redundancy payments and new investment to different communities) might have helped to expand the geographic scale of the struggle for jobs from a series of isolated campaigns to a broader campaign unified across space. Through their actions (some of which were successful, others not), unionists played an active role in shaping the economic geography of the steel industry, not as political dupes who bought into a "false consciousness," but as real-life social and geographical actors who believed that such spatial strategies and the defense of place against class were the best way to ensure their own social existence in light of the local conditions which they found themselves, even if this was at the expense of workers located in other communities.

Although much work on the relationship between unionism and the economic geography of capitalism has focused on the sphere of industrial production, Mitchell's (1996) work on migratory workers in early twentieth-century California and the struggles of the Industrial Workers of the World (the "Wobblies") and other unions illuminates the role played by labor in the physical and ideological making of that state's agricultural landscape. Many studies of California (and of rural regions in general) have portrayed the landscape as an idyllic, bucolic, natural world that has been torn asunder by the forces of modernization and industrialization. Such portrayals are not ideologically neutral, however, for in representing the agricultural landscape as a "natural" one, they hide both the relations of power that have gone into creating such landscapes and the labor of workers to make and maintain the landscape. Furthermore, they fail to examine how the making of the landscape in particular ways can serve as a source of political power. Mitchell highlights the role of workers and their unions' struggles in the fields in the evolution of the California agricultural landscape, and argues that the state's agricultural geography was made in large part by such workers. Workers made not only their own histories à la Marx but their own geographies, contesting through actions large and small, unusual and commonplace, the spatial practices of the growers in making the agricultural landscape (for examples of everyday practices of resistance by agricultural peasant workers in Asia, see Scott 1985). Their activities were central to the spatial and historical evolution of California agriculture.

In his essay examining the links between the economic geography of South Wales and the cultural practices associated with unionism in the area, Cooke (1985) illustrates how the process of unionism was crucial in defining the regional cultural and political geography of South Wales and argues that the miners' union was "the major cohesive force in the [process of] regional formation" (237). For much of the twentieth century, the union dominated the political and cultural life of the coalfields and its influence was felt in religious life (the nonconformism of most miners relative to the Anglicanism of the coal operators), sporting life, the provision of welfare (such as the establishment of convalescent homes for injured workers), and education (with many local union branches establishing their own libraries and reading rooms, and holding lectures and classes for members). It is often assumed, by both mainstream and radical commentators, that it is the spatial structure of capital that is key to understanding the process of region formation (see Smith 1984 for a theoretical analysis that links the geographical organization of capital with the process of region forming). According to Cooke (1985), however, workers and their unions, too, have played significant roles in such processes. This fact raises broader questions about how the geography of labor and unionism shapes the geographic scale at which particular economic processes are organized and operate — for example, how union rules shape the spatial extent of local or regional labor markets, or how union wage gains allow workers to afford to travel greater distances to work, thus affecting the size of urban travel to work areas and the process of urbanization.

Although much of this work on how labor unions have shaped, either directly or indirectly, the economic geography of capitalism has focused on the local, regional, or national scales, some has also sought to show how unions have played important roles in shaping the geography of capitalism on an international scale. Herod (1995) describes how the implementation of a global corporate campaign by the United Steelworkers of America and its supporters on behalf of a union local in Ravenswood, West Virginia, forced a multibillion-dollar corporation to forgo plans to expand its operations into Eastern Europe. Through this campaign, unionists actively helped to shape the spatial organization of the corporation's global investments and the geography of foreign direct investment in the countries of the former Soviet bloc. In a similar vein, Herod (1997c) documents how, by destroying local radical and anti-U.S. unions in the region, the AFL and later the AFL–CIO played significant roles in helping U.S. capital expand into Latin America during the twentieth century. Through such activities, the AFL hoped to create a "spatial fix" (cf. Harvey 1982) whereby the region would be kept open to U.S.-made manufactures — in turn generating jobs for AFL members — although in doing so it contributed greatly to the region's underdevelopment and hemispheric patterns of uneven development. Whereas global patterns of uneven development are often seen as the result of capital's activities (cf. Harvey 1982; Smith 1984), Herod shows how the AFL was an important actor both in the internationalization of the U.S. economy and in making the geography of global capitalist development. This fact suggests that labor's role in shaping patterns of uneven development at the transnational scale is greater than it has usually been theorized to be.

In a slightly different take on union activities at the transnational scale, Holmes and Rusonik (1991) show how the North American auto industry's uneven spatial development had dramatic implications for the geography of unionism in Canada and the United States. Whereas both Canadian and U.S. autoworkers had been represented by the United Automobile, Aerospace, and Agricultural Implement Workers of America (UAW) union for a half century, in 1985 Canadian locals decided to dissaffiliate from the UAW and to form their own independent union, the National Union of United Automobile, Aerospace, and Agricultural Implement Workers of Canada (the CAW). A number of explanations have been offered for this split, including that Canadian workers are generally more militant than their U.S. counterparts and had become tired of U.S. "business union" politics; that Canadian nationalism was an important factor; that the history of and political context within which Canadian and U.S. workers find themselves are so different that a split was inevitable at some point and 1985 just happened to be the time; and that Canadian workers were more determined to resist the introduction of Japanese-type labor relations and work methods into the industry than were the U.S. leaders of the union. According to Holmes

16

and Rusonik, however, a crucial and often underexamined factor in the split, was the uneven development of the industry's economic geography, a pattern of development that forced Canadian and U.S. autoworkers to address very different local conditions.

The widening of production-cost differentials between Canada and the United States in the late 1970s and early 1980s (partly the result of the fall in the value of the Canadian dollar, partly the result of the lower cost of employee benefit packages that result from the fact that in Canada the state rather than employers absorbs the principal costs of health care) meant that production north of the border became increasingly cheaper for the automakers. In turn, this left the Canadian locals in a stronger position to oppose management efforts to introduce more flexible work arrangements than were the U.S. locals, which were more likely to accept such work reorganization in exchange for promises of job security. Ultimately, the Canadian unionists came to believe that their own interests would be best served by restructuring the spatial scale at which they organized themselves, because this would allow them a greater degree of independence to address such changes in the local and regional economic geography of the Canadian industry without being tied into the concessionary positions advocated by U.S. leaders of the UAW for North America as a whole (cf. Herod 1997d for an example from the U.S. longshoring industry in which southern dockers abandoned their union's national agreement in favor of locally negotiated contracts). As Holmes and Rusonik (1991) show, the uneven spatial development of the industry during the 1970s and 1980s and the vastly different economic geographies that the unions on both sides of the border faced led Canadian autoworkers to adopt a deliberate spatial solution, which involved remaking the geography and spatial scale of union representation in their industry.

The Political Geography of Union Organizing

A third area of research involving unions has concerned the political geography of union organizing. The role of space has always been an issue in the politics of union organizing. Early in the history of the U.S. labor movement, for example, there was a fundamental difference of opinion over whether unions should be organized along craft/industry lines (the AFL's position) or along geographical lines (a practice favored by the Knights of Labor). Organizing assumes certain spatial relationships and knowledges, whether it is that some places are more progressive or more conservative than others, that the division of the political landscape into particular administrative units (either of the state or of the union) can be important for the geography of labor regulation, or that some spaces are crucial for unions to organize because they may serve as a spatial "safety valve" to which capital can escape if it does not like conditions imposed on it by organized workers in other places; thus the CIO's "Operation Dixie" in the late 1940s was designed to organize the largely nonunion southern United States, which was seen to be a geostrategically important region that was limiting the abilities of unions in the northern industrial core to secure advances. Indeed, Southall (1988, 466) has argued that unionization is, in fact, a process of "coming together" by workers that is inherently one of "organizing over space."

Much of the debate (at least within the geographic literature) concerning unions' political geographies of organizing across space and their attempts to develop links of solidarity with workers elsewhere has arisen out of a broader interrogation of the politics of geographic scale — specifically the notion that geographic scale is itself a material social construction rather than simply an idealist tool for categorizing space and social processes applied by the researcher (on scale, see Smith 1984, 1988; Smith and Dennis 1987; Taylor 1981, 1987; Herod 1991b, 1997e; Jonas 1994; and the 1997 special issue of *Political Geography* 16.2). Organizing across space is, after all, about developing new geographic scales of support. Expanding the geographic scale of a particular campaign or organization allows actors to draw on a much wider set of social resources to support their activities (cf. McCarthy and Mayer 1977). For example, in the Ravenswood campaign mentioned earlier, the local union and its national organization in the United States developed a global campaign to mount international pressure on a transnational corporation to settle a local labor dispute. By making contact with workers in twenty-eight countries on five continents, the unionists were able to bring a transnational weight to bear on what had started out as a highly localized issue (the lockout of seventeen hundred unionized aluminum workers and their replacement by nonunion workers). Similarly, Bivand (1983) examines the territoriality of the independent union Solidarity in Poland and how its support spread from local disputes to a national movement, a process involving the reconstruction of the union's scale of organization as it brought into its fold more workers.

Drawing on the notion of unionization as a process of coming together over space that also involves organizing at particular geographic scales, Southall (1988) analyzes the geography of early Friendly Societies in Britain and shows how the geographic mobility of artisans during the late eighteenth and early nineteenth centuries laid the basis for the formation of centrally organized, national trade-union bodies. Through their travels, these artisans transmitted ideas about unionism across space, and formal and informal networks were established between the various Friendly Societies operating in trades in different parts of the country (for more on how relocating unionists bring ideas about unionism with them when they move across space, see Wills in this volume). Indeed, Southall suggests, it was the very fact of geographic mobility that contributed to the development of certain types of consciousnesses and attitudes toward unionism in different places and industries. Thus, in the mining industry the particular geologies of coal deposits and the need for locally specific skill to mine them, skill not easily transferable to pits in other localities, discouraged mobility among miners and so encouraged the development of a localist union consciousness based on the pit community. In trades that required less geographically specific and locally situated knowledges, the greater spatial transferability of skill encouraged the development of a more broadly regional and national consciousness and loyalty to others in one's trade born out of the geographic mobility of artisans. Consequently, Southall maintains, although the mobility of artisans laid the basis for a strong centralized national unionism in some trades such as engineering and building, in the mining industry only a weak national federation developed in which local prerogatives have often been jealously guarded, as evidenced in the regional splits that emerged in the National Union of Mineworkers during the 1926 general strike and the 1984–85 strike (discussed in the next section).

Elsewhere, Southall (1996; see also Charlesworth et al. 1996) has illustrated the role played by traveling politicians, union organizers, and agitators in nineteenth-century Britain in creating a national politics. Southall argues that the role of the "outside agitator" has often been theoretically neglected by both those on the Right (who see her/him as creating discontent among otherwise contented workers) and those on the Left (for whom local popular protest is often seen as a spontaneous bottom-up experience), and that, by ignoring the role of spatially mobile "outside agitators," accounts of protest that seek to explain events through reference to local social relations frequently miss much of the picture. This has implications for "locality studies," which often stress the role of local events and processes over those occurring outside the locality being studied (for more on the "localities debate" in geography, see Smith 1987; Cooke 1987; Cochrane 1987; Gregson 1987; Beauregard 1988; Graham 1988; Lovering 1989; Cox and Mair 1989; and the 1987 volume of *Environment and Planning D* 5: 363–434). Southall (1989) has also shown how the international movement of union members and artisans, and their subsequent founding of branches of British trade unions abroad, helped transmit ideas about unionism across vast distances and provided some of the earliest structures around which international networks of union activists could develop. Understanding the spatial mobility of political organizers shows how politics is geographical, for the movements of such organizers link ideas and individuals across the geographic landscape and tie local, regional, national, or international processes and spatial scales of political organization together. In related work, Wills (1996a) too has examined how the geographic mobility of union activists can introduce new ideas and traditions of organizing into particular localities and thereby transform "indigenous" social relations and cultures of unionism. This suggests that processes of forming union traditions have both spatial and temporal dynamics to them.

Whereas Southall's and Wills's work has examined the spatiality of mobility as it relates to the political geography of union organization, Earle (1992a) looks at a different side of the political geography of unionism and suggests that it was the geographic context of workers' organization in the 1880s that fundamentally shaped the nature and development of the AFL. The geography of support and nonsupport for the 1886 general strike in the United States, he argues, particularly the spatial lessons learned by unionists from this pattern of support, was crucial in shaping the political geography of trade-union organizing (for a geographic examination of industrial protest in Britain between 1750 and 1990, see Charlesworth et al. 1996). Earle analyzes the geographical spread of the general strike and shows that it was not general at all but was, instead, spatially concentrated in a few large northeastern cities. This was important because the unionists who came together in late 1886 to found the AFL realized that the U.S. working class was deeply divided along geographic lines and that support for unionism was concentrated in a small number of locations in the industrial heartland. Their failure to mobilize workers across large swaths of the country led the founders of the AFL to conclude that their own interests were best served by a narrow craft-based organization focused on their self-identified constituencies of the urban Northeast. Furthermore, AFL leaders preferred a geographically decentralized organizational structure that would keep any industrial violence localized and thus insulate the wider union federation from the kinds of state repression that had characterized the aftermath of the 1886 Haymarket massacre in Chicago. As Earle comments (1992a, 381), there is a "remarkable paradox [in that] sectarian trade unionists organizing a general strike on behalf of the entire working class in May [1886 had] within eight months withdraw[n] into the sectarian philosophy of pure and simple trade unionism." This paradox is, he maintains, principally geographic, and can be explained by the spatial extent of support for the general strike.

With the dramatic transformation in the spatial and social organization of capitalism during the past several decades, as witnessed by the deindustrialization of many traditional manufacturing hearths, a selective reindustrialization of some of these hearths (though often at different geographic scales; cf. Smith and Dennis 1987), the increasing globalization of economies, the shift from manufac-

20

turing to service-sector employment, the creation of global assembly lines, and the rise of localism in the face of such globalizing processes (for an account of a locally oriented campaign against a transnational corporation, see Jonas in this volume), there has been a growing interest in whether the geographic assumptions on which traditional models of union organizing are based — organizing within national space-economies, identifying union "hot shops," picketing large centralized facilities with regular shift changes and only a few entrances (cf. Green and Tilly 1987) — are still appropriate to the spatial structure of contemporary capitalism (for more on this, see the essays by Savage and Berman in this volume). This is especially so given that contemporary developments are rapidly breaking down established regional and national boundaries to labor markets and are bringing workers from geographically quite distant locations into direct competition with each other. Moreover, the proliferation of new technologies — fax machines, global positioning satellites, the Internet, cyberspace — is causing people to think about spatial relations in entirely new ways (for an account of how new technologies shaped thinking about time and space at the end of the nineteenth century, see Kern 1983). Some unions are making use of these technologies to transform the ways they have traditionally organized in space and are now attempting to use cyberspace to pursue their goals (see Lee 1997). Herod (1998b) examines, for instance, how the United Steelworkers of America and the International Federation of Chemical, Energy, Mine and General Workers' Unions used the Internet to wage a successful cybercampaign against the Bridgestone tire company after it illegally fired some 2,300 workers in 1994 at its U.S. subsidiaries and replaced them with nonunion workers.

A key element of any practice of labor solidarity is the ability to make contacts between workers who live and work in vastly different local, regional, or national contexts. Solidarity across space always involves workers and unions coming to terms with quite different conditions, but doing so across international space dramatically expands the potential variations between workers. Organizing within national territories involves workers who, despite their many differences, often share some common cultural, historical, economic, or political referents (such as a common currency or a common set of national labor laws and political institutions), but organizing across national boundaries introduces a much wider set of geographic issues and variations. Fluctuations in exchange rates, for instance, can dramatically reshape the geography of production costs, thereby impacting the local economies and localities that workers are seeking to tie together through their practices of solidarity (as we have already seen with the case of the UAW split [Holmes and Rusonik 1991]). Yet, it is not impossible for unions to be

21

successful internationally, despite portrayals of capital as globally hegemonic (cf. Herod 1995; Gibson-Graham 1996). Herod (1997c) shows, for instance, how unions in several industries have developed "World Industry Councils" to share information about particular companies with operations in different parts of the world, as well as how several international trade-union bodies have engaged in efforts to standardize some conditions across companies' global operations. Such councils argue that although the geographic realities of different economic contexts, fluctuating exchange rates, and other issues make it difficult for unions to standardize wages, there is no reason that nonfinancial issues (the length of work breaks, the right to organize, etc.) should not be the same for workers at, say, Ford plants in the United States, Australia, Africa, and France.

Johns (1994) has suggested that the impetus for such efforts to develop cross-border solidarity, however, can vary considerably and that, depending on the goals of the workers involved (especially on the part of those in the more developed regions of the world), these efforts can have very different spatial implications. Through an examination of how workers participating in the U.S./Guatemala Labor Education Project set about consciously designing and implementing a transnational solidarity campaign to link work conditions in the United States and Central America, she distinguishes two types of international solidarity that may dominate unions' transnational efforts: "accommodatory solidarity" and "transformatory solidarity." The difference between the two, she argues, is fundamentally related to the geographic objectives that workers share. As workers negotiate the boundaries of class and space, in some instances spatial interests may prevail ("accommodatory solidarity"). Such solidarity is often initiated by workers in more privileged economic spaces as a means of reducing capital flight to other, less developed locations where pay and working conditions are much worse. The goal, clearly, is to defend their own privileged spaces within the global economy and extant social relations against being undercut by workers elsewhere, a goal to be achieved through improving the conditions elsewhere as a way of limiting the attractiveness of mobility for capital. In other instances, however, class interests may prevail ("transformatory solidarity"). In these types of campaigns, workers unite across space to challenge the social power of capital and transnational corporations and to transform the basic social relations of production and consumption. In practice, it may not be easy to draw such distinctions between these different types of solidarity — although in many cases it undoubtedly is. The point is that at different times, as contingent and contextual forces change, workers and their organizations may opt to project either spatial or class interests in their political praxis.[5] As Johns demonstrates, the nature of in-

22

ternational solidarity is clearly dependent on the varying social and *spatial* objectives that propel and inform it.

Local Context and the Power of Place

A fourth focus of geographic work on labor unions has been the role of local context and place in shaping the character of unionism. This work has shown both how union practice varies greatly between places and that the social, historical, and cultural resources of place can play vital roles in shaping the nature of union politics. People's attitudes (including toward unionism) are shaped in large part by the sociospatial context of their everyday existence and experiences. Such attitudes are important in reproducing over time and in space the cultural practices that define particular places. In his examination of the geography of union responses to local government privatization (itself seen as part of a broader shift from a Fordist to a post-Fordist form of the state), Painter (1991), for example, notes that local circumstances have been important influences on the activities of public-sector unions, both because the diversity of local outcomes is important in shaping national union responses to privatization and because local variations in conditions can have dramatic impacts on the success or failure of local and national union policies. Through an analysis of the divergent responses and the geography of successful and unsuccessful opposition to the privatization of local services in Britain, Painter (1991, 224) argues that whereas Marxist state theory has tended to stress the homogeneity of *"the* state," in fact "the transition from a local state form associated with the Fordist regime of accumulation to one suited to its successor [is] tak[ing] place unevenly over space even within one nation state." The uneven geography of public sector union responses to privatization and restructuring, and the spatially divergent successes in opposing such privatization, Painter argues, are playing crucial roles in shaping the geographically uneven development of the state (cf. Peck 1996).

Some geographers have sought to shed light on how place shapes processes and patterns of unionization through examining the geography of the 1984–85 coal miners' strike in Britain. They have done so by focusing on how spatially defined traditions and a clash between geographic scales of political interests (those of the national union hierarchy versus those in some coalfields that wished to preserve local autonomy) shaped the geography of support for industrial action and the split between the national leadership of the National Union of Mineworkers (NUM) and miners in Yorkshire, South Wales, and Scotland on the one hand, and miners in the East Midlands coalfields on the other. Rees (1985, 1986) points out that understanding how the strike played out spatially

23

requires situating coal production in the broader context of the industry's regional historical geography. The new mechanized methods of mining introduced in the 1950s were introduced in a spatially uneven way and led the National Coal Board increasingly to focus production away from peripheral regions such as Wales and toward low-cost central fields such as those in the East Midlands. The changing geography of production and investment in the industry, combined with the way in which the South Wales Area of the NUM has traditionally been organized (with a record of rank-and-file participation in determining policy, in contrast to many other regions, especially those of the East Midlands), resulted in the South Wales coalfield being one of the most solid throughout the strike. Sunley (1986), in contrast, argues that although the changing geography of production may have been a factor, the spatiality of the strike had more to do with various regional cultures of unionism than with the factors examined by Rees, such as the "popular socialism" of South Wales miners compared to the more "individualist" and politically quiescent miners in Nottinghamshire and the East Midlands. Elsewhere, Sunley (1990) compared the geographic pattern of support in the coalfields for the 1926 general strike and the 1984–85 dispute and concluded that the remarkable similarity between the two geographies has much to do with the temporal persistence of regional place-specific traditions of industrial relations.

Griffiths and Johnston (1991) also analyze what the spatiality of the strike has to offer an understanding of "place" as a geographic concept, and they note that cultures of unionism in particular regions and communities were important factors in explaining the geography of the strike. Although the Yorkshire fields were quite profitable and thus one might expect that miners there would have been less perturbed by Coal Board plans to reduce production at less profitable mines in other parts of the country, Yorkshire miners were quite solidly behind the strike, a fact that throws economistic explanations of the dispute into question. In contrast, support for the strike in other areas such as North Wales that had less certain futures and little to lose by industrial action was weak. Furthermore, although the Yorkshire miners supported the strike, miners in East Midland collieries that were also quite profitable were vehemently against striking, a response that might be understandable on purely economic grounds (because they were less threatened by closures) but that also has, Griffiths and Johnston argue, a lengthy historical basis. Indeed, they suggest that much of the divergence in attitude to the strike goes back to long-standing political traditions and conflicts over the scale of power within the NUM, traditions that vary considerably across space. They also see direct spatial parallels between 1984–85 and 1926. In 1926, the majority of the executive board members of the Miners' Federation of Great

Britain (forerunner to the NUM) were influenced by socialist politics, whereas representatives from the Nottinghamshire coalfields were more influenced by traditional Liberal Party politics and Spencerism. Fearing that their interests were not being represented in the national executive organs of the union, they determined to form a more locally controlled union (the Nottinghamshire and District Miners' Industrial Union), which remained separate from the national union until it reaffiliated in 1937. This action was directly concerned with the geographic scale at which power would rest within the union. Significantly, such a struggle over the regional geography of unionism and the spatial scale at which it would be articulated was repeated in 1985 when the East Midlands miners again broke away from the national federation to form the Union of Democratic Miners.

In her study of unionism in the British banking industry, Wills (1996b) similarly observed that local variations in economic conditions and cultures have dramatically shaped the geography of organization. The workers she researched were employed by the same institutions and were members of the same union with the same nationally negotiated terms and working conditions, but the fact that they were from two very different regions of the country led them to adopt different attitudes toward, and practices of, labor unionism. Such differences relate to the distinct geohistorical experiences of the two regions and the differing ways in which they have been incorporated into the broader space-economy of the nation over different historical periods. Workers in Warrington in the northwest of England had a long history of trade-union culture going back to the early days of the industrial revolution from which to draw inspiration, whereas those in Welwyn Garden City (a "new town" built after the 1920s to decentralize the population away from London) in southern England had little such tradition and showed much less social cohesion, given the more recent influx of much of the population. In addition, the broader economic situation within which the two communities found themselves—the "rust belt" of the north versus the relative "boom region" of the south—shaped attitudes toward unionism and industrial action in that the differing economic vitalities of the two areas affected the possibilities of (un)employment. In short, what it meant to join the union and what unionism as a way of life meant varied considerably depending on workers' geographic location, the operation of local labor markets, and the specific work and political traditions in their particular communities.[6] Because such local differences have shaped the geography of union membership in both areas, Wills suggests that any attempt to understand the nature of unionism must be sensitive to the spatiality of local cultures of work and unionism.

Issues concerning the spatiality of cultures of unionism and the influence of place on the geography of unionism have also sparked debates over changing

25

national patterns of union representation in Britain and the existence of "union heartlands." During the 1980s, Doreen Massey and her colleagues examined the changing geography of unionism in Britain as a means to understand structural and other changes taking place in the country's political economy (Massey and Miles 1984; Massey and Painter 1989). Using data on the changing percentage share of unions' membership accounted for by different regions, their work determined that the geography of unionism in Britain in the 1960s and 1970s had undergone a fundamental transformation as a result of the decline of older industrial areas (identified as "heartlands" of unionism), a geographic reorganization of production by capital in search of cheaper labor, the apparant inability of unions to make much headway in organizing such new production regions, and the geographic spread of public sector unionism associated with the decentralization of many government functions to peripheral regions. The result was both a relative and an absolute decline in union membership and power in the heartlands and a "flattening out" of the geography of unionization across the landscape as regions that had been less unionized became more important in the structure of several national unions, a process that probably continued throughout the 1980s. Such geographical changes could be taken to represent a growing "equalization" of unionism across the national space-economy as traditional "hot spots" of union activity became less important and the geography of union membership "spread out" into relatively union-free regions, even if at low levels of overall membership. This finding might suggest that the influence of local union culture had diminished in traditional heartland areas in the face of economic restructuring.

More recent work by Martin, Sunley, and Wills (1993) advances an alternative interpretation of the geography of union fortunes in Britain during the 1980s. They studied the regional density of several national unions' membership during the previous three decades and argue that in fact the traditional heartlands of the British labor movement have remained remarkably resilient and that Britain has not experienced the flattening out of union membership detected by Massey and her colleagues. For Martin et al., the key to explaining this geography of union decline is the failure of unions to organize new sectors and regions of the space-economy, along with a continuing resilience on the part of the older heartland areas. In turn, this leads them to suggest not only that a geographical perspective is important to understand the problems faced by British unions, but that the resilience of traditional heartlands and the resistance of new regions of production to organization by unions demonstrate the importance of local cultures of work and political traditions to unionization. Even in the hardest of times, they suggest, particular geographic "reservoirs" of cultures of labor unionism remain that could serve as the hearths of a future geography of organization.

26

The empirical differences in these two sets of work sparked an intense debate over methodological issues related to studying the geography of unionism (Massey 1994; Painter 1994; and Martin et al. 1993, 1994b; see also Charlesworth et al. 1996 for more on the difficulties of data sources, particularly for historical studies of the geography of unionism in Britain). Whereas Massey et al. had used as the basis for their studies the *proportion* of particular unions' memberships accounted for by different regions, Martin et al. used a measure related to the *density* of memberships in certain regions (with density being calculated in terms of the actual membership divided by a measure of the potential membership available to the union). By using different measures, the two sets of analyses came up with quite different understandings of what constituted the geographic heartlands for the unions studied. In a paper somewhat related to this debate, Church and Stevens (1994) show that spatial differences in union density are closely associated with establishment-level employment change, together with industrial composition, size, and ownership structure, and that, in fact, when adjusted for differences in workplace size and ownership, there is remarkable similarity — though still discernible differences — in union density across the British industrial landscape. As they conclude (p. 117), "this is not to deny the importance of local labour cultures and industrial relations practices, but [does] suggest that any examination of the effect of place-specific social and cultural factors must focus on their interdependency with establishment characteristics which seem to be a crucial influence on spatial differences in union membership." One conclusion to be drawn from this debate is that the geographic scale at which analyses of union density are carried out can be a significant shaper of our understanding of what is occurring in the geography of unionism: at the regional scale, Martin et al. (1993) have identified distinct regional variations in union density, but at certain urban and rural scales, Church and Stevens (1994) suggest that such variations are less distinct. This finding adds a further dimension to the methodological questions raised in the debate.

In other work, Martin et al. (1994a, 1994c) examined how local context has shaped the geography of unionism in the British engineering industry and how the decentralization of industrial relations away from national agreements to agreements tailored to individual plants — a process occurring in many industrialized economies around the world (see Daniel and Millward 1983; Dabschek 1994; Ferner and Hyman 1992; Goetschy and Rozenblatt 1992; Herod 1997a; Howell 1992) — is bringing pressure to bear on the unions to reorganize their own spatial scale of operations to match that of capital (but see Herod 1997d for an example of how it was the employers in the U.S. longshoring industry who had to reorganize their spatial scale of operations to match those of the union). Mar-

27

tin et al. show both how the representation of contemporary developments in labor-management relations is a little partial (for there are important tendencies toward the spatial centralization as well as the spatial decentralization of industrial relations) and how decentralization allows for much greater variation in contracts and work conditions because local concerns come to the fore, increasingly replacing national ones. This latter process itself is contributing to the evolution of a much more geographically uneven landscape of labor regulation and conditions, which means that unions in turn may well have to become much more geographically sensitive as traditional "one size fits all" strategies are no longer appropriate (if they ever were) and as they seek to develop models and strategies tailored to conditions in different areas and localities. Indeed, it is precisely how this sensitivity to geography is an important part of union organizing and operating that all the essays in this volume, in varying ways, seek to address. As I hope will become evident throughout the book, the making of the geography of capitalism in certain ways and not others is crucial to the ability of working people to live their lives. If they are to be successful, labor unions, as organizations of working people, out of necessity must develop strategies that are geographically sensitive to the variations found across the spaces within which they are organizing. This suggests not only that unions can play powerful roles in organizing the very landscape of capitalism itself, but also that a geographical perspective can add much to our understanding of such unions and how they operate.

Conclusion

In this introductory review essay, I have argued that to understand more fully the nature and practice of unionism it is necessary to appreciate the spatiality of social life, the fact that power flows through spatial structures and the landscape, that workers construct their own identities in light of the geographical as well as the historical context within which they live, and that unions must by their very nature as organizations constituted to bring together workers in common cause confront the geographic realities and variations of an unevenly developed global capitalism. I have also provided a broad overview of a body of work conducted within geography that illuminates precisely some of the elements of the spatiality of unionism and the value that a geographical perspective may add to understanding unions and unionism. My goal is to convince geographers that unions are important social entities worthy of study because of the varied ways in which they shape landscapes, but also to encourage labor historians to interrogate in greater depth the spatiality of social life for the insights such an approach may provide. Certainly, many studies and issues have been left out of the review. By providing a broad overview of a number of themes that have dom-

28

inated at the intersection between labor unionism and geography, however, I hope to have provided both a taste of the possibilities that a spatial approach to understanding unionism has to offer and an intellectual context for the essays that follow.

Notes

1. This is not to suggest that all unions seek national agreements. Sometimes local branches may seek to break out of national agreements because they believe they will be better off bargaining locally. Such a belief may stem from the fact that they are strong enough to negotiate a better contract locally than through a national agreement (cf. Herod 1995) or that the conditions set by a national contract are so high that local unions in economically depressed regions feel competitive pressures to sign contracts that reflect local rather than national conditions (cf. Herod 1997d).

2. Since the old ILA union was the legally recognized bargaining agent for the dockers, a situation unaffected by whether or not it was a member of the AFL, the newly sponsored AFL union had to win an NLRB representation election before it could represent waterfront workers in negotiations with the employers.

3. Significantly, such projection of the sanctity of, and need to defend, local rights and privileges against outside forces did not extend to the government's use of the police: constabularies from many different counties frequently shared officers for roadblock, picket-line, and other antistrike duties in counties other than their home ones.

4. Right-to-work (RTW) states are those that outlaw union shops in which all workers at a plant organized by a union must join that union within a certain time after being hired. The right to pass RTW legislation was enshrined in the 1947 federal Taft-Hartley Act. Most RTW states are located in the southern, southwestern, and Rocky Mountain West of the United States.

5. I am not suggesting that space and class are separate from one another, for my purpose has been to stress the spatial constitution of class relations and the class nature of space. Rather, I am suggesting that sometimes workers might see their own interests best served by emphasizing their common class position with workers located elsewhere, whereas at other times they might prefer to emphasize spatial interests (as in nationalistic arguments about the need to protect their communities against products made by foreign workers).

6. David "Dai" Davies, former general secretary of the British Iron and Steel Trades Confederation, makes a similar observation concerning the steel industry. Reflecting on his own experiences as a union organizer in South Wales be-

fore World War II and in the Middlesborough area after the war, he comments that in South Wales the union was seen by many workers with whom he came into contact as a social entity that pervaded their whole life experience, whereas in Middlesborough the prevailing ethos seemed to be that the decision to join the union was based more on a cost-benefit analysis of what the potential member could get out of the union in terms of higher wages, work security, and so on (Davies 1993).

Bibliography

Baruffalo, R. 1996. "National Handling and U.S. Rail Consolidation: Implications for Labor Relations." Unpublished manuscript, Department of Geography, University of Kentucky.

Beauregard, R. A. 1988. "In the Absence of Practice: The Locality Research Debate." *Antipode* 20.1: 52–59.

Bivand, R. 1983. "Towards a Geography of 'Solidarność.'" *Environment and Planning D: Society and Space* 1: 397–404.

Blomley, N. 1994. *Law, Space and the Geographies of Power.* New York: Guilford Press.

Castells, M. 1983. *The City and the Grassroots: A Cross-Cultural Theory of Urban Social Movements.* Berkeley and Los Angeles: University of California Press.

Charlesworth, A., D. Gilbert, A. Randall, H. Southall, and C. Wrigley. 1996. *An Atlas of Industrial Protest in Britain 1750–1990.* New York: St. Martin's Press.

Church, A., and M. Stevens. 1994. "Unionization and the Urban–Rural Shift in Employment." *Transactions of the Institute of British Geographers,* n.s., 19.1: 111–18.

Clark, G. L. 1985. *Judges and the Cities: Interpreting Local Autonomy.* Chicago: University of Chicago Press.

———. 1986. "Restructuring the U.S. Economy: The NLRB, the Saturn Project, and Economic Justice." *Economic Geography* 62.4: 289–306.

———. 1988. "A Question of Integrity: The National Labor Relations Board, Collective Bargaining and the Relocation of Work." *Political Geography Quarterly* 7.3: 209–27.

———. 1989a. "The Context of Federal Regulation: Propaganda in US Union Elections." *Transactions of the Institute of British Geographers,* n.s., 14.1: 59–73.

———. 1989b. *Unions and Communities under Siege: American Communities and the Crisis of Organized Labor.* New York: Cambridge University Press.

Clark, G. L., and M. Dear. 1984. *State Apparatus: Structures and Language of Legitimacy.* Winchester, Mass.: Allen and Unwin.

Cochrane, A. 1987. "What a Difference the Place Makes: The New Structuralism of Locality." *Antipode* 19.3: 354–63.

Cooke, P. 1985. "Class Practices as Regional Markers: A Contribution to Labour Geography." In *Social Relations and Spatial Structures*, edited by D. Gregory and J. Urry, 213–41. New York: St. Martin's Press.

———. 1987. "Clinical Inference and Geographic Theory." *Antipode* 19.1: 69–78.

Cox, K., and A. Mair. 1989. "Levels of Abstraction in Locality Studies." *Antipode* 21.2: 121–32.

Dabschek, B. 1994. "The Arbitration System since 1967." In *State, Economy and Public Policy in Australia*, edited by S. Bell and B. Head, 142–68. Melbourne: Oxford University Press.

Daniel, W. W., and N. Millward. 1983. *Workplace Industrial Relations in Britain.* London: Heinemann.

Davies, D. H. 1993. Interview by the author with David "Dai" Davies, former general secretary of the Iron and Steel Trades Confederation, St. Albans, Hertfordshire, December 31.

Department of Industrial Relations. 1989. *Industrial Relations in Ireland: Contemporary Issues and Developments.* Dublin: Department of Industrial Relations, Faculty of Commerce, University College.

Earle, C. 1992a. "The Last Great Chance for an American Working Class: Spatial Lessons of the General Strike and the Haymarket Riot of Early May 1886." In *Geographical Inquiry and American Historical Problems*, edited by C. Earle, 378–99. Stanford, Calif.: Stanford University Press.

———. 1992b. "The Split Geographical Personality of American Labor: Labor Power and Modernization in the Gilded Age." In *Geographical Inquiry and American Historical Problems*, edited by C. Earle, 346–77. Stanford, Calif.: Stanford University Press.

Fairweather, O., and L. C. Shaw. 1972. *Labor Relations and the Law in France and the United States.* Ann Arbor: Graduate School of Business Administration, University of Michigan.

Ferner, A., and R. Hyman, eds. 1992. *Industrial Relations in the New Europe.* Oxford: Basil Blackwell.

Finch, M., and T. W. Nagel. 1983. "Spatial Distribution of Bargaining Power: Binding Arbitration in Connecticut School Districts." *Environment and Planning D: Society and Space* 1: 429–46.

Fox, E. W. 1971. *History in Geographic Perspective: The Other France.* New York: W. W. Norton.

Genovese, E. D., and L. Hochberg. 1989. *Geographic Perspectives in History.* Oxford: Basil Blackwell.

Gibson-Graham, J. K. 1996. *The End of Capitalism (as We Knew It): A Feminist Critique of Political Economy.* Cambridge, Mass.: Basil Blackwell.

31

Goetschy, J., and P. Rozenblatt. 1992. "France: The Industrial Relations System at a Turning Point?" In *Industrial Relations in the New Europe,* edited by A. Ferner and R. Hyman, 404–44. Oxford: Basil Blackwell.

Gordon, D. M. 1978. "Capitalist Development and the History of American Cities." In *Marxism and the Metropolis: New Perspectives in Urban Political Economy,* edited by W. K. Tabb and L. Sawers, 25–63. New York: Oxford University Press.

Graham, J. 1988. "Post-Modernism and Marxism." *Antipode* 20.1: 60–66.

Green, J., and C. Tilly. 1987. Service Unionism: Directions for Organizing. *Labor Law Journal* 38.8: 486–95.

Gregson, N. 1987. "The CURS Initiative: Some Further Comments." *Antipode* 19.3: 364–70.

Griffiths, M. J., and R. J. Johnston. 1991. "What's in a Place? An Approach to the Concept of Place, as Illustrated by the British National Union of Mine-workers' Strike, 1984–85." *Antipode* 23.2: 185–213.

Gutman, H. G. 1963. "The Workers' Search for Power: Labor in the Gilded Age." In *The Gilded Age: A Reappraisal,* edited by H. W. Morgan, 38–68. Syracuse, N.Y.: Syracuse University Press.

Harvey, D. 1982. *The Limits to Capital.* Oxford: Basil Blackwell.

Herod, A. 1991a. "Local Political Practice in Response to a Manufacturing Plant Closure: How Geography Complicates Class Analysis." *Antipode* 23.4: 385–402.

———. 1991b. "The Production of Scale in United States Labour Relations." *Area* 23.1: 82–88.

———. 1994. "Further Reflections on Organized Labor and Deindustrialization in the United States." *Antipode* 26.1: 77–95.

———. 1995. "The Practice of International Labor Solidarity and the Geography of the Global Economy." *Economic Geography* 71.4: 341–63.

———. 1997a. "Back to the Future in Labor Relations: From the New Deal to Newt's Deal." In *State Devolution in America: Implications for a Diverse Society,* edited by L. Staeheli, J. Kodras, and C. Flint, 161–80. Thousand Oaks, Calif.: Sage.

———. 1997b. "From a Geography of Labor to a Labor Geography: Labor's Spatial Fix and the Geography of Capitalism." *Antipode* 29.1: 1–31.

———. 1997c. "Labor as an Agent of Globalization and as a Global Agent." In *Spaces of Globalization: Reasserting the Power of the Local,* edited by K. Cox, 167–200. New York: Guilford Press.

———. 1997d. "Labor's Spatial Praxis and the Geography of Contract Bargaining in the US East Coast Longshore Industry, 1953–89." *Political Geography* 16.2: 145–69.

Andrew Herod

————. 1997e. "Notes on a Spatialized Labour Politics: Scale and the Political Geography of Dual Unionism in the US Longshore Industry." In *Geographies of Economies*, edited by R. Lee and J. Wills, 186–96. London: Edward Arnold.

————. 1998a. "Discourse on the Docks: Containerization and Inter-Union Work Disputes in US Ports, 1955–1985." *Transactions of the Institute of British Geographers*, n.s., 23.2.

————. 1998b. "Of Blocs, Flows and Networks: The End of the Cold War, Cyberspace, and the Geo-economics of Organized Labor at the *fin de millénaire*." In *An Unruly World? Globalization, Governance and Geography*, edited by A. Herod, G. Ó Tuathail, and S. Roberts, 162–95. London: Routledge.

Holmes, J., and A. Rusonik. 1991. "The Break-up of an International Labour Union: Uneven Development in the North American Auto Industry and the Schism in the UAW." *Environment and Planning A* 23: 9–35.

Howell, C. 1992. "The Dilemmas of Post-Fordism: Socialists, Flexibility, and Labor Market Deregulation in France." *Politics and Society* 20.1: 71–99.

Hudson, R., and D. Sadler. 1983. "Region, Class, and the Politics of Steel Closures in the European Community." *Environment and Planning D: Society and Space* 1: 405–28.

————. 1985. "Communities in Crisis: The Social and Political Effects of Steel Closures in France, West Germany, and the United Kingdom." *Urban Affairs Quarterly* 21.1: 171–86.

————. 1986. "Contesting Works Closures in Western Europe's Industrial Regions: Defending Place or Betraying Class?" In *Production, Work, Territory*, edited by A. Scott and M. Storper, 172–93. Winchester, Mass.: Allen and Unwin.

Johns, R. 1994. "International Solidarity: Space and Class in the U.S. Labor Movement." Ph.D. diss., Department of Geography, Rutgers University, New Brunswick, N.J.

Johnston, K. 1986. "Judicial Adjudication and the Spatial Structure of Production: Two Decisions by the National Labor Relations Board." *Environment and Planning A* 18: 27–39.

Jonas, A. E. G. 1994. "The Scale Politics of Spatiality" (editorial). *Environment and Planning D: Society and Space* 12: 257–64.

Kane, K. D., and T. L. Bell. 1985. "Suburbs for a Labor Elite." *Geographical Review* 75.3: 319–34.

Katz, H. 1993. "The Decentralisation of Collective Bargaining: A Literature Review and Comparative Analysis." *Industrial and Labor Relations Review* 47: 3–22.

Kern, S. 1983. *The Culture of Time and Space 1880–1918.* Cambridge: Harvard University Press.

Lee, E. 1997. *The Labour Movement and the Internet: The New Internationalism.* London: Pluto Press.

Lovering, J. 1989. "Postmodernism, Marxism, and Locality Research: The Contribution of Critical Realism to the Debate." *Antipode* 21.1: 1–12.

Martin, R., P. Sunley, and J. Wills. 1993. "The Geography of Trade Union Decline: Spatial Dispersal or Regional Resilience?" *Transactions of the Institute of British Geographers,* n.s., 18.1: 36–62.

———. 1994a. "The Decentralization of Industrial Relations? New Institutional Spaces and the Role of Local Context in British Engineering." *Transactions of the Institute of British Geographers,* n.s., 19.4: 457–81.

———. 1994b. "Labouring Differences: Method, Measurement and Purpose in Geographical Research on Trade Unions." *Transactions of the Institute of British Geographers,* n.s., 19.1: 102–10.

———. 1994c. "Local Industrial Politics: Spatial Sub-Systems in British Engineering." *Employee Relations* 16: 84–99.

———. 1994d. "Unions and the Politics of Deindustrialization: Some Comments on How Geography Complicates Class Analysis." *Antipode* 26.1: 59–76.

———. 1996. *Union Retreat and the Regions: The Shrinking Landscape of Organised Labour.* London: Jessica Kingsley.

Massey, D. 1973. "Towards a Critique of Industrial Location Theory." *Antipode* 5.3: 33–39.

———. 1994. "The Geography of Trade Unions: Some Issues." *Transactions of the Institute of British Geographers,* n.s., 19.1: 95–98.

Massey, D., and N. Miles. 1984. "Mapping Out the Unions." *Marxism Today* 28.5: 19–22.

Massey, D., and J. Painter. 1989. "The Changing Geography of Trade Unions." In *The Political Geography of Contemporary Britain,* edited by J. Mohan, 130–50. Basingstoke, U.K.: Macmillan.

McCarthy, J. D., and N. Z. Mayer. 1977. "Resource Mobilization and Social Movements: A Partial Theory." *American Journal of Sociology* 82: 1212–41.

Mitchell, D. 1996. *The Lie of the Land: Migrant Workers and the California Landscape.* Minneapolis: University of Minnesota Press.

Moody, K. 1988. *An Injury to All: The Decline of American Unionism.* New York: Verso.

Painter, J. 1991. "The Geography of Trade Union Responses to Local Government Privatization." *Transactions of the Institute of British Geographers,* n.s., 16.2: 214–26.

———. 1994. "Trade Union Geography: Alternative Frameworks for Analysis." *Transactions of the Institute of British Geographers,* n.s., 19.1: 99–101.

Andrew Herod

Parson, D. 1982. "The Development of Redevelopment: Public Housing and Urban Renewal in Los Angeles." *International Journal of Urban and Regional Research* 6:2: 393–413.

———. 1984. "Organized Labor and the Housing Question: Public Housing, Suburbanization, and Urban Renewal." *Environment and Planning D: Society and Space* 2: 75–86.

Peck, J. 1996. *Work-Place: The Social Regulation of Labor Markets.* New York: Guilford Press.

Peet, R. 1983. "Relations of Production and the Relocation of United States Manufacturing Industry since 1960." *Economic Geography* 59: 112–43.

———. 1985. "The Social Origins of Environmental Determinism." *Annals of the Association of American Geographers* 75: 309–33.

Rees, G. 1985. "Regional Restructuring, Class Change, and Political Action: Preliminary Comments on the 1984–1985 miners' strike in South Wales." *Environment and Planning D: Society and Space* 3: 389–406.

———. 1986. "'Coalfield Culture' and the 1984–1985 Miners' Strike: A Reply to Sunley." *Environment and Planning D: Society and Space* 4: 469–76.

Scott, J. C. 1985. *Weapons of the Weak: Everyday Forms of Peasant Resistance.* New Haven: Yale University Press.

Shorter, E., and C. Tilly. 1974. *Strikes in France, 1830–1968.* Cambridge: Cambridge University Press.

Smith, N. 1984. *Uneven Development: Nature, Capital and the Production of Space.* Oxford: Basil Blackwell.

———. 1987. "Dangers of the Empirical Turn: Some Comments on the CURS Initiative." *Antipode* 19.1: 59–68.

———. 1988. "The Region Is Dead! The Region Is Dead! Long Live the Region!" *Political Geography Quarterly* 7.2: 141–52.

———. 1989. "Geography as Museum: Private History and Conservative Idealism in *The Nature of Geography.*" In *Reflections on Richard Hartshorne's "The Nature of Geography,"* edited by J. N. Entrikin and S. D. Brunn, 91–120. Washington, D.C.: Occasional Publication of the Association of American Geographers.

Smith, N., and W. Dennis. 1987. "The Restructuring of Geographical Scale: Coalescence and Fragmentation of the Northern Core Region." *Economic Geography* 63: 160–82.

Soja, E. 1989. *Postmodern Geographies: The Reassertion of Space in Critical Social Theory.* New York: Verso.

Southall, H. 1988. "Towards a Geography of Unionization: The Spatial Organization and Distribution of Early British Trade Unions." *Transactions of the Institute of British Geographers,* n.s., 13: 466–83.

35

———. 1989. "British Artisan Unions in the New World." *Journal of Historical Geography* 15.2: 163–82.

———. 1996. "Agitate! Agitate! Organize! Political Travellers and the Construction of a National Politics, 1839–1880." *Transactions of the Institute of British Geographers*, n.s., 21: 177–93.

Sunley, P. 1986. "Regional Restructuring, Class Change, and Political Action: A Comment." *Environment and Planning D: Society and Space* 4: 465–68.

———. 1990. "Striking Parallels: A Comparison of the Geographies of the 1926 and 1984–85 Coalmining Disputes." *Environment and Planning D: Society and Space* 8: 35–52.

Taylor, P. J. 1981. "Geographical Scales within the World-Economy Approach." *Review* 5.1: 3–11.

———. 1987. "The Paradox of Geographical Scale in Marx's Politics." *Antipode* 19.3: 287–306.

Thelen, K. A. 1991. *Union of Parts: Labor Politics in Postwar Germany.* Ithaca, N.Y.: Cornell University Press.

Undy, R., P. Fosh, H. Morris, P. Smith, and R. Martin. 1996. *Managing the Unions: The Impacts of Legislation on Trade Unions' Behaviour.* Oxford: Clarendon.

van Wezel Stone, K. 1981. "The Post-War Paradigm in American Labor Law." *Yale Law Journal* 90.7: 1509–80.

Weber, A. 1929. *Theory of the Location of Industries.* Chicago: University of Chicago Press (originally published in German in 1909).

Wills, J. 1996a. "Geographies of Trade Unionism: Translating Traditions across Space and Time." *Antipode* 28.4: 352–78.

———. 1996b. "Uneven Reserves: Geographies of Banking Trade Unionism." *Regional Studies* 30: 359–72.

Andrew Herod

Part I

Increasing the Scale of Things
Labor's Transnational Spatial Strategies and the Geography of Capitalism

Andrew Herod

Of the little writing within geography that has examined the issue of labor union-ism, by far the vast majority has looked at unionism in the local, regional, or na-tional context, whether in terms of the impacts of deindustrialization on par-ticular locales or regions (e.g., Hudson and Sadler 1986), the restructuring of the regional geography of unionism in certain countries (e.g., Martin, Sunley, and Wills 1993), the national structure of labor regulation (e.g., Clark 1989), the geography of union elections (e.g., Clark and Johnston 1987), or the re-gional cultural practices engaged in by workers and their unions (e.g., Cooke 1985). In contrast, not much geographic writing has analyzed unions' activities in the international arena. This seems surprising given both the recent focus within geography on processes and implications of economic globalization and the long history of labor internationalism itself. Indeed, examples of labor internation-alism can be traced back at least into the middle of the nineteenth century (van Holthoon and van der Linden 1988; Southall 1989), and more recently much Cold War rivalry was played out in the realm of the international labor move-ment (Radosh 1969; Windmuller 1980; Herod 1997, 1998).

Globalization has fundamentally restructured the economic, political, and ge-ographic contexts within which unions must operate. Through the use of mod-ern telecommunications satellites, fax machines, and the Internet, corporations are increasingly able to manage offshore accounts and factories as easily as if they were situated right next to corporate headquarters. Modern transportation methods such as containerization, intermodalism, and wide-bodied jet aircraft capable of moving large amounts of cargo have dramatically reduced relative dis-tances between places and eroded old regional and national market boundaries. As globalization has become a permanent feature of workers' lives, some unions have increasingly begun to think about ways of addressing the new geographic realities that it brings with it. The three essays in part I of this book examine how unions in three different parts of the world (Eastern Europe, the U.S.-Mexico border area, and East Asia) have attempted to deal with the growing globaliza-

39

tion and interpenetration of local regional economies. Specifically, these unions have had to reconstruct the geographic scale of their operations, either by pursuing international strategies (in the U.S.-Mexico and East Asian examples) or by expanding their already international operations into new regions (in the Eastern European case). Through such actions, workers and unions have been actively involved in shaping the processes of globalization that are the hallmark of contemporary capitalism, both by modifying the impacts of capital's activities and by shaping internationally the very possibilities for those activities.

The first essay (my own) examines the activities of the International Metalworkers' Federation in Eastern Europe since the so-called collapse of communism in 1989. The International Metalworkers' Federation is an international trade secretariat to which unions from different countries working in the metals extraction and processing industries, together with those working in autos, engineering, and several other related sectors, are affiliated. Events in Eastern Europe since 1989 have unleashed powerful geographic forces both within the region and beyond. The geography of trade unionism has been dramatically refashioned (see Herod 1997 and 1998 for more details), while the influx of Western foreign direct investment (especially from Germany and Austria) is raising concerns among labor officials in both the East and the West that Eastern Europe will simply become a low-wage production zone serving Western Europe. If this fear materializes, employers in higher-wage Western European countries might increasingly use Eastern Europe as a geographic safety valve for problems they face, either by exporting large quantities of capital and goods as part of a geographic solution to crises of accumulation in the West (cf. Harvey 1985 for more on the theoretical arguments behind capital's use of space in such a manner) or by using the threat of relocation to undercut conditions enjoyed by Western European workers.

Since 1989, the International Metalworkers' Federation has become especially active in Eastern Europe, conducting numerous seminars concerning collective bargaining, labor law, health and safety, and welfare programs with the goal of training local unionists in the skills of operating in market economies. For the federation, the development of strong unions in Eastern Europe is not only significant in its own right for protecting the rights of workers in the region during a period of transition to an almost anarchic free-market capitalism, but also has important implications beyond the immediate region. It is clear that the federation is operating with distinct geographic objectives in mind. Eastern Europe's proximity to high-wage Western Europe means that it is a region of great geostrategic importance that the federation is seeking to anchor within the fold of Western labor unionism and Western economic and political systems. Not only will this

Andrew Herod

protect conditions in Western Europe and encourage the growth of strong unionism in Eastern Europe, but it will also help to provide a spatial buffer zone with the republics of the former Soviet Union, where the transition is somewhat less secure and the political future less certain. In pursuing these ends, the federation has adopted policies that are sensitive to the variety of cultural, economic, social, and political traditions in the region, tailoring programs to specific countries and situations rather than treating the region as a homogeneous bloc, as was the tendency during the Cold War.

Altha J. Cravey, while focusing on a different empirical example, also examines how unions are attempting to deal with issues raised by the growing economic integration of two regions in great geographic proximity that exhibit markedly different levels of economic development: the two sides of the U.S.-Mexico border. The border between the United States and Mexico is the longest of any in the world between an advanced industrial economy and a less developed country. Historically, the economies of the southwestern United States and of Mexico have been intertwined through trade, labor migration, and cultural links. Between the 1940s and the 1960s, agribusiness interests in California in particular relied heavily on Mexican braceros (literally, "day laborers") to work the fields (see McWilliams 1939 and Mitchell 1996 for accounts of migratory labor flows in California agriculture). With the ending of the U.S.-sponsored "Bracero Program" in the 1960s, however, the Mexican government began to rethink its economic development strategies and to initiate a border industrialization program. This represented a drastic change in the country's geography of industrial development compared to what had existed prior to the 1960s. The availability of cheaper labor and more lax labor laws on the Mexican side of the border, together with the Mexican government's establishment of export processing zones in the border region, attracted investment from many U.S. corporations interested in cutting production costs while still serving the domestic U.S. market. Through establishing *maquiladoras*, such corporations have been able to split up their production by leaving the management and research and development teams on the U.S. side while shipping assembly work to Mexico.

By dramatically reshaping the geography of industrialization in Mexico, the growth of the *maquiladora* factories along the border has had significant impacts on the geography of unionism in the country. Earlier in the twentieth century, the geography of industrialization, focused as it was in central Mexico, spawned close links between the corporatist Mexican labor movement and the ruling Partido Revolucionario Institucional (PRI), which has governed Mexico for most of this century. The new factory regime in the border region, however, is forcing Mexican unions to reorganize their structures and modes of operation. This re- 41 structuring of industry has not only undercut traditional institutional ties between the Confederación de Trabajadores de México (CTM; the dominant union confederation in Mexico) and the PRI apparatus, but has also provided a new space (both material and metaphorical) for more radical unionism to emerge, which is challenging the old corporatist relationship between the CTM and the PRI. Furthermore, the growing integration of the U.S. and Mexican economies, not least as a result of the North American Free Trade Agreement (NAFTA), is spawning growing cross-border organizing efforts as Mexican and U.S. unionists who work for the same transnational corporations seek to confront low wages and conditions in Mexico on the one hand, and, on the other hand, the ability of U.S. corporations to relocate to such border spaces as a means of undercutting wages at home.

The theme of unions remaking the geographic scale at which they operate to address corporate activities and the uneven geography of production and development is also taken up in Robert Hanham and Shawn Banasick's analysis of Japanese labor. They show how a number of unions in Japan have attempted to expand the geographic scale of their activities as a strategy to cope with the internationalization of Japanese manufacturing capital. The reconstruction of Japanese unions during the late 1940s led to the installing of a locally oriented brand of trade unionism that bore great similarities to the U.S. model (cf. Clark 1989). In itself, this is not surprising, given that the process of union reconstruction was largely supervised by the occupying U.S. forces, who were intent on building up the unions to provide a bulwark against the *zaibatsu*, large industrial and financial combines that had supported the Japanese military and war effort. However, the locally oriented nature of unionism in Japan during the postwar period has been key to shaping the geography of the country's labor unionism in two ways. First, it has encouraged many workers to identify their interests with the enterprises in which they work, rather than with unions in other plants, thereby encouraging "plant chauvinism" and geographic divisions between workers. Second, since the 1940s, Japanese labor has spent much time and effort seeking to reconstruct the geographic scale at which unions interact and operate as a way of overcoming the constraints imposed on them by the locally bound nature of the Japanese labor relations system. This has been achieved primarily through the creation of national federations designed to coordinate activities between locally constituted unions.

The growing internationalization of the Japanese economy and manufacturing capital in the 1980s added a new twist to the unions' political and geographic strategies. As Japanese corporations came under competitive pressures, many looked to cheaper production sites in East Asia. The unions in Japan have re-

42

sponded to this in two ways. Seeing the continued profitability of Japanese capital as crucial to maintaining Japanese workers' standards of living, the dominant and conservative Rengo federation has supported the overseas expansion of Japanese corporations to countries such as South Korea and Thailand (there are interesting parallels between Rengo's activities in East Asia and those of the U.S. labor movement in Latin America and the Caribbean during the early to mid-twentieth century; see Herod 1997; Scott 1978). Rengo has played an active role in encouraging the internationalization of Japanese manufacturing capital and in the integration of the East Asian regional economy, even to the point of supporting the breaking of foreign unions so that the profitability of Japanese capital can be assured. Other unions, however, less tied to the model of company unionism and more left-wing in their political orientations, have also been developing international contacts, although in this case with the goal of establishing progressive links with unions abroad so as to challenge Japanese corporations' overseas activities. In essence, the activities of right-wing federations such as Rengo and of Rengo's left-wing rivals have been designed to remake the geographic scale at which they operate and increasingly have involved an international strategy, if for quite different political reasons. Through this process, Japanese unions, whether actively supporting the expansion of Japanese capital overseas or seeking to develop greater solidarity with workers in other East Asian countries, are playing an active role in the processes of globalization of the Japanese economy.

Bibliography

Clark, G. L. 1989. *Unions and Communities under Siege: American Communities and the Crisis of Organized Labor.* New York: Cambridge University Press.

Clark, G. L., and K. Johnston. 1987. "The Geography of US Union Elections I: The Crisis of US Unions and a Critical Review of the Literature." *Environment and Planning A* 19: 33–57.

Cooke, P. 1985. "Class Practices as Regional Markers: A Contribution to Labour Geography." In *Social Relations and Spatial Structures,* edited by D. Gregory and J. Urry, 213–41. New York: St. Martin's Press.

Harvey, D. 1985. "The Geopolitics of Capitalism." In *Social Relations and Spatial Structures,* edited by D. Gregory and J. Urry, 128–63. New York: St. Martin's Press.

Herod, A. 1997. "Labor as an Agent of Globalization and as a Global Agent." In *Spaces of Globalization: Reasserting the Power of the Local,"* edited by K. Cox, 167–200. New York: Guilford Press.

———— 1998. "Of Blocs, Flows and Networks: The End of the Cold War, Cyberspace, and the Geo-economics of Organized Labor at the *fin de millénaire.*"

In *An Unruly World? Globalization, Governance, and Geography*, edited by A. Herod, G. Ó Tuathail, and S. Roberts, 162–95. London: Routledge.

Hudson, R., and D. Sadler. 1986. "Contesting Works Closures in Western Europe's Industrial Regions: Defending Place or Betraying Class?" In *Production, Work, Territory*, edited by A. Scott and M. Storper, 172–93. Hemel Hempstead, U.K.: Allen and Unwin.

Martin, R., P. Sunley, and J. Wills. 1993. "The Geography of Trade Union Decline: Spatial Dispersal or Regional Resilience?" *Transactions of the Institute of British Geographers*, n.s., 18.1: 36–62.

McWilliams, C. 1939. *Factories in the Field: The Story of Migratory Farm Labor in California*. Boston: Little, Brown.

Mitchell, D. 1996. *The Lie of the Land: Migrant Workers and the California Landscape*. Minneapolis: University of Minnesota Press.

Radosh, R. 1969. *American Labor and United States Foreign Policy*. New York: Random House.

Scott, J. 1978. *Yankee Unions, Go Home! How the AFL Helped the U.S. Build an Empire in Latin America*. Vancouver: New Star Books.

Southall, H. 1989. "British Artisan Unions in the New World." *Journal of Historical Geography* 15.2: 163–82.

van Holthoon, F., and M. van der Linden, eds. 1988. *Internationalism in the Labour Movement 1830–1940*, vols. 1 and 2. London: E. J. Brill.

Windmuller, J. P. 1980. *The International Trade Union Movement*. Deventer, The Netherlands: Kluwer.

Andrew Herod

Chapter 1 • The Geostrategics of Labor in Post–Cold War Eastern Europe

An Examination of the Activities of the International Metalworkers' Federation

Andrew Herod

Today, the deterioration of the economic landscape in Eastern Europe gives rise to concern and anxiety.

The East-West Cold War may be over. The North-South divide grows day by day. But if we can consolidate democratic trades unionism in Eastern Europe, if we can help create societies based on social and economic justice, if we can stop the banks and the multinationals from exploiting workers, if we can harness the energy and democratic commitment of Polish and Czechoslovakian and other workers to build solid unions of metalworkers, then this will help the task of metalworkers everywhere in the world.

Marcello Malentacchi, general secretary, International Metalworkers' Federation[1]

"Geopolitical analysis," Saul Cohen has written, relates "international political power to the geographical setting" (Cohen 1964, 24). Historically, students of geopolitics and international political power have focused their attention on the state in order to examine and understand how the "geographical setting" shapes the practice of statecraft (cf. O'Sullivan 1986). In the early 1990s, some political geographers and political scientists began to move beyond the traditional focus of geopolitics and its concern with issues of military power and strategic location to examine questions of international economics and their effect on statecraft (what is sometimes referred to as a "geo-economic" approach) (e.g., Luttwak 1990; Grant 1993; O'Loughlin 1993; Ó Tuathail 1993). Others, working from a more critical perspective, began to use discourse analysis to examine how language and symbols are used to create particular geopolitical understandings of the world (Dalby 1990, 1994; Dodds 1994; Ó Tuathail 1994; Ó Tuathail and Agnew 1992; Popke 1994; Sidaway 1994). In both the traditional brand of geopolitical analysis and its nascent critique, however, political geographers have largely ignored trade unions as international geopolitical and geo-economic actors. This is a surprising

45

omission given the long history of international trade-union activities, which stretches back to the mid-nineteenth century (van Holthoon and van der Linden 1988), and the fact that much Cold War geopolitical rivalry was played out in the realm of international labor politics (see Foner 1989; Godson 1984; Morris 1967; Radosh 1969; and Herod 1997, 1998a).[2] In this essay, I wish to push further the critical reexamination of geopolitical analysis as traditionally practiced to investigate how the geographical setting is shaping the international activities of an international labor organization — the International Metalworkers' Federation (IMF) — and how, in turn, these activities are helping to reshape the geopolitical and geo-economic order of post–Cold War Europe. Headquartered in Geneva, the IMF is an International Trade Secretariat (ITS) with which unions operating in the metals processing, engineering, aerospace, automobiles, shipbuilding, telecommunications, and several other industries throughout the world are affiliated (Harmon 1959 outlines the IMF's general structure; Casserini 1993 provides a history of the federation since it was founded in 1893). It provides information and resources to its various affiliates concerning wages, work conditions, labor laws, and strikes, and consults with, and brings pressure to bear on, employers and governments concerning matters that affect its affiliates (see Herod 1995 for a case study of a global corporate campaign in which the IMF was involved). The federation had few formal contacts with unions in Eastern Europe during the period of the Cold War, but since 1989 it has been very active in developing links between Western unions and unions that have emerged or democratized in Eastern Europe and the new republics of the former Soviet Union, several of which have now become IMF affiliates.

As the statements by the IMF's general secretary, Marcello Malentacchi, reproduced at the beginning of this chapter indicate, Eastern Europe represents at once both a "problem region" and, potentially, a "keystone region" of great importance to the IMF. The federation is keen to ensure the growth of strong, democratic, and independent trade unionism as a means to protect workers' rights in Eastern Europe but also to prevent the region from becoming a low-wage competitor for metalworkers in other parts of the globe, especially in neighboring Western Europe. This is of concern in view of the fact that some former Soviet satellite states might become full members of the European Union, which would allow their products to flow freely across national boundaries within the union. Indeed, the Czech Republic, Poland, and Hungary have already taken steps toward becoming associate members of the union and were admitted to NATO in 1997. The availability of both skilled and unskilled workers at relatively low wages so close to Western Europe has encouraged many Western corporations to set up operations in the region, causing some West European workers to fear

Andrew Herod

that their jobs might be threatened by competition from imports of more cheaply produced commodities. In seeking to aid metalworkers in Eastern Europe, the IMF is not only carrying out age-old principles of internationalism in the trade-union movement, but is also thinking in geographic and geostrategic terms about the transition in the East and how the breakdown of the old geopolitical and geo-economic blocs of the past half century might affect workers in the West. The federation is, in fact, seeking to play a significant role in shaping the new order in post–Cold War Europe (and beyond).

The purpose of this essay is twofold. First, it examines the effects of the transformations in Eastern Europe on trade unions. Although there is a burgeoning geographic literature on the transition in Eastern Europe, it has focused predominantly on the geography of foreign investment (Murphy 1992; Michalak 1993; Buckwalter 1995), economic restructuring (Pavlínek 1992; Smith 1994), the region's foreign debt (Gibb and Michalak 1993), problems of implementing democratic political structures and of gaining legitimacy (Frankland and Cox 1995), and the implications of the transition for international geopolitics. Relatively little has been written on the new geographical relationships unions must deal with during the transition to the market economy and the ways they are seeking to shape the economic and political geographies of the post–Cold War period. The first section of the essay, then, fills in some of the gaps in the geographic writing about the transition by examining some of the changes that have taken place since 1989 in Eastern Europe as they affect workers and trade unions. The end of the Cold War brought with it an economic and political transformation that is posing significant challenges for workers and trade unions throughout Europe (see Clarke, Fairbrother, and Borisov 1995 and Herod 1998b). For workers in the former Soviet bloc, the shift from a centrally planned system of production and distribution to a market economy is changing the relationships between enterprise managers, the workforce, the state, and the trade unions, while the end of state control over the official trade-union movements has seen the emergence of a multitude of new trade unions, labor organizations, and workers' groups vying for influence.

The influx of Western capital, too, is affecting the geography of production and consumption in the region. Not only are Western companies' new facilities often more modern and better able to compete in local markets than locally owned facilities, but many local producers are finding it difficult to hire and/or retain skilled (and even unskilled) workers in the face of higher wages and benefits offered by Western companies. This is reshaping labor markets and migration patterns throughout the region. At the same time, the introduction of Western-style management and labor relations is forcing many workers in Eastern Europe to learn new ways of working and is transforming the manner in which the "regimes" (Burawoy 1985) of labor control operating in the workplace are articulated. In turn, this has raised fears that foreign investors will try to introduce work methods that workers in their home countries have been successful in prohibiting but that the nascent labor organizations in Eastern Europe may still be too weak to prevent.

Second, this essay considers some of the IMF's activities designed to help trade unionists in the region adapt to, and operate in, a market economy. The IMF is playing an important role in shaping the economy and politics of post–Cold War Europe, at least in the field of labor relations and trade-union politics. This suggests (1) that political geographers should pay greater attention to the international activities of trade unions during the transition (and more generally), and (2) that understanding the specific geographic context within which the IMF finds itself provides insights into its activities in Eastern Europe and the federation's geostrategic thinking with regard to the transition. Such a geographic perspective, I argue, can add significantly to an understanding of unions' economic and political behavior.

Effects of the Transformations in Eastern Europe for Trade Unions

The fall of the Berlin Wall, the collapse of the Soviet Union, and the ongoing economic and political transformations in Eastern Europe represent a fundamental restructuring of the geopolitical order that dominated Europe for the past half century. In this section, I address some of the implications of these transformations for trade unions in the region as they struggle to redefine their roles and come to terms with the new economic and political forces unleashed during the transition to the market economy (see Herod 1997 and 1998a for a discussion of Cold War international trade-union politics). I examine the effects of privatization on the economies of the region, the rise of new trade-union and workers' groups, the new roles such groups are attempting to define, and the influx of foreign capital.

Privatization

For many "reformers," the future success of the Eastern European economies is seen to lie in the ability to break up and demonopolize the state sector — particularly the massive enterprises built up during the Communist period — and to encourage the formation of smaller-sized firms in order to establish a system in which autonomous, decentralized production units can compete with each other and on the world market.[3] Privatization is viewed as the principal means by which such a transformation will be brought about (Gaudier 1991). However, privatization is raising serious questions and posing problems for workers and trade unions in the region, in particular with regard to the codification of property rights, compensation to former owners of businesses seized after World War II, how state-run enterprises are to be valued, who will control such enterprises after privatization, and whether restructuring them should be carried out by the state prior to privatization or by the new private owners after purchase. This latter question, particularly, is proving to be a source of major conflict as many of the old *nomenklatura* seek to use their position of influence in the state sector to acquire economic and political power in the market economy sector.

Although privatization is seen in all the region's countries as the catalyst by which to bring about the transition to a market economy, the rate at which privatization has been occurring and the manner in which it is being implemented vary widely. Czechoslovakia, Romania, and Russia were among the first countries to undertake mass privatization programs with sales of enterprises in 1992. These were followed by Estonia and Lithuania in 1993. The remaining countries of the former Soviet Union and other transition economies did not develop programs until later. By 1996, most of the countries of the region had introduced some kind of mass privatization program. Even the term *privatization* has been taken to mean different things by different people, including the sale of assets, the sale of shares, transfer of shares to workers, cutting off public funding to force enterprises to look to private sources, deregulation, the breaking up of monopolies and the sale of subsidiaries, and privatization of management through the replacement of state-appointed managers by private ones (see the discussions in Daintith 1993 and Estrin and Stone 1996 on different forms of privatization). In the Czech Republic, for instance, small and medium-sized enterprises (mostly services, retail stores, and small cooperatives) have been sold at auction under the auspices of district privatization commissions appointed by the central government, whereas privatization of large enterprises has been carried out through a system in which citizens can buy vouchers to be used to bid for shares of state enterprises. In Poland, in contrast, large enterprises have been privatized mainly through a process of capitalization in which they are first converted into government-controlled joint-stock companies and shares or stock are subsequently transferred to third parties. Small and medium-sized enterprises, though, have usually been privatized by liquidation and the direct sale of assets. In Romania, some thirty profitable small-sized enterprises were among the first to be partly privatized through the auction of assets in 1992, although the government later launched a larger privatization campaign in which citizens were entitled to receive free of charge 30 percent of the capital of former state-owned companies held in a number of mutual

49

funds (called Private Ownership Funds) (International Metalworkers' Federation 1993).

Whereas some governments (e.g., in Hungary and Poland) were early proponents of privatization, others (e.g., in Bulgaria, Slovenia, and Romania) have been slower to develop such programs. As Poul-Erik Olsen (1995) of the International Metalworkers' Federation has observed about the early days of the transition: "In Romania and Bulgaria, everybody spoke about privatization but in fact very little happened." Although in Hungary, Bulgaria, and the Czech Republic privatization (particularly in the early days of the transition) was often little more than a legal change in ownership, in Poland and Slovenia it has more frequently gone hand in hand with attempts to bring about a rapid restructuring of enterprises (see Šarčević 1992 for case studies of several countries' privatization plans). Moreover, although legislation authorizing privatization was adopted throughout the region, in many instances procedures for implementing it have frequently not been clearly established. Even in the Czech Republic, where the government of Prime Minister Václav Klaus has been one of the most fervent proponents of neoliberal policies, trade unionists in the mid-1990s were still complaining that the process of privatization had taken on the aura of a somewhat artificial "crypto-privatization," and that even after nearly a decade of transition there was still "zero mechanism established for the functioning of any capital trade" and that much privatization was little more than speculative activity of the part of banks and portfolio investors (Falbr 1996). Although official policy in all countries is to push privatization, the absence of other necessary economic and political institutions (banks that can provide venture capital, stock exchanges, taxation and insurance policies, etc.) means that privatization is not unproblematic.

The process of privatization, then, has been very uneven throughout the region, with different consequences for different groups of workers (Smith 1997). Nevertheless, workers are facing a number of common challenges that go beyond the specifics of their particular country's privatization process. Foremost among these is the rise in unemployment levels as many enterprises are sold off and/or shut down because they are ill prepared to compete according to "free-market" principles. Rising levels of unemployment have gone hand in hand with a dramatic collapse in real wage levels associated with often rapid and substantial price increases in food, housing, transportation, and consumer goods to their "true" market levels. Many workers are also losing access to state-provided social services on which they have traditionally relied (such as universal and free education and health care, family allowances, uniform old-age pensions). These services either are being discontinued because of cutbacks in government expenditures or are being privatized (as with the rise in private medicine, growing numbers of

50

employee-funded, contribution-defined pension plans, etc.). Combined with the loss of "existential security" (the triumvirate of job, income, and housing security formerly provided by the state), many workers are finding that they are increasingly unable to provide for themselves and their families, a situation that is fueling social unrest and has sparked strikes and demonstrations. Such unrest has been directed especially against the widening income gaps between the majority of workers and the relatively small class of affluent entrepreneurs, often former Communist managers of newly privatized enterprises.

Privatization also augurs dramatic shifts in the industrial structure and economic geography of the region, shifts that will undoubtedly be quicker and deeper in some areas and sectors than in others. The probable turn away from heavy industry and toward consumer durables' production, together with the growth of subcontracting, the breakup of large collective units of production, greater market penetration by high- and low-quality imports, and the de-specialization and respecialization of many enterprises, will have very disruptive effects on millions of workers and their communities as old factories need to retool and new ones are built (Gaudier 1991). In addition, thousands of new small, private enterprises have been established and thousands of old (and new) establishments have shut down. This is causing problems for unions trying to organize the workplace because they frequently cannot keep up with the rapid pace at which some of these businesses open and close. Most unions have also reported difficulty in winning bargaining rights from invariably hostile employers (even when the workforce overwhelmingly favors unionization), especially in the smaller private firms (International Metalworker's Federation 1994). Thus, although they have generally supported privatization, many unions fear that the economic and social dislocation it is bringing will expose workers to the worst excesses of capitalist development — leading many to refer to the region as the "Wild East" — unless the unions have the freedom and ability to organize workplaces and unless they can prevent the total withdrawal of the state from the provision of social services and enforcement of pro-worker protective legislation (Mureau 1995a).

Trade Unions and Labor Relations

The transition from centrally planned economies to market economies and the end of state control over the trade unions are leading to dramatic changes in the roles played by unions and in the way in which labor markets function. During the Communist period, trade unions served primarily as "transmission belts" by which directions concerning production were transmitted from central planners to workers on the shop floor and (theoretically at least) information about shop-floor conditions was made known to the central planners and party officials.

Unions had a dual role of mobilizing and disciplining the workforce for production and "socialist emulation," while also representing members' legal rights and interests in the face of management (i.e., state) arbitrariness (see Herod 1998b). In practice, however, the former role usually took precedence and the unions' primary consideration was the promotion of party and government policy. Certainly, there were variations on this model. Both East Germany and Czechoslovakia, for instance, were relatively industrialized societies prior to the Communist period and both had well-established pre-Communist social democratic traditions. Consequently, the Communist parties and trade unions in those countries were more inclined to follow relatively egalitarian wage policies, especially during the 1950s and 1960s, and to adopt policies designed to protect workers in the factory than were the unions in countries such as Bulgaria and Romania, which were predominantly agrarian societies at the end of World War II. In these latter countries, the pre-Communist tradition of trade unionism was much weaker and the unions tended to act in the postwar period as agents of modernization and enforcers of industrial discipline on workforces more attuned to the rhythms of agricultural production than to those of the factory floor (Pravda and Ruble 1986). Nevertheless, a number of commonalities did run through the role played by Communist trade unions and their practice of industrial relations.

The Soviet model of unionism imposed after World War II involved a centralized structure of union control in which key union positions were appointed by party officials (Clark 1966; Herod 1998b). As Pravda and Ruble (1986, 4) put it, "trade unions remain[ed] closely subordinated to the party yet organizationally distinct from it, [a] distinction [that] afford[ed] a degree of administrative latitude but exclude[d] policy neutrality, let alone union autonomy." Only at the enterprise level did unions enjoy even a limited degree of local control, although the legal structure severely limited what they could negotiate with management (Nagy 1984). Furthermore, unions tended to adopt an organizational structure in which all those employed in a particular sector were eligible for membership, even managers. Although most countries in the region had both sectoral and enterprise-level contracts, there was little collective bargaining of the sort that Western unions would recognize, and collective agreements rarely included provisions covering wage rates or basic working conditions such as working time and leave (International Metalworkers' Federation 1994). Disputes between workers and management were often settled by higher authorities through mediation or arbitration rather than by industrial action (resolution was supposed to be through amicable negotiation and not adversarial collective bargaining). Indeed, strikes were seen as failures of the system rather than as legitimate union weapons for improving the lot of the membership (Pravda and Ruble 1986). The fact that

52

the state played the role of employer and manager of enterprises meant that there were few employers' organizations of the sort that exist in most advanced capitalist economies. In their place existed a network of trade associations and chambers of industry, commerce, or economy — usually little more than extensions of the Ministry of Trade — that had very little to do with the conduct of labor relations (International Metalworkers' Federation 1994). Although some limited efforts to develop less state-controlled collective bargaining were made in the 1980s (particularly in Hungary and Poland), these had few tangible effects because the state continued to retain control over the principal elements of the employment relation (e.g., wage determination) (Héthy 1991).

This situation has already changed in dramatic ways. The state no longer controls the trade unions the way it once did. Two models of independent unionism have emerged: the growth of new unions now allowed under the law (the "Polish model"), and the taking over of formerly Communist-controlled unions by reformist elements and their restructuring along democratic, autonomous lines (the "Czech model") (Héthy 1991; Brewster 1992). In addition, some unions are still dominated by the old *nomenklatura* but have declared their independence from state institutions (see Herod 1998a and 1998b for details). These developments have had two major sets of consequences.

First, the ending of state control over the union movement is giving rise to a new role for unions. Although some countries lag behind, efforts have been made in all of them to lift some legal barriers to collective bargaining, to bring about the separation of government, trade unions, and employers' associations, to exclude political parties from being labor relations actors, to provide legal recognition of the right to strike (although this is still severely limited in some countries), and to create tripartite institutions that, while recognizing that collective bargaining should be free of government interference, bring unions, employers, and government representatives together to address matters of "national interest" such as inflation and minimum wage rates (Héthy 1991; Musil 1991).[4] As a result, unions are increasingly taking on the role of representatives of workers' interests and rights in dealings with government officials and the still small number of employers' associations. Furthermore, the withdrawal of the state from the unions' activities has led many to adopt decentralized confederative organizational structures in an attempt to prevent the centralization of power reminiscent of the Communist era and to preserve local autonomy. This is, however, hampering the ability of the national leadership of many unions to address national issues concerning wages, working conditions, and the like. In the former Czechoslovakia, for instance, the national chamber of trade unions (ČSKOS) that replaced the old Communist body in 1990 initially adopted a voluntaristic model patterned after the AFL–CIO in the United States, although the successor chambers to it in the Czech and Slovak Republics (the Českomoravská Komora Odborových Svazů [ČMKOS] and the Konfederácia Odborových Zväzov Slovenskej Republiky [KOZ SR]) are now seeking to develop stronger centralized control in order to present a more unified front to the employers and the government (Falbr 1996). Nevertheless, some 75 percent of union dues collected still remain with the local union at the enterprise level, with the remainder being divided between regional and national organizations (OS KOVO n.d.). Similar proportions are reported throughout the region (International Metalworkers' Federation 1994; Olsen 1995). Such a "localist" structure has the potential to lead to a veritable geographic patchwork of wage rates and working conditions, which could provide companies the opportunities to play workers in different plants and regions against each other — a situation that U.S. workers have increasingly faced as employers have broken up national agreements in several industries (cf. Herod 1991).

Second, there has been a proliferation of new unions under the revised labor laws. The Charter of Fundamental Rights and Liberties of January 1991 in the former Czechoslovakia, for example, stipulated that "trade union organisations shall be established independently of the State" and that "it shall be inadmissible to limit the number of trade union organisations" (article 27, 2, quoted in International Metalworkers' Federation 1994, 23–24). Similar legislation has been passed in other countries. In the Czech Republic, for instance, as few as three workers can charter a trade union, whereas in Romania a 1993 law allows as few as fifteen workers to do so. Although the growth in the number of independent trade unions will ensure workers' rights to organize unions of their own choosing, it is proving problematic as workers become divided between a plethora of old and new unions, which are often very small (Mureau 1995b).[5] Some employers have taken advantage of these laws to encourage breakaway groups of workers to form their own unions with which the employers then negotiate, a practice that threatens to weaken the bargaining power of organized labor (International Metalworkers' Federation 1992b). Something of a paradox exists in this regard. The old unions may be tainted in the eyes of many workers because of their activities during the Communist period, but they often are the only ones with operational structures in place and financial assets on which they can draw. The new unions, on the other hand, are frequently short of cash and sometimes must rely on donations from Western unions to function. Thus, although workers may shy away from the old unions because of their Communist past, workers may also be reticent to join the new unions, which are often seen as ineffective.

54

The situation for many unions has been exacerbated by efforts in some countries to establish German-style "works councils" at the plant level with the right to confer with management on certain issues independently of the union (Thelen 1991).[6] These councils allow for labor participation in some work-related affairs but they are formally separate from the unions. Although collective bargaining at the plant and branch level is still the purview of the unions, the works councils have the right to consult with management on a range of issues, including safety rules, the introduction of new technologies and work methods, changes in wages and salaries, personnel decisions, and welfare arrangements. Worker representatives on these councils are often union members, but in no country is that a legal requirement. Thus, although many government and management officials have pushed such councils as bodies for representing workers within the workplace, many union officials fear that they are being established as a way for managers to avoid having to deal with the unions directly, especially given that the unions are still too weak in many countries to dominate such councils as they do in Germany (Uhlíř 1994). Furthermore, on the basis of experience with the German works council system, which is serving as something of a model for Eastern Europe, some union leaders have argued that councils foster "plant egoism" in which the parochial interests of particular plants are placed before broader union interests, a situation that can lead to problems of fragmentation for the national union — especially in the kind of decentralized union structure outlined earlier. Others contend that the councils are at present unable to defend the interests of workers because they are easily co-opted, given their legal obligations to work with management for the good of the plant (Thelen 1991).

Not only are the roles of the unions changing but so is the way in which labor markets operate. A number of characteristics concerning the operation of labor markets during the Communist period can be identified (Freeman 1992). Foremost among these was the tendency for workers to be hired on the basis of the need to meet *politically* determined production quotas, regardless of the labor costs involved. Moreover, the shortage of raw materials in many countries encouraged enterprises to hoard labor so that workers would be on hand when components and other production inputs arrived, whereas the shortage of consumer goods meant that enterprises frequently remunerated their workers with nonmonetary compensation (housing allotments, special permits to buy scarce goods, vacations in enterprise or union-owned resorts, etc.). Because wages were determined centrally by the planning agencies, they bore little relation to productivity or availability of skills. In addition, enterprises frequently paid their workforce with add-ons, so that sometimes as little as a quarter of a worker's wages consisted

55

of base pay. Finally, to a greater or lesser degree, labor mobility was restricted as a way of retaining skilled workers in particular enterprises and regions.

The political and economic transformations currently taking place in Eastern Europe are dramatically changing the way labor markets operate. This is causing consternation and confusion for many workers and trade unions. The main concern has been the rise in unemployment rates as many enterprises have laid off workers or closed down completely. This has been combined with growing levels of worker migration, particularly from regions with a disproportionate share of heavy industries, which have been among the hardest hit by the transition. Although some migrants have relocated within their home countries, the lack of employment opportunities and housing has forced many to move further afield to more developed East European countries such as the Czech Republic and Hungary, to West European countries (Germany, Austria, France, Sweden, Norway, Denmark, and the Benelux nations), and to Canada, the United States, and Australia. This is causing a number of problems. In the metals industry, for instance, migrants are disproportionately men between twenty and forty years of age who are relatively well educated and skilled (International Metalworkers' Federation 1992a). Not only is this having significant effects on civil and social life (women and children are frequently left behind, either temporarily or permanently), but it is depriving many enterprises and communities of their most skilled workers. Additionally, because such workers also represent a source of cheap labor, some West European unions have expressed fears that they might exert a downward pressure on wages in the West. In Germany, agreements have been established with several East European governments in which these countries' firms can use their own imported specialized labor (subject to an upper limit) while operating in the German market. Even within Eastern Europe, the influx of low-wage foreign workers is potentially a problem in (relatively) higher-wage countries such as the Czech Republic and Hungary, which have been the destination for thousands of migrants from farther east.

The withdrawal of the state from activities in which it formerly participated, together with the restructuring of the unions and their adoption of new roles, is changing the way wages and benefits are determined. Efforts have been made to decentralize the wage determination process, shifting it from the realm of the state to the enterprise or plant level. Many labor rights that were formerly guaranteed by law are devolving to the realm of collective bargaining, to be settled on a case-by-case basis, a situation that raises the specter that some workers will lose basic rights if they fail to secure them in their contracts or if employers simply ignore these contracts (as many are doing). Unions are pushing for collective bargaining to be adopted throughout the region, but in many instances

Andrew Herod

the lack of employers' associations or the unions' failure to convince employers to bargain collectively and in good faith, especially in the smaller private firms, makes this problematic — especially in view of the fact that in several countries employers have no legal obligation to bargain collectively.[7] This has several consequences for unions. Not only does it mean that throughout the region the procedures and mechanisms for collective bargaining often operate on an ad hoc basis with few formal guidelines, but unions invariably find it difficult to gain access to basic information from the company that is necessary for realistic bargaining to happen.[8] Given that there is usually no legal obligation to do so, most employers steadfastly refuse to disclose information that is often provided to Western unions as a matter of course. Furthermore, the lack of legal requirements to bargain collectively also frequently causes confusion over which union has the right to negotiate for, and sign agreements on behalf of, the workers (International Metalworkers' Federation 1994). This sometimes results in the employer choosing to bargain with the union it perceives to be most favorable to management's goals. At the plant level it is usually fairly obvious which union is favored by the workforce, but at the national level this is often not the case, sometimes leading the government (which is still often the enterprise owner) to make a political decision to negotiate with some unions and not with others.

In most East European countries, the lack of effective employers' associations means that collective bargaining is focused at the level of the individual enterprise or plant. Although this provides local unions the freedom to negotiate agreements sensitive to local conditions, it means that they are often unable to bring national political and economic power to bear on the employers and/or state. Agreements can be negotiated voluntarily at higher levels if an employers' association exists, but many employers and government officials have opposed formal regional or national contracts because they fear that these would give unions greater political and economic leverage. Furthermore, legislation throughout the region also allows workers to sign *individual* contracts with employers, who often offer higher wages to workers if they will do so rather than join the union, a practice that undermines the power of trade unions (Mureau 1994). In addition, a large number of enterprises are using wage tariff systems established by the government according to skill levels and length of employment with the company (International Metalworkers' Federation 1994) rather than through the process of collective bargaining, while still other employers simply impose conditions of remuneration unilaterally on their workers.

Significant variation also exists in Eastern Europe in how unions settle disputes and in the legal environment in which they operate. In Bulgaria, for example, the Law for Settlement of Collective Labor Disputes provides for negotiation and 57 arbitration of industrial disputes, with parties allowed to resort to arbitration after a minimum of two weeks of negotiations. Although the right to strike is enshrined in law, the employer must be notified in writing ahead of time of the union's intention to strike and of the expected duration of the strike. Spontaneous "work stoppages" (the equivalent of "wildcat strikes" in the United States) are limited to one hour's duration. In Romania, the law calls for obligatory mediation and conciliation before a union can strike while the Law on the Settlement of Collective Trade Disputes (law no. 15/1991) forbade strikes over issues that require adoption of a government decree, such as increases in the guaranteed minimum wage. Workers are prevented from striking to protest violations of the collective bargaining agreement, making it virtually impossible to legally defend workers' interests through industrial conflict. In Poland, the right to strike was granted to all nonpublic-sector workers in 1991. A strike may be initiated only after a vote and only if employers are given five days' notice of a planned action. In Hungary, new labor laws made no legal obligation for the two parties to conclude an agreement and strikes aimed at changing the provisions of the collective agreement before its expiration have been prohibited. Strikes with "unconstitutional aims" (however defined) have also been declared illegal.

Clearly, the legal protections offered workers with regard to their ability to strike vary widely, as does the propensity of workers to use the strike as a weapon to settle disputes. In the early 1990s, in particular in the Czech Republic, Slovakia, and Hungary, the unions were reticent to strike and preferred instead to use other means (such as public demonstrations) to achieve their goals — although strikes were used more frequently later on. In Poland, Bulgaria, and Romania, on the other hand, strikes (often illegal) have been used frequently and in a more overtly political manner since the first days of the post-Communist period, with strikers' goals often geared more toward changes in government policy than to workplace issues (International Metalworkers' Federation 1994). Evidently, as the transition progresses, the models of unionism and industrial relations adopted throughout the region, and the implications these have for workers, are likely to vary considerably as each country seeks to develop its own road to the market economy (cf. Herod 1998b).

Foreign Investment

Eastern Europe's transition to the market economy offers considerable business opportunities for Western corporations. The region represents a potential market of more than 400 million people (if the republics of the former Soviet Union are included) that is chronically short of consumer durables and other services, but that has large reserves of natural resources, a plethora of skilled manual workers in some countries, and relatively low wages. In addition, government officials and workers are often willing to ignore or relax work safety and environmental regulations. These factors and the region's proximity to Western Europe have encouraged investment and led to a slow but steady flow of Western capital into the region (Morawetz 1991). Furthermore, many governments and enterprises, strapped for cash and keen to attract Western capital — which they see as a means to jump-start their economies — have pushed joint ventures, direct acquisition of enterprises, franchising, and other forms of collaboration with Western corporations. Despite the many problems in doing business in the region — not least of which is how to repatriate their profits in hard currency — some Western corporations have taken the plunge and invested substantial quantities of capital.

Although the volume of foreign investment has been rather low relative to early expectations, between 1991 and 1996 the countries of Central and Eastern Europe and the former Soviet Union received a net inflow of $42.2 billion in foreign direct investment (a figure that represented only about 4 percent of the transition economies' GDP compared to inflows of about 6 percent of GDP for Latin America and 13 percent for the East Asian developing economies [International Monetary Fund 1997, 106]). Much of the investment in the region by Western governments has been in the form of credits and has gone toward rescheduling debt payments (*Le Monde* 1995). A large proportion of private foreign investment has been in the form of purchases of state-owned enterprises by Western companies seeking to establish subsidiaries in the region. Frequently, foreign acquisition has required restructuring and labor shedding before a deal has been possible; only when foreign companies have bought monopolies has this requirement for restructuring prior to purchase been outweighed by the race to gain access to monopoly profits (United Nations 1994).

Not all regions in Eastern Europe have received investment equally. Generally speaking, the more industrially developed economies of Central Europe (the Czech Republic, Hungary, and Poland) and the Baltic countries — and particularly those countries such as Hungary and Estonia that chose a privatization method that allowed major sales to foreign investors — have attracted the lion's share of foreign direct investment (FDI), about 70 percent between 1991 and 1996. Between 1991 and 1996, Hungary received a net influx of $12.8 billion in FDI, Poland $4.9 billion, and the Czech Republic $6.4 billion, compared to Bulgaria's $588 million, Slovenia's $650 million, and Romania's $1.4 billion (International Monetary Fund 1997, 107).[9] The dominant streams of investment have been in manufacturing and goods production, yet this investment emphasis varies geographically. In the Czech Republic, investment has been primarily in manufacturing and transport, whereas in Hungary the leading recipients have been manufacturing and the financial sector. Moreover, with the exception of a number of large joint-venture projects launched by Western corporations such as Volkswagen, ABB, General Motors, Siemens, and Fiat, the majority of foreign direct investment has been invested by small and medium-sized firms (International Metalworkers' Federation 1992b). During the early 1990s, Germany and Austria were the main countries of origin for such investment, with corporations from other West European countries, the United States, and Canada, together with a number of Asian nations, investing to a lesser degree. German and Austrian firms have invested particularly in the German-speaking areas of the Czech Republic, Poland, and Hungary. Japanese firms have been relatively slow to invest in the region, at least in the more industrialized countries, with most early Asian investment coming from South Korea and the People's Republic of China (Michalak 1993).

The growth of Western foreign direct investment entails several implications for workers and unions, of which three warrant mention. First, many union officials in the region fear that Western companies will seek to pursue labor relations practices that unions in their home countries have successfully prevented. Despite the relatively slow rate of Japanese investment, a primary union concern is that Western firms will adopt a model of labor relations based on the "Japanese model" of industrial development, namely, one with few skill divisions, a system of work organization based on teams, quality of work-life circles in which workers must do multiple tasks, company unionism, and so on (Uhlíř 1994). Given the lack of indigenous traditions of industrial relations on which they can draw, based on an experience of market economies, union officials are concerned that they might find it difficult to resist such models of "flexible" employment practices.

Second, many worry that the low wages and lack of work safety provisions in the region will encourage a branch plant economy to develop that services Western Europe in a semicolonial relationship. Such an economic relationship would have implications not only for workers' rights but also for the type of economic development that will take place in the region, development that will be determined to a large degree by foreign decision makers. Many union officials see in such an arrangement a future for Eastern Europe that more closely resembles that of, say, Mexico with its *maquiladoras* than of the Western European economies to which they aspire.

Third, many workers in Western Europe question how the growth of Western investment in Eastern Europe will affect their own wage rates, job security, and working conditions. The availability of very skilled, low-wage labor in the Czech Republic, Hungary, and Poland in particular, together with these countries'

Andrew Herod

efforts to gain full membership in the European Union, mean that higher wage-workers in countries such as Germany and Austria may face increasing competition for work. Eastern Europe may in fact come to serve as a geographic safety valve for Western employers, who can use the threat of relocation to undercut demands for wage increases, improvements in working conditions, or even unionization itself. Furthermore, if Eastern European countries do eventually gain full membership of the European Union, Western European employers could import lower-cost labor from the east, which would have the same effect as relocation, while also allowing them more easily to use ethnic, linguistic, and cultural differences to divide their domestic workforce.

The Role of the International Metalworkers' Federation in Remaking Labor Relations in Eastern Europe[10]

The disintegration of the relatively stable bipolar political and economic system that for almost half a century divided Europe between "West" and "East," capitalist and Communist, and its replacement with a seemingly more complex economic, political, and cultural landscape are posing many problems for the International Metalworkers' Federation. Amid the fragmentation of the old world order and the genesis of the new, the IMF's main objective in Eastern Europe has been to ensure that strong and democratic unions develop that will be able to defend the rights of workers and prevent them from being subjected to the worst excesses of capitalist development. In order to encourage a strong trade unionism capable of asserting itself as a negotiating power, the IMF has initiated a number of projects with metal unions in the region.

Perhaps the clearest example of the IMF's involvement in reconstructing trade unionism in Eastern Europe is its sponsorship of training seminars designed to familiarize the region's workers with the roles played by unions in market economies. Initiated in response to requests for information from trade unionists in the transition economies, these seminars have covered topics ranging from basic matters concerning trade-union structure in the West European and North American labor movements to specific information on putting together collective bargaining agreements, developing welfare and benefits programs (e.g., pension schemes), health and safety, workers' education, privatization, "lean" and just-in-time (JIT) production, converting military production to civilian production, how to read company balance sheets, negotiating and organizational skills, and various aspects of Western labor law (Olsen 1995). The IMF has translated manuals and handbooks on union structure and operation into several of the region's languages. In 1994 alone it conducted some forty seminars in Bulgaria, Romania, the Czech Republic, Slovakia, Slovenia, and Poland, while laying out a 61 framework for similar programs in some of the republics of the former Soviet Union. The federation also sent a delegation to Macedonia in late 1994. Although it initially adopted a cautious attitude with regard to the countries of the former Yugoslavia for fear that becoming too embroiled in the Balkan conflict might compromise its ability to work in the area after the end of the war (Mureau 1994), it did affiliate metalworkers from Macedonia in June 1995, set up a pilot scheme to gather information on problems local unionists face, and had some informal contact via third parties with opposition workers' groups in Serbia and Kosovo (Olsen 1995). In the early days of the transition, staff from the IMF's Geneva office conducted these seminars, but more recently the federation has involved some of its Western affiliates (Finnish unionists went to the Slovak Republic in 1995, for example, to train local unionists) while training East European unionists to develop their own training structures and run the programs themselves.

Despite much success, the IMF's efforts have run into some difficulties. In particular, the absence among Eastern European unions of a genuine collective bargaining tradition has been a major handicap. Unions often do not have sufficient technical expertise to understand company finances and macroeconomic analysis, and they are not always sufficiently familiar with the content of (rapidly changing) new laws (Mureau 1995a). Moreover, there are still few employers' associations with whom unions can negotiate and, where state ownership continues to be the dominant feature of the economy, the role of the employer has not been clearly defined (Olsen 1995). In addition, many terms and concepts that are second nature to Western trade unionists are unfamiliar to Eastern European workers (International Metalworkers' Federation 1994).[11] This situation is sometimes further complicated by the fact that the IMF's own staff and the representatives from its Western affiliates themselves come from different union traditions and may have different appreciations of such terms. Rivalry between different ethnic groups (the division of Czechoslovakia, for instance, was matched by the division of the country's metalworkers' union into two separate unions), between new and "reformed" unions (e.g., between the new union federation Podkrepa and the reformed CITUB in Bulgaria), as well as among new unions, have also sometimes made it difficult to coordinate IMF educational seminars. Indeed, on occasion the federation has been forced by the intensity of this rivalry to develop separate programs for new and reformed unions.[12] Nevertheless, the IMF hopes that by projecting an image of cooperation it can encourage the independent unions throughout Eastern Europe to work together on issues common to them all — such as the implications of privatization — and prevent fragmentation and multiplication of unions in the metals sector that, the federation fears, will weaken workers' collective bargaining power (Mureau 1994). As a practical way of encouraging such cooperation, in 1995 the IMF asked its Czech and Slovak affiliates to send a delegation to Bulgaria to share information on their privatization experience.

The political instability in the region has also presented problems for the IMF. In the early 1990s, rivalries and high worker expectations about the ability of unions rapidly to increase their standards of living produced a high turnover of union officials, which in turn has made it more difficult for IMF officials and representatives from the federation's Western affiliates to develop consistent long-term working relationships with some unions. In addition, serious problems of corruption on the part of many government officials have made dealing with some state agencies difficult. Many workers are still suspicious of trade unions because of their previous role under central planning as transmission belts for the Communist parties; many others fear a centralized union structure. As a result, both new and reformed unions have had a tendency to adopt a decentralized, locally oriented brand of trade unionism. IMF officials, however, are concerned that such a model of trade unionism, although pluralist in nature, will hinder efforts to develop strong national organizations capable of addressing issues resulting from privatization and confronting multiestablishment employers.

In general, the IMF has been careful not to advocate particular models of labor relations and has preferred to let the region's unions make their own way. Typically, the federation's position has been one of "We do not say 'this is the model for your development' but that 'we will assist you in your development.' ... We try to discuss with them what is required by the union in that particular country in that particular situation ... and where we can step in to help" (Olsen 1995). At the same time, however, it has been actively seeking to impress upon its new affiliates the importance of developing strong branch federation structures (Mureau 1994). Not only will this provide a structure in which the same union represents workers in different plants of the same company, but it will also begin to break down the old Communist structures in which the unions were organized to a great degree on the basis of the local political jurisdiction of the party rather than enterprise structure. One way the IMF has sought to do this is by providing information to the national union leaderships on the proportion of union dues that the federation's Western affiliates spend locally, regionally, and nationally, and on the roles that such affiliates' regional and national organizations play in wage bargaining, health and safety issues, legislative lobbying, and the like. In turn, the national leaderships have used this information to try to persuade local unions of the need for some greater degree of power and union funds to be placed in the hands of the national unions.

63

The federation has paid particular attention to the great variation of economic conditions, histories, political situations, local cultures, and needs across Eastern Europe in developing its programs in a process that might be described as the "glocalization of labor." For example, whereas the unions in the Czech Republic have tended to work more independently of the IMF and have consulted with it more on issues related to privatization, the IMF has been much more active in developing links with workers in the Slovak Republic, especially around the issue of trade unions and electoral politics, which has concerned its Slovak affiliate (OZ KOVO) since the election of Vladimir Meciar in 1994. Indeed, as the IMF's Poul-Erik Olsen (1995) has commented, in recognizing the wide variation in conditions across the region, the federation has tried to devise "programs that are really tailor-made." Olsen points out that "it is quite obvious that Romania and Bulgaria with their type of privatization and their type of problems, they are facing different problems than are Hungary, Poland, and the Czech Republic. . . . This means priority will be given to different things." With time, the issues unions are interested in have also changed: "Early on it was privatization and restructuring, now it's more on what is the role of the unions in the various countries." In Poland, for example, the federation's early seminars with the independent union Solidarity focused on general issues, whereas by 1995 it was running individualized seminars for union officials in each of the four main industrial sectors (steel, aerospace, automobiles, and machine building) that Solidarity represents. In designing its activities, the federation has been cognizant of the emerging geopolitical situations in various parts of Eastern Europe. Consequently, it has organized a series of events solely for the four Visegrad countries (Hungary, Poland, the Czech Republic, and the Slovak Republic) plus Slovenia, which, with the exception of the Slovak Republic, all have long industrial histories — unlike other Eastern European countries such as Romania or Bulgaria — and which are the countries in the region that the European Union is looking to incorporate first. Similarly, in seminars on the conflict and labor situation in the Balkans, the IMF has been keen to include also metalworkers from both Bulgaria and Romania so as not to "split the region . . . [since] we have no interest in having any division between the unions [in the area]" (Olsen 1995).

In response to concerns by its Western affiliates that lower workplace safety and environmental standards in Eastern Europe might serve as an incentive for employers to shift investment from Western Europe and North America, the IMF has conducted seminars addressing the issue of environmental degradation and workers' health and safety. It has also worked with unions in Japan concerning work conditions in Suzuki's plant in Hungary. The federation has encountered some difficulties in this area, however, not least of which is a low awareness among many East European workers of the importance of health, safety, and environmental issues (Mureau 1994). Many workers seem willing to work in substandard conditions if it means that they can attract foreign investment, retain their jobs, and improve their wage and benefits packages. Nevertheless, IMF seminar leaders have stressed the importance of health, safety, and environmental issues for workers' quality of life and feel that some progress is being made (Mureau 1995a). Related to the issue of workplace safety has been that of the status of female workers. In the metals industries in Eastern Europe, women make up approximately one-third of the workforce and, typically, experience the worst working conditions and the lowest remuneration rates. As part of its workplace health and safety education effort, the federation has attempted to develop programs geared particularly to women workers and women trade unionists in the transition.

In addition to such direct contact with unions in Eastern Europe and the federation's encouragement of its Western affiliates to cooperate in these training programs, the IMF seeks to ensure that codes of conduct regarding the operation of multinational corporations and a social charter guaranteeing basic labor rights including freedom of association, the right to organize and bargain collectively, and the right to strike are extended to Eastern Europe (International Metalworkers' Federation n.d.b).[13] It has encouraged its affiliates to pressure their governments and international agencies with regard to the region's foreign debt, economic growth, and balanced development. IMF officials recognize, however, that the narrow constituencies of individual unions and even of the federation itself make it difficult to influence institutions such as the World Bank and the International Monetary Fund regarding investment policies. Therefore, they have decided to work closely with the International Confederation of Free Trade Unions (ICFTU) on such matters. With its membership made up of national trade-union centers rather than unions in particular crafts or industries, the ICFTU is much more broadly based, both sectorally and geographically, than is the IMF (see Windmuller 1980 for more on the Confederation's history and structure). The IMF is working with the ICFTU to pressure the World Bank and the International Monetary Fund to adopt less austere policies in Eastern Europe and "to bring all their weight to bear to counter the anti-labour fundamentals of these organisations' recommendations and ensure that they pursue investment policies which do not reduce workers' living standards and employment opportunities but encourage pro-worker economic development" (Mureau 1995a).

Conclusion

The International Metalworkers' Federation has been intimately involved in remaking the political and economic geography of post–Cold War Europe. Already by

1992 the IMF had come to represent nearly two million metalworkers in Eastern Europe and was helping to rebuild the region's trade-union movements (International Metalworkers' Federation 1992a). The future, however, remains unclear. Many of the nascent trade unions in the region are very weak and the loss of benefits, reduced living standards, and general hardships have made some workers nostalgic for the days of Cold War stability, raising questions about the path these unions will take in the future and how far and how fast the process of marketization will take (cf. Herod 1998b). A real possibility also exists that if the metal unions of the former Soviet Union ever affiliate with the IMF, they might come to dominate the organization because of their large size. This, in turn, could lead to shifts in the internal balance of power of the IMF. Consequently, the federation has been cautious in its dealings with these unions, especially in view of the political instability in Russia, although it has had contact with groups of instrument makers in the Moscow region through its Norwegian affiliate (Olsen 1995). Furthermore, the IMF's activities in Eastern Europe have raised questions from some quarters about whether the added financial and organizational burdens on the federation will impact its ability to conduct similar programs in other parts of the globe, especially the less developed countries.

The activities of the IMF raise significant conceptual issues for political and economic geographers. To date, geographers have largely ignored the international activities of trade unions and other workers' organizations when examining the operation of the global economy and the practice of geopolitics. Analyses of the restructuring of the economies of Eastern Europe and of the rescripting of geopolitical discourses in the post–Cold War period have tended to focus on the activities of capital and the state. Yet, as evidenced by the IMF's activities, workers and their organizations are playing important roles in the processes of economic and political transformation in the region. This suggests that greater attention should be paid to the ways in which unions are remaking the economic and political spaces of Eastern Europe. A geographic perspective not only provides insights into the mosaic of economic and political conditions, cultural values, labor laws, union organization, and types of labor markets operating throughout the region, but it can also help to explain the thinking and geographical praxis of social actors such as trade unions. The IMF sees Eastern Europe in very clear geostrategic terms. The region's geographic proximity to high-wage Western Europe and the possibility that the boundaries of the European Union will one day be extended to include all the countries of the region mean that Western capital may increasingly come to use Eastern Europe as something of a "spatial safety valve" by which it can reorganize and expand production into spaces

66

Andrew Herod

not available to it during the Cold War. The threat of moving production to the region or of importing labor and commodities from it are arguably far more potent weapons that capital can use to undermine workers' wages and working conditions in Western Europe than are threats to move to, say, Southeast Asia or Latin America. In many ways, Eastern Europe's proximity makes these threats more tangible to Western European workers because a large supply of very skilled labor exists in Eastern Europe that does not exist in many "less developed" parts of the world, and because labor markets and production links are more likely to become highly integrated between European countries in any future expanded European Union than they are between Europe and other parts of the world. Ensuring the emergence of strong unions in the region is thus key to the IMF's ability to defend workers' rights both in Eastern Europe and beyond.

The fact that Eastern European unions are adopting for themselves some elements of trade-union praxis developed in other countries raises significant questions about the transmission of ideas across space and national boundaries, and between cultures. The diffusion of knowledge is an inherently geographical (and political) process. Geographers have an important contribution to make to the study of trade unionism because they can provide insights into the spatial component and content of trade-union practices and how these are developed in one place yet adopted, modified, and remade in other places. Furthermore, developing new models of trade unionism in Eastern Europe requires an explicitly spatial sensitivity. Not only do conditions vary considerably throughout the region and not only do issues such as centralized versus decentralized union structures clearly relate to the question of the geographic scale (national or local) at which power will be held in the unions, but the issue of how place and geographic context affect the development of new models is also important (Herod 1998b). The variety of cultural, economic, social, and political traditions throughout Eastern Europe means that ideas that work in one context might not work elsewhere. Geographic context is important. Blanket, aspatial solutions will not work, as the IMF is keenly aware. As general secretary Marcello Malentacci has commented:

> It will take some years before new models of labour relations emerge in Central and Eastern Europe. They may be partly based on models from other countries and integrate some of their characteristics but, in the end, their configuration will lie in the hands of the change makers themselves who will have to build up their own models, using their innovative abilities while taking into account their historical and cultural

67

traditions, their specific needs and aspirations. Systems cannot be simply transferred from one country to the other but the experience and knowledge gained during [IMF] seminars will be valuable assets in the reconstruction process and the search for a new role in societies at the crossroads. (Quoted in International Metalworkers' Federation 1994, 3)

Clearly, the IMF is thinking explicitly about issues of geographic context, international economic and political geography, place, and space. It is also clear that understanding the IMF's behavior, and the behavior of trade unions more generally, requires a geographic perspective and sensitivity.

Notes

I would like to thank the following individuals for help with this essay: David Fowler, former assistant general secretary of the International Metalworkers' Federation; Anne-Marie Mureau, former coordinator for Central and Eastern Europe, International Metalworkers' Federation; and Poul-Erik Olsen, director, Education and Working Environment Group for Eastern and Central Europe, International Metalworkers' Federation. All provided documents and time during research trips to Geneva. I would also like to thank several people who commented on earlier drafts of the paper: Anne-Marie Mureau, Poul-Erik Olsen, Erica Schoenberger, and Gearóid Ó Tuathail. This research was funded by a grant from the University of Georgia Research Foundation titled "Implications of the Transition to a Market Economy for Trade Unionism in Eastern and Central Europe."

1. The first quote comes from International Metalworkers' Federation (1992a, 2); the second quote comes from International Metalworkers' Federation (n.d.a, 3).

2. For instance, in late 1945 an international trade-union body, the World Federation of Trade Unions (WFTU) was formed to continue the work of a similar prewar organization. However, in 1949 the international labor movement split along ideological lines as many non-Communist unions left the WFTU, which they accused of having become a pawn of Soviet foreign policy (the Soviets formed the largest contingent in the federation), and formed the International Confederation of Free Trade Unions (ICFTU). Throughout the period of the Cold War, most of the world's trade-union centers were split between the largely pro-Western ICFTU on the one hand, and, on the other, the WFTU, whose membership was made up principally of unions from the Communist and Arab countries (see Windmuller 1980 for more details; see Herod 1998a for an account of the WFTU in the post–Cold War period).

68

Andrew Herod

3. The degree to which various plants were horizontally or vertically integrated into enterprises varied throughout the region. In Czechoslovakia, state-owned enterprises were characterized by a high degree of horizontal integration, with an "average" enterprise in the manufacturing sector consisting of eight or nine plants producing similar products. In East Germany, too, giant vertically integrated combines (*Kombinate*) dominated the industrial and construction sectors of the economy. In Hungary, by way of contrast, prior to 1980 there was a high degree of organizational centralization with about 45 percent of state-owned enterprises having more than a thousand employees; during the early 1980s, however, many of these large conglomerates (called "trusts") were dissolved. Furthermore, most of these large organizations had been integrated only administratively and remained geographically and technologically separate units. Nevertheless, despite such differences, throughout Eastern Europe the average size of enterprises was much larger than in the Western market economies and their breakup has been seen as crucial to the success of the privatization process (United Nations 1994).

4. Despite efforts to separate the unions from the political parties, many unions remain extremely politically active (e.g., Solidarity in Poland, Podkrepa in Bulgaria, and Fratia in Romania).

5. The text of the Romanian law is reproduced in English in "Law on Trade Unions," Law no. 54, August 1, 1991, in *Monitorul Oficial* (official gazette of Romania), part I, no. 164, August 7, 1991.

6. In Hungary, for example, works councils are required by law in all establishments with more than fifty workers. The first free elections to these councils were held in May 1993.

7. In Hungary, the labor code requires employers to cooperate with trade unions and provide them with information necessary for collective bargaining but does not require them to actually bargain collectively; in Poland, the Trade Union Act prevents an employer or the government from contesting a union's registration but, again, does not require employers to bargain collectively. In Bulgaria, in contrast, the labor code does require an employer to negotiate a collective bargaining agreement in good faith with the workers' representatives (International Metalworkers' Federation 1994).

8. In Romania, for example, the 1991 Law on Trade Unions contained no legal regulations regarding the bargaining procedure and scope of the bargaining unit, which were to be determined on a case-by-case basis. Likewise, in Hungary there are no legally enforceable guidelines concerning the composition of the bargaining committee. In Slovenia, the composition of the bargaining

unit is not governed by either the law or the collective bargaining agreement but is determined by the parties involved (International Metalworkers' Federation 1994).

9. The differences between these countries become particularly pronounced when foreign direct investment is calculated on a per capita basis. Hungary's predominance is quite clear. Between 1991 and 1996, Hungary received a cumulative net inflow of FDI valued at $1,256 per capita, the highest amount for any transition economy. Per capita amounts for transition economies have varied tremendously for this period, as shown by the following figures: Azerbaijan $120; Belarus $5; Bulgaria $65; Croatia $123; Czech Republic $617; Estonia $558; Georgia $6; Lithuania $65; Moldova $43; Poland $126; Romania $61; Russia $42; Slovak Republic $128; Slovenia $325; Tajikistan $10; and Ukraine $23 (International Monetary Fund 1997, 107).

10. Much of the information provided in this section comes from IMF documents and from information supplied by Anne-Marie Mureau, the IMF's former coordinator for Central and Eastern Europe, and Poul-Erik Olsen, director, IMF's Education and Working Environment Group for Eastern and Central Europe. Both are based in the federation's Geneva office.

11. This has been particularly true of the term "works council" (Olsen 1995). The European Union has issued a directive that compels companies to form works councils, a move supported by both the IMF and the European Metalworkers' Federation. Under this directive, works councils serve as bodies in which workers (who do not have to be members of the union, though in practice they usually are) are granted some say over some plant and production issues (see Thelen 1991 for a discussion of Germany's works councils system). Many trade unionists in Eastern Europe, however, appear suspicious of works councils because they associate them with the types of joint management-union committees that operated in plants during the Communist period.

12. Although new and reformed unions often work together at the plant level, at the regional and national level in their home countries their political rivalry frequently makes it impossible to conduct joint seminars (Mureau 1995b).

13. At a meeting of the IMF central committee in Marseilles in May 1994, the federation laid out a charter that included demands to stimulate economic growth, to respect political democracy, human rights, and environmental protection, to reverse the "shock therapies" being implemented in Eastern Europe, to encourage international assistance to stabilize employment and production in the region, to make available capital to finance necessary imports into the region, to regulate international financial markets so as to prevent instability, to support social safety nets and encourage tripartism with regard to negotiating

70

changes in such provisions, and to implement education and training programs for workers (International Metalworkers' Federation n.d.b).

Bibliography

Brewster, C. 1992. "Starting Again: Industrial Relations in Czechoslovakia." *International Journal of Human Resource Management* 3.3: 555–74.

Buckwalter, D. W. 1995. "Spatial Inequality, Foreign Investment, and Economic Transition in Bulgaria." *Professional Geographer* 47.3: 288–98.

Burawoy, M. 1985. *The Politics of Production: Factory Regimes under Capitalism and Socialism.* London: Verso.

Casserini, K. 1993. *International Metalworkers' Federation, 1893–1993: The First Hundred Years.* Geneva: International Metalworkers' Federation.

Clark, E. C. 1966. *Soviet Trade Unions and Labor Relations.* Cambridge: Harvard University Press.

Clarke, S., P. Fairbrother, and V. Borisov. 1995. *The Workers' Movement in Russia.* Aldershot, U.K.: Edward Elgar.

Cohen, S. A. 1964. *Geography and Politics in a Divided World.* London: Methuen.

Daintith, T. C. 1993. "Legal Forms and Techniques of Privatisation." In *Legal Aspects of Privatisation.* Proceedings, Twenty-First Colloquy on European Law, Budapest, October 15–17, 1991, 50–87. Strasbourg: Council of Europe Press.

Dalby, S. 1990. "American Security Discourse: The Persistence of Geopolitics." *Political Geography Quarterly* 9: 171–88.

———. 1994. "Gender and Critical Geopolitics: Reading Geopolitical Discourse in the New World Disorder." *Environment and Planning D: Society and Space* 12: 595–612.

Dodds, K.-J. 1994. "Geopolitics in the Foreign Office: British Representations of Argentina 1945–1961." *Transactions of the Institute of British Geographers,* n.s., 19.3: 273–90.

Estrin, S., and R. Stone. 1996. "A Taxonomy of Mass Privatization." *Transition: The Newsletter about Reforming Economies* 17. 11–12 (November–December) (New York: World Bank).

Falbr, R. 1996. Interview by the author with Richard Falbr, president, Czech Moravian Chamber of Trade Unions (Českomoravská Komora Odborových Svazů [ČMKOS]), Prague, Czech Republic, August 20.

Foner, P. S. 1989. *U.S. Labor and the Viet-Nam War.* New York: International Publishers.

Frankland, E. G., and R. H. Cox. 1995. "The Legitimation Problems of New Democracies: Postcommunist Dilemmas in Czechoslovakia and Hungary." *Environment and Planning C: Government and Policy* 13: 141–58.

71

Freeman, R. B. 1992. "Getting There from Here: Labor in the Transition to a Market Economy." In *Labor and Democracy in the Transition to a Market System: A U.S.–Post-Soviet Dialogue*, edited by B. Silverman, R. Vogt, and M. Yanowitch, 139–57. London: M. E. Sharpe.

Gaudier, M. 1991. "Economic Reform, Social Change and Institutional Perspectives in Central and Eastern Europe: An Analysis of the Literature." *Labour and Society* 16.4: 439–66.

Gibb, R. A., and W. Z. Michalak. 1993. "Foreign Debt in the New East-Central Europe: A Threat to European Integration?" *Environment and Planning C: Government and Policy* 11: 69–85.

Godson, R. 1984. *Labor in Soviet Global Strategy.* New York: Crane Russak.

Grant, R. 1993. "Trading Blocs or Trading Blows? The Macroeconomic Geography of US and Japanese Trade." *Environment and Planning A* 25: 273–91.

Harmon, J. L. 1959. *The International Metalworkers' Federation.* Washington, D.C.: U.S. Department of Labor, Office of International Labor Affairs.

Herod, A. 1991. "The Production of Scale in United States Labour Relations." *Area* 23.1: 82–88.

———. 1995. "The Practice of International Labor Solidarity and the Geography of the Global Economy." *Economic Geography* 71.4: 341–63.

———. 1997. "Labor as an Agent of Globalization and as a Global Agent." In *Spaces of Globalization: Reasserting the Power of the Local*, edited by K. Cox, 167–200. New York: Guilford Press.

———. 1998a. "Of Blocs, Flows and Networks: The End of the Cold War, Cyberspace, and the Geo-economics of Organized Labor at the *fin de millénaire.*" In *An Unruly World? Globalization, Governance and Geography*, edited by A. Herod, G. Ó Tuathail, and S. Roberts, 162–95. London, Routledge.

———. 1998b. "Theorising Unions in Transition." In *Theorising Transition: The Political Economy of Change in Central and Eastern Europe*, edited by J. Pickles and A. Smith. London: Routledge.

Héthy, L. 1991. "Towards Social Peace or Explosion? Challenges for Labour Relations in Central and Eastern Europe." *Labour and Society* 16.4: 345–58.

International Metalworkers' Federation. N.d.a. *Metalworkers in Eastern Europe.* Geneva: International Metalworkers' Federation.

———. N.d.b. *A Metalworkers' Charter for Social and Economic Alternatives.* Geneva: International Metalworkers' Federation.

———. 1992a. *Industrial Restructuring and East-West Migration: The Impact on the Metal Industry.* Geneva: International Metalworkers' Federation.

———. 1992b. *Investissements étrangers et droits syndicaux en Europe Centrale et Orientale.* Geneva: International Metalworkers' Federation.

Andrew Herod

————. 1993. *Metalworkers and Privatisation Worldwide.* Geneva: International Metalworkers' Federation.

————. 1994. *Collective Bargaining in Transition Economies.* Geneva: International Metalworkers' Federation.

International Monetary Fund. 1997. *World Economic Outlook.* Washington, D.C.: International Monetary Fund.

Le Monde. 1995. "Les investisseurs sont peu attirés par l'Est." April 30–May 2.

Luttwak, E. N. 1990. "From Geopolitics to Geo-economics: Logic of Conflict, Grammar of Commerce." *National Interest* 20: 17–23.

Michalak, W. Z. 1993. "Foreign Direct Investment and Joint Ventures in East-Central Europe: A Geographical Perspective." *Environment and Planning A* 25: 1573–91.

Morawetz, R. 1991. *Recent Foreign Direct Investment in Eastern Europe: Towards a Possible Role for the Tripartite Declaration of Principles concerning Multinational Enterprises and Social Policy.* Working Paper no. 71, Multinational Enterprises Programme. Geneva: International Labour Office.

Morris, G. 1967. *CIA and American Labor: The Subversion of the AFL–CIO's Foreign Policy.* New York: International Publishers.

Mureau, A.-M. 1994. Interview by the author with Anne-Marie Mureau, coordinator for Central and Eastern Europe, International Metalworkers' Federation, Geneva, August 30.

————. 1995a. Letter to the author, dated May 2.

————. 1995b. Personal communication by telephone, February 20.

Murphy, A. B. 1992. "Western Investment in East-Central Europe: Emerging Patterns and Implications for State Stability." *Professional Geographer* 44.3: 249–59.

Musil, J. 1991. "New Social Contracts: Responses of the State and the Social Partners to the Challenges of Restructuring and Privatisation." *Labour and Society* 16.4: 381–99.

Nagy, L. 1984. *The Socialist Collective Agreement.* Budapest: Akadémiai Kiadó.

O'Loughlin, J. 1993. "Geo-economic Competition in the Pacific Rim: The Political Geography of Japanese and US exports, 1966–1988." *Transactions of the Institute of British Geographers,* n.s., 18: 438–59.

O'Sullivan, P. 1986. *Geopolitics.* New York: St. Martin's Press.

Ó Tuathail, G. 1993. "Japan as Threat: Geo-economic Discourse on the USA-Japan Relationship in US Civil Society, 1987–91." In *The Political Geography of the New World Order,* edited by C. H. Williams, 181–209. London: Bellhaven Press.

————. 1994. "(Dis)placing Geopolitics: Writing on the Maps of Global Politics." *Environment and Planning D: Society and Space* 12: 525–47.

Ó Tuathail, G., and J. Agnew. 1992. "Geopolitics and Discourse: Practical Geopolitical Reasoning in American Foreign Policy." *Political Geography* 11.2: 190–204.

Olsen, P.-E. 1995. Interview by the author with Poul-Erik Olsen, director, Education and Working Environment Group for Eastern and Central Europe, International Metalworkers' Federation, Geneva, September 24.

OS KOVO. N.d. "Základni Informace." Leaflet published by OS Kovo, Prague (in Czech).

Pavlínek, P. 1992. "Regional Transformation in Czechoslovakia: Towards a Market Economy." *Tijdschrift voor Economische en Sociale Geografie* 83.5: 361–71.

Popke, E. J. "Recasting Geopolitics: The Discursive Scripting of the International Monetary Fund." *Political Geography* 13.3: 255–69.

Pravda, A., and B. A. Ruble, eds. 1986. *Trade Unions in Communist States.* Boston: Allen and Unwin.

Radosh, R. 1969. *American Labor and United States Foreign Policy.* New York: Random House.

Šarčević, P., ed. 1992. *Privatization in Central and Eastern Europe.* London: Graham and Trotman.

Sidaway, J. 1994. "Geopolitics, Geography and 'Terrorism' in the Middle East." *Environment and Planning D: Society and Space* 12: 357–72.

Smith, A. 1994. "Uneven Development and the Restructuring of the Armaments Industry in Slovakia." *Transactions of the Institute of British Geographers*, n.s., 19.4: 404–24.

———. 1997. "Breaking the Old and Constructing the New? Geographies of Uneven Development in Central and Eastern Europe." In *Geographies of Economies*, edited by R. Lee and J. Wills, 331–44. London: Edward Arnold.

Thelen, K. A. 1991. *Union of Parts: Labor Politics in Postwar Germany.* Ithaca, N.Y.: Cornell University Press.

Uhlíř, J. 1994. Interview by the author with Jan Uhlíř, national president of the Czech Metalworkers' Federation (OS Kovo), Prague, August 24.

United Nations. 1994. *Economic Survey of Europe in 1993–1994.* Report prepared by the Secretariat of the Economic Commission for Europe, Geneva.

van Holthoon, F., and M. van der Linden, eds. 1988. *Internationalism in the Labour Movement 1830–1940*, vols. 1 and 2. London: E. J. Brill.

Windmuller, J. P. 1980. *The International Trade Union Movement.* Deventer, The Netherlands: Kluwer.

Andrew Herod

Chapter 2 • Cowboys and Dinosaurs
Mexican Labor Unionism and the State

Altha J. Cravey

Workers in contemporary Mexico face a decentralized production geography that is a radical change from the past. The previous concentration of industry in Mexico City played a pivotal role in the historical project of national political consolidation. In the effort to centralize political power in the early twentieth century, postrevolutionary governments forged an alliance with the emerging industrial labor movement, while at the same time creating a comprehensive regulatory framework for labor relations. Through this state-worker alliance, political power and industrial capital coalesced in a densely concentrated geographical pattern; that is, postrevolutionary political leaders, bureaucrats, industrial workers, and capitalists were increasingly clustered in Mexico City. The political elites of this primate city gradually overpowered provincial *caciques* and, as the federal bureaucracy expanded, industry was distilled into an analogous configuration centering on the capital city.[1] Workers enjoyed a mutually beneficial relationship with the state for several decades during which the unions ceded a measure of control to the corporatist state in return for secure jobs and adequate wages for their members. The state also provided many social benefits to workers and their families through such programs as the Mexican Social Security Institute (a massive public-health program) and, somewhat later, a housing program. During these years, union leaders were also powerful political actors, who frequently rotated from labor union positions into elected and appointed government posts.

Since the mid-1970s, however, a new geography of production has emerged in Mexico that brings with it both new challenges and new possibilities for organized labor. As the old industrial geography of Mexico has been increasingly replaced by a new border-focused pattern, old corporatist arrangements between the state and organized labor have begun to break down. New arrangements are being forged in the border zone in which the official unions have much less influence among workers and in which more radical unions may begin to emerge. This transformation is occurring within the context of the reorientation of the state's

75

development strategy—from a state-led industrial program of import substitution to a neoliberal agenda that transformed the relationship between the workers and the state. The increasingly acrimonious nature of this new state-labor relationship has been tied up with the declining ability of the state itself to regulate capital flows (especially given pressure from the World Bank to deregulate the economy). At the same time, there has been an increase in labor union organizing in both official and unofficial movements.

The transition from a state-led to a market-led industrial strategy has been facilitated by a geographical shift of industry from production sites centered around the capital to dispersed northern locations. (A schematic representation of this transition is presented in table 2.1 and figure 2.1.) Much like the recent movement of U.S. industrial investment to the Sunbelt, a new factory regime in Mexico emerged in places that were remote from the influence of the powerful unions and entrenched industrial practices.[2] New relationships rapidly supplanted the previous model of capital accumulation and the coherent industrial policy that had undergirded the strategy. The speed with which the earlier factory regime was dismantled can be explained partly by geography, which made it difficult for the official unions to formulate a coherent strategy of organizing in the far-flung northern sites. Decentralized regulatory structures created additional barriers to collective action. At the same time, the shifting allegiance of the Mexican state, which favored transnational corporations at the expense of official unions, weakened workers vis-à-vis their employers.

This chapter examines the relations between the state and labor as they illuminate a changing geography of power. A strong centralized union movement is shown to have been closely aligned with national political power for more than forty years. In the shifting and menacing international and national economic terrain of the last two decades, however, a new geography of unionization has been emerging as workers devise strategies for both resistance and survival. The spatiality of the ongoing struggle is examined at the local scale within one northern community, Nogales Sonora. This case study is then linked to larger transnational efforts to strengthen worker solidarity in ways that transcend the U.S.-Mexico border.

The State and Labor during the ISI Years (1930–76)

The union movement has evolved in close collaboration with the modern Mexican state. Parallel projects of consolidating a nation-state and cultivating a network of labor unionists helped to produce analogous geographical patterns during the years of import substitution industrialization (ISI): a centralized and concentrated network of production sites and a centralized regulatory apparatus to over-

Altha J. Cravey

Table 2.1. Transition in Mexican industrial strategy

	Old factory regime	New factory regime
Period	1930–76	1976–present
Location	Centralized (Mexico City and nearby)	Northern region, dispersed sites
Strategy	State-led import substitution industrialization (ISI)	Market-led neoliberal
	Some Fordist aspects (effort to increase production)	Some post-Fordist aspects (effort to lower cost of social reproduction)
National alliances	State and trade unions	State and transnational capitalists
Workplace control	High wage (family wage)	Low wage (individual)
		Wage fixing among local and regional employer groups
	Secure long-term employment	High turnover (15–16-month tenure)
		Elaborate system of "bonuses" as necessary part of the wage
		Quality circles
	Centralized bargaining structures	Decentralized bargaining structures
		Some in-factory benefits, depending on employer
Regulatory control		Lax enforcement of labor law
		Geographic containment of grievances
		Round-the-clock control for those in dormitories
	Centralized regulatory structure	Decentralized regulatory structures
	State social programs	Social goods bound tightly to employment relationship
		State retrenchment; programs underfunded in northern region; social provision by larger transnational corporations
	Public child care	Private (household) child care
	Worker housing assistance	Severe housing shortage, squatters meet needs outside the market
	Comprehensive state medical care for worker and family	Health care is commodified, but some doctors within factories

● Industrial Sites of the New Factory Regime (1976–95)
▲ Industrial Sites of the Old Factory Regime (1930–76)

Figure 2.1. Geographic shift of Mexican industry from production sites around the capital to dispersed northern locations.

see labor relations at these sites. Geographical patterns of production during the ISI years were striking. With the exception of steel and related industries in Monterrey that had been located near extensive iron ore deposits, industrial production was concentrated in central urban areas, particularly in Mexico City. Guadalajara, to the northwest of the capital, was a secondary industrial location. The state's regulatory apparatus displayed an identical pattern. Power was concentrated in a hierarchical set of institutions clustered in Mexico City. The structure of the labor unions themselves and their network of national federations also took on a hierarchical form in which power was concentrated in central Mexico. The emergence of these patterns underscores the extent to which the two processes were interconnected during these years.

The close connection between political consolidation and collective labor organizing did not result in co-optation of the popular class-based labor movement. On the contrary, the two projects were highly interdependent. The state-building impulse gave strength to the labor movement and vice versa. The relationship also had a cyclical character, in which periods of increased state control alternated with cycles of greater labor militancy. At times, however, labor militancy was explicitly encouraged by the state and, *throughout the period,* labor unions—

Altha J. Cravey

through their intimate alliance with the federal state and through its regulatory framework — enjoyed a superior position in the labor-capital relation. Nonunion workers did not receive special privileges, however, and in many respects subsidized the protected position of industrial workers.

The roots of the labor movement predate the modern postrevolutionary Mexican state (which itself may be dated from the 1917 Mexican Constitution). Although workers played only a limited role in the revolution, their participation established a foundation for future close cooperation with other political actors. During the years of struggle, urban workers demonstrated their potency by organizing themselves into revolutionary "Red Battalions." The revolution itself offered the labor movement new opportunities for organizing, while the activities of the mass actors contributed to a body of new political ideas, the "ideology of the Mexican Revolution" (Middlebrook 1991).

After the revolution, political elites used two strategies to institutionalize opportunities for worker participation in the emerging polity. Within the larger project of state building, they first developed a comprehensive regulatory framework that established specialized agencies to mediate labor conflicts and provide social services to workers. The main agencies were the Department of Labor (1911), the Ministry of Industry, Commerce, and Labor (1917), the Autonomous Department of Labor (1932), and the Ministry of Labor and Social Welfare (1940). The 1917 Constitution also established conciliation and arbitration boards (based on social justice criteria), which were expanded into a federal system in 1927 with subsidiary regional branches. The 1931 federal labor code further elaborated the new institutional arrangement among government-labor-business actors (Middlebrook 1991; Roxborough 1984).

In addition to this regulatory apparatus, the new national leadership employed a second strategy, creating a political alliance with the emerging industrial labor movement. The earliest linkages were with the Mexican Regional Labor Confederation (CROM), which quickly expanded as it moved to centralize and control much of the labor movement's political activity. The CROM accepted political and financial rewards from presidents Álvaro Obregón and Plutarco Elías Calles in exchange for restraining the militancy of its own members. Although the assassination of Obregón in 1928 splintered CROM into rival factions, by 1936 a new labor organization, the Confederation of Mexican Workers (CTM), had moved in to fill the vacuum and was formally acknowledged as one sector of the governing party, the Partido Revolucionario Mexicano (PRM).[3] The reorganization of the state's sectoral organizations divided urban from rural workers (peasants and agricultural workers were removed to a *separate* sector) in the 1930s and the alliance that united the CTM and the state in 1936 was particularly strong and has survived until today. The sectoral structure of the ruling party has reinforced the national political position of organized labor, with labor as a powerful branch of the governmental hierarchy. At times, however, labor's privileged position within the government apparatus has been a source of weakness. The official labor movement's ability to chart policy and select independent-minded leaders has been circumscribed and at times abrogated by the authoritarian actions of the larger bureaucratic entity.

Restrictions on labor autonomy were particularly evident in the 1940s as the Mexican economy began to expand at such a rate that it was widely invoked as a development "miracle." Radical groups (especially those based in powerful national industrial unions) mobilized to such an extent that the state-labor alliance was threatened. Seeking a measure of autonomy from the state, radicals formed a rival labor confederation in 1947. In response, the government purged the member organizations (railroad, petroleum, mining-metalworking, and telephone workers) of their independent leaders and by the early 1950s defeated the "most important labor opposition movement in Mexican history" (Middlebrook 1991, 7; de la Garza 1993). The radical leaders were replaced with handpicked leaders who were willing to behave in a more cooperative manner. Government-imposed union leaders have since been known by the deprecatory term "cowboys" (charros), from the nickname of one of these leaders.[4] This defeat of an independent labor union movement in the late 1940s consolidated the CTM–PRI alliance in a very resilient form that remained basically unchanged from the 1940s to the early 1980s (Middlebrook 1995).

The Neoliberal State

Close state-labor cooperation no longer exists in Mexico. A radical reorganization of the geography of production has had a salient impact on changing state-labor relations. Northern regions along the U.S.-Mexico border have attracted more new investment than the old industrial cores. Moreover, urban border sites have become a prototype for a new model of accumulation that underpins a new state development strategy. The northern pull of investment is evident in the pattern of new business creation for 1992 (see figure 2.2; Pardo-Maurer and Rodríguez 1992). Some notable recent investments have been located in the interior cities of northern states. Within the sparsely populated northern regions of Mexico, new sets of labor relations reflecting the new state-labor relationship have been negotiated in dispersed factory sites that are remote from the influence of Mexico's labor unions. Many of the workers in these new spaces were drawn from rural areas and were inexperienced in wage labor and collective bargaining. The older spaces, particularly the Mexico City agglomeration and the

Altha J. Cravey

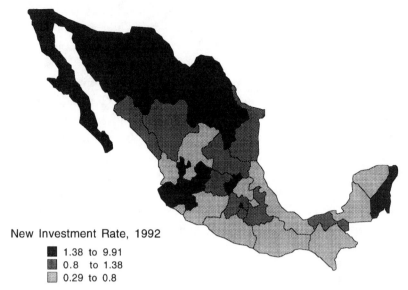

New Investment Rate, 1992
- ■ 1.38 to 9.91
- ▨ 0.8 to 1.38
- ▢ 0.29 to 0.8

Figure 2.2. Pattern of new business creation in Mexico in 1992, showing the northern pull of investment. The values reflect the extent of deviation for the state's investment rate from the overall average.

remote production site centered on Monterrey in the north, continue to be significant industrial centers. The practices of the new production territories, however, have been used to undercut the position of labor in these traditional production spaces.

Some institutional links from the old state-labor alliance do remain in place (e.g., the CTM's relationship to the PRI), but these connections have become tenuous and are certainly less beneficial for unions and workers than in the past.[5] The state has aggressively singled out and disciplined dissident unions and union leaders, signaling a new antagonism to labor unionism and an indifference to the concerns of workers. Other actions also illustrate the deterioration of this previously intimate arrangement: the loss of employment resulting from the privatization of state-owned enterprises; the state's effort to cultivate new sources of mass support through the community-based Solidarity program;[6] and the supervision of national business and labor pacts that have effected devastating reductions in wages.

What are the new labor practices of northern Mexico? And how uniform are they in this huge region of dispersed industrial development? Although there are some intriguing variations within the region, the pattern is surprisingly consistent. The homogeneity of the new factory regime is reinforced by competitive global processes whose short-term trends are closely watched by even the largest transnational employers. The norms of the new factory regime entail the reorganization of the labor process and the larger regulatory environment, changes that have been overwhelmingly disadvantageous to labor.

The best example of the reversal of the old development strategy is in the *maquiladora* sector, which originated as an ad hoc arrangement but quickly demonstrated a potential for rapid growth and for meeting a large share of the nation's foreign exchange needs. Several factors allowed *maquiladora* owners to devise new labor practices in this sector, a *maquiladora* factory regime. First, the owners recruited a young, mostly female workforce that had little experience with waged work or with collective action. Second, the Mexican state did not actively encourage unionization in these new foreign-owned plants. Third, the new production spaces were virtually all remote from the areas of entrenched labor unionism. Whereas the state's developmentalist logic during the ISI period had been to generate growth by increasing productivity, the goal of the current neoliberal period is to decrease the costs of social reproduction. This is seen clearly in the *maquiladora* sector, where repression of labor keeps wages low. Moreover, low wages and poor conditions in the *maquiladoras* can be used to undercut the conditions and wages in other sectors and in other regions.

Geographical patterns of unionization within the *maquiladora* sector illustrate the way that space was used creatively by capital to create a new factory regime. Although there is some variation within the border zone, it must be emphasized that northern production practices are sufficiently distinct and homogeneous to be considered a new entity (table 2.1). Variability that does exist along the border reflects historical divisions of labor in the region (Carrillo V. 1985; Williams and Passe-Smith 1991). With the exception of the east end of the zone, low unionization rates result from the recruitment of a youthful labor force to emerging industrial sites within the predominantly agricultural zone. Thus, at the far western end of the U.S.-Mexico border, Tijuana has a 30 percent rate of unionization (1990) and is an important location of *maquiladora* investment with more than five hundred plants. And Ciudad Juárez, with the largest concentration of *maquiladora* employees in Mexico (129,000 in 1990), has only a 13 percent rate of unionization. At the eastern end of the U.S.-Mexico border, in contrast, the three cities in Tamaulipas have high rates of organization. Nuevo Laredo, the westernmost of the three, has a 95 percent rate, while the labor force in both Reynosa and Matamoros is almost 100 percent organized. The high rates in Tamaulipas result from a history of entrenched labor union power that flourished among petroleum workers. Workers at this end of the border have slightly

82

better pay scales and better working conditions, but still nothing comparable to the working conditions under the earlier ISI factory regime.

This new state-labor relationship reflects a restructuring of the Mexican state, as it moved to dismantle its former comprehensive development policy and the import substitution industrialization project that had been its centerpiece. This ISI model had stimulated high growth rates for nearly forty years, but began to falter in the mid-1970s. Faced with an increasingly contradictory development strategy and escalating problems with external (international) relations, the state abandoned the old ISI strategy. The state-led development program was replaced with a market-led neoliberal approach.

Labor and the Neoliberal State

Labor unionists remain a sizable and important national force in the new era. Approximately ten million Mexican workers, nearly 35 percent of the total, are members of unions. During the 1980s, as Mexico was embracing a neoliberal model of development and becoming more integrated with the U.S. economy, these workers and their nonunion counterparts saw their real wages decline precipitously. Real wages—which had already declined 20 percent from 1977 to 1982, declined an additional 66 percent between 1982 and 1990 (Cook 1994, 148; U.S. Congress 1993, 81). Tracing the geographical pattern of resistance to these changes is complex but enlightening. The shift in the terrain of conflict has weakened labor's collective strength during the neoliberal years, but the labor union movement may yet learn how to use new spaces to its advantage.

In addition to the wage declines of the 1980s and 1990s, workers witnessed an assault on labor unions that was coordinated by the state. Many of these antilabor moves employed space creatively to undermine the strength of the union movement. One of these—the adoption of a new developmental model predicated on less-favorable labor relations' practices in the new production regions of the north—was discussed earlier. A side effect of the border industrialization program was that it undermined old spaces of union control while opening up a space for non-PRI militant unionism. In general, the rural agricultural population in the northern states had little previous experience with collective bargaining when they confronted their new transnational employers and therefore were, at least at first, ill prepared to articulate and demand the satisfaction of their most basic needs.

A second antilabor (and explicitly geographical) approach by the state was to attack the centralized structure of the unions by attempting to destroy industry-wide contracts (*contracto ley*). Where this has been successful, it has effectively diluted the concentrated national power of the unions, unions that the state

83

had previously encouraged. An example of this approach with far-ranging social implications was a 1992 agreement by the teachers' union to decentralize not only their own union, but also the entire national school system (Cook 1995). A third strategy was to privatize and close major state-owned enterprises, which contributed to massive employment cuts and contract and work rule changes that "sapped the strength of Mexico's most important industrial unions" (Middle-brook 1995, 297).

A fourth approach employed a familiar routine in state-labor relations but added a creative new twist. The familiar routine, known to all participants in Mexican politics, was to cultivate various groups of workers (usually in rival national organizations) and play them off against one another. This time the state developed a network of mass actors who were organized according to community and neighborhood membership, but *not* as workers. The community networks were funded from massive capital accounts that had resulted from the sale of state-owned enterprises. The Solidarity program (PRONASOL) targeted neighborhood, community, and rural networks where opposition parties were particularly strong. In this way, entire social networks of mass-based community support were created that could substitute for the traditional labor sector of the ruling party, the PRI. The political payoff was twofold: the strongholds of the opposition political parties were undermined, and the message was delivered to traditional labor unions that they were not indispensable as one sector of the PRI.

A geographical approach helps to explain the way these social struggles have evolved. North has been played against south, the center against the provinces, cores of labor union power have been disciplined and dismantled, and neighborhood groups have supplanted shop-floor organizations. As workers have organized, they have encountered social barriers with complex spatial expressions.

An Example from the *Maquiladora* Factory Regime

The spatiality of social struggle and the hostility of the neoliberal state to labor unionism are well illustrated with a concrete instance of state-labor relations in the northern *maquiladora* region. In this case study we trace the history of labor struggle in Nogales, Sonora, in order to put the new era of state hostility to labor unionism under the microscope. Although the Nogales environment is hostile to union organizing, an exploration of this case illuminates some of the intractable challenges faced by Mexican unions. The local specificity of this case also provides a window on the ways in which this new type of production may open new spaces for organizing. Although there are some unusual features in this (and other) *maquiladora* sites, there are considerable commonalities in the practices of the new factory regime along the entire border zone (table 2.1).

84

Altha J. Cravey

Decentralization and devolution of labor union power through the geographical balkanization of labor regulation characterizes the new factory regime. Localized regulation of labor conflicts has worked to the disadvantage of efforts to engage in regional or national organizing in the northern regions, similar to the local operation of the National Labor Relations Board in the United States (Clark 1989). In the new factory regime, each labor grievance must proceed through the bureaucratic layers of newly decentralized regulatory structures. The fact that these layers are widely dispersed in space creates an additional restraint for workers, who must assemble sufficient resources to cover transportation expenses and forgo regular incomes in order to travel and pursue an appeal beyond the immediate locality. Unsympathetic arbiters in the neoliberal years have made these geographical barriers all the more potent in that local worker issues tend to be confined to small geographical and jurisdictional units.

Nogales is a typical northern industrial city, exhibiting many hallmarks of the new factory regime (table 2.1). Workplace control is asserted by individual factory managers who reinforce their individual strengths by harmonizing the practices of larger factories. Collaborating through the Nogales Maquiladora Association, local managers keep a downward pressure on wages and benefits, while minimizing interfactory competition for labor. Thus, most *maquiladora* workers earn the minimum wage, which has come to be an individual wage in the new factory regime. Although workers change jobs frequently, they find that this action provides little leverage for improvement in such a tightly controlled context. Furthermore, a large percentage of workers in the local labor market relies on *maquiladora* incomes. An elaborate system of "bonuses" (which are actually an *essential* part of the wage) disguises the fact that this minimum is hardly a living wage for an individual. To survive, many workers create extended households in which they pool multiple factory wages, or live temporarily in company-run single-sex "dormitories." In contrast to the old factory regime, jobs are insecure. Job turnover rates in Nogales in 1992 averaged fifteen to sixteen months. Transnational employers experiment with quality circles and other new techniques of workplace control.

Several of the largest factories have union contracts, but these function as protection against genuine collective bargaining (discussed later in this chapter). The local reorganization of social provision has increased the power of the employer in Nogales. This is because many social goods that were abundantly provided by the state in the old factory regime are only available through the employment relationship in Nogales. Workers thus are less able to challenge employers, because they rely on their jobs for these essential social goods.[7]

Changes in the regulatory environment in Nogales also reflect the enhanced power of employers. The lax enforcement of labor laws includes such things as

85

the employment of underage workers, wage payments below the legal minimum, firings without compensation, and the disregard for occupational health regulations. At the same time, every effort is made to contain local labor grievances so they do not proceed to another jurisdiction. The state itself uses the decentralized regulatory structure of the conciliation and arbitration boards (where grievances are filed and adjudicated) to spatially contain worker discontent and suppress labor unrest. *Maquiladora* owners and managers share information and blacklist individuals who have filed grievances or initiated protests. All of these measures work together to produce an environment of intimidation and insecurity that makes genuine collective action extremely difficult.

The *maquiladora* industry dominates the Nogales economy, employing more than half the local workforce. Since the late 1960s, when local industrialization began, periods of labor strife have corresponded to economic downturns that entailed workforce reductions and high rates of unemployment. During the earliest of these events, in 1974 and 1975, six thousand local workers lost their jobs when seventeen factories closed down, and half the remaining plants curtailed some of their operations and imposed draconian cuts in the workforce (Orantes 1987).[8] Table 2.2 lists some of the significant events in the evolution of the Nogales factory regime.

Most labor complaints during this time concerned the loss or possible loss of employment. In spite of guarantees in the Constitution and federal labor law, many of the thousands of workers who lost their jobs were not compensated adequately. The state responded to the unstable and difficult circumstances by granting further concessions to local industry and by further relaxing the enforcement of labor law. All *maquiladoras* (which, at the time, were confined to a strip

Table 2.2. The evolution of the Nogales factory regime

Date	Event
1965	*Maquiladora* program established
1974–75	Industry-wide crisis — U.S. recession
1980	AIRCO (now Jefel) strike
1981–82	2d industry-wide crisis — recession
1981	12 factories sign CTM union agreement
1982	National crisis — peso devaluation
1983	*Maquiladora* program extended to all of Mexico
1992	Jefel protests—collective grievance

Sources: *Nogales International,* December 26, 1974; April 10, 1975; May 22, 1982; Orantes 1987; author's field notes.

Altha J. Cravey

of land within twelve miles of the U.S. border) were offered additional financial inducements and further remission of taxes from the federal government.

Efforts at the local level focused on promotion of the *maquiladora* industry. For instance, city officials acting in conjunction with the neighboring state of Arizona prepared and distributed a seventy-two-page promotional *International Community Prospectus* (1977) describing the available female labor pool, the facilities of the modern industrial park, and the community services of Nogales. Within the state of Sonora, the governor also granted a five-year extension of free zone status (Ramírez 1988). The free zone status streamlined importation procedures for the *maquiladoras*, which were already permitted tariff-free importation of goods through the federal *maquiladora* program. The state of Sonora also acted to reduce the expense of medical insurance payments that factory owners were required to pay to IMSS, the Mexican Social Security Institute, which classifies all workplaces according to five levels of risk. According to federal law, employers are assessed higher payments for higher-risk sites. In this case, Sonoran officials simply decided to lower the risk level evaluations of individual plants, thereby reducing the IMSS payments of *maquiladora* owners so that high investment levels could be maintained in Sonora.

At this time, the industry pushed for and won more control over the workforce through relaxation of federal labor law enforcement. The actions of Bowmar, one of the *maquiladoras* beset with labor protests, demonstrate the growing power of the employers in the new factory regime. In 1975 the factory closed and then reopened as a new company named IFR (Orantes 1987). Forming a new legal entity allowed Bowmar to rid itself of activist employees who had been leading the protests, and at the same time facilitated the hiring of former employees, who had no seniority at IFR, at reduced wages.

This action by Bowmar was part of a comprehensive strategy in which the state cooperated with industry to stifle incipient union activity. Another effective part of the plan was the manipulation and repression of local labor grievances so that they would not be pursued at the regional or state level (Ramírez 1988). This involved Mexico's system of conciliation and arbitration boards, which are the legal mediators of all labor disputes. Local grievances are heard by a board in Nogales. If unresolved there, disputes proceed to a board in the state capital Hermosillo, 180 miles away. In the aftermath of the 1970s recession, under intense pressure from the *maquiladora* owners and the U.S. Chamber of Commerce who threatened a corporate exodus, every effort was made to prevent grievances from advancing to Hermosillo. Workers were offered cash settlements, usually an amount that was much less than that requested. Those workers who did reach Hermosillo with a grievance faced a protracted hearing at great personal 87 expense, a guaranteed adverse decision, and a probable blacklisting in the Nogales *maquiladoras* (Ramírez 1988).

Problems in Nogales in the Early 1980s

Nogales employment levels recovered in 1978 and 1979, but low international demand and falling prices, particularly in the electronics sector, began to create instability in Nogales *maquiladoras* again in the early 1980s. Several smaller and medium-sized plants closed. For workers, months of insecurity over job tenure were followed by a steep overnight increase in the cost of living when, on February 18, 1982, the Mexican peso was devalued 45 percent. This hardship stimulated labor unrest and work stoppages. These labor conflicts had unfortunate consequences for many workers. In May 1982, the owners of the Señor Ricardo factory, having experienced labor unrest during both the early and current crises, closed their plant and laid off the 186 remaining employees. In violation of the law, the company refused to pay severance pay to former employees. In other cases, workers were blacklisted for marching to protest the peso devaluation and fired for speaking to reporters or participating in work stoppages.

By far the most dramatic activity occurred at AIRCO, a company that also had severe problems during the 1974 crisis. In August 1980, some 840 workers went out on strike. The CTM, the most powerful union federation in Mexico, became involved but undermined the strength of the AIRCO workers. In this case, the local director of the CTM, Raúl Olmos, allied himself with the company and the strike eventually failed (Orantes 1987). Olmos has continued to be a local labor union leader and has used his position to become an alderman in the city council. After the strike failed, AIRCO was closed and resurrected as Jefel in February 1981. As in the Bowmar maneuver of 1975, the AIRCO action circumvented labor law by firing employees without just cause and without adequate compensation.

This type of contradictory behavior on the part of official unions is not unusual in the *maquiladora* industry (Carrillo V. 1991). As noted earlier, the official unions have historically been organized at the national level and their leaders intimately linked with the PRI. A hierarchy of power within the official unions has often been used to manipulate local labor organization. In the far-flung spaces of the new factory regime, there is heightened concern that radicals will take over and challenge the union hierarchy. Consumed with this fear, the CTM *completely undermined* an attempt at collective bargaining in Nogales. This could *not* have happened in the older production sites or anywhere during the era of ISI growth; the labor union leaders who assumed powerful political positions in the ISI years achieved those positions by representing workers and articulating

88

their collective demands. In this case, the CTM director chose to barter the confidence of the activist workers at the AIRCO plant for an improved position in local politics.

Nevertheless, labor unrest continued at the plant. In April 1982, one hundred workers marched to protest working conditions. Their demands were for a wage increase, running water, drinking water, an end to mandatory overtime, and an end to supervised bathroom privileges. These issues of basic human dignity and health would not have been contentious in the old factory regime. The early 1980s was a rocky period for the new regime. Plant closures and sharp wage cuts created an uncertain environment for Nogales workers. Work stoppages were followed by protest marches and a large strike at the AIRCO/Jefel electronics plant. Although (or perhaps because) the official unions collaborated with the state to undermine the strike, the factory itself remained a local trouble spot through the mid-1990s.

"Company Union" Contracts in Nogales

In February 1981, immediately following the AIRCO/Jefel strike, fourteen of the largest factories in Nogales signed labor contracts with the CTM, the union that had worked to defeat collective bargaining at AIRCO.[9] These agreements were the first collective agreements in the city's factories. They are best understood as protection contracts, which, by installing a company union, protect *maquiladora* owners from other labor unions and from grassroots organizing. Local businessmen themselves refer to the agreements as "desk drawer" contracts, because they can be filed away and forgotten. Some clauses contravene federal labor law by relaxing the conditions under which workers may be dismissed and by permitting mandatory overtime without pay. Most surprising of all, workers in these plants are often *unaware* that they have a union representing them or a collective bargaining agreement pertaining to their workplace relationships (Denman 1988; Orantes 1987; Ramírez 1988).

The invisibility of the CTM in the Nogales *maquiladoras* demonstrates that the union is actively working to subvert worker organization and genuine collective bargaining. The election of the CTM leader Olmos to a prominent role in the Nogales city administration crystallized the local alliance of industry and the CTM. And the signing of CTM union contracts by a core group of large *maquiladoras* consolidated the new factory regime in Nogales. The triumvirate of industry, city government, and the official union guaranteed a stifling degree of control over local working conditions and ushered in a period of *relative* stability. In spite of overwhelming odds, workers in Nogales have continued to resist. Grassroots organizing is a feature of daily life in squatter neighborhoods and

89

on shop floors. In 1991, *maquiladora* workers in one plant created an independent coalition in order to file a collective grievance against an employer — the first action of its kind in Nogales's history (Cravey 1993).

The history of labor struggles in Nogales *maquiladoras* suggests that the state helped to undermine collective bargaining activity throughout the evolution of the new model of industrialization. In 1980, the unions themselves collaborated with the state to suppress the largest strike in the history of Nogales. Within six months, a core group of large *maquiladoras* signed (and certainly paid for) "protection" contracts with the official union federation to ensure labor peace. The decentralized bargaining structures and decentralized regulatory structures of the new factory regime facilitated this contradictory behavior on the part of the unions. Union leaders acted in opposition to their membership in order to consolidate an alliance with local politicians and maintain their history of intimacy with the PRI. Whereas the state had aligned itself with the labor union movement during the ISI years so that labor enjoyed a superior position in the labor-capital relation, it now moved forcefully to tip the balance of power toward capital in the Nogales factory regime. The realignment of labor union and state actors in this city reflected a broader realignment of social forces in northern Mexico that quickly spread throughout the entire country. In turn, the dynamic new growth and development strategy set in motion a new wave of labor resistance.

Labor's New Spatial Strategies

Throughout the 1980s, Mexican labor unions and their leaders began to experience a new vulnerability in their political position. The long-standing alliance between labor unions and the state became increasingly fragile, while at the same time union legitimacy was frequently called into question by the rank and file. Unions devised a variety of survival strategies in this changing political economic context. One of the most promising projects that emerged in the 1980s and 1990s has been the explicitly spatial strategy of building links beyond the borders of Mexico through transnational labor solidarity. As the Mexican economy became increasingly integrated with the U.S. economy during the 1980s, labor unionists began to consider the political leverage that could be gained through alliances with labor unionists in the United States.

Mexican labor unionists have faced tremendous barriers in contemplating these broader alliances. First, the Mexican state is actively opposed to transnational union alliances. Of course, this opposition is more evident in the official (CTM) labor union sector than among independent labor unionists because of the close historical connection to the state. A second factor is the well-founded belief that labor law is more favorable to workers in Mexico than in the United

Altha J. Cravey

States. Third, the ethic of revolutionary (and anti-Yankee) nationalism that has been a central organizing ideal for many segments of the official labor movement inspires a grassroots reluctance to participate in *any* international alliances, especially with U.S. affiliates.[10]

What geographical patterns have characterized cross-border organizing in recent years? Two broad generalizations can be made: (1) most cross-border initiatives have been launched from Canada or the United States; and (2) the majority of the Mexican counterparts in these emerging alliances are from the northern industrial region. These geographical patterns deserve further consideration.

The fact that most North American initiatives have emanated from the north may have several explanations. I would argue that the material and ideological barriers to transnational organizing are more salient in Mexico than in the United States and Canada. Mexican labor unionists also may have fewer resources available to commit to international networking. It also seems clear that North American economic integration is a greater threat to U.S. and Canadian labor unionists than to Mexican ones. After all, factories that relocate in Mexico provide jobs and the potential to swell the ranks of the labor union movement. Nevertheless, the north-south flow of ideas and proposals may be problematic. If these transnational alliances proceed without attention to creating greater symmetry through the give-and-take of genuine respect, then chances of institutionalizing some of the worst paternalistic and protectionist impulses of U.S. and Canadian labor unionists increases. These impulses in turn could destroy the transformative potential of the emerging movement (Barkin 1994; Carr 1994).

The implications of the second geographical pattern are also significant. Mexican workers in the northern industrial regions have had a different experience with labor unionism than the workers in central Mexico. Fewer of them have participated in unions, and even those in unionized sectors have not had the same opportunity for participation nor have they savored the benefits that were available in the old factory regime (in central Mexico). For this reason, they may be more willing to redefine the terms of Mexican labor unionism and create entirely new forms of political activity and organization. The border region could potentially become a space for new practices beyond the reach of the old institutional spaces controlled by the CTM. The emerging cross-border alliances could facilitate this project. These workers may also be more amenable to transnational organizing because they share a particular employer with U.S. or Canadian workers. New informational networks with these workers can be very useful when confronting a common employer.

It is important to note that there are some historical precedents for cooperation between Mexican and U.S. labor unionists, particularly in the early twentieth century. Categories of workers in which mobility was built into the nature of the job itself such as sailors (particularly members of radical maritime unions) are one example. Miners in the border zones and migratory Mexican agricultural workers were also active in cross-border organizing in these earlier years (Carr 1994). Cooperation between labor unionists was uncommon during the period after World War II but began to pick up once again during the late 1980s.

One of the early alliances in this most recent period has united Mexican and U.S. employees of the Campbell's Soup Company. This is an active and mutually supportive alliance. It is also significant because it is the only case of a union that is affiliated with the CTM participating in this type of transnational alliance. The union in this case is the Mexican National Union of Salaried Field-workers (SNTOAC), which has been building a long-term alliance with the Ohio-based Farm Labor Organizing Committee (FLOC) (Cook 1995). The two unions are working to develop common policies, information exchanges, and a wage parity model. Union leaders say that the joint strategy has resulted in wage and benefit increases for members in both countries, although Mexican wages lag far behind. The alliance was initiated in 1987 by FLOC leaders, who obtained support from the CTM and the AFL–CIO to set up a commission for ongoing talks between the two unions. Support from these national labor confederations "appears to have been crucial in making transnational cooperation successful" (Cook 1994, 151).

Some cross-border alliances have had the specific goal of enforcing the provisions of the North American Free Trade Agreement (NAFTA) that protect labor organizing.[11] The first three legal complaints filed under the labor side agreement of NAFTA concern labor union organizing in the new production regions of the north: Ciudad Juárez, Chihuahua; Chihuahua (City), Chihuahua; and Nuevo Laredo, Tamaulipas. A Mexican independent labor union federation, The Frente Auténtico del Trabajo (FAT), which represents some fifty thousand workers, has been central to this effort (Alexander and Gilmore 1994). FAT has worked with U.S. Teamsters and the United Electrical, Radio and Machine Workers of America (UE) to prepare and file these grievances with the U.S. National Administrative Office (NAO). The NAO has very limited scope beyond issues of minimum wages, child labor, or health and safety laws; however, it can make investigations and recommendations. The unions asked the NAO to investigate firings and other labor-rights violations committed by General Electric and Honeywell at two plants that had been the targets of organizing campaigns. Although a 1994 decision of the NAO rejected these complaints, a third complaint against a Sony plant at Nuevo Laredo was more complex because it challenged the government's regulatory and enforcement role as well as corporate firings of

Altha J. Cravey

pro-union workers. Sony was accused of collaborating with Mexican police to harass workers who demonstrated outside the plant.

My discussion thus far has centered on labor union solidarity as distinguished from the larger arena of labor solidarity and the even larger arena of community-labor solidarity. The outlook in these larger contexts is actually more hopeful than the narrow issue of labor union alliances, although the two are intertwined. The proliferation of cross-border linkages of labor solidarity (among organized and unorganized workers) and community-labor issues literally exploded in North America in the wake of NAFTA. Environmental activists, women's advocates, religious groups, and community organizers have all sought to create larger North American networks during the 1990s. Some have been successful in opening and using new "transnational spaces" to gain greater political leverage at home. One such example is the Mexican Action Network (RMALC), a coalition of religious, environmental, and community groups that might have been inconsequential in Mexican politics had it not played a very visible public role during the debate over NAFTA in the United States, providing information about Mexican labor and environmental conditions to the U.S. Congress, unions, and other groups (Cook 1994, 155). Some efforts have concentrated on unorganized workers. For example, Mujer a Mujer, an organization based in San Antonio, Mexico City, and Toronto, facilitates contacts among women workers in all three NAFTA countries. It sponsors tours that have allowed many unorganized women, especially garment workers, to begin a dialogue across national borders (Alexander and Gilmore 1994). Another informational exchange tour was arranged by food-processing workers from a Teamster's local at a Green Giant factory in California who went to Irapuato, where production had been transferred, to tell Mexican workers how their wages compared with what U.S. workers had been paid. In these and many other examples, workers and community activists have used transnational spaces to create a new dialogue and new political possibilities.

As the political and economic contexts change, new strategic opportunities continue to open up for Mexican labor unionists who are able to find creative ways of organizing the new transnational spaces. Some problems persist in the asymmetry of cross-border alliances formed in the early 1990s, but if the groups involved can recognize the inherent tensions between labor unionism in a developed and a developing context, they may find greater common ground. Beyond the labor unions themselves, a tremendous potential exists in alliances among community groups that give attention to workers that historically have not been organized and that seek to build links between labor and community issues; Carr provocatively terms this "social movement unionism" (Carr 1994, 30). These emergent strategic alliances also reflect spatial strategies. By moving be-   93 yond the limits of national borders, workers can expand the scope of individual and local struggles. Of course, these early efforts face many obstacles. It will be interesting to see if workers can utilize innovative information media, such as the Internet, to overcome some of the problems of spatial fragmentation and geographical isolation, or whether access to such media will be effectively controlled by corporations.

Conclusion

A geographical shift in production during the 1970s and 1980s was useful to the Mexican state, which aligned itself with transnational employers to establish a radically different factory regime in dispersed northern locations distant from Mexico City. This new regime was used to undercut the state-labor alliance, which was strongest in centralized production sites (in and near Mexico City) and which had characterized the years of import substitution industrialization. In some superficial ways, this alliance still appears to be intact — the CTM still wields a measure of power at the national level and still binds a significant percentage of workers to the PRI's official party structure. As the Nogales case study illustrates, however, the labor federation has taken contradictory stands in some cases. In that context of extreme vulnerability, local labor leaders collaborated with local political and business leaders to stifle grassroots organizing efforts in the 1980s and to contain future complaints within the local jurisdiction. Workers in Nogales have had to find alternatives to the official labor unions in order to attend to the most basic workplace issues.

Decentralization of political and union power has also weakened the union movement in Mexico, but this particular spatial change may have unintended consequences in the future. It could be that the decentralization of bargaining structures and regulatory structures will become a useful tool for labor and community organizers, because the increasingly diffuse pattern of struggle will be more difficult for the centralized CTM to control. In the Nogales case study, however, decentralization worked to the advantage of the transnational employers, whose tightly disciplined manager enclave used sociospatial arrangements to circumscribe and contain potential protests while establishing systems of labor control that reinforce their dominance — the most extreme form of the latter being in the huge single-sex dormitories where twenty-four-hour guards regulate the most intimate aspects of the lives of workers (see Cravey 1993 for details). In these former factory buildings, the spaces of resistance have been reduced in scope but are nevertheless important sites of struggle. Neighborhood-based community organizing also provides an alternate space in which to raise labor issues that have resulted from a decentralized geographical pattern. These sorts of micro-

94

spaces may be useful locations for organizing resistance to the new labor practices because they are less subject to centralized control.

One way that labor unionists are confronting the new production regime is through transnational labor solidarity. As the two economies have become more closely integrated, numerous links have been established between Mexican and U.S. labor unionists. These enlarge the scope of the labor union struggle beyond the locality and beyond the boundaries of the nation. In Mexico, many of the workers who have created these connections are in northern and north-central locations. A common employer often serves as the basis for an initial contact between worker groups in the two countries.

These recent examples hint at the potential *usefulness of space* in redefining the terms of union struggles to recover the power that Mexican unionists lost in the reversal of industrial policy nearly two decades ago. These developments are only suggestive, but may indicate that by enlarging the scope of the struggle Mexican labor unionists may regain a measure of influence over the geography of production. The new types of production in the northern region are opening up spaces for new types of labor militancy that will not be supervised by the CTM. Whatever emerges in the future, however, unionists must chart a difficult path, because the central labor movement's historical alliance with the Mexican state has been a source of strength and, more recently, a source of weakness. It remains to be seen whether Mexican labor unionists have the political will to renegotiate or transcend their alliance with the "dinosaurs" and other elements of political leadership in the Mexican state.[12] The task is all the more treacherous in the intensely competitive global environment of the 1990s, in which the factories at the expanding frontier of job creation in northern Mexico must compete in a complex new spatial dynamic that places them in competition with U.S. sites, as well as with many other low-wage sites throughout the industrializing world.

What do we learn from the example of Mexican labor unionism? Above all, it demonstrates that *organizing space* is a key element for *organizing labor.* To be effective in the rapidly changing global environment, unions must be alert to the spaces of the shop floor, the spaces of the community, regional spaces within the country, and the competitive global spaces in which their employers operate. The Mexican experience also demonstrates the profound impact that the state, particularly a developmentalist state, can have on labor unions. The intimate alliance between the Mexican state and the labor unions affected the internal organizational structure of both the unions and their national confederations, as well as the regulation of workplace relations and the daily practice of collective representation. The centralization of power that occurred during the parallel process of state building and unionization was a great source of strength for unionists. In the 1970s and 1980s, the geographical shift northward and the dispersion of industrial sites allowed the state to reverse industrial policy, and this development strategy has presented the labor union movement with a knotty dilemma. Labor unionists must find new ways and new spaces in which to reinvent themselves.

Notes

1. Before the *maquiladora* program, the only sizable industrial investments outside the capital were a corridor stretching from Mexico City to Guadalajara; Guadalajara; and the more distant northern city of Monterrey.

2. The concept of factory regime is borrowed from Michael Buroway (Buroway 1985) and encompasses the apparatus of production regulation and the organization of production.

3. The dominant political party is now known as the Partido Revolucionario Institucional (PRI).

4. Jesús Díaz de León earned his nickname as an enthusiast of Mexican popular rodeos (*charrería*). His forcible takeover of the railroad union offices in the late 1940s became known as the *charrazo.*

5. The broad-based power of the CTM has declined steadily since the early 1980s. Union leaders have signed off on labor contracts that have cost members about 60 percent of their wages in inflation-adjusted terms. Longtime labor boss Fidel Velázquez rallied the unions within CTM to support further concessions within yearly business-labor compacts (*pactos*) until his death in the summer of 1997. A new coalition of 132 union groups, led by the telephone workers guild, that formed within two months of Velázquez's death may signal the emergence of democratic union organizations that will have more autonomy from the state and the ruling party.

6. The Solidarity program (PRONASOL) was initiated in 1988 by President Carlos Salinas de Gortari in order to rebuild the state's social base. Privatization funds were geographically targeted to community, neighborhood, and rural infrastructure projects.

7. See my article in *Economic Geography* for a discussion of the changing channels of social provision in the new factory regime and the lower social wages that result (Cravey 1997).

8. One prominent *maquiladora* owner, computer component manufacturer Packard Bell, moved its local operation to Taiwan in September 1974 (Orantes 1987). In March 1975, a unionization struggle erupted among four hundred workers at the Señor Ricardo shirt factory (Irvine Industries in the United States),

96

while one hundred workers at the Bowmar calculator assembly plant staged a public protest after being laid off (*Nogales International*, March 27, 1975). By April, problems at Bowmar had escalated to the point that workers, accompanied by workers from Micromex, an electronics firm, "stormed the state labor office in Hermosillo" 180 miles away demanding reinstatement of their jobs (*Nogales International*, April 10, 1975).

9. The companies and their products were Avent (disposable medical products), Jefel (inductors), Samson (luggage), Permamex (garage door openers and security systems), Tecnología Mexicana (ceramic capacitors), Charles E. Guillman (wire harnesses), Cambión Mexicana (capacitors), Metro-Mex de Nogales, Rockwell Collins (microwave and lightwave transmitters and receptors), Foster Grant (sunglasses), Micro-Mex (electronic assemblers), Badger Meter (fluid meters), D.P.I. de México (disposable medical goods), and Sonitronies (shelter operator). The union at these companies is the Sindicato Industrial Progresista de Trabajadores de Empresas Maquiladoras del Área de Nogales Sonora de la CTM.

10. This reluctance stems from a history of U.S. interference in Mexican affairs.

11. NAFTA, signed by Canada, the United States, and Mexico and implemented on January 1, 1994, institutionalized the integration of the Mexican economy with the U.S. economy that had been occurring throughout the 1980s.

12. Mexico's political leadership has shown increasing signs of fragmentation in the last few years. The most traditional group, as distinguished from the foreign-educated *técnicos*, is frequently referred to as *los dinosaurios*, to underscore a popular notion that they are relics of the past.

Bibliography

Alexander, R., and P. Gilmore. 1994. "The Emergence of Cross-Border Labor Solidarity." *NACLA: Report on the Americas* (July–August): 42–51.

Barkin, D. 1994. "Building Trinational Labor Solidarity in an Era of Free Trade." *Latin American Labor News* 9.3–11.

Buroway, M. 1985. *The Politics of Production: Factory Regimes under Capitalism and Socialism.* London: Verso.

Carr, B. 1994. "Labor Internationalism in the Era of NAFTA: Past and Present." In *Latin American Labor Studies Working Paper #14.* Durham: Duke–University of North Carolina Program in Latin American Studies.

Carrillo V., J. 1985. *Conflictos laborales en la industria maquiladora.* Tijuana: Centro de Estudios Fronterizos del Norte de México.

———. 1991. "The Evolution of the Maquiladora Industry: Labor Relations in a New Context." In *Unions, Workers and the State in Mexico*, edited by K. Middlebrook, 213–41. San Diego: Center for U.S.-Mexican Studies.

Clark, G. 1989. *Unions and Communities under Siege.* Cambridge: Cambridge University Press.

Cook, M. L. 1994. "Regional Integration and Transnational Labor Strategies Under NAFTA." Paper read at the conference "Regional Integration and Industrial Relations in North America" at New York State School of Industrial and Labor Relations, Cornell University, October 1–2, 1993.

———. 1995. "Mexican State-Labor Relations and the Political Implications of Free Trade." *Latin American Perspectives* 22 (winter): 77–94.

Cravey, A. 1993. "The Changing Relationship of the State, Market and Household: Industrial Strategies in Mexico." Diss., University of Iowa.

———. 1997. "The Politics of Reproduction: Households in the Mexican Industrial Transition." *Economic Geography* 73.2: 166–86.

de la Garza, E. 1993. *Restructuración productiva y respuesta Sindical en México.* Mexico City: Universidad Nacional Autónoma de México, Instituto de Investigaciones Económicas.

Denman, C. 1988. "Repercusiones de la industria maquiladora de exportación en la salud: El peso al nacer de hijos de obreras en Nogales." Thesis, El Colegio de Sonora.

Middlebrook, K. 1991. "State-Labor Relations in Mexico: The Changing Economic and Political Context." In *Unions, Workers and the State in Mexico,* edited by K. Middlebrook, 1–25. San Diego: Center for U.S.-Mexican Studies.

———. 1995. *The Paradox of Revolution: Labor, the State and Authoritarianism in Mexico.* Baltimore: Johns Hopkins University Press.

Orantes, L. 1987. "La industria maquiladora y su impacto sobre la fuerza de trabajo: El caso de Nogales 1960–1986." Thesis, Department of Social Science, University of Sonora, Hermosillo.

Pardo-Maurer, R., and J. Rodríguez. 1992. *Access Mexico: Emerging Market Handbook and Directory: 1992–1993 Edition.* Arlington, Va.: Cambridge Data and Development.

Ramírez, J. C. 1988. La nueva industria sonorense: El caso de las maquilas de exportación. In *La nueva industrialización en Sonora: El caso de los sectores de alta tecnología,* edited by J. C. Ramírez, 5–119. Hermosillo: El Colegio de Sonora.

Roxborough, I. 1984. *Unions and Politics in Mexico: The Case of the Automobile Industry.* Cambridge: Cambridge University Press.

U.S. Congress. 1993. *U.S.-Mexico Trade: Pulling Together or Pulling Apart?* Washington, D.C.: U.S. Government Printing Office.

Williams, E., and J. T. Passe-Smith. 1991. *The Unionization of the Maquiladora Industry: The Tamaulipan Case in National Context.* San Diego: Institute for Regional Studies of the Californias, San Diego State University.

Altha J. Cravey

Chapter 3 • Japanese Labor and the Production of the Space-Economy in an Era of Globalization

Robert Q. Hanham and Shawn Banasick

Japanese capital has been extremely successful in shaping and reshaping the space-economy of Japan to ensure its profitability and the reproduction of capitalist social relations within the country since the end of the Second World War. In recent years, Japanese capital has extended the scale of this process internationally as it searches for a spatial fix, which involves geographical expansion and restructuring of production in an increasingly globalized economy (Harvey 1982, 1985). Frequently overshadowed in the telling of this familiar story, however, has been the role of Japanese labor in shaping the country's economic geography. If it is considered at all, the working class in Japan is simply regarded as having played a willingly cooperative role in the reproduction of Japanese capitalism since the end of the Second World War. Yet, this is a simplistic, one-sided view of a complex and multidimensional struggle. In fact, organized labor and the working class have played a far more active, and at times proactive, role in the production of the space-economy over the past half century.

In this essay, we examine a small part of this story, namely, Japanese labor's attempt to deal with the increasing internationalization of Japanese manufacturing capital. Following Herod (1997), we argue that labor, far from being solely a reactive or passive agent as often implied by both radical and orthodox theories of regional development, has instead played an active role in shaping the economic geography of Japan and, more recently, of the world. Not only organized labor has played this role; other labor groups — female workers, minority workers, and unorganized workers — have all participated in significant ways in trying to create a spatial fix for Japanese labor. Unfortunately for labor, however, we find that Harvey's assertion that labor tends to be more effective at organizing in place while capital is more effective at commanding space is certainly true in Japan (Harvey 1989, 1993). The story of Japanese labor's attempts to shape the space-economy from the end of the Second World War to the present is primarily one of a struggle to overcome the local dependence (Cox and Mair 1988, 1991) partially created by labor's place-bound spatial fix of the late 1940s. The production of geographic scales of organization is a key component of this struggle (Herod 1997). This is a major theme that runs throughout this essay.

Labor's successes and failures in asserting greater control over the production of Japan's economic geography have been strongly conditioned by the labor law and constitutional framework established soon after the Second World War ended. This framework, which has changed very little to the present day, on the surface gives labor considerable power, at least in comparison to other capitalist countries. In reality, though, Japanese labor laws have been used effectively by capital to divide and control labor. The details and implications of this legal framework are summarized in the first section of this essay.

The development of the Japanese space-economy since 1945 can be divided into four periods (Itoh 1994). They represent phases in which the roles of capital and labor in shaping the economic geography of the country changed in significant ways. The four are characterized by (1) an initial period of struggle over the renewal of capitalism in the late 1940s; (2) a period of rapid accumulation from the 1950s to the early 1970s; (3) a period of domestic restructuring from the early 1970s to the mid-1980s; and (4) a period of international restructuring from the mid-1980s to the present. Although this essay largely concerns the fourth of these periods, the activities of labor during the most recent period cannot be understood without reference to key events that took place in the three earlier periods. An examination of these events is presented in the second section of this essay.

Since the mid-1980s, Japanese labor has been confronted by a major international restructuring of Japanese capital. Labor's response has generally been assertive. The response has varied, however, according to the nature of the groups involved. For example, mainstream unions have employed different strategies than have more radical unions, organized labor has responded differently than has unorganized labor, and women's groups have devised their own distinctive strategies. The fourth section of this essay discusses labor's role in the production of the global space-economy. This will be followed by a concluding section that will review the key findings.

Legal Framework

After the Second World War ended, the United States was determined to ensure that the Japanese economy, powered by monopolistic, family-held financial combines (*zaibatsu*), was no longer a threat to its interests and those of its allies. Initially, it did so by weakening the power of capital and increasing the power of labor. The United States insisted on the passage of antitrust legislation to break up the *zaibatsu* and demanded that capital stock be transferred to countries that

100

Robert Q. Hanham and Shawn Banasick

had been victims of Japanese aggression during the war (Tsuru 1993; Seiyama 1989). The Americans also decided to use organized labor as a means to regulate capital, surely a rarity in the history of capitalism. One month after Japan's defeat in 1945, the U.S. government prepared a document titled "Post-Surrender Policy for Japan," which contained a provision in a section titled "Promotion of Democratic Forces" that included the statement that "encouragement shall be given and favor shown to the development of organizations in labor, industry and agriculture organized on a democratic basis" (Gould 1984, 17).

Within two years, under the guidance of the United States, Japan had enacted a new constitution and two major labor laws that together appeared to give labor unprecedented power to organize itself and shape the space-economy of the country. This legal framework has remained largely intact until the present. Some observers claim, however, that this legal framework is far less effective in promoting the interests of labor than commonly assumed, and that it was devised to protect the interests of capital as much as those of labor (Woodiwiss 1992). Yet, one thing that is not in doubt is that capital has been able to exploit this legal framework in its efforts to control Japanese labor over the past half century.

The Japanese constitution of 1947 guarantees the right of workers to organize, bargain, and act collectively, and stipulates that standards on wages and working conditions are to be fixed by law. These provisions, which appear to be unique in the capitalist world, seem on the surface to give labor considerable power. Certainly they do help to explain why the Japanese state has rarely attempted to pass laws that weaken labor rights (Hanami 1985). Nevertheless, the state has managed to accommodate capital's interests in three ways. First, it has vigorously pursued policies, both domestic and foreign, that benefit capital (Seiyama 1989). Second, it has weakly enforced labor and antitrust laws (Garon and Mochizuki 1993; Molony 1995; Woodiwiss 1992). Third, the state ensured that the two major labor laws enacted after the war both contained provisions that would allow capital to subvert them.

The first of these postwar laws is the Trade Union Law of 1947, which outlines the rights of labor to organize, bargain, and act collectively, including the right to strike (Hanami 1985). It privileges collective agreements over all others, and creates a mechanism, the labor relations commissions, for settling disputes. There are, however, some substantial drawbacks to this legislation, which capital has used effectively to undermine labor. First, there is no requirement for representational exclusivity. This has made it easy for capital to form cooperative second unions to compete in the workplace with the more radical first unions established after the Second World War. The constitutional right to organize has, ironically, facilitated this process, since capital and the state argue that every employee is entitled to representation from any union he or she chooses. Second, the law permits supervisors to join the same union as those workers who are being supervised, which undermines worker solidarity. Third, the law prohibits unions from engaging in political activities or acting as a social movement, which clearly limits their efforts to shape state policy in radical ways. Fourth, the law was not designed to democratize the workplace but was, rather, an attempt to establish order and use unions to discipline a core group of regular employees. The law's goal is to establish an orderly system of industrial relations and all the activities this implies, and goes on to privilege the union rather than the individual workers as the recipient of the rights granted by the law (Woodiwiss 1992). Fifth, the law does not give temporary, part-time workers the right to join a union. This has greatly facilitated capital's strategy of controlling labor by establishing a deeply segmented labor market, a large share of which consists of such workers (Chalmers 1989; Woodiwiss 1992).

The second major piece of postwar legislation is the Labor Standards Law of 1947, which sets out the minimum standards for working conditions as prescribed by the constitution. These standards are typical of such laws and govern such things as duties, hours, reasons for dismissal, and payment of wages (Hanami 1985). The law does have three significant weaknesses, however, at least from the perspective of labor. First it does not distinguish between regular and temporary employees, but rather between those on contracts of indefinite or definite length. Employers are therefore able to set different standards of work for these two kinds of workers (Hanami 1985). Japanese capital has made effective use of this loophole by labeling employees as definite contract workers, but employing them indefinitely simply by repeatedly reappointing them. Japanese capital is therefore able to employ a large proportion of its long-term workforce as temporary workers who receive much lower pay and far fewer benefits. Second, although the law requires businesses to draw up work rules specifying the conditions of work for employees, those businesses that employ fewer than ten regular employees are not required to do so (Ohta 1988). Clearly, this gives small businesses enormous freedom to exploit their workers and large firms the incentive to subcontract work to such business. Today, almost 90 percent of private sector firms have fewer than ten regular workers, and these firms employ more than 40 percent of the total workforce, 25 percent of the full-time workforce, and 60 percent of the temporary workforce (Chalmers 1989). Third, the law instituted major constraints on the employment of women in full-time positions that allowed capital to employ them primarily in temporary and part-time positions with lower pay and fewer benefits. For example, the law stipulated that women could not work at night and set limits on the amount of overtime they could work (Hanami 1985).

102

Robert Q. Hanham and Shawn Banasick

The application of the Labor Standards Law has been mediated by the Japanese courts in two significant ways. First, the courts have tended to use a legal model rather than a contractual model to determine the rights of workers who wish to challenge employers who unilaterally change work rules. The courts have generally accepted the argument that these rules are the law of the enterprise, which employees must obey, rather than a contract to which both parties must adhere. For example, the courts used the legal model in deciding both the Shuhoku Bus case of 1968 and the Takeda System Company case of 1983, both of which challenged an employer's right to change work rules unilaterally (Ohta 1988). This interpretation of employer authority over work rules has proven beneficial to those businesses wishing to restructure the production process during times of crisis. Second, the courts have made a civil law distinction between contracts of commission and contracts of employment (Hanami 1985). The courts recognize an employment relation only where the employee is in a position of subordination. Consequently, the Labor Standards Law has been interpreted as only relating to contracts of employment and not to contracts of commission. Because contract labor is considered to be a contract of commission rather than of employment, Japanese capital has been able to develop a postwar economy based heavily on subcontracting. This system has absolved larger corporations of the responsibility of adhering to the Labor Standards Law; they have instead passed this responsibility on to smaller capitals, most of whom are too small to be legally bound to the law in any event. In fact, a high proportion of subcontractors in Japanese industry are offshoots of big capital, created to give the illusion of independence. In this way, capital is able to maintain a high degree of control over its own subcontracted workforce without the constraints of the Labor Standards Law (Chalmers 1989).

The Geography of Organized Labor and Postwar Development

Enterprise unions are an important component of the class accord between Japanese capital and labor that developed in the postwar period (Kenney and Florida 1988), but the focus on the enterprise as the appropriate scale of organization has its roots in the prewar and wartime periods. Gordon (1985) has argued that when the Japanese economy began to industrialize in the late nineteenth century, the scale of organizing activity tended to be at the workshop or factory level because, unlike workers in Europe or the United States, Japanese workers lacked a tradition of regional or national craft organizations. National policy reinforced labor's attachment to the enterprise in 1938, when the Japanese government created the industrial patriotic movement Sanpo. Its purpose was to reduce labor- **103** management conflict during a period of vigorous Japanese imperialism (Notar 1985). Sanpo associations took the place of unions that had been organized in the prewar era, and were also established in each industrial and commercial workplace in the country. It has been argued that this legacy influenced the development of enterprise unions in the postwar period (Gordon 1985; Notar 1985). Furthermore, both white-collar and blue-collar workers participated in the Sanpo associations, which may have been the reason for the inclusion of white-collar workers in the enterprise unions that formed after the war (Gordon 1985).

The institutional memory and organizational experience created by the Sanpo movement help to explain the rapid pace of unionization in the immediate postwar period. Taking advantage of the permissive policies of the occupation authorities, labor leaders undertook a massive organizing drive, which peaked in 1949 when 56 percent of the workforce was unionized and almost thirty thousand enterprise unions had been established (Utada 1993; Williamson 1994). The great majority of these were independent unions established in particular workplaces. Time has greatly reinforced this form of labor organization. More than forty years later, by the 1990s, there were seventy thousand enterprise unions, making up 94 percent of all unions (Utada 1993).

Another factor that contributed to the emergence of enterprise unions was labor's determination to gain the equality in the workplace that it had failed to achieve before the war (Gordon 1993; Kumazawa 1996). Organizing in the workplace and changing the conditions of employment in the workplace became the dominant aims of workers. Efforts to organize at a broader scale were undertaken, but these were secondary to transforming the workplace. If we view these actions as labor's efforts to create a particular spatial fix, then its scale clearly had a local bias (cf. Clark 1989 for a comparison with the United States). Organized labor was not unaware of the limitations of enterprise unionism in the postwar period, and sought to overcome them by establishing various industrial and national federations of unions whose task was to coordinate the actions of individual enterprise unions and to present a common front in labor's struggle with capital. The first major postwar federation, Sanbetsu, was militant and quite effective in this regard (Gordon 1993).

In the years immediately following the war, however, labor's success and militancy proved to be excessive for American interests and for Japanese capital. Confronted by major strikes, many instances of workers taking over factories and controlling production, and an unwillingness by Japanese capital to invest in production, the United States changed its policies. In the late 1940s the Supreme Command for Allied Powers (SCAP) withdrew the right of public workers to bargain collectively and strike, purged thousands of workers accused of being

Robert Q. Hanham and Shawn Banasick

communists, stopped reparations of Japanese capital, allowed the disbanded *zaibatsu* to re-form as monopoly enterprise groups, and forced the Japanese government to reduce public spending (Garon and Mochizuki 1993; Gordon 1993; Sumiya 1989; Tsuru 1993). Underlying these changes was the emerging American policy that a strong Japanese economy was needed to combat a growing communist movement in Asia (Williamson 1994).

SCAP also stage-managed the breakup of Sanbetsu and encouraged the establishment of alternative centrist and right-wing federations whose policies were far less confrontational. The new federations were organized in such a way as to devolve power to individual enterprise unions, thus reinforcing organized labor's fragmentation along enterprise lines. In addition, SCAP allowed capital to revive the prewar industrial and national business federations to counter the interests of organized labor, further enhancing capital's command of the space-economy.

Japanese capital took immediate advantage of the changed circumstances and rapidly set about establishing its own spatial fix within the space-economy. The key to its strategy was to maximize its command of space, while at the same time locking labor into an enterprise dependency that built on the locally dependent structure of labor's postwar unionization. Japanese employers set about accomplishing this in three ways.

First, firms systematically marginalized the militant enterprise unions that had formed after the war by encouraging white-collar employees to form second unions in each enterprise in return for permanent employment status. The second unions adopted a more cooperative labor-management consultation system of labor relations and rejected the traditional adversarial system employed by first unions (Chalmers 1989; Gordon 1993; Ohta 1988). This shifted the character of unions away from being organizations dedicated to improving workplace conditions to being instruments for regulating and controlling a core labor force.

The second strategy was for large firms to develop new ways of deepening, integrating, and organizing the social division of labor (Sayer and Walker 1992; Kenney and Florida 1988). On an interfirm basis, this was accomplished by increasingly locking small and medium-sized businesses into subcontracting relationships. The lack of investment capital available to smaller firms in the late 1940s and early 1950s made this process easier, since often the lack was made up for by supplies of capital from banks that were part of the monopoly enterprise groups (Tsuru 1993). The spatial outcome of these interlocking business relationships was a higher degree of local dependency for medium-sized and small firms, and the development of integrated regional production complexes along much of the Pacific coast, each consisting of a hierarchy of tiered subcontractors clustered around a much larger firm or firms (Taira 1993; Huddle and Reich

.Japanese Labor and the Space-Economy

1987; Kornhauser 1976; Sayer and Walker 1992). Toyota's regional production complex in central Japan is illustrative of this process. It has been estimated that Toyota's regional production complex in Aichi prefecture includes at least five layers of subcontractors, with a total of more than forty thousand firms (Fujita and Child-Hill 1993; Sumiya 1989).

On an intrafirm basis, the second strategy was accomplished by deepening the detail division of labor within the workplace. Worker hierarchies were expanded as large firms increased their use of contingent workers and replaced many full-time workers with part-time, disproportionately female, workers (Chalmers 1989; Gordon 1993; Upham 1993). The segmentation of the workforce was reinforced by greater disparities in wages and benefits between full-time and part-time workers, and between workers in large firms and subcontracting firms (Fujita and Child-Hill 1993; Steven 1988). Full-time workers in this new division of labor became increasingly enterprise-dependent through the introduction of salary, benefit, and bonus incentive schemes that discouraged labor mobility (Steven 1988).

The third of capital's strategies was to penetrate the state at all levels. At the national level, the ruling Liberal Democratic Party became heavily influenced by business interests (Carlile 1994). A similar strategy was carried out by many firms at the local level. For example, Fujita and Child-Hill (1993) found that Toyota was able to shape local industrial development policy by sponsoring the election of a number of Toyota union officials to the Toyota (formerly Koromo) City Council from the 1950s to the 1970s. The policies of the council during this period greatly facilitated the creation of Toyota's regional production complex. It is particularly instructive to note the role played by organized labor in this process.

By the early 1950s, Japanese capital had set in place the key ingredients of its new spatial fix, and for the next twenty years achieved a phenomenal rate of accumulation. During this period capital was able to impose two significant changes on its organized workers. First, wages were increasingly tied to individual performance and less to seniority. Dohse, Jurgens, and Malsch (1985), Gordon (1993), and Kumazawa (1996) have argued that the widely regarded lifetime seniority-based wage system is largely a myth in Japan, and that in reality much of the productivity gains in Japanese industry from the early 1960s to the present can be attributed to a ruthless performance-based pay system that was imposed on an enterprise-dependent workforce. Second, capital was able to impose a whole range of new production techniques aimed at increasing productivity (Gordon 1993; Dohse et al. 1985). Some techniques, such as quality control circles and small-group self-management, were designed to externalize the costs of labor

106

control away from management onto labor itself. Other techniques, such as just-in-time delivery methods, were mainly designed to externalize the cost of inventory onto suppliers.

Organized labor tried to counter the weakness of its own local dependence by expanding the power of the national union federations. For example, it used the federations to coordinate wage bargaining at a national scale among the many thousands of enterprise unions (cf. Moody 1988 for a discussion of how U.S. unions did likewise in the wake of passage of the 1947 Taft-Hartley Act). This yearly spring wage offensive, or Shunto, eventually became institutionalized in the early 1960s. Although resistant at first, capital was forced to accept the practice, not least because full-time labor shortages were quite significant in the 1960s (Utada 1993). However, capital was able to ensure that individual industry and firm differentials were factored into this national bargaining system and that working conditions were excluded from it.

In the early 1970s, the Japanese economy became caught up in the global crisis. The rising cost of primary products, the breakdown of the Bretton Woods international currency system, and an overaccumulation of capital relative to the Japanese working population marked the end of the favorable conditions that had facilitated the growth rates of the previous two decades (Fujiwara 1989; Itoh 1994). Japanese capital embarked on a three-pronged restructuring strategy throughout the 1970s for dealing with the crisis, which not only reshaped the geography of the Japanese economy but was also able to take advantage of labor's local enterprise dependence. One component of this strategy was for firms in industries such as autos, textiles, and electrical machinery, to shift their assembly plants away from the high-cost core region on the Pacific coast to more peripheral, low-cost locations in the northern and southern parts of the country. This involved a substantial restructuring of the space-economy, as many subcontracting firms were also forced to relocate, resulting in the almost wholesale shift of some regional production complexes (Ogawa 1994).

Organized labor played an important role in these geographic shifts. Large enterprises with more cooperative second unions either tended to remain in place or were able to delay relocation for a longer period of time. This can be seen in the Japanese auto industry. While Nissan and Mazda were relocating extensive production complexes to peripheral regions in southern Japan in the late 1970s and early 1980s, Toyota, with its more compliant unions, did not set up production in this region until 1992 (Ogawa 1994). We have already discussed the role that Toyota's union played in shaping the local development policies that facilitated the growth of Toyota's regional production complex in Aichi prefecture. In addition, the union cooperated with management in the development 107 and implementation of the just-in-time production system. The manager responsible for developing Toyota's production system, Ono Taiichi, maintains that it was this cooperation that gave Toyota a distinct advantage over its competitors (Cusumano 1985). Ono argues that Nissan found it difficult to meet the productivity and profit rates of Toyota because in many cases Nissan's second union chose to challenge management's policies, making it difficult for Nissan to compete with Toyota.

The second component of capital's restructuring strategy in the 1970s involved the widespread restructuring of the labor process, primarily through capital substitution and switching (Sumiya 1989), work intensification (Dohse et al. 1985), and increased use of part-time labor (Kodera 1994). The net result was an unprecedented cutback in the full-time workforce (Dore 1986). Unions responded initially with a flurry of strikes. As the crisis continued and unemployment rose further, most unions changed course and made concessions to hold on to their dwindling membership (Chalmers 1989; Edwards 1988). From the early 1970s to the early 1980s, union membership fell from 35 percent to 30 percent (Utada 1993). Enterprise unions, however, were unwilling to organize the growing number of part-time workers who were taking the place of full-time workers (Gordon 1993).

Capital's third restructuring strategy in the 1970s was to greatly accelerate the export of its products to foreign markets. Japan had the largest growth in exports of any major industrialized country during the 1970s, with an average annual growth of about 22 percent (Fujiwara 1989).

The Japanese economy was hit even harder by the global crisis of the 1980s (Itoh 1994). In addition to expanding the strategies that were used during the 1970s, it soon became clear that to remain competitive in the world economy, Japanese capital would have to devise another spatial fix, that of moving production overseas. Foreign direct investment by Japanese capital had begun in a modest way during the 1970s. At that time it involved the movement of labor-intensive component assembly to low-wage Asian countries and a shift in production to selected developed countries, in North America, Western Europe, and Oceania, to ensure market access (Dicken 1988).

During the 1980s, however, Japanese capital dramatically shifted the emphasis of its restructuring strategy toward investment in production complexes overseas. After the sharp appreciation of the yen in 1985 following the Plaza Accord, a currency and trade agreement among the G5 (group of five) countries, foreign direct investment accelerated rapidly and Japanese capital began to create integrated production complexes in regions throughout the world (Edgington 1993). Regionally, investment is strongest in North America and Asia, though it is growing fastest in the latter. Japanese capital has been able to greatly improve its command and mobility over global space since the 1980s. This new global spatial fix has been all the more effective in that not only does Japanese labor lack global mobility but, as we argued earlier, core elements of labor are also enterprise-dependent. In the following section, we describe in greater detail labor's role in shaping the global space-economy and the internationalization of Japanese capital.

Japanese Labor and the Global Space-Economy

In the 1990s, Japanese organized labor has become dominated by the second union movement. About 80 percent of organized workers today are represented by enterprise unions belonging to Rengo, the conservative national federation of unions established in the late 1980s. Rengo and its member unions play a strong role in the production of the Japanese and global space-economy, not only by virtue of their size but also because of their policies of cooperation with management. However, Rengo represents only 19 percent of Japanese workers. Of the remainder, 5 percent are represented by more radical unions and federations, and 76 percent are unorganized. The latter are disproportionately female, low-waged, and employed in small to medium-sized firms. Non-Rengo workers, too, play a significant and growing role in shaping the policies of Japanese capital in the global economy. Whereas Rengo's actions tend to reinforce the actions of capital and the state in shaping the space-economy, non-Rengo groups and coalitions are more confrontational to those actions, with a particular concern for protecting both their own interests in the hollowing out of the Japanese space-economy and the interests of workers in foreign countries exploited by Japanese capital.

Historically, Japanese labor's role in the global economy has been shaped by American geopolitical concerns as much as by those of Japanese capital. More often than not, those concerns match each other. The result has been a long-standing tension between factions of Japanese labor that have been willing to cooperate with American policies and those of Japanese capital, and other factions that have been unwilling to cooperate. This conflict dates back to the immediate postwar period.

The marginalization of postwar radical unions in the late 1940s and early 1950s was not only a domestic issue. It was also caught up in the swirling currents of international politics at the time. Sanbetsu, the left-wing, national union federation had joined the Soviet-oriented World Federation of Trade Unions (WFTU) in 1950. Fearful of the consequences, the United States was instrumental in the breakup of Sanbetsu and the formation of the more moderate Sohyo national federation (Levine 1958). It was expected that Sohyo would join the pro-Western International Confederation of Free Trade Unions (ICFTU). 109

However, radical elements in Sohyo canceled those plans and established a rigorously neutral international policy (Shirai 1983). Its plans frustrated, the United States began to encourage more conservative unions to leave Sohyo and form Zenro (later Domei), a right-wing national federation whose primary goal was to affiliate with the ICFTU.

Throughout the high-growth phase from the early 1950s to the early 1970s, the more moderate Sohyo pursued an independent international relations policy while Domei pursued a pro-enterprise and pro-Western policy. During the domestic restructuring period of the 1970s, Sohyo began to compromise its neutral policies. Recognizing Japan's increasing global economic influence, Sohyo started to interact more with the AFL–CIO and with Germany's equivalent national labor federation, weakened its links to union movements in Communist countries, and began to explore ICFTU membership (Williamson 1994). Sohyo had begun to move closer to Domei's pro-enterprise policies. In the 1970s, Domei, now an ICFTU member, began to dominate the Asian/Pacific Regional Organization (APRO) of ICFTU and strengthened its ties to American unions. Domei was considered at the time to be one of the most conservative members of the ICFTU (Williamson 1994). The underlying goal of Domei was to support the international competitiveness of Japanese business. Wage demands were moderated throughout the 1970s by Domei unions and the implementation of restructuring strategies by business was widely accepted. In its contacts with unions in Western countries, Domei invariably stressed the importance of free trade (Muto 1984).

During the 1980s, Sohyo moved even closer to Domei. Although supportive of independent national trade-union movements such as those in South Korea, which Domei was strongly against, Sohyo moved to consolidate its links with mainstream union federations throughout Asia and the Pacific, many of which expressed an interest in learning the secrets of Japan's economic success, including its cooperative industrial relations policy (Williamson 1994). Domei continued its explicitly pro-enterprise policy during the 1980s, supporting pro-government and pro-business union movements throughout Southeast Asia. Its goal continued to be to support the expansion of Japanese capital and enterprise unionism, which it saw as being profitable to its enterprise-dependent member unions in Japan. In the mid-1980s, Domei even went so far as to promote overseas investment of Japanese capital and the revaluation of the yen, both seen as boosts to Japanese monopoly enterprise groups in an increasingly global economy (Okimoto 1988). As such, Domei was playing an important role in the globalization of the Japanese economy (cf. Herod 1997 for a comparison with the activities of the AFL–CIO).

Robert Q. Hanham and Shawn Banasick

In 1987, the right-wing Domei national federation and the more moderate Sohyo federation joined forces to form Rengo, the second-largest national union federation in the capitalist nations of the world after the AFL–CIO. Representing 80 percent of unionized workers (though only 19 percent of all workers) in Japan, this federation now dominates organized labor at the national scale. Rengo is the ultimate achievement of the cooperative, enterprise-dependent union movement, a movement that represents the overwhelmingly male, permanently employed workforce in big business and national government. The remaining 20 percent of organized workers are members of two much smaller, left-wing federations, Zenroren and Zenrokyo, whose members typically work for smaller companies or local government.

Rengo's birth was itself conditioned by the increasing globalization of the Japanese economy. A key requirement for the merger between Domei and Sohyo was that Rengo be affiliated with the capitalist-oriented ICFTU. Rengo was designed in part to represent Japan's fragmented enterprise unions at the global scale and it is one of ICFTU's most conservative affiliates. Rengo's primary goal in the production of the global space-economy is largely to support attempts by Japanese capital to maintain its international competitiveness and improve its profitability. As we saw in the previous section with the example of Toyota's second union's participation in local government, there is a long-standing history of involvement by elements of organized labor in the production of the space-economy on behalf of the interests of capital as well as their own. Rengo's members, the elite of organized labor, benefit directly from their enterprises' attempts to cut costs by moving labor-intensive operations to low-wage sites overseas.

Rengo's policies support Japanese capital's internationalization in two ways. One way is by pressuring the Japanese government to increase Japan's role in foreign affairs, particularly in Asia. This includes greatly increasing the amount of foreign development aid in countries that supply Japan with raw materials, serve as current or potential markets, and host Japanese transnational corporations (TNCs), a strategy very much akin to that generally attributed to capital itself (Harvey 1985). Rengo pushes hard to be included in these international efforts, arguing that it can function as an effective agent, along with business and government, in expanding Japanese interests overseas (Rengo 1993).

Another way Rengo actively supports the internationalization of production is by promoting Japanese-style industrial relations. Rengo has chosen to ignore most independent union movements in Asia, choosing instead to support government (military-industry)-controlled union organizations in South Korea, Indonesia, Taiwan, the Philippines, and Singapore (Williamson 1994). Furthermore,

111

Japanese Labor and the Space-Economy

Rengo argues that disputes involving specific Japanese TNCs overseas are the responsibility of the relevant enterprise union in Japan.

Rengo's most important international program is the Japan International Labor Foundation (JILAF). Funded generously by Rengo, JILAF's purpose is to bring union leaders from overseas, primarily from underdeveloped countries, to attend workshops in Japan at which the benefits of Japanese capitalism and industrial relations are extolled, much as the AFL–CIO has done at its union school in the United States for Latin American and Caribbean unionists. Interestingly, however, these workshops have been criticized by foreign participants for discouraging interaction between union leaders from different countries (Williamson 1994). It appears that Rengo is less interested in establishing coalitions among workers across space than it is in shaping the policies of organized labor in places where it has a vested interest. No other country's national union federation expends anywhere near the effort and expense in such an endeavor, though it has been pointed out that it resembles the policy of the AFL–CIO in the 1950s and 1960s (Williamson 1994).

With the accelerating globalization of Japanese manufacturing capital in the late 1980s and early 1990s, individual Japanese enterprise unions have been confronted by a growing conflict between their relationship with Japanese TNCs on the one hand, and their relations with workers in other countries on the other hand. At the heart of this tension lies the character of enterprise unionism and, in particular, the locally dependent spatial fix in which it has become trapped. Individual enterprise unions have been very reluctant to assist workers employed by Japanese TNCs overseas. The evidence seems to suggest that Japanese enterprise unions are most likely to defer to the interests of the TNCs, their own employers. Most unions have no international connections at all, and those that do are primarily concerned with looking after the interests of their own Japanese members who are working abroad. For example, the Labor Union of Hitachi Workers sees itself as being responsible for the employment conditions of its five hundred members working in Hitachi's forty foreign plants, but does not have any regular or structured contact with the eighteen thousand foreign workers in those plants (Williamson 1994). Most Japanese enterprise unions, whose members are elite, full-time employees of large firms with a high degree of employment security, are not even hostile to foreign direct investment by Japanese TNCs. They view such investment as an integral component of industrial restructuring that is necessary to keep the company profitable, and as such are generally supportive of it (Williamson 1994; Okimoto 1988).

Unions in the larger TNCs, particularly in autos and electronics, are more likely to maintain regular contacts with their foreign counterparts employed by

112

the same company. Even these unions, however, see these contacts as an extension of, and complement to, labor-management relations in Japan (Williamson 1994). These contacts are rarely sanctioned by international labor organizations — the International Metalworkers' Federation, for example — because they fail to meet the requirement of independence from management control. Japanese unions in turn tend not to seek support from international labor organizations in their overseas contacts for fear of being pressured to involve more militant, independent unions in their exchanges with foreign workers (Williamson 1991).

Even when foreign workers employed by Japanese TNCs request help, Japanese enterprise unions typically either ignore them or claim that it is inappropriate for Japanese unions to interfere in the management of their employers' foreign operations. Japanese TNCs tend to be more antiunion than do European and North American TNCs, particularly in Asia, where most Japanese foreign investment is currently targeted (Ogle 1990; Williamson 1994). Employment conditions, pay, and job security for workers in Japanese TNCs overseas are far inferior to those of Japanese workers employed by the same TNCs in Japan. Furthermore, Japanese TNCs have a strong reputation, in Asia particularly, for resisting and breaking unions. For example, soon after the largely female workforce formed an independent union in Sumida Electric Company's plant in South Korea in 1987, the Japanese company closed the plant without notice. Sumida's enterprise union in Japan refused a request to help the South Koreans, arguing that it was more concerned about the employer's profitability, and went so far as to support Sumida's proposed move of the South Korean plant to China (Williamson 1994). This is not an uncommon story among Japanese transnational corporations and their unions in the 1990s. The South Korean workers eventually did receive compensation from Sumida with the help of a coalition of Japanese militant unions, citizen's groups, and churches.

A similar situation concerned a thousand workers in Hitachi's plant near Kuala Lumpur in Malaysia who were fired after they went on strike in 1990 to demand union recognition. When asked to help, the Hitachi enterprise union in Japan declined, arguing that Hitachi's Malaysian management had a right to fire its workers in the Malaysian context (Williamson 1994). Meanwhile, in Thailand workers employed by Yazaki, a Japanese TNC, had for many years asked their counterparts in Japan to help improve their working conditions to no avail. Eventually, the Japanese union agreed to meet to exchange information, but Thai union leaders were apparently skeptical of a meaningful outcome (Williamson 1991).

Although Japanese enterprise unions are loath to assist directly their counterparts overseas, they are more likely to try to pass that responsibility on to the domestic industrial or national union federation of which they are a member. In the Malaysian case just mentioned, for example, the relevant industrial federation from Japan did at least provide the Malaysian workers with information to use in their struggle against Hitachi (Williamson 1994). Japanese industrial federations tend to be weak, however, with little control over their members' actions. Internationally, they function primarily as a means for enterprise unions to belong to an international union organization.

Despite being the overwhelming majority of workers in Japan (81 percent), non-Rengo unions, other workers' groups, and unorganized labor play a much smaller role in shaping the global space-economy. Their role is significant, however, in that they tend to be much more concerned with challenging the policies of Japanese capital both at home and abroad. In Japan, these groups are often concerned with retaining capital and making it harder for Japanese firms to internationalize production. Abroad, these groups are active in providing assistance to foreign workers interested in challenging Japanese transnational corporations. In both cases, non-Rengo labor groups are actively involved in attempts to reshape the space-economy produced by Japanese capital. The minority left-wing federations, the Communist-oriented Zenroren in particular, have been critical of Rengo's pro-business approach and of programs such as JILAF. Zenroren organizes regular conferences to which it invites minority, independent unions, primarily from Asian countries, the purpose of which is to assist foreign workers in devising strategies to challenge Japanese transnational corporations (Williamson 1994).

Alternative social movements in Japan, often in coalitions with militant unions, are also increasingly turning abroad to seek help, offer help, or simply develop solidarity with foreign workers in dealing with the problems of an increasingly integrated world economy. Some groups, such as the EW = EW (Equal Work = Equal Wage) Tokyo Circle, appear to be concerned primarily with generating international solidarity to pressure Japanese capital to change its domestic policies. This group fights for women's rights in the Japanese workplace. Its strategy has been to force more militant, minority unions, many of which are remnants of the first unions established after the Second World War, to deal more aggressively with female worker issues. Groups such as these are attempting to escape their place-bound constraints and enhance their limited command over space by coalition building across separate workplaces. EW = EW Tokyo Circle attended the Beijing Women's Conference in 1995 as a nongovernmental organization to build links with foreign social movements (EW = EW Tokyo Circle 1995).

Other Japanese social movements, again often in coalitions with militant labor groups, focus their attention on assisting workers in various parts of the world,

114

primarily in Asia, that are being exploited by Japanese TNCs. For example, the Asian Pacific Workers' Solidarity Links — Japan Committee supports workers in Asian and Pacific rim countries trying to organize; the Asian Women Workers' Center aims to protect the interests of rural women from exploitation by TNCs in Asia; the Solidarity Network Asia and Minamata group works with people in Asian countries who have been exposed to TNC pollution and toxic poisoning; the Peoples' Action Network to Monitor Japanese TNCs campaigns against TNC violations of human rights in Asia; and numerous similar social movements exist whose interests are country-specific, for example, the Philippines Support Group (Williamson 1994). The policies of groups such as these are typically designed to change the way in which Japanese transnational corporations are shaping the global space-economy. Social movements such as these are growing and, along with the minority left-wing unions and federations, they represent the major voices in Japan opposing the exploitative consequences of the globalization of Japanese capital.

Conclusion

Geography has played an important role in the story of Japanese labor. This essay has argued that labor has developed a number of geographic strategies since the Second World War, ranging from assertive attempts to create a spatial fix to promote its own interests vis-à-vis capital, to defensive measures to protect previously won gains. We have demonstrated that labor's strategies have evolved in scale from local to national, and more recently to the global scale in response to the international expansion of Japanese production, and that Japanese labor is, and always has been, multifaceted and that different groups of labor have employed different geographic strategies to promote or defend their varying interests.

Japanese labor was more unified immediately after the Second World War than at any other time before or since. Given the freedom to organize, labor responded by creating a localized spatial fix for itself in the form of enterprise unionism. Subsequent attempts to forge links to form industrial unions across national space were successfully countered by captial and the state. Japanese corporations were then able to exploit the localized nature of labor's spatial fix to divide and control the workers. However, labor's spatial fix also had an impact on the way in which capital restructured the Japanese space-economy. It can be argued, for example, that the geographic scale of labor's fix significantly influenced the formation of regional production complexes. Unwilling to move the recently invested fixed capital to other locations, large Japanese enterprises responded by developing regional subcontracting production systems based on unorganized, contingent, and female labor employed by small firms, and by co-opt-   115 ing their core organized workers in large enterprises into supporting company policies to maintain competitiveness and profitability.

From the 1960s to the present, mainstream organized labor, in the form of the second union movement, has developed policies that allow it to play an active role in supporting capital in shaping the domestic and global space-economy, such as its failure to organize contingent and female workers and its unwillingness to provide meaningful assistance to workers overseas employed by the same enterprises. Minority and unorganized labor groups, on the other hand, have tended to adopt strategies that try to challenge capital's production of the space-economy. These groups often resist Japanese capital's efforts to move labor-intensive production abroad, and in cases where Japanese firms are already operating overseas, work to educate and organize foreign workers to confront rather than cooperate with their Japanese employers.

This essay shows that labor plays a significant role in the production of the space-economy at a variety of scales. It needs to be recognized, however, that different factions of labor, having different goals, adopt different geographic strategies to accomplish those goals. Finally, although it may appear that the actions of some factions of labor are passive in their acceptance of the way in which capital produces and reproduces the space-economy, we have argued that in the case of Japanese organized elite workers, for example, their active support of capital has had no less of an impact on the production of the space-economy than those who challenge capital to produce an alternative economic geography.

Bibliography

Carlile, L. 1994. "Party Politics and the Japanese Labor Movement." *Asian Survey* 34.7: 606–20.

Chalmers, N. 1989. *Industrial Relations in Japan: The Peripheral Workforce.* London: Routledge.

Clark, G. L. 1989. *Unions and Communities under Siege: American Communities and the Crisis of Organized Labour.* Cambridge: Cambridge University Press.

Cox, K. and A. Mair. 1988. "Locality and Community in the Politics of Local Economic Development." *Annals of the Association of American Geographers* 78.2: 307–25.

———. 1991. "From Localized Social Structures to Localities as Agents." *Environment and Planning D: Society and Space* 23: 197–213.

Cusumano, M. 1985. *The Japanese Automobile Industry: Technology and Management at Nissan and Toyota.* Cambridge: Harvard University Press.

Dicken, P. 1988. "The Changing Geography of Japanese Foreign Direct Investment in Manufacturing Industry: A Global Perspective." *Environment and Planning A* 20: 633–53.

116

Robert Q. Hanham and Shawn Banasick

Dohse, K., U. Jurgens, and T. Malsch. 1985. "From 'Fordism' to 'Toyotism'? The Social Organization of the Labor Process in the Japanese Automobile Industry." *Politics and Society* 14.2: 115–46.

Dore, R. 1986. *Flexible Rigidities: Industrial Policy and Structural Adjustment in the Japanese Economy, 1970—1980.* London: Athlone Press.

Edgington, D. 1993. "The Globalization of Japanese Manufacturing Corporations." *Growth and Change* 24: 87–106.

Edwards, L. 1988. "Equal Employment Opportunity in Japan: A View from the West." *Industrial and Labor Relations Review* 41: 240–50.

EW = EW Tokyo Circle. 1995. *We Are Fighting for Equality in the Japanese Workplace.* Tokyo: Nippon Shintaku Ginko Workers' Union.

Fujita, K., and R. Child-Hill. 1993. "Toyota City." In *Japanese Cities in the World Economy*, ed. Kuniko Fujita and Richard Child-Hill, 175–200. Philadelphia: Temple University Press.

Fujiwara, S. 1989. "Foreign Trade, Investment, and Industrial Imperialism in Postwar Japan." In *Japanese Capitalism since 1945*, edited by T. Morris-Suzuki and T. Seiyama, 116–206. Armonk, N.Y.: M. E. Sharpe.

Garon, S., and M. Mochizuki. 1993. "Negotiating Social Contracts." In *Postwar Japan as History*, edited by A. Gordon, 145–66. Berkeley: University of California Press.

Gordon, A. 1985. *The Evolution of Labor Relations in Japan: Heavy Industry, 1853–1955.* Cambridge: Harvard University Press.

———. 1993. "Contests for the Workplace." In *Postwar Japan as History*, edited by A. Gordon, 373–94. Berkeley: University of California Press.

Gould, W. 1984. *Japan's Reshaping of American Labor Law.* Cambridge: MIT Press.

Hanami, T. 1985. *Labour Law and Industrial Relations in Japan.* Deventer, The Netherlands: Kluwer Law and Taxation.

Harvey, D. 1982. *The Limits to Capital.* Oxford: Basil Blackwell.

———. 1985. "The Geopolitics of Capitalism." In *Social Relations and Spatial Structures*, edited by D. Gregory and J. Urry, 128–63. New York: St. Martin's Press.

———. 1989. *The Condition of Postmodernity: An Enquiry into the Origins of Cultural Change.* Oxford: Basil Blackwell.

———. 1993. "From Space to Place and Back Again: Reflections on the Condition of Postmodernity." In *Mapping the Futures: Local Cultures, Global Change*, edited by J. Bird, B. Curtis, T. Putnam, G. Robertson, and L. Tickner, 3–29. New York: Routledge.

Herod, A. 1997. "From a Geography of Labor to a Labor Geography: Labor's Spatial Fix and the Geography of Capitalism." *Antipode* 29.1: 1–31.

Huddle, N., and M. Reich. 1987. *Island of Dreams: Environmental Crisis in Japan.* Cambridge, Mass.: Schenkman Books.

Itoh, M. 1994. "Is the Japanese Economy in Crisis?" *Review of International Political Economy* 1.1: 29–51.

Kenney, M., and R. Florida. 1988. "Beyond Mass Production: Production and the Labor Process in Japan." *Politics and Society* 16.1: 121–58.

Kodera, K. 1994. "The Reality of Equality for Japanese Female Workers: Women's Careers within the Japanese Style of Management." *Social Justice* 21.2: 136–54.

Kornhauser, D. 1976. *Urban Japan: Its Foundations and Growth.* New York: Longman.

Kumazawa, M. 1996. *Portraits of the Japanese Workplace: Labor Movements, Workers, and Managers.* Boulder, Colo.: Westview Press.

Levine, S. 1958. *Industrial Relations in Post-War Japan.* Urbana: University of Illinois Press.

Molony, B. 1995. "Japan's 1986 Equal Employment Opportunity Law and the Changing Discourse on Gender." *Signs: Journal of Women in Culture and Society* 20.2: 268–302.

Moody, K. 1988. *Injury to All: The Decline of American Unionism.* London: Verso.

Muto, I. 1984. "Class Struggle on the Shopfloor: The Japanese Case 1945–1984." *AMPO* 16.3: 38–49.

Notar, E. 1985. "Japan's Wartime Labor Policy: A Search for Method." *Journal of Asian Studies* 44.2: 311–28.

Ogawa, Y. 1994. "Shinkou Jidousha Kougyou Chiiki Ni Okeru Jidousha Ichiji Buhin Meekaa No Seisan Tenkai" [The development of the automobile industry in the peripheral region of Japan]. *Keizai Chirigaku Nenpo* 40.2: 105–25.

Ogle, G. 1990. *South Korea: Dissent within the Economic Miracle.* London: Zed Books.

Ohta, T. 1988. "Work Rules in Japan." *International Labor Review* 127: 627–39.

Okimoto, D. 1988. "Political Inclusivity." In *The Political Economy of Japan,* edited by T. Inoguchi and D. Okimoto. Stanford, Calif.: Stanford University Press.

Rengo. 1993. *The Spring Struggle for a Better Living.* Tokyo: Japanese Trade Union Confederation.

Sayer, A., and R. Walker. 1992. *The New Social Economy: Reworking the Division of Labor.* Cambridge, Mass.: Basil Blackwell.

Seiyama, T. 1989. "A Radical Interpretation of Postwar Economic Policies." In *Japanese Capitalism since 1945,* edited by T. Morris-Suzuki and T. Seiyama, 28–73. Armonk, N.Y.: M. E. Sharpe.

Shirai, T. 1983. "Japanese Labor Unions and Politics." In *Contemporary Industrial Relations in Japan,* edited by T. Shirai. Madison: University of Wisconsin Press.

Robert Q. Hanham and Shawn Banasick

Steven, R. 1988. "The Japanese Working Class." In *The Other Japan*, edited by E. Patricia Tsurumi, 91–111. Armonk, N.Y.: M. E. Sharpe.

Sumiya, T. 1989. "The Structure and Operation of Monopoly Capital in Japan." In *Japanese Capitalism since 1945*, edited by T. Morris-Suzuki and T. Seiyama, 105–30. Armonk, N.Y.: M. E. Sharpe.

Taira, K. 1993. "Dialectics of Economic Growth, National Power, and Distributive Struggles." In *Postwar Japan as History*, edited by A. Gordon, 167–86. Berkeley: University of California Press.

Tsuru, S. 1993. *Japan's Capitalism: Creative Defeat and Beyond.* Cambridge: Cambridge University Press.

Upham, F. 1993. "Unplaced Persons and Movements for Place." In *Postwar Japan as History*, edited by A. Gordon, 325–46. Berkeley: University of California Press.

Utada, T. 1993. *Labor Unions and Labor-Management Relations.* Tokyo: Japan Institute of Labor.

Williamson, H. 1991. "Japanese Enterprise Unions in Transnational Companies: Prospects for International Co-operation." *Capital and Class* 45: 17–26.

———. 1994. *Coping with the Miracle: Japan's Unions Explore New International Relations.* Boulder, Colo.: Pluto Press.

Woodiwiss, A. 1992. *Law, Labour and Society in Japan: From Repression to Reluctant Recognition.* New York: Routledge.

Part II

Geographic Mobility, Place, and Cultures of Labor Unionism

Andrew Herod

The essays contained in part II focus on ideological and cultural aspects of the spatiality of unionism. They examine how traditions of organizing are constituted geographically and how they may be spatially translated across the landscape as part of a subversive geography of mobility and solidarity. Both essays highlight the importance of placing the reproduction of tradition and cultural practices associated with union organizing within a spatial context, although they do so in different ways. As both authors show, cultural practices are spatially defined and constituted. They do not merely play out across space. Rather, geography and spatial relations are intimately bound up in the very genesis and reproduction of traditions and cultures. In fact, the geographical context within which the cultural practices associated with union organizing are developed and transformed is paramount. Hence, similar events may produce quite different outcomes in different places depending on the local context within which they develop. In the United States, the ability of individual states to enact right-to-work legislation means that union practices that are legal in one state (for example, insisting on a "union shop" in which everyone must join the union) may be illegal in others. On the other hand, different practices may also be adopted in response to similar events occurring in the same place. As Hudson and Sadler (1983) point out, the threat of job loss in the French steel industry was met in Lorraine by vociferous opposition in 1979, yet by 1981 the threat of job loss provoked little more than a whimper from affected workers. Equally, similar practices may have different meanings in different locations (a nod of the head means "yes" in some parts of the world but "no" in others, for instance) or at different times (the Churchillian "V-sign" representing "V for Victory" over fascism in the 1940s became a sign for peace and the counterculture in the 1960s).[1]

The development of traditions and ideologies concerning union organizing and politics, then, would seem to be fundamentally a geographical matter. Yet, typically, examinations of working-class traditions related to union organizing have tended to emphasize how the cultural practices that represent and exemplify

123

such traditions are reproduced historically (cf. Thompson 1963) and have paid less attention to their spatial aspects, except in the narrow terms of delineating the locations in which these traditions predominate. Such historical examinations have often focused on the continuities and/or discontinuities in the temporal reproduction of particular traditions and their associated cultural practices. Although it has been relatively easy conceptually to account for continuities in traditions over time — it is assumed that new generations of workers are simply inculcated with the already extant traditions of the regions in which they grow up — accounts that focus solely on how traditions are reproduced historically often find it more difficult, however, to account for temporal *discontinuities* in traditions. If traditions are inculcated in new generations of workers as they grow up in particular regions, why, then, do new generations of workers from regions known for their union and/or radical politics sometimes adopt less militant positions than their forebears at particular historical junctures? Why do groups of workers who themselves may have had a history of militancy sometimes later adopt quiescent stances toward particular issues? In other words, why are places with a history of militant labor politics not always militant? As Jane Wills points out in her essay, for example, Nottinghamshire miners did not join the national coal strike of 1984–85, but they were actively involved in those in 1972 and 1974. If traditions are analyzed solely in temporal terms of how the cultural practices that have predominated in an area are reproduced historically, how can we explain radical breaks with the past?

Part of the explanation for such discontinuities may lie in the changing contingent historical contexts within which workers find themselves. As areas suffer the effects of widespread layoffs and unemployment, for example, workers who have traditionally been quite militant may become more tempered in their politics, perhaps out of fear that signs of overt militancy might dissuade new investors from the region (see Herod 1991 for an example of this). Yet, in many ways such discontinuities in which formerly radicalized workers drop their militant politics often seem easier to explain — on the basis that the decline in the local economy has tempered militant politics — than is the reverse process in which workers who do not have a tradition of labor organizing or militant politics begin to build one. If traditions of quiescence (Gaventa 1982) are inculcated historically in ways similar to how militancy is reproduced temporally, how do new and dramatically different traditions of militancy or oppositional politics evolve in particular places? How do workers with no tradition of organized labor politics create one where none has existed before? This is a crucial question for those on the left, for it goes to the heart of concerns about how political practice originates in particular places at particular historical junctures. Again, part of the

124

reason for such discontinuities in tradition may lie in the changing historical conditions in which such workers live (for instance, layoffs in formerly booming regional economies may lead to growing opposition to governments whose policies were previously seen as underpinning the boom). But this is only a partial explanation.

By viewing the creation and reproduction of tradition not merely as a historical process but also as an explicitly *geographical* one, a more complete explanation of discontinuities in traditions is possible. In particular, by examining how traditions are introduced to areas from outside — that is, how they are transmitted across space — we can begin to develop fuller explanations of historical discontinuities in patterns of militancy and/or quiescence. It is this spatial nature of traditions and cultures of labor organizing, especially how such traditions and cultures are transmitted across space, that the essays in part II address.

In her chapter, Jane Wills suggests that through their geographic mobility workers and labor organizers may bring to nonunion areas traditions of militancy and labor politics developed elsewhere. The arrival of organizers from elsewhere, from locations that may be quite distant, can serve as the catalyst of radical change in formerly nonunionized labor forces and lead to the "invention" (Hobsbawm and Ranger 1983) of new traditions of organizing, so that the invention of tradition itself takes on a spatial aspect. In Britain during the 1930s and after World War II, for example, workers migrating to the new towns built to reduce growth pressures on cities such as London brought with them traditions of militancy born out of shared experiences in older industrial areas (Croucher 1982). Similarly, regions that had a history of militancy may over time exhibit less militant politics as workers from outside the region who are not inculcated with the same labor history and cultural traditions arrive in search of work — for example, as rural workers migrate to heavily unionized manufacturing or mining areas. At the same time, through information campaigns and solidarity actions with workers in other locations, ideas about labor organizing and unionism may be spread from one place to another in a "demonstration effect," without the need for the physical movement of organizers themselves. Likewise, the "dampening effect" of union defeats elsewhere may serve to reinforce local quiescence.

Wills's case study of the Greenings wire-making factory located in Warrington in northwest England illustrates how the arrival of organizers from outside the plant, combined with the involvement of Greenings workers with workers and disputes in other plants throughout the region, had a dramatic impact on changing the antiunion tradition at the plant. Understanding how ideas are translated across, and constituted in, space can thus help to explain how temporal discontinuities in tradition are generated. This is not to say that such traditions of organi-

125

zation were adopted unchanged from elsewhere and superimposed on Greenings; rather, they were reworked within the historical and geographical specificities of the conditions and preexisting traditions at Greenings. Wills highlights how a geographical sensitivity is important to understand how cultural practices and traditions of organizing are constituted and reproduced across space and in place, and how discontinuities in such practices and traditions can be explained.

If Jane Wills's essay provides an example of how organizers and ideas concerning unionism were successfully imported into an area from the outside, Don Mitchell's essay examines how powerful agricultural interests in California sought to use a series of spatially grounded ideological constructions concerning what constituted the geographic scale of "legitimate local interests" precisely to exclude such "nonlocal," and therefore supposedly "illegitimate," organizers and traditions from contaminating their farm labor with notions of radical labor unionism. Specifically, he analyzes how agribusiness manipulated spatial images and the ideological construction of geographic scales as part of a well-orchestrated political campaign to undermine union activity in the fields of California during the 1930s. Through their valorization of "the local," agribusiness interests and local law enforcement were able to create a rhetoric of "insiderness" and "outsiderness" in an effort to control agricultural labor. Such localism, Mitchell suggests, has long been used in U.S. political life and popular culture as a surrogate for legitimacy — the more local the actors, supposedly the more legitimate their claims on the rights and privileges of the community. Drawing on this long tradition, agribusiness interests sought to label union activists as "outsiders" and hence nonlegitimate persons who did not have the right to intrude upon the local contractual relationships established between farmers and migrant labor, and, at the same time, to present themselves and nonmilitant labor as "insiders" and hence legitimate local representatives and defenders of the public good. The creation of a rhetoric of union organizers as "outside agitators" was crucial to capitalist farmers' efforts to delegitimize them and limit their claims to the resources of the community — such as the right to speak, leaflet, or picket in public places — and to subject them to local ordinances regarding, in particular, vagrancy.

What is ultimately paradoxical about this strategy, Mitchell observes, is that the agribusiness interests involved in such a campaign were themselves often not "local" at all but were, rather, huge commercial enterprises whose activities stretched across the United States and even internationally. Indeed, the big players in Californian agriculture were at least as much outsiders as were many of the union organizers and sympathizers they tried to vilify — in many cases more so because agricultural laborers did not actually have to be from outside the local community to be labeled "outsiders"; exhibiting sympathy for the union cause was

Andrew Herod

sufficient. Mitchell shows, however, it was precisely through their geographic mobility, combined with the demonstration effects of struggles elsewhere, that organizers attempted to subvert the growers' ideological and spatial strategy. By moving around the state from harvest to harvest, from disturbance to disturbance, strikers, migrant workers, and union organizers were able to link together struggles in different parts of California.

Just as Wills describes how workers take ideas about trade unionism and political culture with them when they relocate, Mitchell shows how geographic mobility on the part of organizers was crucial to overcoming the growers' rhetoric of localism because it allowed workers in different parts of the state to see the connections between their own struggles and those of workers elsewhere who were often laboring for the same agricultural interests. By appealing to a larger notion of justice, California workers were able to contest capital's efforts to create a scale of legitimacy based only on the local. For the organizers, the ability to move through the California agricultural landscape was the key to their efforts to spread unionism in the fields and to expand the scale of their struggle for social justice. Not only did workers use mobility as a subversive tool, but their strategy was designed to construct a larger geographic scale of struggle than that preferred by the farming interests, a scale that went beyond the local to link together strikes, disturbances, and conditions throughout California and beyond.

Notes

1. Relatedly, during World War II the BBC often opened its coded messages to the resistance movements in France and some other occupied countries with the first four notes of Beethoven's Fifth Symphony, since the notes sound the same as the Morse code for "V" (dot, dot, dot, dash) signifying "victory" in English and *victoire* in French. Populations in the occupied countries would sometimes tap out the Morse code sounds or hum the opening bars to the symphony as a form of opposition to the Germans while being able to claim, if challenged, that they were actually pro-German by favoring Beethoven's music. Such an opportunity, however, was not open to the Germans in their own propaganda broadcasts, since in German the word for victory is *Sieg*. Clearly, the success of such practices for the Allies and the resistance was shaped by the cultural context within which they were employed, in this case by the underlying geography of language.

Bibliography

Croucher, R. 1982. *Engineers at War 1939–1945*. London: Merlin.
Gaventa, J. 1982. *Power and Powerlessness: Quiescence and Rebellion in an Appalachian Valley*. Urbana: University of Illinois Press.

127

Herod, A. 1991. "Local Political Practice in Response to a Manufacturing Plant Closure: How Geography Complicates Class Analysis." *Antipode* 23.4: 385–402.

Hobsbawm, E., and T. Ranger, eds. 1983. *The Invention of Tradition.* Cambridge: Cambridge University Press.

Hudson, R., and D. Sadler. 1983. "Region, Class, and the Politics of Steel Closures in the European Community." *Environment and Planning D: Society and Space* 1: 405–28.

Thompson, E. P. 1963. *The Making of the English Working Class.* London: Penguin Books.

Andrew Herod

Chapter 4 • Space, Place, and Tradition in Working-Class Organization

Jane Wills

The spatial division of working-class organization underwrites many of the key foci of human geographic scholarship: the location and relocation of capital, the creative destruction of place, the politics of resistance, urbanization, and collective consumption are all geographical themes that rest on a spatialized understanding of class. Class divisions and capacities are understood to be spatially differentiated, and it is argued that this geography of class plays a key part in the constant transformation of the sociopolitical landscape. Yet, despite the centrality of class to human geography, existing scholarship has remained remarkably muted in its theorization of class. In their book *Class and Space*, Thrift and Williams (1987, 12), for example, felt moved to declare that "no systematic account of the place of space in class analysis has been given." Spatializing class analysis is a project still awaiting completion.

This essay introduces an argument that might form the basis of a greater understanding of the spatial nature of working-class organization. It makes the case for a more explicit consideration of labor as geohistorical agent. I unpack the concept of tradition and argue that workers' traditions of organization should be conceived as simultaneously spatial and temporal in formation. This geohistorical approach is then developed through a case study of workplace trade unionism in northwest England. Active traditions of trade-union organization in the factory are shown to be processual, developing over time through a combination of the specificity of location and the translation of traditions across considerable distances of geographic space. Trade unionism is simultaneously connected to both proximate and spatially distantiated social relations and sources of power. Rather than being a historical product in place, traditions are analyzed as being simultaneously spatialized in their constitution.

Geographies of Workers' Organization

Geographical scholarship in the area of trade unionism and class relations has tended to take one of two directions: either an economic orientation in which 129 the social implications of economic restructuring are explored and reciprocally related to economic decision making,[1] or a more explicitly political approach in which geographical patterns of class organization are the prime focus.[2] In practice, these two approaches have porous boundaries, and both focus on the spatial unevenness of trade-union organization and collective traditions. Organizational resources and the capacity of workers to resist are known to be differentiated across space, as Lash and Urry (1984, 42) remind us:

> If we consider individual workers within a given society then their 'preference structure' will be largely determined by the cultural and organizational resources that the working class in that society possess, such as the cultural resources of 'norms of solidarity', or the organizational resources of a union able to enforce a closed shop...these resources are *spatially and historically variable*, so that we can talk of a set of repertoires for collective action. (Emphasis added)

Yet in focusing on uneven patterns of trade unionism, geographers have tended to neglect the importance of historical discontinuities and conflicts in the social and political practices deployed in particular places. In our attempts to draw boundaries around places on the basis of their class composition or organizational traits, we are in danger of freezing social processes and losing sight of their dynamic development over both space and time.[3]

The problems of oversimplifying the spatial divisions of working-class organization are clearly illustrated by the debate between Rees (1985, 1986) and Sunley (1986, 1990) over the events of the 1984–85 miners' strike. In highlighting the recurrence of certain forms of trade unionism within particular coal-mining communities of Britain, Sunley suggested that "coalfield cultures" had been established whereby new generations of workers were initiated into local union traditions through their experiences of work. Pointing to the actions of Nottinghamshire miners during the 1926 and the 1984–85 national strikes, he argued that union traditions were being socially reproduced over time. Rees, on the other hand, stressed the contingency of social practices, suggesting that Sunley's approach neglected the importance of discontinuities in union traditions and underplayed the role played by labor institutions and political agency in shaping trade-union practices. Rather than coalfield cultures being automatically reproduced over time, he argued that "industrial and political actions are *contingent*, spatially and temporally (as are other determinants of class practices)" (Rees 1986, 470). In defense of this position, he highlighted a number of examples where union practices have been discontinuous in time, changing dramatically from one period to another. Although the Nottinghamshire miners refused to support national strike action in 1926 and 1984–85, for example, they whole-heartedly supported strike action in 1972 and 1974. Similarly, the Spencerite South Wales Miners' Industrial Union, which was actively supported by the coal employers and operated in opposition to the Miners' Federation of Great Britain (forerunner to the National Union of Mineworkers), recruited at least two thousand members in Welsh mining communities during the 1930s. For Rees, this phenomenon is "difficult to reconcile with the supposed 'popular socialism' of the region" (1986, 473); he suggests that the contingency of collective action is a result of the complexity of social relations. He argues that working-class traditions are multidetermined, processual, and never predictable on the basis of past events. Social practices can change in a remarkably short space of time (see also Fantasia 1988).

Rees's analysis echoes the work of Raymond Williams (1989), for whom cultural dynamism is a necessary part of the historical process. The collective resources of ideas and organization will change over time within any population, as he writes of Welsh culture: "It depends on which period you take. Think of Catholic, Royalist Wales, as late as the Civil War. Are these the same people as the radical nonconformists and later the socialists and militants of the nineteenth and twentieth centuries? It was not the race that changed; it was the history" (1989, 102).[4] This temporal fluidity of workers' traditions cannot be separated from spatial unevenness in collective organization, and both processes operate at the same time (see Stedman-Jones 1974; Hall 1981; Church, Outram, and Smith 1990; Fisher 1993).

In recent years, traditions of trade unionism have been disrupted by capital mobility, state reregulation, major economic restructuring, and political change (Burawoy 1985; Peck 1996). With the creative destruction of place and community, traditional heartlands of trade unionism have been undermined, leaving the unions with fewer resources to reach growing nonunionized spaces of economic activity. As the spatial dynamics of production, political regulation, and contestation constantly undermine the places in which labor is able to organize, unions are forced to seek new ground among new sections of workers if they are to survive. Whether the translation of union traditions to such new locations is successful depends very much on the political and economic climate and the reserves of trade-union activists who agitate to bring about new recognition.

Social practices can never predictably be reproduced through time, nor fixed in geographic space. Rather than conceiving cultures and traditions as tightly scripted sets of social rules, we can better understand them as being negotiated social activities, with participants having "a role in constantly making and remaking the culture — an active role as participants rather than as performing spec-

Space, Place, and Tradition

tators who play out their canonical roles according to rule when the appropriate cues appear" (Bruner 1986, 123). If social action is the result of a negotiation in and over place, then our understanding of the geography of trade unionism will necessarily involve an exploration of the way that workers are making and remaking the map of union traditions as conditions and perceptions of those conditions change over space and time.

The Spatial and Temporal Constitution of Tradition

The idea that workers can make and shape their own history is central to the work of E. P. Thompson (1978, 1980, 1991). Thompson argues that class relationships take their shape through the impact of experience, class being a social and cultural formation in which workers can play an active part, with their experiences shaping their activities and ideas.[5] For him, such relationships are historical ones: "the notion of class entails the notion of historical relationship. Like any other relationship, it is a fluency which evades analysis if we attempt to stop it dead at any given moment and atomize its structure" (1980, 8). Yet, understanding geographies of trade-union organization involves more than looking at the historical development of class relations in particular places. As a number of critical geographers have argued, social relations are also spatial relations (Gregory 1978; Harvey 1973; Soja 1989; Massey 1992; Merrifield 1993):

> Spatial structure is not, therefore, merely the arena within which—and in part, through which—class relations are constituted, and its concepts must have a place in the construction of the concepts of determinate social formations. . . . spatial structures cannot be *theorized* without social structures *and vice versa*, and . . . social structures cannot be *practised* without spatial structures, *and vice versa*. (Gregory 1978, 120; emphasis in original)

Class thus entails geographical as well as historical relationships, and an excavation of the *geo*historical development of class relations might lead us to a retheorization of working-class agency (Herod 1994, 1995). Spatiality makes a difference to historical process—not only because of the social relations within particular places, but also because places are interconnected by networks of social relations stretching across space. In this sense, traditions of trade unionism can be understood as having both spatial and temporal moments within them.[6]

In many ways, the geographical constitution of trade-union tradition is becoming ever more complex through what Harvey (1989) calls "time-space compression." The globalization of production and economic activity is drawing workers into social relationships forged over ever larger distances. Workers in Britain, for example, are affected by wage rates in China, political events in Rus-

132

sia, and trade-union decision making in Europe. The geographical constitution of workers' traditions in place is immensely complicated, not least because so many different relations of power and agency are involved. As Gramsci (1977, 111) argued, for example, workers need to understand the spatial interconnectedness between themselves and others if local resistance is to be effective. He uses the example of autoworkers in Turin, arguing that once they see the fruits of their labors as part of an ever-expanding geographical hierarchy of social organization, reaching out beyond the borders of the factory to the globe, the political task of transforming capitalist social relations might begin. Today, it is impossible to draw a boundary around the workers in one place and explain their social relations and traditions of organization in isolation from those taking place elsewhere. Geographical location makes a difference to workers' concrete experiences and perceptions of those experiences, but geography means more than simply location. Although workers' traditions are shaped by specifically local historical conditions, by the actions of local trade-union activists, and through the formation of collective repertoires, institutions, and memories of resistance, at the same time the external is perennially influential.[7]

The transmission of ideas across space as well as time has always been central to the organizational dynamics of the international labor movement. And it is this translation of trade-union traditions on which I focus in the remainder of this essay. I explore three different avenues through which local trade-union traditions can be shaped by the translation of ideas and practices across space. First, ideas and traditions can move as people migrate to new places, some of them taking particular traditions and experiences with them. Second, ideas about trade unionism can be communicated across space through the media and union campaigns to spread information and organization. These "demonstration effects" involve the translation of traditions (including both pro-union and antiunion traditions) from one place to another, without physical movement on the part of particular workers. Third, translation can occur when workers seek solidarity from others, taking their own lessons of struggle to trade unionists and supporters in other places. Solidarity involves a search for allies in spatially distant places, and workers and their organizations have historically relied on such secondary support to undermine their opponents.

The history of labor movements in the nineteenth and early twentieth centuries is testimony to the extraordinary influence of particular individuals who acted as labor organizers as they moved across borders (see Hobsbawm 1988; van Holthoon and van der Linden 1988). The connections forged between New Unionism in Britain, the International Trade Secretariats in Europe, and the Industrial Workers of the World (IWW) in America were generally reliant on such individuals. But the mass migrations of European people within the Continent and to the Americas and Australasia also involved the movement of trade-union experiences, traditions, and organizational forms across space. At every spatial scale, the movement of people involved the transportation of experiences and ideas, even if they were never transplanted in their original form. Even within a country like Britain, such translation has been recorded when individuals relocate from one region to another (moving to the new towns of the postwar years, for example) (see Croucher 1982; Wills 1996a).

Union organization has also been spatially translated through more indirect mechanisms of communication. The lessons of workers taking action in one place can be translated to those elsewhere by the media, union campaigns, and publicity. A "demonstration effect" can spread ideas from one place to another, sparking an increase, or a decrease, in the level of union activity in other industries and locations. Historians of the labor movement have noted how cycles of conflict and union organization have spread in this way across industries and national borders, only to be interspersed by downturns in activity and mobilization (Cronin 1979, 1987; Hobsbawm 1964; Screpanti 1987; Luxemburg 1986; Kelly 1988; Haimson and Tilly 1989). Periods of upturn in activity have been associated with the spread of union organization to new sectors and new locations, sometimes politicizing new layers of union cadre (see Hobsbawm 1964; Fishman 1990; Fishman and Mershon, 1993). But "demonstration effects" can be negative as well as positive, as the downturn in union activity across industrialized nations during the 1980s and 1990s shows. As major sections of the working class have been economically and politically defeated through unemployment, political reform, and workplace retreat, a feeling of powerlessness has spread to all corners of the labor movement. In the United Kingdom, the defeat of the 1984–85 miners' strike had a major impact in this regard; it imparted the message to workers across the country that resistance is ineffective, even futile, eroded confidence, and reinforced union decline (see Hyman 1989; Kelly 1988; Millward 1994).

Finally, the active organization of solidarity across space has always played a major, if episodic, part in the labor movement. By consolidating and broadening the scale of contestation, workers have been able to increase their bargaining strength and sustain collective action for longer periods. It was for these reasons that Marx established the First International in 1864, which aimed to unite the workers of the world and overcome racial and national barriers to solidarity as the capitalist class forged a new world market (Hobsbawm 1988; van Holthoon and van der Linden 1988). In attempting to share common concerns with others, workers who request or give solidarity support are reconfiguring social relations

134

in, and across, space. The use of flying pickets is a particularly clear illustration of the importance of spatial strategy, vividly demonstrating the potential power of spatial extension in class confrontation (Blomley 1993). Indeed, by outlawing secondary action during the 1980s, successive Conservative governments in the United Kingdom brutally demonstrated the threat of geographic mobility and solidarity across space to the ruling class (for a fuller discussion of scale in trade union organization, see Herod 1991, 1995). The active creation of spatial networks of supporters can have important ideological effects beyond the victory, or defeat, of any dispute. And in the case study presented in this essay, solidarity from other workers helped to cement the confidence of strikers in their own abilities to sustain industrial action.

These processes of translation by movement, demonstration, and solidarity are explored with regard to trade-union organization among one group of engineering workers at the Greenings factory, Warrington, England.[8] Union traditions in this factory have been shaped by the translation of practices and ideas from other workplaces in the locality, and by the transfer of labor movement activists into the plant. The heightened class struggle of the late 1960s and 1970s was also translated into social relations within the factory, giving confidence to union members and leaders alike. In addition, as we shall see, five protracted strikes between 1965 and 1983 had a major impact on the development of union traditions and shared memories within the workplace. In 1976, 1979, and 1983, workers built networks of supporters across the country, sustaining strike action through donations and emotional solidarity from the broader labor movement. This active spatial translation of experience on the part of the workforce increased the scale at which each dispute was fought out and ultimately strengthened the hand of the union. The legacy of these disputes was found to be inscribed in union practices, traditions, and shared memories at the plant during the early 1990s. Experiences of conflict and the lessons of union organization in the past were still shaping union practices and traditions in the present.

The Greenings Factory, Warrington: Building the Union during the 1960s and 1970s

Nathaniel Greening set up his first wire-drawing factory in 1799, and during the 1830s he revolutionized the wire industry by inventing the first steam-driven loom for weaving wire. In 1905, the company moved to its present site in Bewsey Road Warrington, occupying twenty-seven acres and employing several thousand workers, many of them women, who wove wire mesh on looms as though it were cloth (Mais 1949). By the 1960s, the company was still in family ownership, employing more than a thousand workers, specializing in wire weaving and perforating metal. The company is one of the oldest in Warrington, with its roots in the industrial revolution and the wire industry, for which the town was famous (the rugby team is still known locally as "The Wires").

When Arthur Conheeny arrived at Greenings in 1961, he found the company dominated by a tradition of paternalism, and recalled: "Trade unions were established, but in a very company style, it was paternalistic and very fragmented. There was no sense of solidarity in the place at all."[9] He described working conditions at the factory as "Victorian," which for him symbolized the weakness of the unions in Greenings: "When I went to Greenings in 1961 the washing facilities were on the clock. The hot water came on automatically to wash your hands, and it only came on at finishing times. . . . It was a sort of Victorian thing; we were part of the machinery. It was a measure of the trade unions in Greenings at the time." By the time Conheeny retired from Greenings in 1988, the workplace was on the national map, renowned for its traditions of strong organization and solidarity. In twenty years, the union tradition had shifted to being independent, tightly organized, and resolutely solidaristic. Moreover, at the time of writing, union organization had been retained in the very difficult circumstances that have prevailed in recent times. Despite devastating job losses and new management strategies, the union remained influential in the workplace and trade unionists were still able to defend and improve working conditions.

Union activists such as Arthur Conheeny came to Greenings bringing a wealth of working experiences gleaned from other workplaces within the locality. He served his time at Ruston Paxman Diesels (starting work in 1938), worked on the railway in Manchester, in the steel plant in Warrington, and at the Sankey Sugar Company in Newton-le-Willows, and arrived at Greenings with a knowledge of the trade-union movement, a determination to change things, and a skill for organizing working people. For him, solidarity and loyalty to the union could only be built with "patience and time," and he started to convince people that they could do something to change their environment. He explained that when he first arrived, workers took their poor conditions for granted:

> These things were accepted as normal then, and you can't change them overnight. It would be nice to put a wedge in it and break it at one go. But you can't do that, it's too powerful . . . you've got to chip away at it. A gain here, maybe a loss there, but gradually you know that change is possible.

Conheeny translated his experiences and leadership skills into the new workplace, and on Friday, November 5, 1965, he was elected into union office as a shop steward. Three days later, he was called into the manager's office and sacked

136

for allegedly breaking his contract. The minutes of the Newton and Warrington District Committee of the Amalgamated Engineering Union (AEU)[10] describe these events as follows:

> Agreement had been reached for Saturday afternoon overtime for maintenance fitters on a rota basis each week. The fitters on rota would be excused working if a replacement was provided. On Saturday 6th November, the engineer insisted that a fitter on rota must work Saturday afternoon even though he didn't wish to do so. On Monday, 8th November, he was called into the office and sacked. This member had been elected shop steward in place of a retiring one on Friday, 5th November, 1965. The District Secretary arranged a meeting with management on Monday morning to discuss the matter. Management refused to reinstate the newly elected shop steward. Our maintenance members held a meeting at lunch time and decided to withdraw labor.
>
> Moved: That we support our members, and insist on the reinstatement of the newly elected shop steward.
>
> Carried.

Being elected steward on Friday, sacked on Monday, and embroiled in strike action by Monday afternoon must surely be something of an industrial relations record. And it was not until Tuesday, November 16, that the AEU members forced management to rescind their decision, negotiating a return to work.

This dispute was the first in a long litany of strikes; with each one, more workers took part and attitudes at the factory hardened. In line with national trends, there was a general increase in the number of strikes and working days lost in Warrington during the late 1960s and 1970s (see figure 4.1),[11] and there were three major disputes at Greenings during the 1970s (in 1974, 1976, and 1979).[12] In each case, victory strengthened the union, and with each success, support and loyalty to the organization grew. A tradition of resistance was gradually built through conflict, and shared experiences and memories became increasingly important to social relations within the plant. These experiences of conflict and the lessons taken from each dispute acted as a resource in each subsequent dispute, thereby aiding collective resistance and solidarity. As Shorter and Tilly (1974, 238) write of strikes in particular communities, a collective repertoire of resistance was developed at Greenings:

> Traditions of industrial conflict themselves represent a force of enormous momentum in shaping the collective action of a working class population. If people strike in a place, it is partly because their fathers

and grandfathers also struck, or because they find themselves in a community with firmly rooted conflictual institutions and with collective mentalities of ancient pedigree. If people strike, it is not solely because they are boilermakers or machine assemblers or masons, though the structure of their jobs may limit or shape the exact forms their collective action assumes. It is also because they are enmatrixed in a certain community with certain acquired habits of joint action.

As the strike at Greenings in 1976 attests, such collective sentiments can develop during a very short period of time. The 1976 strike action lasted for ten weeks, and it again centered on Conheeny's dismissal. He and a colleague were sacked for an alleged breach of health and safety involving the use of a crane, and the 120 engineers took immediate action, not only to defend their colleagues but in recognition of the attack made on their union organization.[13] The strike proved to be a major turning point in the development of union traditions at Greenings, and cemented a new attitude toward the union within the factory. As Conheeny explained: "The strike acted as something of a catalyst as people began to see me as part of a broader thing, not merely an engineering steward, but as part of the organized working class." The 1976 strike involved the mobilization of workers beyond the Greenings establishment for the first time. Donations and collections were made by AUEW members across the country, enabling the strikers to see the potential for sustaining their action through solidarity.[14] As the place of the dispute embraced space, workers' power strengthened immeasurably. Greenings workers recognized that they were part of something broader than their own place-bound union, which in turn helped to reconfigure their attitudes toward the union within Greenings.

After ten weeks of disruption, the Greenings management met with John Tocher, the district organizer of the AUEW, to negotiate an end to the dispute.[15] The strike ended with the reinstatement of Conheeny and his colleague, and when Conheeny eventually returned to the factory, his position was stronger than ever. In the opening provided by the strike victory, trade unionists established a joint shop stewards committee, uniting union members under one organizational umbrella for the first time. Union traditions grew by breaking down sectional divisions within the workforce, which helped to expand the scale of union influence within the factory.[16] The balance of power had shifted in favor of the union, granting workers the wherewithal to develop and strengthen their union traditions in place and across space.[17] At Greenings, struggle allowed the workers to build new traditions on the foundations of the old, adding the experiences of workers in other locations to their repertoire of resistance.

138

Jane Wills

Figure 4.1. Locally based industrial disputes, Warrington, 1969–91. These data represent only local strikes; all national (and hence most public-sector) strikes are excluded.

Source: Original analysis of Department of Employment strike records

Building a Network of Solidarity: The 1983 Strike

Within Greenings, the development of union traditions appears to have gathered momentum over a very short period of time. With each successive strike, union practices and traditions were rehearsed and reworked according to the circumstances of each dispute. This process is most clearly illustrated by the twenty-three-week strike in 1983.

In April 1983, the Johnson Firth Brown management[18] produced a nine-page document (which had not been negotiated) in which it announced its decision to make eighty-nine workers compulsorily redundant, institute a wage freeze, abolish all negotiated holidays, end canteen and club facilities, terminate the full-time convenor's position, and close half the factory site (with more redundancies in the pipeline). Not surprisingly, given the history of industrial relations at the factory, four hundred workers responded by taking indefinite strike action.

To organize the strike, the joint shop stewards' committee (JSSC) was expanded into a strike committee, including all workers who wanted to play an active leadership role within the dispute. This committee coordinated picket lines, organized the writing of letters and bulletins, arranged finance to sustain the strikers, and planned strategy. From the outset, the JSSC presented the strike as being about general principles that mattered to every trade unionist in the country,

139

encouraging others to identify with their struggle. Here, they argued, was a small group of workers resisting redundancy and defending their union organization amid the devastation of the national manufacturing sector. While the Conservative government was determined to undermine the power of organized labor, Greenings workers presented themselves as a beacon of resistance to the assault, defending the rights of organized workers everywhere. They were determined not to lose the gains they had made in the past, as the wording of one of their solidarity leaflets makes clear: "Agreeing to management terms and conditions means a return to the 'cap in hand' days of the 1920s and 1930s. Our struggle has been long and hard—we must close ranks in solidarity against management's attempts at dictatorship. The tide is now in our favour! Demonstrate that we *demand* the right to negotiate our future!" (emphasis in original).

As the strike progressed, the JSSC put increasing resources into the organization of solidarity, because emotional, financial, and physical support from other trade unionists was vital to the continuation of the dispute. Len Blood, one of the shop stewards at the time, was crucial to this solidarity operation. Using the names of trade unionists and supporters who had helped the Gardners workers in Eccles (Manchester) during their strike in 1981, Blood was able to contact a vast network of potential supporters. The geographical scale of these contacts is illustrated by the collections made at Trades Council meetings across the country (see figure 4.2). Many trade unionists made collections for the strikers, relating their own experiences to the resistance at Greenings. In this way, solidarity effectively deepened and broadened the geographic scale of the dispute from the local to the national arena, from being a matter of local concern to an issue of national political significance.[19] The strike forged a new constellation of struggle as workers sought to translate their experiences across space to workers in other locations.

This translation involved delegation work conducted by the strikers themselves in which small groups of workers traveled by car to workplaces in other towns in order to seek support from fellow trade unionists. From late July 1983 each of these trips was recorded on delegation sheets, naming the workplaces visited and the responses received.[20] Strikers went as far afield as Norwich and Glasgow, and at least 270 workplaces outside Warrington were contacted in this way (see figure 4.3). Arthur Conheeny recalled one group of four middle-aged men who were particularly active in this solidarity work:

> They had a car and were very mild, not militant in any way, shape or
> form. They travelled miles, calling in at different factories all over the

140

Figure 4.2. Trades Council donations to the Greenings strike, 1983.
Source: Strike records

country. We'd give them money for petrol and cups of tea in the morning and you wouldn't see them for the rest of the day, they'd be off collecting money and raising support.

From the records on the delegation sheets, these four men made fourteen different trips by car between July 26 and August 30. They visited Ellesmere Port, Chester, Birkenhead, Speke, Liverpool, Preston, Rochdale, Bolton, and Bury, cov-

Space, Place, and Tradition

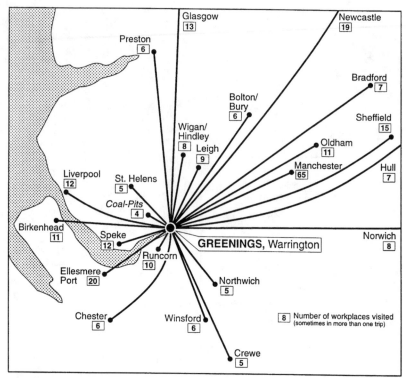

Figure 4.3. Workplaces visited by Greenings workers between July 26 and August 30, 1983.
Source: Strike records

ering a vast area and a large number of workplaces. Rather than waiting for solidarity to happen automatically, these workers reached out to kindred spirits, spreading the news of their strike and actively shaping the future of the dispute.

After attempting to lead two returns to work, taking out an injunction against an occupation of the plant, sacking all those who refused to return to work, and threatening to close the factory, Greenings management was eventually forced to negotiate with the unions. Ultimately, a return to work was agreed upon on Monday, September 9, 1983, and workers came back to the factory after twenty-three weeks on strike. All redundancy notices were rescinded and all proposed changes in working practices and union facilities were withdrawn.[21] The strike was an absolute vindication of the workers' actions and the union position and it left a strong legacy in the union organization after the return to work.

Reworking Traditions at Greenings in the 1990s

Through shared experiences during the strikes at Greenings, a strong loyalty developed among the workers, both to one another and to their union. As Hobsbawm (1964, 144) wrote of working-class organization: "The habit of industrial solidarity must be learned." In Greenings it was learned directly through practical experience. Workers took part in strike action and learned that solidarity was a real possibility, a means to sustain their action and achieve their aims. Fishman and Mershon (1993) suggest that such episodes of collectivity can be foundational, particularly for shaping the longer-term trajectory of working-class organization. As they explain, foundational experiences can "continue to shape collective worker action for years or even decades through their enduring impact on the beliefs and behaviour of the many workplace leaders formed or brought forward by those experiences and through the institutions or organizations that set the framework for collective action" (81). As implied here, workplace union leaders can play an elemental part in evolving union practices and traditions. At Greenings, Arthur Conheeny and Len Blood played a central role in evolving union traditions, translating their experiences of trade unionism and socialist politics into the factory. By offering leadership and direction to union members during the regular periods of conflict, workers could see the value of their ideas and methods in practice (see also Lynd 1990). Len Blood, for example, proved that solidarity was a viable strategy in sustaining the strikes. Through his knowledge of the labor movement, his ability to organize solidarity collections and delegation work, and his familiarity with a national network of socialist activists, Blood successfully coordinated the collection of thousands of pounds to support the 1983 strike. Through the work of dedicated union activists, workers came to understand the value of labor solidarity through their own experiences of conflict (see Gramsci 1971).[22]

During the early 1990s, when this research was carried out, Len Blood was still the convenor at Greenings and, despite difficult economic circumstances during the years since the 1983 strike, he worked hard to preserve union organization. The number of workers at Greenings had fallen dramatically since 1983; because of a division of the company, retirements, resignations, and voluntary redundancies, the hourly paid workforce numbered only seventy individuals.[23] All were still in the union, and they were represented by three stewards, of whom Blood acted as convenor. Formal meetings were much less frequent because of the size of the workforce, and there had been no strike action at the factory since 1983. Union organization had necessarily evolved to meet new and difficult circumstances, but despite this, industrial relations were still described by a

143

management representative as "extremely difficult." During the early 1990s, management was unable to reach agreement with the workforce about holiday entitlements, redundancies, and rates of pay and, at the time of interview, an unofficial overtime ban on Saturday work had just come to an end after eighteen months.[24] A management representative who was interviewed could not explain the strength of feeling and loyalty to the union that sustained this action among local employees: "If you went round and asked the men to work on Saturdays they'd say they hate the shop stewards for losing them so much money and they'd love to do the work. All they want is to be able to do the job. But, when it comes to it they won't break the union decision." Loyalty to the union thus remained central to workplace relations even in the changed circumstances of the 1990s. As this manager acknowledged, the history of industrial relations and the resultant politics of trade unionism were key determinants of workplace relations:

> The union leaders will convince the men that if they do what management want they aren't serving their best interests. I can't really explain it but the moderates have a terrible fear of the union. A lot of them are fairly old, they were involved in the 1983 strike and they haven't worked anywhere else for years. They think this is the normal way for things to go on with the union!

Through their experiences, the workers established a set of traditions that were different for each of them, but together they were able to form a serious obstacle to management within the plant. Len Blood, in particular, continued to play a central role in keeping the history of the union alive. He maintained workplace collections of fifty pence a week from all seventy workers in order to fund future disputes and solidarity donations for other workers involved in strike action. During March 1993, one of the Timex strikers from Dundee came to the factory to make a collection, and many of the workers remembered the support given to them by workers at Timex during the 1983 strike. These traditions of solidarity were also illustrated by the enormous contribution the Greenings workers made to the AEU "Drive for 35" working hours campaign during 1989–91, contributing more than £13,074 to sustain the national action. Traditions of solidarity on this scale were probably unparalleled anywhere else in the United Kingdom at this time.

Shared memories and determined leadership have facilitated the survival of a strong union presence among Greenings workers. Yet, despite this continuity, union traditions have had to evolve with changing economic and political circumstances. By the early 1990s the number of workers had dwindled, jobs seemed

144

insecure, and the union was less powerful than it had been. Keeping the union together was extremely difficult during these years, as Blood explained during an interview: "I don't sleep well these days. I do find it very difficult. You see, I've lived through this glorious climate, this glorious period when we really made things happen and built the union.... Now I'm getting repudiations from the union for an overtime ban against redundancy. I feel we're somehow very alone at the moment." The national political climate in the 1990s had shifted considerably since the days of the 1970s, which Blood recalls as a "glorious period." Although the union at Greenings remained strong in relative terms, being a declining industry undermined its position and strength. The union had evolved over time, but without an economic foundation the translation of tradition was very hard to sustain. Service work had come to dominate the economic landscape of Warrington by the 1990s and union practices in the new industries were very different from those in the old. As Harry Howard, the AEEU district secretary remarked, the traditions of unionization at Greenings were always an exception, even among engineering workplaces in the town. Newer workplaces tended to have less of a political tradition, and increasing numbers of establishments in the town were not even unionized as a result of management hostility and resistance to union recognition:

> Greenings has a history of trade unionism in the classic form, the right to challenge the employer has been fought for. There's more of a deep tradition of solidarity and a belief in the union as an organization. In other newer workplaces, trade unionism is based upon more immediate things like their terms and conditions, and unfortunately, that type of tradition is less resilient. Things have really changed today, though, and we don't have the power to force the employers to concede recognition anymore. There's a firm near Skelmersdale where we had 109 members from the 130 employees but the boss wouldn't agree to recognition. We had a ballot and an overtime ban but it only lasted a fortnight. There's no legal channel we can turn to, so we keep plodding away at it, leafleting the factory and pushing the employer. It's almost back to the last century; the employers have got harder and they're much more determined to break the unions.

The economic and political climate has clearly served to interrupt the spatial translation of union traditions from workplaces such as Greenings into other establishments while also reshaping the temporal translation of union traditions within Greenings. Although the legacy of the past is still felt within Greenings,

145

the hostile economic situation and the shifting industrial relations climate made union organization in the plant and the town much more difficult than it was in the past. In many ways, then, the experience of trade unionism at Greenings bears testimony to the trade unionism of the past; Greenings acts as a symbol of the resistance to which organized workers can aspire, but the translation of this set of traditions has been difficult in the harsh economic and political climate of Britain in the 1990s.

Conclusion

To conclude, I return to the themes that began this essay, endeavoring to develop a spatialized understanding of class relations and trade-union organization. The Greenings example illustrated that class organization embeds itself and takes on a meaning in place, and that this set of ideas and traditions can then be translated over space, shaping organization and ideas in other locations. The Greenings case demonstrated that material practices in place often result from the importation of ideas and traditions generated elsewhere. Individuals (such as Conheeny and Blood) brought their own experiences and traditions into the factory, transforming inherited union practices. Cyclical trajectories in the balance of class forces at a wider scale also marked local union traditions, strengthening confidence during the 1970s and undermining it during recent years. Finally, the solidarity support given to striking Greenings workers played a vital part in the development of union traditions, widening the spatial scale of their disputes and ultimately helping to secure their success. As a unique product of workers' geohistory, union traditions can thus only be understood as being simultaneously spatial and temporal in formation.

I have argued that union traditions are ideas, grounded in place while also circulating in space. But, just as any characterization of capital as geographically footloose understates the importance of fixed location to the accumulation process, so too workers' traditions are more than simply free-floating ideas. Ideas need to "take place" in some material sense if they are to be reproduced and reinvented.[25] Ideas can only be reproduced and reinvented in the long term — among workers, at any rate — through being materially grounded in some way. Hence, as events "take place," workers can "prove" their ideas against the others on offer, reformulating their traditions in the process — a process that will itself be highly uneven across space.

Recentering workers' agency within critical human geography has important implications for understanding the role that capital has in fashioning the historical geography of capitalism. How workers respond to their conditions, and what

146

they achieve or do not achieve, makes a difference to processes of uneven development. In Greenings, workers were able to defend their union and limit the impact of economic recession on their wages, conditions, and rights to organize. In so doing, these workers changed their own conditions, but they also affected the terrain beyond the walls of their workplace. In making their own history and geography, Greenings workers were also shaping the landscape in which others make theirs. Because the geographical landscape is a product of social relationships, and class conflict (benign or otherwise) is a key part of this social equation, uneven class relations and organizational capacities matter to the production of space. Even when it appears that workers are not able to make any adequate response to the hegemony of capital, the inactivity of workers in one part of the country is still affecting the contours of class for those in other locations. These contours are never fixed in time and space, and the pressure gauge of class conflict is constantly fluctuating, shaping the landscape in which decisions are made. Just as the movement of capital is described as seesawing across the landscape in search of profit (Smith 1990), so too labor traditions and organization have a geographical dynamic. Embedded in place, yet also mobile across space in a way that defies prior delimitation, the translation of tradition is a fundamental part of the geographical landscape, shaping the arena in which capital investment is made.

Such a spatialized understanding of class relations has been fundamental to Conservative governments since 1979. Groups of trade unionists in particular localities have been confronted by the government, invariably one at a time, and, with each defeat, the conflict has been superseded by that with another group of workers (Coates 1989; Kelly 1990). In a strategy that climaxed with orchestrated set-piece battles for the coalfields and the print industry, each defeat seemed to lead inexorably to the next. The ruling class had a geographical strategy to defeat labor, localizing struggle through outlawing secondary action and taking on one group of workers at a time. In this scenario, working-class defeat has been a geographically uneven process. It is only by challenging the spatial despotism of capital through organization and struggle in particular places that workers can begin to reverse this decline. By drawing new contour lines on the map of class power, workers' activity can shape the terrain in which economic processes and social relationships unfold. Whereas workers' agency helped to rework the landscape of class to the benefit of labor in the late 1960s and early 1970s, those gains have been at least partially reversed during the 1980s and 1990s, leaving workers in a weak position from which to make geohistory in their favor. Even at a time of such apparent weakness as in the 1980s and 1990s, however,

147

workers' activity, or lack of activity, still shapes the production of space. By highlighting the geography of such processes, workers can be viewed as active agents, shaping the landscape of capitalism on which they depend.

Notes

I would like to thank Andrew Herod for his supportive interest and feedback and Arthur Conheeny, Len and Janice Blood, and Harry Howard for their time and involvement in this project. Certainly, more could be done to document the history of trade unionism in northwest England before workplaces like Greenings close down altogether. The material presented here forms part of a Ph.D. thesis undertaken at the Open University, and I am grateful to Doreen Massey and John Allen, whose encouragement and gentle guidance proved invaluable to its completion.

1. Massey's (1984) *Spatial Divisions of Labour* is the key text in this school. Massey outlines the reciprocal relationships between processes of economic restructuring and local political cultures. The themes of this work were taken up in a number of localities research projects during the 1980s (see Cooke 1985, 1986, 1989; Harloe, Pickvance and Urry 1990; the Lancaster Regionalism Group 1985; Bagguley et al. 1990; Savage et al. 1987; Duncan and Savage 1991; Massey 1991). Class formations and traditions were seen to make a difference to, and be affected by, processes of economic change in place. Other writers who have taken an economic approach to understanding union change are Massey and Painter (1989), Clark (1989), Painter (1991), and Martin, Sunley, and Wills (1993, 1994, 1996).

2. For these authors, local social relations and political traditions occupy central place in their analyses of trade-union practices (Mark-Lawson, Savage, and Warde 1985; Warde 1985, 1988, 1992). Work in this vein reached its height during the miners' strike of 1984–85 as geographers sought to explain spatial disparities in trade-union activity and popular perceptions of the strike (Sunley 1986, 1990; Rees 1985, 1986; Griffiths and Johnston 1991; Gilbert 1992).

3. The clearest example of this problem is research into so-called radical regions (see Cooke 1985; Morgan and Sayer 1988). This body of scholarship has tended to obfuscate temporal discontinuities in workers' organization and emphasize social cohesion in working-class life within these locations. In practice, any set of traditions is contested from within, multiple in its divisions, and often exclusionary to those who do not belong. (For a critique of radical regions research, see Jackson 1991.)

4. Despite this reference to the complexity of local culture, Williams's work has been criticized as overromanticizing working-class culture in Wales. Although

Jane Wills

he acknowledges a temporal dynamic to culture in this example, he pays less attention to the social divisions within places, and the spatial dynamic of local cultures and processes of cultural reproduction (see Said 1989; Harvey 1995).

5. It is important to note that Thompson's prioritization of experience as the key component of class formation has been subject to robust criticism from a wide variety of sources. Hall (1981, 384), for example, disputes Thompson's rejection of class structure in explaining class relations and argues that reducing class to an active relationship loses the central Marxist dialectic between structure and agency. Callinicos (1987, 224) writes that experience is never unmediated, being subject to multiple interpretations and the influence of particular ideologies within everyday life. In addition, experience is open to reinterpretation after the event, and, as oral historians know only too well, the recollection of events may tell us more about the present ideas of the raconteur than it does about the events themselves (Portelli 1981, 1990; Samuel 1994). Nevertheless, Thompson's work has been enormously influential in highlighting the role of workers' agency in making history, and, even if it is problematic, this essay seeks to argue that this approach can be applied (with care) to geographical analysis.

6. Although this essay is focusing on the spatial constitution of tradition, this is not to neglect other complications in our use of the word *tradition*. As Beynon and Austrin (1994, 4) remark, *tradition* is "a term which explains, while explaining away, the question of continuity and discontinuity in social life." As I have argued elsewhere, traditions are multiple and conflictual as well as unitary and consensual, reactionary as well as radical, and based on the present as much as the past (Wills 1995, 1996a, 1996b). New inventions and breaks with the past constantly interrupt the reproduction of historical tradition, as practices are changed to meet the needs of the present (see Calhoun 1983, 1987; Hobsbawm 1983, 1984; Tilly and Gerome 1992; Samuel 1994). It is perhaps not surprising that Williams describes *tradition* as one of the most complicated words in the English language (1976, 319).

7. For examples of work that explores the rich local constitution of working-class life, see Shorter and Tilly (1974), Smith (1984), Golden (1988), Williams (1989), Hayter and Harvey (1993), Fisher (1993), and Beynon and Austrin (1994).

8. This research has involved numerous interviews with Harry Howard, the district secretary of the Amalgamated Engineering and Electrical Union (AEEU), Arthur Conheeny, previous convenor (1961–88), Len Blood, convenor at the time of research (1975–96), a management representative, and a regional official from the Engineering Employers' Federation (EEF). Secondary sources such as union records and minutes, newspaper reports, and library materials have been used to

build up a fuller picture of the events described. During other research into trade unionism in Warrington, of which this example forms a small part, Greenings often came up in conversation, cited as a well-established trade-union stronghold in the area. Special thanks must go to Len Blood, the convenor during the time this research was undertaken, who spent many hours recounting tales of union organization within the factory. His subsequent redundancy is a mark of the decline of this industry and its workers.

9. Trade unions had been recognized at Greenings before the Second World War, and no one was able to remember when, and how, this occurred. Engineering trade unionism has a very long history in the region, and records show that union organization in Warrington predates the establishment of a national engineering union in 1851 (Jeffreys 1945). As Greenings belonged to the Engineering Employers' Federation, recognition would have been automatic upon membership, even if it had not been granted previously. At the time of research, three different unions were still operating in the factory—the AEEU, the General and Municipal Boilermakers (GMB), and Manufacturing, Science and Finance (MSF)—and all three were involved in a joint shop stewards committee. This research has focused on the engineering union members and organization within the plant, whose workers were primarily fitters and maintenance workers, all of them men.

10. The engineering union has changed its name on a number of occasions during its history. On its founding in 1851, the collection of local unions was called the Amalgamated Society of Engineers (ASE), and became the Amalgamated Engineering Union (AEU) in 1920, the Amalgamated Engineering and Foundry Union (AEF) in 1967, the Amalgamated Union of Engineering Workers (AUEW) in 1971, reverting to the AEU in 1986 and becoming the Amalgamated Engineering and Electrical Union (AEEU) in 1992 following the merger with the Electrical, Electronic, Telecommunications and Plumbing Union (EETPU). Here, the name has been used as appropriate to the historical period in question.

11. It is important to note that although Warrington recorded a large number of strikes during this period, they were very unevenly distributed: 93 of the 212 local disputes recorded between 1969 and 1991, for example, occurred within the engineering industry, and 29 percent of them actually occurred in one factory, Ruston Paxman Diesels. Assessing the impact of strikes on local union organization is thus problematic. Such events are not shared by all workers and, moreover, are not experienced or interpreted in the same way by all those involved.

12. The engineers also took part in two one-day strikes as part of the campaign against the proposed Industrial Relations Bill during 1971 (see Harman 1988, 240). These strikes were called by the broad left in the AUEW and were

purely political and aimed at defending national rights to organize as trade unionists.

13. Toward the end of the 1976 strike, Greenings's management provided a vivid illustration of the importance it attached to Conheeny's influence within the factory by offering him thirteen years' pay (£60,000) if he would leave Greenings for good. This action was met with incredulity by those involved in the strike, and the astonishment grew when he refused to accept the money. Conheeny's rejection of the money is legendary among engineering trade unionists within the town. Such action also indicates the importance of Greenings's management in the development of union traditions. Processes of trade unionism are inextricably linked to management decision making.

14. The arrival of Len Blood at the factory during 1975 was also important to the organization of union solidarity at Greenings. Blood brought an enormous wealth of organizing experiences with him to Greenings, having moved from Ford Halewood after a period of employment at Ruston Diesels and thus having work experience in two of the most militant workplaces in the region. Between 1967 and 1976 he was involved in at least five strikes at other workplaces, and this had an immense impact on the organizational resource base he added to the union at Greenings. He brought new knowledge and experience to the Greenings tradition. He was very active in the trade-union movement and (Trotskyist) Socialist Workers Party, and provided leadership in the coordination of union solidarity.

15. John Tocher was a longtime Communist Party member and engineering union official with a rich history of organizing workers in the northwest. He was involved in the famous Roberts-Arundel strike in Stockport during 1966–67 (Arnison 1970), led the 1972 Manchester pay disputes, was involved in the Gardners' strike in Eccles in 1980–81, and played a central role in many other disputes in the region. His wholehearted support for the strikers was also important in the development of union traditions in Greenings. Geographical location clearly made a difference to the union resources available to the strikers and the political hue of the union officials in the region.

16. Blood recalled how slow the union was to make serious attempts to organize the women workers in Greenings, having assumed that they were not interested in union organization. In the event, the women were encouraged to elect representatives onto the new joint shop stewards committee, and they made a number of improvements to women's position within the factory.

17. Couto (1993) similarly finds the reinvention of workers' traditions during conflict at the Pittston mine in Appalachia during a strike in 1989–90. Drawing on the work of Evans and Boyte (1986), he suggests that the strike extended

the "free social space" available to the miners, allowing them to draw on their shared experiences and memories of the past in public, collectively contemplating and rethinking their experiences. Moreover, the Pittston strike did not involve a simple repetition of past practices but gave workers the opportunity to remember the past while re-creating their traditions of resistance, thereby introducing the "traditions of other free spaces" to the workers of Pittston (Couto 1993, 185). Learning the lessons of the civil rights movement, the union drew the wider community into demonstrations, sit-downs, occupations, and local events at the strike centers.

18. By 1979, the Greenings family had sold the company to the Johnson Firth Brown group, which also had sites in Sheffield and Glossop.

19. Herod (1995) presents a similar example from a strike by workers at the Ravenswood Aluminum Corporation (RAC) in West Virginia during 1990–92. These workers used international pressure and solidarity to win their dispute, and the scale of community action, as at Greenings, was crucial to the outcome of the strike. As Herod explains: "Workers successfully extended their understanding of community to operate on a number of different scales. By expanding the scale of conflict geographically they were able to draw upon social resources which would not otherwise have been available to them and which provided a greatly enlarged resource base for mobilizing against RAC" (355).

20. Although the records of the strike indicate that this delegation work began after July 26, 1983, Conheeny and Blood recalled such activity being organized much earlier in the dispute. Indeed, reports in the *Socialist Worker* (April 30, 1983, 14) suggest that as early as April 30, strikers were out collecting money and visiting other disputes. They went to the Firth Derihon occupation in Sheffield and the Aire Valley strike over recognition. The report for May 14 states: "The lessons that have been learned in the previous struggles at Greenings are being applied today. Delegations are being sent out all over the country to raise support for the strike. This week strikers will be in London, Manchester and Coventry, while others are travelling to Brighton for the Civil Servants' Union Conference" (*Socialist Worker*, May 14, 1983, 16).

21. Of the eighty-nine workers originally made redundant, only twenty-three chose to return to work, the others having taken their redundancy money and left the company during the strike.

22. In her discussion of the persistence of syndicalist trade-union practices within Italian politics, Golden (1988) points to the importance of industrial conflict as a means of transmitting traditions. During the hot autumn of 1969, older workers shared their experiences of the factory councils of 1919–20 with their younger colleagues. "When militants evaluated strategic options for the

future, they drew on and reinvented their own past, and in context that meant they looked directly to the formative experiences of the Italian workers' movement, especially to the period after World War I. They did so quite explicitly and self-consciously, as illustrated, for instance, by the decision during the hot autumn by the FIOM-CGIL to reprint a whole volume of *Ordine Nuovo* articles dealing with the factory councils of 1919–20" (Golden 1988, 22).

23. In 1988, Greenings was divided in two as some of the managers bought out the wire screen part of the business, which now operates under the name Screen Systems Ltd. and employs some one hundred workers at the Greenings site. The metal perforating side of the company was sold by the Johnson Firth Brown group to a holding company, which then sold it to CI Industries. In the period since the completion of this research, the plant has been sold again and large numbers of workers, including the convenor Len Blood, have been made redundant.

24. This action to increase overtime rates after the thirty-seven-hour agreement reached in 1990 was unofficial until the management contacted the general secretary of the AEEU, asking him to repudiate the unofficial action and call the stewards into line. In response, the local unions held a workplace ballot and secured a good majority for the action, forcing the management to make a new agreement over rates of pay. The results of this ballot in June 1993 were AEEU 18 in favor, 2 against; MSF 28 in favor, 3 against; GMB 4 in favor, none against.

25. As Neil Smith (1990) has pointed out, if the reassertion of spatiality in social theory is to mean anything beyond metaphor, space and place must be understood as central components in the materiality of political practice.

Bibliography

Arnison, J. 1970. *The Million Pound Strike.* London: Lawrence and Wishart.

Bagguley, P., J. Mark-Lawson, D. Shapiro, J. Urry, S. Walby, and A. Warde. 1990. *Restructuring: Place, Class and Gender.* London: Sage.

Beynon, H., and T. Austrin. 1994. *Masters and Servants: Class and Patronage in the Making of a Labour Organization.* London: River Oram Press.

Blomley, N. K. 1993. *Law, Space and Power.* London: Guilford Press.

Bruner, J. 1986. *Actual Minds, Possible Worlds.* Cambridge: Harvard University Press.

Burawoy, M. 1985. *The Politics of Production.* London: Verso.

Calhoun, C. J. 1983. "The Radicalism of Tradition: Community Strength or Venerable Disguise and Borrowed Language." *American Journal of Sociology* 88.5: 886–914.

Space, Place, and Tradition

————. 1987. "Class, Space and Industrial Revolution." In *Class and Space: The Making of Urban Society*, edited by N. J. Thrift and P. Williams, 51–72. London: Routledge and Kegan Paul.

Callinicos, A. 1987. *Making History*. Cambridge: Polity Press.

Church, R., Q. Outram, and D. M. Smith. 1990. "British Coal Mining Strikes 1893–1940: Dimensions, Distribution and Persistence." *British Journal of Industrial Relations* 28.3: 329–49.

Clark, G. 1989. *Unions and Communities under Siege: American Communities and the Crisis of Organized Labor*. New York: Cambridge University Press.

Coates, D. 1989. *The Crisis of Labor: Industrial Relations and the State in Contemporary Britain*. Oxford: Philip Allan.

Cooke, P. 1985. "Radical Regions? Space, Time and Gender Relations in Emilia, Provence and South Wales." In *Political Action and Social Identity: Class, Locality and Ideology*, edited by G. Rees, J. Bujra, P. Littlewood, H. Newby, and T. L. Rees, 17–41. London: Macmillan.

————, ed. 1986. *Global Restructuring, Local Response*. London: Economic and Social Science Research Council.

————. 1989. *Localities: The Changing Face of Urban Britain*. London: Unwin Hyman.

Couto, R. A. 1993. "The Memory of the Miners and the Conscience of Capital." In *Fighting Back in Appalachia: Traditions of Resistance and Change*, edited by S. L. Fisher, 165–94. Philadelphia: Temple University Press.

Cronin, J. E. 1979. *Industrial Conflict in Modern Britain*. London: Croom Helm.

————. 1987. "Strikes and Power in Britain, 1870–1920." *International Review of Social History* 32.2: 144–67.

Croucher, R. 1982. *Engineers at War 1939–1945*. London: Merlin.

Duncan, S., and M. Savage, 1991. "Commentary: New Perspectives on the Locality Debate." *Environment and Planning A* 23: 155–64.

Evans, S. M., and H. C. Boyte. 1986. *Free Spaces: The Sources of Democratic Change in America*. New York: Harper and Row.

Fantasia, R. 1988. *Cultures of Solidarity: Consciousness, Action and Contemporary American Workers*. Berkeley: University of California Press.

Fisher, S. L., ed. 1993. *Fighting Back in Appalachia: Traditions of Resistance and Change*. Philadelphia: Temple University Press.

Fishman, R. M. 1990. *Working Class Organization and the Return to Democratic Spain*. Ithaca, N.Y.: Cornell University Press.

Fishman, R. M., and C. Mershon. 1993. "Workplace Leaders and Labor Organization: Limits on the Mobilisation and Representation of Workers." *International Contributions of Labor Studies* 3: 67–90.

Jane Wills

Gilbert, D. 1992. *Class, Community and Collective Action: Social Change in Two British Coalfields 1850–1926.* Cambridge: Cambridge University Press.

Golden, M. 1988. "Historical Memory and Ideological Orientations in the Italian Workers' Movement." *Politics and Society* 16: 1–34.

Gramsci, A. 1971. *Selections from Prison Notebooks.* London: Lawrence and Wishart.

———. 1977. *Selections from Political Writings, 1910–1920.* London: Lawrence and Wishart.

Gregory, D. 1978. *Ideology, Science and Human Geography.* London: Hutchinson.

Griffiths, M. J., and R. J. Johnston. 1991. "What's in a Place? An Approach to the Concept of Place, as Illustrated by the British National Union of Mineworkers Strike 1984–1985." *Antipode* 23.2: 185–213.

Haimson, L. H., and C. Tilly, eds. 1989. *Strikes, Wars, and Revolutions in an International Perspective.* Cambridge: Cambridge University Press.

Hall, S. 1981. "In Defence of Theory." In *People's History and Socialist Theory,* edited by R. Samuel, 378–85. London: Routledge and Kegan Paul.

Harloe, M., C. Pickvance, and J. Urry. 1990. *Place, Policy and Politics: Do Localities Matter?* London: Sage.

Harman, C. 1988. *The Fire Last Time: 1968 and After.* London: Bookmarks.

Harvey, D. 1973. *Social Justice in the City.* Oxford: Basil Blackwell.

———. 1989. *The Condition of Postmodernity.* Oxford: Basil Blackwell.

———. 1995. "Militant Particularism and Global Ambition: The Conceptual Politics of Place, Space and Environment in the Work of Raymond Williams." Paper presented at Southampton University, March 1995.

Hayter, T., and D. Harvey, eds. 1994. *The Factory and the City.* London: Mansell.

Herod, A. 1991. "The Production of Scale in United States Labour Relations." *Area* 23.1: 82–88.

———. 1994. "On Workers' Theoretical (In)visibility in the Writing of Critical Urban Geography: A Comradely Critique." *Urban Geography* 15.7: 681–93.

———. 1995. "The Practice of International Labor Solidarity and the Geography of the Global Economy." *Economic Geography* 71.4: 341–63.

Hobsbawm, E. 1964. *Laboring Men.* London: Weidenfeld and Nicholson.

———. 1983. "Introduction: Inventing Traditions." In *The Invention of Tradition,* edited by E. Hobsbawm and T. Ranger, 1–14. Cambridge: Cambridge University Press.

———. 1984. *Worlds of Labor: Further Studies in the History of Labor.* London: Weidenfeld and Nicholson.

———. 1988. "Working Class Internationalism." In *Internationalism in the Labour Movement 1830–1940,* edited by F. van Holthoon and M. van der Linden, 3–16. London: E. J. Brill.

Space, Place, and Tradition

Hyman, R. 1989. *Strikes.* London: Macmillan (originally published 1972 by Fontana).

Jackson, P. 1991. "Mapping Meanings: A Cultural Critique of Locality Studies." *Environment and Planning A* 23: 215–28.

Jeffreys, J. B. 1945. *The Story of the Engineers: 1800–1945.* London: Lawrence and Wishart.

Kelly, J. 1988. *Trade Unions and Socialist Politics.* London: Verso.

———. 1990. "British Trade Unionism 1979–1989: Changes, Continuity and Contradictions." *Work, Employment and Society* (special issue, May): 29–65.

Lancaster Regionalism Group. 1985. *Localities, Class and Gender.* London: Pion.

Lash, S., and J. Urry. 1984. "The New Marxism of Collective Action: A Critical Analysis." *Sociology* 18.1: 33–50.

Lee, R., and Wills, J., eds. 1997. *Geographies of Economies.* London: Edward Arnold.

Luxemburg, R. 1986. *The Mass Strike, the Political Party and Trade Unions.* London: Bookmarks.

Lynd, S. 1990. "Youngstown, Ohio: Rebuilding the Labor Movement from Below." In *Fire in the Hearth — the Radical Politics of Place* (vol. 4 of *The Year Left*), edited by M. Davis et al., 177–94. London: Verso.

Mais, S. P. B. 1949. *The History of Greenings 1799–1949.* Warrington: Mackie, Guardian Press.

Mark-Lawson, J., M. Savage, and A. Warde. 1985. "Gender and Local Politics: Struggles over Welfare Policies, 1918–1939." In Lancaster Regionalism Group, *Localities, Class and Gender.* London: Pion.

Martin, R., P. Sunley, and J. Wills. 1993. "The Geography of Trade Union Decline: Spatial Dispersal or Regional Resilience?" *Transactions of the I.B.G.* 18.1: 36–62.

———. 1994. "Local Industrial Politics: Spatial Sub-systems in British Engineering." *Employee Relations* 16.2: 84–99.

———. 1996. *Union Retreat and the Regions: The Shrinking Landscape of Organised Labour.* London: Jessica Kingsley.

Massey, D. 1984. *Spatial Divisions of Labor: Social Structures and the Geography of Production.* London: Macmillan.

———. 1991. "The Political Place of Locality Studies." *Environment and Planning A* 23: 267–81.

———. 1992. "Politics and Space/Time." *New Left Review* 196: 65–84.

Massey, D., and J. Painter. 1989. "The Changing Geography of Trade Unions." In *The Political Geography of Contemporary Britain,* edited by J. Mohan, 130–50. Basingstoke, U.K.: Macmillan.

Jane Wills

Merrifield, A. 1993. "Place and Space: A Lefebvrian Reconciliation." *Transactions of the I.B.G.* 18.4: 516–31.

Millward, N. 1994. *The New Industrial Relations?* London: Policy Studies Institute.

Morgan, K., and A. Sayer. 1988. "A 'Modern' Industry in a 'Mature' Region: The Remaking of Management-Labor Relations." In *Uneven Re-Development*, edited by J. Allen and D. Massey, 167–87. London: Sage.

Painter, J. 1991. "The Geography of Trade Union Responses to Local Government Privatisation." *Transactions of the I.B.G.* 16.2: 214–26.

Peck, J. 1996. *Work-Place: The Social Regulation of Local Labour Markets.* London: Guilford Press.

Portelli, A. 1981. "The Peculiarities of Oral History." *History Workshop Journal* 25: 96–107.

———. 1990. "Uchronic Dreams: Working-Class Memory and Possible Worlds." In *The Myths We Live By*, edited by R. Samuel and P. Thompson, 143–60. London: Routledge.

Rees, G. 1985. "Regional Restructuring, Class Change and Political Action: Preliminary Comments on the 1984–1985 Miners' Strike in South Wales." *Environment and Planning D: Society and Space* 3: 389–406.

———. 1986. "Coal Culture and the 1984–1985 Miners' Strike: A Reply to Sunley." *Environment and Planning D: Society and Space* 4: 469–76.

Said, E. (with Raymond Williams). 1989. "Media, Margins and Modernity." In *The Politics of Modernism*, edited by R. Williams, 177–97. London: Verso.

Samuel, R. 1994. *Theatres of Memory.* London: Verso.

Savage, M., J. Barlow, S. Duncan, and P. Saunders. 1987. "Locality Research: The Sussex Programme on Economic Restructuring, Social Change and Locality." *Quarterly Journal of Social Affairs* 3.1: 27–51.

Screpanti, E. 1987. "Long Cycles in Strike Activity: An Empirical Investigation." *British Journal of Industrial Relations* 25.1: 101–24.

Shorter, E., and C. Tilly. 1974. *Strikes in France 1830–1968.* Cambridge: Cambridge University Press.

Smith, J. 1984. "Labor Tradition in Glasgow and Liverpool." *History Workshop* 17: 32–56.

Smith, N. 1990. *Uneven Development: Nature, Capital and the Production of Space.* Oxford: Basil Blackwell.

Soja, E. W. 1989. *Postmodern Geographies: The Reassertion of Space in Critical Social Theory.* London: Verso.

Stedman-Jones, G. 1974. "Working Class Culture and Working Class Politics in London, 1870–1890." *Journal of Social History* 7: 460–508.

157

Sunley, P. 1986. "Regional Restructuring, Class Change and Political Action: A Comment." *Environment and Planning D: Society and Space* 4: 465–68.

———. 1990. "Striking Parallels: A Comparison of the Geographies of the 1926 and 1984–1985 Coalmining Disputes." *Environment and Planning D: Society and Space* 8: 35–52.

Thompson, E. P. 1978. *The Poverty of Theory and Other Essays.* London: Merlin.

———. 1980. *The Making of the English Working Class.* London: Penguin Books.

———. 1991. *Customs in Common.* London: Merlin.

Thrift, N., and P. Williams, eds. 1987. *Class and Space: The Making of Urban Society.* London: Routledge and Kegan Paul.

Tilly, L., and N. Gerome. 1992. "Tradition and the Working Class." *International Labor and Working-Class History* 42 (fall): 1–4.

van Holthoon, F., and M. van der Linden, eds. 1988. *Internationalism in the Labor Movement 1830–1940.* London: E. J. Brill.

Warde, A. 1985. "Spatial Change, Politics and the Division of Labor." In *Social Relations and Spatial Structures,* edited by D. Gregory and J. Urry, 190–212. London: Macmillan.

———. 1988. "Industrial Restructuring, Local Politics, and the Reproduction of Labor Power: Some Theoretical Considerations." *Environment and Planning D: Society and Space* 6: 75–96.

———. 1992. "Industrial Discipline: Factory Regimes and Politics in Lancaster." In *Skill and Consent: Contemporary Studies in the Labor Process,* edited by A. Sturdy, D. Knights, and H. Willmott, 97–114. London: Routledge.

Williams, R. 1976. *Keywords.* London: Fontana.

———. 1989. *Resources of Hope.* London: Verso.

Wills, J. 1995. "Geographies of Trade Union Tradition." Ph.D. thesis, Open University, Milton Keynes.

———. 1996a. "Geographies of Trade Unionism: Translating Traditions over Space and Time." *Antipode* 28.4: 352–78.

———. 1996b. "Uneven Reserves: Geographies of Banking Trade Unionism." *Regional Studies* 30.4: 359–72.

Jane Wills

Chapter 5 • The Scales of Justice
Localist Ideology, Large-Scale Production, and Agricultural Labor's Geography of Resistance in 1930s California

Don Mitchell

With the recrudescence of agricultural labor militancy beginning in 1928 and bursting into radical visibility in 1933 (Daniel 1981; Mitchell 1996a), growers in California faced a strong, well-organized, and seemingly lasting resistance to their traditional hegemony in labor relations. Communist-backed unions such as the Agricultural Workers' Industrial League (1930) and the Cannery and Agricultural Workers' Industrial Union (CAWIU, 1932–34) vied with activist ethnic unions (such as the Filipino Labor Union of the Salinas Valley) and the American Federation of Labor's halfhearted effort to organize field and cannery workers. Labor historian Cletus Daniel (1981) called 1933 the "Great Upheaval," and organized growers and workers saw it as just that. In famous battles in the Alameda County pea harvest (April 1933), the San Joaquin Valley fruit and grape harvests (June–September 1933), the San Joaquin Valley cotton harvest (October 1933), and the lettuce, pea, and cantaloupe harvests in the Imperial Valley (November 1933–July 1934), as well as in dozens of other smaller battles, militant workers organized striker encampments and "flying pickets" to press their claims for higher wages, better conditions, and union recognition (Mitchell 1996a). Worker successes, in terms of demands met, were both partial and tenuous, but they were clearly portentous. They served warning on industrialized farmers that they could no longer do business as they had grown accustomed to doing it, that is to say, with little or no regard for the desires and rights of the workers who made California agriculture so successful and profitable.

Strikes around the state were connected by migratory workers moving from one harvest to another and by a core of committed organizers, many of them young communists, who traveled and lived with harvest workers, seeking both to organize strikes in advance and to strengthen wildcat strikes. Indeed, many growers and local and state officials were increasingly coming to see migrancy itself as subversive. The very ability of workers to connect battles separated by hundreds of miles threatened the landed, industrial interests of the state. For radical workers and organizers, connecting crop- and site-specific struggles to   159 each other was a conscious strategy. In the words of a "Monthly Handbook for Functionaries," distributed to CAWIU organizers in March 1934: "No campaign should be allowed to run as a separate campaign by its self, but must be tied up with every other campaign and the contacts made should be utilized for all the mass activity" (LFC [La Follette Committee], *Hearings*, Part 49, Exhibit 8306, 18180). Thus, as Earl Warren, then the Alameda County district attorney argued, the goal for growers and local law enforcement officials after the 1933 "upheaval" was to find a way to "break the continuity" of migrant workers by hiring locally unemployed workers (with the cooperation of officials who would cut off their relief payments, even though it was doubtful that unskilled workers could make a living wage in most harvests) or by reinforcing the sacred rights of community over the needs and desires of those they called "outsiders" (*San Francisco Examiner*, April 8, 1934).

The creation of a rhetoric of "outsiders" was crucial to grower and law-enforcement strategy for controlling worker unrest. Naming striking workers "outside agitators," or simply "outsiders," delegitimized their claims to the resources of community—such as the right to speak in public spaces, to picket on public highways, or even to gain access to local sympathizers—even as it reinforced the growers' claims to local legitimacy. The ability to name some in the community "outsiders" rode on historically developed ideological arguments about the scale of legitimacy. This argument presumes that the more local the actor, the more legitimate his or her claim on the rights and privileges of community.[1] California agricultural-ists had a well-honed sense of the "legitimate" local. A director of the antiunion Associated Farmers declared:

> We have never refused to bargain with our people collectively, but we do find in many instances that it is not our own people, our own work-ers, that they wish us to bargain with, but it is people who have come in from the outside and who are constantly agitating for demands in which they have no experience, and in work in which they have never been employed, and never had employment on that particular ranch or in that particular area. They come from the outside. (LFC, *Hearings*, Testimony of Henry L. Strobel, Part 53, 19504)

Defining "the local" is a process of determining boundaries and the nature of legitimacy within those boundaries. As this Associated Farmer went on to remark, "I want to talk to the people I am going to employ. I don't want to put the loy-alty or the trust of those people in some *outside* influence which has ... no con-cern and does not tend to do the worker any good, or myself" (ibid.; emphasis added). The invocation of "outsiders" draws on a deep ideological fund that

Don Mitchell

argues that the right to determine access to political voice and the structure of social relations begins and ends in the (ideologically defined) *local* community. Drawing on classical notions of republicanism, Americans have long held that a republic "had to be small both in size and in population. Its people had to be virtuous, thinking of the common good rather than private interests" (Levine et al. 1989, 167). Against that has been a federalist strain, which has argued, along with James Madison in the *Federalist Papers*, that, in an "extensive" republic, the "public good" could be served by numerous private interests competing with each other—the classically liberal position (ibid., 168). In both instances, however, community is developed, as it were, from the bottom up, either with a small group of citizens determining the nature of community, or with *individuals* acting in their own, usually local, self-interest. The locus of legitimacy, whether political or economic, remains the locality, even as federation created an extensive common market.

Localism, then, while drawing on this fund of ideology and common sense for legitimacy, exists within, and is often in objective conflict with, the continual political-economic production and negotiation of material or geographic scale (Herod 1991; Smith 1990, 1992). Herod (1991, 82) argues that "geographical scale is produced as the resolution of processes of cooperation and competition between and among social groups in building landscapes." Smith (1990; see also Smith and Dennis 1987) asserts that understanding the constant negotiation and renegotiation of the scales of production is essential to understanding both the uneven development of capitalism and its continued survival. But, as Herod (1991, 84; emphasis in original) points out, understanding scale as being produced nearly exclusively as the result of the internal logic of capital turns attention away from the degree to which geographic scale is a "*contested* social construction" in which "other struggles and experiences," such as the hard ideological work of defining community, struggles over reproduction within the household (and beyond), or the promulgation of laws and regulations, "modify the law of value in different geographic locations."[2] Or, as Smith (1992, 66; emphasis in original) has remarked, "scale demarcates the sites of social contest, the object as well as the resolution of contest.... It is geographical scale that defines the boundaries and binds the identities around which control is executed *and* contested."

This essay will take Herod's and Smith's argument one step further by showing how the production of geographic scales—particularly "extralocal" scales—rests on the ability to define the local and to assure one's place in it, that is, to determine who constitutes the "legitimate" local community. The production of geographic scales is, in part, a function of ideological arguments *about* scale. In the terms of the federalist debate that has animated so much American political ideology, an understanding of the interaction between ideological invocations of scale and the production of geographic scale shows that classical republicanism is not so much opposed to the creation of larger-scale "common markets" but is actually a necessary component of that creation. The production of national and international scales of production, consumption, and economic control has rested on the ability to sanctify the local as a place of decision and community. To illustrate this claim, I will first examine the ideological invocation of the local (and resistance to this invocation) as a tool of power in violent labor struggles during the 1930s in agricultural California. I will then explore the material scales of production within which ideological scales of the local were organized. Or, put another way, I will show that the valorization of "the local" by growers and law-enforcement officers served to legitimate a repressive social order that in fact was crucial to making national and global agricultural production possible. In this way, "the local" was put to work in service of larger-scale operations.

For agricultural workers in California in the 1930s, concern with intersecting geographic and ideological scales was no academic exercise. Rather, as the following analysis shows, the contradictions inherent in this intersection determined, in a very important and concrete sense, both the geography of labor's resistance to agricultural capital and the nature of social justice — what the muckraking Senate La Follette Committee called "economic democracy" — within a quite iniquitous set of labor relations.[3] "Economic democracy and all that it holds for the civil liberties of labor," the La Follette Committee declared in its report on agricultural labor relations in California, "must be established in industrialized agriculture, or civil rights will continue to be violated in a wholesale and violent fashion whenever and wherever they are exercised by labor in such a manner as to affect agricultural interests" (LFC, *Report*, Part VIII, 1944, 1130). California growers' "resistance to economic democracy, established around 'industrialized farmers,' financed by antiunion groups" (ibid.) hinged precisely on their ability to establish their own local legitimacy (by reinforcing an ideology of localism) at the expense of farmworkers.

Violence, Justice, and the Ideology of the Local

At the beginning of March 1934, the Growers' and Allied Industries' Association of San Jose was formed by growers and canners as part of a concerted effort to avoid the sort of worker militancy that had marked the 1933 season. The *San Francisco Chronicle* (March 2, 1934) reported:

> One of the [association] moves will be to determine a standard uniform wage for fruit pickers, and to publish this for public consideration and

Don Mitchell

approval. Once approved it will be considered the standard wage for the county and workers refusing to accept it will be considered as agitators and malcontents who *have come into the county* for the purpose of making trouble. They will be treated accordingly. (Emphasis added)

Farmers, and indeed "real workers," the Growers and Allied Industries Association claimed, were beleaguered locals beset from beyond by dangerous pests who had little understanding of the mores of the community. But, like other pests, they could be eradicated with community effort. Indeed, growers often made this comparison with pests explicit. Three years after the San Jose association was formed, the secretary-manager of the Associated Farmers of the Imperial Valley, Inc., informed a correspondent: "We have a strong and enthusiastic organization in the Valley, and the effectiveness of our work is evidenced by the lack of strikes in our county. We have an excellent formula for getting rid of cockroaches, grasshoppers and CIO agitators" (LFC, *Hearings,* Part 55, Exhibit 8953, 20347).

The "formula" was hard-won. In 1934, growers and workers in the Imperial Valley were engaged in a set of the most violent strikes of the "Great Upheaval." Beginning with the lettuce harvest in November 1933 and extending through the cantaloupe harvest the following summer, the valley was convulsed by protests, beatings, tear-gas bombings, violent dispersals of strikers' encampments, and deportations. Investigative commissions sponsored by both the federal New Deal government and organized growers came to research conditions in the valley. There they met an army of labor conciliators, American Civil Liberties Union (ACLU) attorneys, and state agricultural labor-relations experts drawn to the conflict. They also found unrepentantly violent growers and quite radicalized workers. The federal Leonard Commission learned from incensed growers that the Cannery and Agricultural Workers' Industrial Union was a conspiracy of "Statewide proportions, led by men and women alleged to be 'Communists', 'reds', 'radicals' and 'outside agitators' to quote some of the more polite names we have heard" (LFC, *Hearings,* Part 54, Exhibit 8766, 20047).

In response to the "communist invasion" of their valley, growers formed the Imperial Valley Anti-Communist Association, which simultaneously sought to promote "Americanism" and to recruit labor spies (LFC, *Report,* Part IV, 1942, 458–60). Created concurrently with the Anti-Communist Association was the Imperial Valley Growers and Shippers Protective Association, which "sought to project the image of a completely independent local farmers' group dedicated to the protection of the valley's yeomanry from Communist diabolism" (Daniel 1981, 238). The general tenor of this campaign was captured by an obliging article in the *Los Angeles Times Farm and Garden Magazine*:

163

Then clouds began to mar a peaceful sky [in Imperial Valley]....[A] hundred too many [migratory workers] began flocking in where they were not needed, demanding work of an industry that can only accommodate so many. And with them came agitators, gentry of the stamp of those who had played the devil with the cotton harvest in the San Joaquin Valley a few months before. Then the strike was on.... When it was finally over and the threat of trouble-makers had been removed the always willing pickers went back to work on the overloaded vines to salvage what they could of the crop. Both they and the growers had been victimized by the agitating group which is threatening the stability of California agriculture. (McFadden 1934, 3)

The imagery is exact: "agitators" are "outsiders," not members of the community, not interested in the survival of its members. Real local workers, on the other hand, are "always willing," except when influenced by that ultimate destructive outsider, the Devil, and that most devilish of ideologies, communism.

Such a language of localism beset by dangerous outsiders was both diagnostic and important to the survival of agricultural production in California. In the Imperial Valley, growers and their allies in local (and, to an extent, state) law enforcement met worker militancy with all the violence they could muster. When strikers organized caravans to picket fields, the police responded with clubs and tear gas. They violently broke up strike meetings and, in one widely publicized case, locked strikers in an assembly hall and fired tear gas into it. The Imperial County sheriff declared all meetings of two or more workers to be illegal (Daniel 1981, 229). Concerned about the abuse of workers' rights, A. L. Wirin, a Los Angeles attorney and board member of the American Civil Liberties Union, sought permission from each of several law agencies in the Imperial to allow workers to meet. Wirin had no success and so sought, and received, a federal injunction in San Diego barring local law officers and growers from interfering with a scheduled workers' meeting. Just before the start of the meeting, Wirin was kidnapped from his Imperial Valley hotel (according to Wirin, the kidnapping party included a uniformed member of the state highway patrol). He was robbed and then dumped barefoot in the desert eleven miles from town. When he got back to his hotel he was greeted by a mob of three hundred vigilantes who demanded that he immediately leave the valley. The workers' meeting was canceled and the lettuce strike soon fizzled (Daniel 1981, 231).

When strike efforts were rekindled among pea pickers in February 1934, local growers and police responded just as violently and this strike too was quickly broken (Mitchell 1996a; Daniel 1981). Growers were in no mood to deal with outside meddlers of any kind and claimed that the growers themselves knew what was best for the valley. Two labor mediators, one from a regional labor board in Los Angeles and the other the state labor commissioner, were warned by the local captain of the state highway patrol to "get out of here.... We know how to handle these people, and where we find trouble makers we'll drive them out, even if we have to 'sap' them" (LFC, *Hearings*, Part 54, Exhibit 8765, 20039).

One successful strategy for "driving them out" — and thereby reinforcing the borders of the legitimately local — was the selective enforcement of vagrancy laws. During the January 1934 lettuce strike, twenty-eight of eighty-six strike-related arrests were for "vagrancy" (most of the rest were for disturbing the peace) and scores of other men and women were " 'picked up' but not booked." Local police defined as vagrant anyone opposed to growers' interests who could not establish permanent residency in Imperial County. As the Leonard Commission commented, "Only by a prostitution of the State vagrancy law could some of the prisoners be arrested or held. This group includes two attorneys, one from the State of Arizona, and the other a resident of San Bernardino County, California" (LFC, *Hearings*, Part 54, Exhibit 8766, 20049). But the letter of the law was clearly not the concern. Rather, it was "interference" in valley affairs by "outsiders" that was at issue.

The San Bernardino and Arizona attorneys jailed for vagrancy were in the Imperial Valley to serve writs of habeas corpus for organizers who had been arrested. Both lawyers missed their court dates because they were in jail. The cases were continued to the following day and when the organizers and their attorneys were finally released, one of the attorneys, Grover Johnson, was savagely beaten outside the courthouse by growers (and a county supervisor) while the sheriff and deputies stood idly by (LFC, *Hearings*, Part 54, Exhibit 8765, 20038; Mitchell 1996a). The passivity of the sheriff in this instance is hardly surprising because he himself was a large landowner in the valley, as, in fact, were the police chiefs of the major towns, Brawley and El Centro, the head of the local office of the state highway patrol, an undersheriff, and the police judge (who was also justice of the peace). As the report of a state labor commissioner noted, the only law-enforcement official without a direct interest in ranching in the valley was the district attorney (LFC, *Hearings*, Part 54, Exhibit 8765, 20038). Local justice, then, took on a decidedly peculiar cast in the Imperial Valley.

The nature of local justice was well described by the Leonard Commission:

> It is regrettable that men who have put heroic effort into the reclamation of desert wastes are threatened with the loss of their hard earned fortunes. It is deplorable that many workers are not able to earn sufficient

165

to maintain even a primitive, or savage, standard of living, and consequently are forced upon charities. It is horrible that children are reared in an environment as pitiable as that which we saw in more than one locality. But worse than these is the harsh suppression of that which we in the United States claim as our birthright, the freedom to express our lawful opinion and legally to organize to better our lot and that of our fellow men. (LFC, *Hearings*, Part 54, Exhibit 8766, 20049)

The commission's nine recommendations for the long-term settlement of agricultural labor relations in the Imperial pivoted on the fact that local "justice" and local control over conditions were both unjust and undesirable. It recommended:

1. That the *Federal* and *State* Governments exercise every power and authority to maintain in fact the rights of free speech, free press and free assembly, and that men, either citizens or aliens, shall not be harassed by permanent, temporary, amateur, or self-appointed officers of the law....

2. That the *Federal* Government encourage the organization of workers, in order that collective bargaining may be effective in matters of wages and conditions ... and the right to strike and peacefully to picket shall be maintained....

3. That a "Labor Coordinator" be appointed by the *Federal* Government to equalize and balance the labor supply, and that, *through this Coordinator*, preference be given to permanent residents.[4]

4. That a permanent board or an impartial administrator be set up by the *Federal* Government, to act in matters of dispute regarding wages [and conditions].... We recommend this because we believe there are no codes for the protection of workers.

5. That State and County authorities be urged by the *United States* Public Health Service to improve living quarters ... and all other determining factors in the health and welfare of the *entire* community.

6. That the *Federal* Government cooperate with the State and County to establish subsistence farms or gardens....

7. That the *California State* Department of Education promote a program of social and economic education....

8. That both *State* and *Federal* Governments encourage the growers and the shippers to organize, that they handle more intelligently the various problems relating to the successful conduct of their business.[5]

9. That steps be taken to repatriate aliens (*a*) who are undesirable and are subject to deportation, and (*b*) who desire of their own free will to

Don Mitchell

return to their respective countries. (LFC, *Hearings*, Part 54, Exhibit 8766, 20052; emphasis added)

Explicit in these recommendations is the assumption that local governments and growers were incapable of providing either justice or decent living conditions. Only a larger, national-scale intervention could protect "that which we . . . claim as our birthright."

Outraged by the meddling of the federal Leonard Commission, Imperial Valley growers sponsored their own investigative committee, the Hutchison Committee, composed of a dean of the College of Agriculture at the University of California, a right-wing state Assembly member (who in the late 1930s professed great admiration for the disciplined societies of Germany and Italy), and an administrative assistant for the State Department of Agriculture. The Hutchison Committee countered the Leonard Commission's recommendations with a dozen recommendations of its own, which, while also calling for intervention at a larger scale than the local, did so in order to protect the interests of a narrowly defined community. Prominent among the Hutchison Committee's recommendations was a demand that the state bar "investigate the activities of attorneys employed to defend persons who advocate the overthrow of the present government and who disparage the efforts of courts to mete out impartial justice" (*San Francisco News* April 21, 1934, in LFC, *Hearings*, Part 70, Exhibit 12463, 25720). And, where the Leonard Commission recommended that local, state, and national law-enforcement and governmental agents be mobilized to protect the civil rights of workers, the Hutchison Committee responded that although it "supports the right of free speech and assemblage, . . . it is time to make a distinction between free speech and unlicensed speech" (LFC, *Hearings*, Part 54, Exhibit 8767-B, 20067).

Despite their rather different takes, the issue itself remained one of legitimacy. And legitimacy remained clearly defined in terms of scale. The question debated by these two investigative bodies was simply this: Which was more important, the abstract, universal rights of those who may be out to destroy community and government, or the local, concrete, palpable rights of those threatened by outside menace to determine the fate of their community? As the *Pacific Rural Press* (April 28, 1934), organ for agricultural-industrial interests in the state, opined: "disturbances such as the one in the Imperial Valley are not actually a contest over wages, nor a genuine public protest against housing conditions, but are part of a definite Communistic plot of discontent, organization and world revolution, undeniably hatched in Moscow." In such besieged circumstances, when international conspiracies were apparently threatening the rights of local citizens to make a decent living, there could be no room for meddling "outside" labor organizers and lawyers—or even wrongheaded federal commissions. A local mayor was more direct: "We simply will not have them here. We will put the law of self-preservation into effect if necessary.... You know we have dealt with those who have endeavored to destroy our crops and who have been striking at the very heart of American government.... We are decent, law-abiding citizens and will brook no interference with our constitutional rights" (*Brawley News*, April 24, 1934).[6] Perhaps the mayor was referring to radical workers. But the vigilante assaults on the ACLU's Wirin, the attack on attorney Grover Johnson, the threats to labor conciliators, and, finally, another brutal attack in June on an ACLU attorney who had been guaranteed protection by a federal labor mediator (Daniel 1981, 247–48) suggest that the sights of the "community" were set more broadly than that.

The Los Angeles *Examiner* (April 7, 1934; in DIR [Division of Industrial Relations] Records, Carton 86) reinforced the sense that the battle in Imperial was one structured in terms of a local community beset by meddlesome and dangerous outsiders:

> Deportation of Communistic, alien, trouble-making Mexicans of the floating class is held by many *citizens* of Imperial Valley to be the right answer to threats of agitators to produce warfare here unless demands which they have formulated are met.... For more than four months the melon pickers are in the class of plasterers and bricklayers as wage earners. That is why valley citizens are fairly confident there will not be a strike of melon pickers as threatened by the Communist *outside* leaders of the Cannery and Agricultural Workers Industrial Union. (Emphasis added)

The language here is telling and it points directly to the problem that long-developed and ever-evolving ideologies of racial "fitness" to do agricultural work presented to growers and their allies.[7] They wanted to believe that Mexican workers were somehow naturally fit to do stoop labor happily under oppressive conditions—as they had likewise been eager to embrace similar ideologies about Asian workers in the past. With each racially marked group growers recruited, however, there eventually came a time when worker militancy gave the lie to the convenient, paternalistic language of race. At such times, growers typically evolved—as they did in the Imperial Valley—a racist ideology of local patriotism that explained away worker militancy as the result of corrupting outside influences. Mexican workers, susceptible as they were to influences that they presumably did not understand, turned from being willing workers to troublesome agitators deserving of deportation.

168

Don Mitchell

The Los Angeles *Examiner* article (which a state labor camp inspector called "garbled" in its representation of valley conditions [DIR Records, Carton 86]) was based on, and seconded the extensive comments of, Alvin N. Jack, president of the Imperial Valley Growers' and Shippers' Protective Association (which presumably represented the citizens of the valley). After a lengthy disquisition on the increasingly problematic Mexican workers, Jack widened his compass and ended with a dire warning:

> [The] prevalence of many Filipino laborers in the Valley now adds to the menace of the situation. They are trouble makers. Chester Williams of the American Civil Liberties Union is planning a meeting of Mexican and Filipino malcontents in Azteca Hall in Brawley's "east of the track" section tomorrow afternoon. He wired to General Glassford [the federal labor conciliator sent to the valley by federal Secretary of Labor Frances Perkins] today asking if he might bring along John Packard[,] another Civil Liberties lawyer. (Ibid.)

All this work — vigilante violence, calls for deportation, the ideological work of constructing racial stereotypes and of stressing yeomanry threatened by "outsiders" — served to make the violent protection of local boundaries into "the highest and most graphic expression of regional and class patriotism" (Daniel 1981, 228). Such work has not been unique to 1930s California. In his analysis of the 1984 British National Union of Mineworkers' coal strike, for instance, Nicholas Blomley (1994, 64) has argued that the denial of rights to workers, whether workers "stranded" by highly mobile capital or workers forced on the road by strikes and job structure, rests on a "resonant language of decentralization and localism." In both 1930s California and 1980s Britain, the ideology of localism has been closely tied to an economic system that itself produced the legitimized scales of everyday life *and* the scales of capitalist production. This localism is quite specific in its effects, as Lord Wedderburn (1985, 43) noted in his analysis of the British coal strike:

> *The collective strength of workers is to be limited by the boundaries of their employment units.* These boundaries are of course set not by the workers but by capital in the private sector, and in the public sector by the state and capital together. Industrial action across the boundaries is unlawful; the concept of a trade dispute is not to flow over them; each subsidiary company in a small national or giant multinational group is to retain its own boundaries. (Quoted in Blomley 1994, 180; emphasis in original)

Capital thus establishes the boundaries of the local within which worker legitimacy is defined.[8]

But, clearly, these boundaries exist within a continually developing web of re-lationships, within nested hierarchies of produced scales that structure the real-ization of surplus value from local production. For all their appeal to the value of local community and the prerogative of "citizens," Imperial Valley growers were themselves national and even global in their reach and organization. When the Leonard Commission curiously recommended that the state and federal gov-ernments assist growers and shippers to organize, the Hutchison Committee re-sponded with puzzlement: "The Committee does not understand this recom-mendation. The Growers and Shippers are already organized and have been for years. They must and do handle their problems cooperatively" (LFC, *Hearings*, Part 54, Exhibit 8767-B, 20068). Unlike what the growers and the shippers ex-pected of the harvest workers, their cooperative affiliations did not stop at the borders of the Imperial Valley; their own scale of organization stretched far be-yond the local area. As we will see, it was precisely this extralocal scale of organi-zation that ultimately lay at the heart of growers' and shippers' strategy for defin-ing who constituted legitimate insiders and illegitimate outsiders in the agricultural communities of the state.

The Organization of Growers and the Production of Geographic Scale

Over the eighty years of Anglo-American agriculture in California, growers had evolved a complex set of institutions to organize their production, marketing, and labor relations. These included national marketing cooperatives, regional labor supply and strikebreaking organizations, and statewide employers' and antiunion organizations that crossed not only crop boundaries but also boundaries between enterprises traditionally considered "urban" and "industrial," and those consid-ered "rural" and "agricultural." "In my opinion," C. C. Teague (1944, 76), the director of the massive Limoneira citrus ranch in Santa Barbara, wrote in 1944, "cooperative marketing, more than any other factor, has brought about the phe-nomenal expansion of the citrus business in California during these past 50 years." The same could be said of cooperatives in walnut, cotton, lettuce, pea, and numer-ous deciduous fruit crops. Teague was instrumental in establishing the Califor-nia Fruit Exchange (Sunkist) and the California Walnut Growers' Association (Diamond Brand). By World War II, Teague (1944, 85) estimated, Sunkist con-trolled "approximately three-fourths of the entire movement [to market] of packed citrus fruit" from California and Arizona. The Walnut Growers' Associ-ation accounted for 85 percent of the California walnut crop (ibid., 111). The degree of control achieved by such cooperatives over markets is an indication of their power. But it is also important that this control was not always easily at-

170

tained. First, local growers had to be brought on board. The Sun-Maid Raisin Growers' Association, for example, achieved complete control of raisin production in California during the 1920s by employing methods that "would have done credit to the carpet-baggers of the post–Civil War south" on reluctant (usually Armenian) growers, according to one commentator (La Peire 1930; quoted in McWilliams 1971, 187). "The story of those months will never be told; all that can be said is that desperation resulted in the worst mob violence which Fresno County has ever seen" (ibid.).

Cooperatives like these not only arranged for the marketing of crops in distant markets. They also set wage rates for the member growers, ran subsidiary firms (like the Fruit Growers Supply Company), lobbied in Sacramento and Washington, D.C., and fixed prices (by "pooling" produce from numerous growers and local member associations). Between 1907 and 1940, Sunkist spent more than $37 million in advertising around the nation (Teague 1944, 86). Such "commodity organizations" were (and remain) extremely powerful in California. Cooperative cotton gins, for example, disciplined small growers when they paid more than "prevailing wages" to pickers by refusing loans on the next year's crop (LFC, *Report*, Part IV, 1942, 419–553).

Complementing the "commodity organizations" in California agriculture were numerous "area associations" (regional organizations of growers, often organized through the Farm Bureau Federation or the State Chamber of Commerce), such as the Western Growers' Protection Association (WGPA). The WGPA was formed in 1926 by large growers of vegetables and melons. The first purpose of the organization was to reduce transportation costs by grouping shipments and then demanding volume discounts. In 1930, one-quarter of all vegetables shipped by rail in the United States was grown in California and Arizona, and Imperial Valley growers shipped lettuce to every state except New Hampshire and Delaware. Indeed, the majority of melons and vegetables produced in these states were marketed east of Denver (LFC, *Report*, Part IV, 1942, 438–39).

Large growers styled themselves "grower-shippers," and the name was accurate. Grower-shippers operated vertically integrated growing, processing, packing, shipping, and marketing industries. With many controlling in excess of thirty thousand acres, vegetable grower-shippers were, according to the WGPA trade journal, "practicing the oft expressed theory of industrialized farming." Indeed, some 75 percent of California vegetable and melon acreage was controlled by large-scale firms and individuals (*Western Grower and Shipper*, December 1929, 16; January 1933, 11–12). These were impressive, and spatially quite extensive, operations. As the *Western Grower and Shipper* (July 1930, 16) gloated, "Most of the large factors have headquarters in Los Angeles, and thousands of acres of land   **171**

---

in the Imperial, Salt River, and Salinas Valleys hundreds of miles away, are actually 'farmed by phone' from the western metropolis. . . . Several factors travel exclusively by plane." In the Imperial Valley, more than half the cropland was owned by individuals and corporations outside the valley. By 1936, some 83 percent of all melon and vegetable land was owned by only fifty-one grower-shippers. Similarly, forty grower-shippers controlled 84 percent of the lettuce crop (LFC, *Report*, Part IV, 1942, 437).

These patterns of industrialized farming, coupled with California's growing specialization in intensive specialty crops, called up an incredible system of "casual" labor.[9] During the 1920s, all types of farming (with the exception of field crops — grains, alfalfa, cotton,[10] etc. — which had a labor demand of 88 percent of their pre–World War I level) recorded intensified seasonal labor demands. Labor demand in truck crops increased to 233 percent of prewar levels, fruit and nuts to 168 percent, and livestock to 110 percent (Fuller 1939). A weighted average of labor demand for the decade (considering the effects of acreage and share of labor force devoted to each crop) showed an increase to an average 137 percent of prewar demand. The problem for California agriculturalists and workers in all this, however, was that labor demands were highly seasonal. During 1935 and 1936, for example, nearly 150,000 agricultural workers *in excess of those permanently employed* were needed in California during September; more than 130,000 temporary workers were needed in August and October; and between 100,000 and 110,000 workers were needed for temporary work on farms in each of May, June, and July. By contrast, during March, the month of lowest labor demand, only around 50,000 temporary workers were needed on the farms of the state (CSRA 1936). This seasonality demanded a mobile, ephemeral labor force. Growers argued that they could not pay the yearly reproduction costs of seasonal labor power and evolved a spectacular set of rationalizations, often grounded in a racist ideology of "fitness to work," for assuring that *necessary* labor did not become *local* labor (Fuller 1939; Daniel 1981).

While migratory labor traveled extensive distances up and down the state in search of work, large-scale farmers also spread across the landscape, controlling land in districts throughout the West and beyond, and creating associations like the WGPA to safeguard their collective interests in securing proper markets and proper labor. But organizations like the WGPA were not simple, democratic associations of small-scale *farmers* with common interests, the epitome of Jefferson's yeomanry. Rather, they were closely controlled by a handful of large firms, with 70 percent of the membership providing only 15 percent of its funds and 4 percent of the membership (eleven companies) providing 38.8 percent. The four largest contributors (giving 20 percent of WGPA's total income) were the Ameri-

Don Mitchell

can Fruit Growers, Inc., incorporated in Delaware and created by the merger of companies in Pittsburgh, Chicago, upstate New York, central Florida, and Los Angeles; S. A. Gerrard Co., incorporated in Ohio and a farmer of land in several parts of California, Arizona, and Colorado; the H. P. Garin Co., owner of farms in Imperial, Salinas, and the Brentwood (Contra Costa County) areas of California; and A. Arena and Co. of Los Angeles, which farmed in Imperial, Salinas, and the Salt River Valley (LFC, *Report*, Part IV, 1942, 442–43).

These details are important precisely because they point directly to the issue of scale understood in Herod's (1991, 82) terms as "the resolution of processes of cooperation and competition." In fact, the WGPA had *created* the Imperial Valley Growers' and Shippers' Protective Association as a local strikebreaking subunit during the 1933–34 strikes in the Imperial Valley and was instrumental in organizing and directing the Imperial Valley Anti-Communist Association (LFC, *Report*, Part IV, 1942, 457–58). The Imperial Valley Growers' and Shippers' Association was, for all intents and purposes, synonymous in membership and leadership with the WGPA, "even though it sought to create the public impression that it was a local body formed and conceived by local citizens" (ibid., 457). Similarly, in the Salinas Valley, south of San Francisco, the Grower-Shipper Vegetable Association, ostensibly a local organization concerned with protecting local farmers, was simply a branch of the WGPA. Thirteen of its fifteen directors between 1933 and 1940 also served on the board of directors of the WGPA (ibid., 472). Given that most of the large Imperial vegetable and melon growers were also large growers in Salinas, this overlap is hardly surprising. It is even less surprising when we recall that many workers, too, continually wove connections between Salinas and Imperial (and on to the Salt River Valley in Arizona) in their yearly migratory paths (ibid., 469–70). What is surprising, however, is the degree to which organizations like this could *represent* themselves as *local*, as pillars of the *local* community, as in no way "outsiders."

But such representations did not go uncontested. The contradiction of state and national industrial associations posturing as besieged local farmers often rushed to the fore. In the Salinas Valley (Monterey County), a local paper worried in 1935 that "there is distinct danger that Monterey county will be made a battle ground for industrial warfare.... Lettuce shippers and speculators elsewhere in this state look cynically upon the peace in Monterey county.... The *outside influences* that are in the game to break union labor in California agriculture want Monterey county in the same game, too" (LFC, *Hearings*, Part 73, Exhibit 13765, 27078; emphasis added). In the face of such opposition (and in response to increased calls for the federal government to intervene in a meaningful way in labor relations in California), organizations like the WGPA and the marketing coop- 173 eratives, coupled with the California State Chamber of Commerce, the California Farm Bureau Federation, and numerous urban industrial, utility, and transportation concerns, formed the Associated Farmers of California, Inc., which, though originally a top-down, statewide organization, was meant to represent the interests of local, small-time farmers in their battles against radical workers and the state.

The Associated Farmers and the Reassertion of the Local

By Whom Organized

By Farmers; run by farmers, with a farmer directorate, and financed (except for emergency expenditures) by farmers—in spite of all propaganda to the contrary put out by those whose subversive efforts are handicapped by the existence of such organizations as the Associated Farmers of California, Inc....

How Financed

By a nominal assessment upon agricultural commodities in this State....Roughly it may be understood to be 1¢ a ton on all fresh fruits and vegetables; 2¢ a ton on strawberries; 1¢ a ton on milk; 10¢ a ton on hops; 1¢ a bale on cotton; and 75¢ per car on nuts. (LFC, *Hearings*, Part 68, Exhibit 11490, 25025)

So declared the Associated Farmers (AF) in one of its pamphlets. Very little in this statement was true, except, perhaps, the claim that AF "handicapped" the "subversive efforts" of farmworkers to organize. The AF was created—significantly given the ongoing battles in Imperial and the threat of continued unrest elsewhere in the state as the harvest moved north—on March 28, 1934. It was the brainchild of large, urban-based, industrial corporations and associations that, through the state Chamber of Commerce, "marshalled and unified existing local and regional groups in industrialized agriculture into a State-wide coordinating unit" (LFC, *Report*, Part IV, 1942, 573). The connections between farmers' organizations such as the Farm Bureau Federation, individually powerful growers, allied industrial concerns (such as packing companies), urban industrial concerns, and large banks, railroads, and utilities in the formation of the AF are byzantine but, as the La Follette Committee reported, for its first two years this "farmer's" organization "was financed...almost entirely by industrial interests located in San Francisco" (ibid., 588).

Even so, the Associated Farmers presented itself as a *local* organization. Its executives claimed that the state-wide organization existed only to coordinate

174

the activities of the various county-level Associated Farmers organizations — and, in fact, the statewide organization had no members. Rather, it consisted of a board of directors, which, presumably, represented the different county units. (In practice, membership on the state board of directors rotated between several quite powerful independent growers or managers for powerful corporate farmers) (ibid., 583–88). During the first two years of operation, the La Follette Committee concluded, the AF "was to all practical purposes a subsidiary of 'area' and 'commodity' employers' associations, created specifically to deal with the wave of agricultural strikes which had their inception in 1933" (LFC, *Report*, Part VIII, 1944, 1137).

The AF was formed for several reasons, not the least of which was to help assure "the passage of antipicketing legislation ordinances in every county in the State" (LFC, *Hearings*, Part 55, Exhibit 8857, 20251). These ordinances at the county level were instrumental in reinforcing the boundaries of the local as a means of controlling radical labor. In the first month of its existence, one of the AF's organizers noted proudly: "More than 20 counties . . . passed picketing ordinances. . . . In addition, the respective counties in most instances have perfected some type of organization to meet whatever communistic troubles may develop" (LFC, *Hearings*, Part 68, Exhibit 11465, 25009). The AF was also formed to provide financial and ideological support for a campaign to gut the radical unions (both agricultural and industrial) in the state by arresting and convicting their leaders under criminal syndicalism charges. The organization worked closely with county and state prosecutors to secure criminal syndicalism convictions for most of the leadership of the CAWIU and, in so doing, "delivered to the CAWIU, and to agricultural unionism in California, a stunning and debilitating blow" (Daniel 1981, 254).[11] By the middle of 1935, however, without an effective union in the fields of California and with the conviction of radical organizers assured, the AF drifted with little purpose and "found itself without a program, without an interested membership, and with a considerable debt" (LFC, *Report*, Part VIII, 1944, 1133).

All that changed when the Associated Farmers of California was revived in 1936 (largely thanks to the fund-raising activities of Leonard Wood, an official of the California Packing Corporation headquartered in San Francisco) to meet the renewed threat of both rural and urban labor organization attendant upon the passage of the 1935 Wagner Act, which guaranteed workers the right to unionize.[12] With the reorganization, the AF remained controlled by interests other than local farmers. In the organization's bylaws, members were not required to pay membership dues to the statewide organization, which instead was financed

175

The Scales of Justice

by a charge to employer associations, railroads, packing companies, utilities, banks, oil companies, sugar companies, and paper and box manufacturers (LFC, *Report*, Part VIII, 1944, 1157–66). Where the AF claimed financing from an assessment on farmers by commodity, the real source of its income was a myriad assortment of corporations and organizations that were sometimes directly associated with agricultural production and at other times simply interested in advancing the antiunion cause in the state. It was policy of the AF not to divulge the names of its financiers (ibid., 1171; LFC, *Hearings*, Part 67, 24492).

Although the AF was formed from "above," its revival fostered the organization and maintenance of county units, in part to allay the impression that AF was simply an antiunion arm of powerful state employer associations and industrial companies. What money was raised by the county AFs, whether for their own use or for the state organization, in fact came from precisely the industrial companies, railroads, banks, and so forth that had funded the state AF, except that now they channeled their contributions through county units. In Los Angeles County, for example, from 1937 to 1939 only $248 of a total budget of $17,527.25 was collected directly from farmers (LFC, *Report*, Part VIII, 1944, 1182–85, 1193).

With financial obligations guaranteed by large corporations and employers' organizations, the state AF turned in 1936 to the task of developing a mass membership among farmers. Most of the county AFs were "set up through the diligent efforts of the State organization" (ibid., 1190). Less organizations of independent small farmers than cabals of industrially organized agribusiness interests, the county units typically drew their directorships from existing, large grower-controlled "area" associations like the Imperial Valley Growers Protective Association or the Diablo Valley Public Relations Committee (cf. Mitchell 1994). When actual crop assessments were made at the county level, they were often made coercively by cooperative packers and cotton ginning companies (LFC, *Report*, Part VIII, 1944, 1195–99). The degree to which county-level AFs were supported by farmers is questionable. Throughout the 1930s, the Associated Farmers of California claimed a membership of 50,000 farmers. Investigators for the United States Senate were able to verify only a total of around 6,000 dues-paying members through 1939 and a conceivable membership of 11,200 when mailing lists (which included libraries and oppositional organizations that subscribed to AF publications) were counted (ibid., 1199–206).

Nonetheless, the Associated Farmers continued to stress that it was "run by farmers." "Who are the Associated Farmers?" the organization asked in its newsletter as it was being investigated by the La Follette Committee:

176

You, the individual members, not only are the Associated Farmers, but you know that in your county, and the state as a whole, the AF are you, your neighbors, and thousands of farmers banded together in order to grow your crops.... Our strength has lain in the strong membership of our county units. Our effectiveness has been that tillers of the soil have stood shoulder to shoulder in protection of their civil rights. (*Associated Farmer*, April 15, 1940, 3–4; quoted in Chambers 1952, 51)

What were the farmers actually doing as they "stood shoulder to shoulder" protecting their rights? Speakers for the AF declared that the reason they had not sought farmer-members prior to 1936 was that membership in the AF would make farmers ineligible to sit on juries trying radical workers for criminal syndicalism and lesser local crimes. With reorganization, however, the directors of the AF "made up our minds that it is more important to enforce the law than to sit on juries" (LFC, *Hearings*, Testimony of Walter Garrison, Part 50, 18270–271). County AF units were designed, in large part, to function as private "law-enforcement bodies." With this change of focus, the AF became what the La Follette Committee called "one of the most serious vigilante movements which has developed in this country" (LFC, *Report*, Part VIII, 1944, 1208). The AF posses were well integrated with local police forces:

In each county our members contact the District Attorney, the Sheriff, the Chief of Police, and the Town Constable. The Peace authorities are furnished with a list of our members. The authorities are informed that our members may be called upon to serve as deputies in case of an emergency. The sheriff has the list before him. He can call up the men he wants, those he knows can be trusted to give good service.... To illustrate our strength — in Stanislaus County the Sheriff has a list of 1,000 farmers he can call to duty; in Imperial County there are 1,200, in Monterey County 800, in San Joaquin County 900, in Sonoma County 1,100. (LFC, *Hearings*, Part 50, Exhibit 8365, 18272–73)

Indeed, the membership of county AF units fluctuated directly with the threat of strikes or organizational efforts by agricultural workers in their counties. The county AFs functioned, quite simply, as posse comitati whenever workers threatened the presumed "peace" of the county (LFC, *Report*, Part VIII, 1944, 1371–75).

Posse comitatus — literally, a county (or community) posse — is derived from the word for companion. The language is redolent. Strictly speaking, a sheriff can compel able-bodied citizens into a posse comitatus in order to put down riots

177

and preserve the peace. But the language masks what was at work here. Not all community residents were part of these posses; rather, only those who "can be trusted to give good service" as determined by the leadership of the Associated Farmers were considered as reliable local citizens and thus potential deputies. In short, state-level organizations of national and global capitalists called up local citizens to enforce the rights of property and the mores of community against "outside agitators," so that national and global production could be protected. With California agriculture, markets were distant, labor was recruited from around the world (Fuller 1939), growers' organizations were regional, statewide, and national, and growers cooperated across boundaries of geography and crop type, even as they stressed their localist, yeoman ideology through organizations like the Associated Farmers.

"Geographical scale," Smith (1990, 173) noted, "is political precisely because it is the technology according to which events and people are, quite literally, 'contained in space.'" In the case of California agriculture, this containment process was made possible by a violent reassertion of "the local" in support of the national and global markets agriculturalists had created — as in the Imperial Valley and numerous other places where county-level Associated Farmers' organizations forcefully maintained the "rights" of community in the face of unionizing or striking workers (LFC, *Report*, Part VIII, 1944, sections 3 and 4, 1298–1611). This process was also clear, as the next section makes plain, in the Associated Farmers' (presumably less violent) sponsorship of antipicketing ordinances around the state.

County Antipicketing Ordinances and the Nature of Local Justice

For the La Follette Committee, as it investigated violations of free speech and the rights of labor in California, the adoption of county-level antipicketing ordinances up and down the length of California was a matter of grave concern. Analyzing the purpose and effect of these ordinances, the committee contended that

> from time immemorial, men who seek to enslave or restrict the rights of their fellow men find it easier to sustain such restraint through the power of government rather than private action. It was this type of tyranny of the State that was uppermost in the minds of the founding fathers, receiving expression in the Bill of Rights. Indeed that is the very lesson that the spectacle of totalitarian government presents to the world today.... The spectacle in Europe of the progress of totalitarian rule over the powers of a dismembered trade-union movement should

give pause to legislative "lynching bees" of labor's civil rights. (LFC *Report*, Part IX, 1944, 1642–43)

The Senate committee argued that the antipicketing movement in California was part of an "organized drive to defeat an advancing economic democracy" inaugurated with the New Deal (ibid., 1643). As we have seen, New Deal proponents like the Leonard Commission saw the promotion and guarantee of "economic democracy" to be a national imperative. It was precisely the local promulgation of antilabor laws and vigilantism that threatened this larger-scale struggle for justice.

Sponsors of these initiatives saw the matter differently. One of the first county-level antipicketing ordinances was passed, at the urging of District Attorney Earl Warren, by the Alameda County Board of Supervisors just before the start of the 1934 pea-picking season (see LFC, *Hearings*, Part 70, Exhibit 12464, 25723–24). Warren urged the passing of this ordinance (along with another requiring adequate housing facilities for migratory workers) because the county wished "to avoid the riots and other disturbances which resulted in bloodshed in many counties of California during the year 1933–1934" (LFC, *Hearings*, Part 70, Exhibit 12463, 25717). Together with a program to release unemployed workers from relief roles to substitute for migratory labor, these legislative actions and improvements to living conditions came to be known as the "Alameda Plan." Warren argued that implementing the Alameda Plan was necessary because "in the year 1933, the uprisings that took place from one end of the state to the other started in Alameda County," and he wanted to assure that did not happen again (*San Francisco Examiner*, April 8, 1934; Federal Writers Project 1938, 53). The pea crop had "been harvested for years by migratory workers," according to Warren, and some four to six thousand workers were employed at the height of the harvest in Alameda County (LFC, *Hearings*, Part 70, Exhibit 12463, 25717). But in 1933, Warren averred, there had been "a mere handful of agitators who followed" the "workers who came to the county in good faith to harvest the crop" (ibid.). Warren therefore concluded that the Alameda antipicketing restrictions were necessary to deter these outside "agitators" from returning in subsequent years.[13]

Alameda County Ordinance No. 282 expressly forbade the blocking of highways, streets, and walkways by any person or persons. It also established a permit system "for any parade, march or procession of any kind other than a funeral procession to make any display of, or to use, beat or operate any wind instrument, stringed instrument or musical instrument, in or upon any public highway, public parks or public places" (LFC, *Hearings*, Part 70, Exhibit 12464, 25723). To

179

secure a permit (which was nontransferable and could be "revok[ed] for good cause" by the board of supervisors) an applicant had to provide "a certificate signed by at least three reputable residents of the County of Alameda, certifying to the good moral character and reputation of the person or persons making such application. No permit [would] be granted to any person who does not bear a good character and reputation for peace and quiet *in the neighborhood in which he resides*" (ibid.; emphasis added).

Earl Warren and the Alameda County Board of Supervisors were making a clear appeal to the notion that reasonableness is local and that local communities have the right to sanction political activity. To obtain a permit, an applicant needed to be a resident of, and known in, some neighborhood of Alameda County. This provision is of crucial importance because, as Warren noted, the harvesting of a crop "so perishable that if [it] is ripe in the morning and it is not harvested until afternoon it is not marketable" (LFC, *Hearings*, Part 70, Exhibit 12463, 25717), was conducted almost entirely by "outsiders" — by migratory workers. The target of the ordinance was very specific. It was aimed alone at the migratory workers so crucial to the harvest. That this is so is borne out by a comparison with the 1917 Oakland antipicketing ordinance that outlawed "any person in or upon any street, sidewalk, alley, or public place in the City of Oakland [from making] any loud or unusual noise, or to speak in a loud or unusual tone . . . for the purpose of inducing or influencing or attempting to influence or induce" people to quit work and join a strike or to boycott a place of business. Likewise, the Oakland ordinance made it illegal to picket or display banners, buttons, or signs near businesses (LFC, *Hearings*, Part 70, Exhibit 12466, 25725). There were, however, no residency requirements in the Oakland law. Oakland's industry, after all, did not rely on migratory labor.

This legal construction of the local became even more evident in the next few years, as antipicketing ordinances were adopted in thirty-four (of fifty-two) California counties, "roughly corresponding to the major agricultural areas in California" (LFC, *Report*, Part IX, 1944, 1643). Many of these ordinances resemble the Oakland city ordinance more than they did the Alameda ordinance in that they sought to outlaw all protests and pickets, rather than institute a permit system.[14] Even so, the sense of ideological scale implicit in antipicketing ordinances was highlighted in the "urgency clause" contained in most of them. The Sonoma County ordinance was typical:

> The Ordinance is hereby declared to be an urgency measure and necessary for the immediate preservation of the public peace, health and safety, for the reasons that there threatens to exist in the County of Sonoma

Don Mitchell

a serious situation involving the interference of persons not directly or indirectly interested therein in the conduct of lawful enterprises; the purpose of such persons being to agitate and disturb the peace of the people of the County... by inciting and prolonging disputes between employers and employees..., that unless the prevention of people congregating upon the streets and highways and other public places for the purpose of unlawfully interfering with lawful business is discontinued, such practice will tend to attract criminal, vicious, and undesirable characters and to cause great disorder and many breaches of the peace and quiet of the County of Sonoma, and constitute a menace to life, limb, and property. (LFC, *Hearings*, Part 61, Exhibit 9500, 223440)

As with the organization of the Associated Farmers posses, the passage of anti-picketing ordinances enacted a quite restricted notion of community and local rights in the service of globalized production. As the secretary of the Sutter County Associated Farmers boasted after noting the AF's role in passing anti-picketing ordinances in the county and local cities, Sutter County is "known as [the] world's 'Peach Bowl,' and ships cling peaches" around the world (LFC, *Hearings*, Part 61, Exhibit 9491, 22269).

It is no accident that each of the county ordinances in the state bore a family resemblance. With the exception of the Alameda ordinance, nearly every anti-picketing ordinance was sponsored by the Associated Farmers, usually through its county units. As noted earlier, after an organizing tour by Associated Farmers officials in May 1934, twenty counties immediately passed antipicketing ordinances and, in 1937, the AF was still involved in the campaign against picketing. "Has your county an anti-picketing ordinance?" the AF executive secretary wrote to all the county associations. "If not, would it be of assistance if we sent you copies of such ordinances now in effect in this state?" (LFC, *Hearings*, Part 61, Exhibit 9492, 22339). The minutes of the 1937 Associated Farmers convention provide telling evidence of both the concerted nature and the success of this effort. Many of the county reports for the year read like that of Colusa County, which had "secured passage of [an] antipicketing ordinance along the lines of Sutter and Yuba [County] ordinances" (LFC, *Hearings*, Part 61, Exhibit 9491, 22269).

In just three strikes during 1939, 363 people were arrested under various county antipicketing ordinances (LFC, *Report*, Part IX, 1944, 1656). But in Alameda County, District Attorney Warren proudly claimed that no one was ever arrested under the terms of the ordinance, and that the county never denied a permit. Indeed, Warren boasted, there were no "disturbances" in the county after

The Scales of Justice

the antipicketing ordinance was passed (LFC, *Hearings*, Part 70, Exhibit 12463). Where the La Follette Committee saw threats of tyranny, Alameda County, Earl Warren, and even the liberal *San Francisco News* (March 10, 1934) saw the establishment of industrial peace.

To further this "industrial peace" many counties incorporated "antiparading" sections in their antipicketing bills (or passed restrictions on parading separately). Most often, parading restrictions required that parade organizers secure a permit similar to that required in Alameda County. "In agricultural communities where strikers seek to publicize a labor dispute to workers on large and widely separated ranches," the La Follette Committee noted, "the antiparading ordinances are in effect a form of antipicketing prohibition" (LFC, *Report*, Part IX, 1944, 1653). The committee emphasized that a permit system such as that in Alameda and other counties was patently unjust, quoting from a 1940 U.S. Supreme Court decision (*Thornhill v. Alabama*, 310 US 88): "It is not the sporadic abuse of power by the censor but the pervasive threat inherent in its very existence that constitutes the danger to freedom of discussion.... One who might have a license merely for the asking may therefore call into question the whole scheme of licensing when he is prosecuted for failure to procure one" (LFC, *Report*, Part IX, 1944, 1653). The Associated Farmers understood this point clearly. As the district attorney for Mendocino County told the La Follette Committee: "No arrests have been made under the above mentioned [antipicketing] Ordinance. However, numerous union organizers have called at this office to determine whether or not the ordinance would be enforced. All have been advised in the affirmative. The result has been no union organizing in this county" (LFC, *Hearings*, Part 61, Exhibit 9506, 22274).

In Shasta County (as in many others), county supervisors argued that allowing picketing would "agitate the peace of mind of the people of the County of Shasta . . . [would] foment resistance to said union activities, and [would] bring about a condition of open physical violence and a state of riot and uncontrollable mob action" against unionizing workers (LFC, *Report*, Part IX, 1944, 1654). The La Follette Committee made the point even more strongly in the conclusion to its report on the antipicketing campaigns: "anti-union legislation [such as anti-picketing ordinances] may become the device by which organized employers hostile to collective bargaining substitute the forces of law and community opinion for labor spies and strikebreakers as union-busting or union-preventative devices" (ibid., 1695).

The movement for county-level antipicketing ordinances, then, once again shows the value of a localist ideology for the furtherance of large-scale goals on the part of "self-appointed protectors of 'public order' and 'rights' of individual employers" such as the Industrial Association of San Francisco, the Merchants and Manufacturers Association of Los Angeles, and, through them (and numerous industrial, transportation, and utility concerns), the Associated Farmers of California (ibid., 1693). The problematic of scale, however, can cut both ways, and as these organizations attempted to "jump scales" (Smith 1992) and take their movement statewide, they reached the limits of their own localist ideology. Precisely *because* scale is ever a contested construction and is not given, workers and their sympathizers found that they *could*, in fact, defeat growers at their own game if they too "jumped scales."

Jumping Scales: Labor's Geography of Resistance and the State Antipicketing Ordinance

Migratory labor in California was, of necessity, extralocal. Like the commodity markets in which California growers sold their produce, agricultural labor markets had long been organized at scales much larger than the local. Early labor, of course, had been Chinese and Japanese (Daniels 1962; Saxton 1971; Chan 1986), though by World War I much of that labor had been replaced by white migratory workers (especially single men displaced by recurrent economic crises in the eastern United States and Europe). Records of migratory patterns from World War I show that many white male workers migrated between the agricultural harvests of California, the lumber camps of the Pacific Northwest, and the copper mines of Alaska. Many others moved over a seasonal or longer-term pattern between the agricultural, mining, construction, and lumber camps of California, coupling crop work in California with stints in munitions factories in Iowa, grain harvests in the Dakotas, and mining in the Rockies (Military Intelligence Division, U.S. Army, 1984, Reels 1 and 2; Mitchell 1996a). As farmers turned to Mexican labor during World War I and to Mexican and Filipino labor during the 1920s, California agricultural labor markets once again took on a clearly international dimension. During the 1930s, the influx of refugees from the economic and ecological disasters of the Dust Bowl tied California migratory patterns to the Midwest, Southwest, and Southeast (Stein 1971).

The most successful organizing campaigns among migratory workers in California during the early part of the century had also been extralocal. Or, more accurately, these campaigns had sought to tie local events (riots, strikes, appalling conditions) to the fact of migration. The Industrial Workers of the World (IWW), for example, connected various place-based struggles together by making the union local itself migratory. Organizers "carried the local under their hats," setting up shop wherever migratory workers could be found, seeking to assure that the riots in the northern part of the state were understood to be connected to protests in   183 southern California, as well as to events in the Northwest, South, Midwest, and Northwest (Mitchell 1996a; Foner 1964; Dubofsky 1988). Where growers sought to emphasize the "local" nature of their enterprise, migratory workers continually worked to expose its larger-scale connections. Radical migratory workers trans-formed the historically developed spatial practices of California agriculture — huge farms, rapid labor turnover, enforced tramping — into tools of subversion precisely by appealing to more universal notions of justice than were possible in the appeals to community that were the stock-in-trade of growers and their orga-nizations. The CAWIU operated in much the same way, rushing organizers to the scene of labor conflagrations and continually reminding workers that struggles in the Imperial were connected materially (and also in the way they were denied justice) to struggles in Salinas, Marysville, San Francisco, and elsewhere in the world (such as the fight against fascism in Europe) (Daniel 1981).

Given the extensive migratory patterns that did in fact connect farmworkers in spatially distant struggles, and given the (limited) success of the CAWIU and later unions affiliated with the CIO, the Associated Farmers worried that their own piecemeal, county-by-county approach to dismantling worker rights through antipicketing ordinances was not sufficient. In 1938, the group sought to enact an amendment to the California state constitution that would have the effect of outlawing all picketing and much union organizing in California. Meeting at Del Monte in April, executives of several prominent employers associations and large corporations developed the objectives for such an antiunion amendment:

1. To prohibit secondary boycott.
2. To prohibit the use of coercion or intimidation upon employers and employees in connection with industrial relations.
3. To regulate picketing.
4. To prohibit any interference with the free and unobstructed use of public streets, highways, sidewalks, docks, and other public places in the State of California by workers, irrespective of affiliation with any particular organization, and also to prohibit the exercise of any intimidation or coercion toward such workers in the exercise of such rights. (LFC, *Hearings,* Part 61, 22291)

The proposed amendment (dubbed Proposition 1) developed as a result of this conference was lengthy and convoluted. Attorneys working for its passage advised their clients that "the bill itself, even to attorneys, is an 'unsaleable package.'" They therefore suggested promoting a "condensed version" to the public (LFC, *Hearings,* Part 61, Exhibit 9525, 22373; Exhibit 9526, 22374–75).

184

Don Mitchell

The condensed version of the initiative claimed that the "only restriction on the right to strike ... is the *prohibition* of *sit-down* strikes" and that the bill was designed only to "closely regulate what acts [strikers] may do in connection with a strike" (LFC, *Hearings*, Part 61, Exhibit 9526, 22374). In fact, the initiative did much more than closely regulate how picketing was conducted (even as it did so by severely restricting picketing as to "time, place, and manner," that is, by limiting picketing to one person at each entrance to a place of business and by outlawing all picketing not directly connected with a primary strike).[15] For example, Proposition 1 would have made it permissible for only "bona fide employees" of a particular firm to picket that firm: picketing to encourage people "to become, refrain from becoming, remain, or cease to remain, a member or participant of any labor organization" was to be expressly prohibited. It would also have been illegal to attempt to deter the delivery of any goods or people to a struck firm through "hot cargo" bans, secondary boycotts, or blockades. The initiative additionally would have made it unlawful "for any employee, labor organization, or [labor] officer" to "intimidate or coerce any other person" in any manner into joining a union, quitting work, or boycotting a shop. The word *coerce* was given a specific meaning that would have all but outlawed unionism itself. It was defined as follows:

> to mean and include, but not be limited to, the infliction of threat, directly or indirectly, (i) of injury to the person or damage to the property of another person ... or (ii) of loss of employment [or wages] ... or (iii) of the imposition by any labor organization of any fine [on members] ... or (iv) of any *momentary* loss, injury to business or reduction in earnings or profits, or (v) of loss or impairment of the ability to obtain workers, materials, supplies, goods ... or (vi) of the exercise of power possessed, or supposed to exist or to be possessed, by the party coercing over or with respect to the part coerced; provided, however, that such words shall not include the infliction or threat of a voluntary strike or of lawful picketing [as permitted in other sections of the initiative]. (LFC, *Hearings*, Part 61, Exhibit 9524, 22366; emphasis added)

The definition of "intimidation" was nearly as broad. In essence, this bill outlawed all union activity *except* a primary strike by "bona fide employees" — and even *that* was thrown into question by a provision that declared it unlawful for "any person" to picket "in a manner calculated or with the intent to coerce or intimidate any person ... approaching, entering, occupying or leaving, or who is in or on, any place of business or place of residence, or who is attempting or

185

seeking to do any of the foregoing" (ibid.). What little picketing remained legal was further jeopardized if it could be shown to cause harm in any manner (including economic harm) to the picketed establishment.

The La Follette Committee concluded, unsurprisingly, that the amendment was "designed to crush and destroy the effective power of unions to maintain their membership and enforce their rights by peaceful means" (LFC, *Report*, Part IX, 1944, 1667). Of course, that was also the goal of the county-level ordinances sponsored by the Associated Farmers and its industrial allies. The difference here, however, is one of scale. The growers' goal now was not just to control localities but to control the whole economic and political space of the state. "Those who command space," argues David Harvey (1989, 234–35), "can always control the politics of place." The industrial and agricultural employers around the state, those who "refuse[d] to accept finally the principles of industrial democracy" being developed by New Dealers and radical unionists alike (LFC, *Report*, Part IX, 1944, 1694), sought to cement this control, beyond what was possible with locally organized violence, with the state initiative.

Sponsors of Proposition 1 went out of their way to stress the need, the fairness, and the popular nature of the initiative:

> In preparing PROPOSITION NO. 1 for the November ballot, the starting point was the factor of JUSTICE and FAIRNESS as the first requirement in establishing ideal human relations. Labor Relations have come to be among the most important Human Relations. That is the reason why this people's statute has been placed before the voters. It will be a foundation upon which California citizens can build a structure of employment relations in which workers and employers can sit down together in peace and good order. (LFC, *Hearings*, Part 75, Exhibit 14421, 27771; emphasis in original)

In other words, employers' organizations (banded together as the California Committee for Peace in Employment Relations) were arguing that by utterly controlling the political and economic space of the state, workers and employers could form a community of interest founded on the community ideals of peace and order. The right to bargain collectively was to be tightly circumscribed to that most local of interactions, the individual employees of a firm and the (presumably) just as individual employer. Bargaining was to be confined to a negotiation between an employer and "our own people, our own workers," just as the directors of the Associated Farmers wished.

The Associated Farmers maintained that opposition to Proposition 1 was confined to "so-called labor leaders who have a snap. Every worker pays for their support. And if Proposition Number One wins, those fellows won't have any pay for agitating trouble . . . they won't have rough neck shock troopers and goon squads hired, at fancy prices to beat the workers into submission" (LFC, *Hearings*, Part 75, 27790). (Presumably, success on Proposition I would, however, maintain the AF's right to beat workers into submission.) Elsewhere, Associated Farmers executives maintained that CIO unions, and indeed AFL unions, were no different than Communist unions in this regard. They had no support beyond the support induced by coercion (LFC, *Report*, Part VIII, 1944, section 3; Bancroft 1962, 354, 362). Farmer rhetoric was identical to the antiunion, antipicketing rhetoric employed at the county level. But here resistance was of a different nature.

"Locals" of all sorts lined up to oppose the statewide initiative and together their power was formidable. The newly formed United Cannery, Agricultural, Packing, and Allied Workers of America—the first truly national farmworkers union since the IWW[16]—joined forces with urban-based AFL and CIO unions, civil liberties activists, New Dealers, and progressive urban residents in opposition to the AF and the "Peace Committee." Workers and their allies called upon just as resonant a rhetoric of justice and fairness, but one that was more universal in scope than that of their opponents.

Interestingly, the California State Grange, an organization of small farmers, opposed Proposition I. The Grange's attorney wrote in its newsletter:

> Today, we are asked to adopt on November 8, Initiative Proposition No. I . . . sponsored by . . . the Associated Farmers (an association composed largely of the agencies of banks and public utility corporations) which initiative, if adopted, will deprive the people of California of each and all of these cherished rights so guaranteed by every Federal and State Constitution in our land. . . . Said by its proponents to be needed legislation for industrial peace, this initiative proposition would really take away the constitutional rights of labor; it is dangerous because the layman does not recognize the fascistic provisions hidden within the proposal. . . . This initiative Amendment No. I is the most un-American, most vicious ever submitted to the American people. (*California Grange News*, November 5, 1938; quoted in Chambers 1952, 104–5)

Again the language is redolent: appeals to national, even universal, rights and to the imminent dangers of fascism suggested the degree to which "local" or "community" interests were not so much legitimate as they were oppressive.

The proposition lost, and with this labor victory a "Little New Deal" government was swept into the California statehouse (Burke 1953, 32–33). The   **187** growers' attempt to "jump scales" ideologically had been rebuffed in part by the fact that labor was *already there*, organized at the state and national level in a concerted effort to defeat employers' attempts to further solidify their hegemony. The rhetoric of localism did not work at the state level precisely because workers could not be as easily isolated as "outsiders" by employers claiming to speak for the whole of the "community."[17] The Associated Farmers recognized this and sought to regain power by taking the organization national. Beginning first with the formation of the Associated Farmers of the Pacific Coast and then seeking influence in the Midwest (LFC, *Report*, Part VIII, 1944, 1594–1611), the goal of the AF was to find a means whereby a national organization could once again valorize the local such that, across vast spaces, workers would always be outsiders in their own communities. "The record of [the Associated Farmers] is one of conspiracy — developed on a far-flung scale covering an entire region. That conspiracy designed to prevent the exercise of their civil liberties by oppressed wage laborers in agriculture, was executed ruthlessly with every device of repression that antiunionism could muster" (ibid., 1612). So determined the La Follette Committee in its investigation of the Associated Farmers. Going one step further, the committee concluded: "That record also constitutes a warning to the organized trade-union movement that the security of its rights in urban industrial areas may depend to a considerable extent upon the rights of those who labor in the fields and farm factories outside the city gates. A nation cannot exist 'half slave, half free'" (ibid.).

Conclusion: Scale, Justice, and Labor Geography

The events in California show that the production of globalized capital, resting as it does on ideologies of localism and community, is contradictory. Hence, oppositional worker movements must be cognizant of scale, of how it is produced and negotiated, of how different processes interact at different scales, and of how "the production and representation of scale ... lie[s] at the centre of a spatialized politics even if in much political discourse this spatial struggle is often implicit in arguments over nomenclature, naming places, as much as explicit in boundary struggles" (Smith 1990, 173). David Harvey (1989, 234–35) was quoted earlier to the effect that those who command space can control the politics of place. Harvey's fuller passage, which he designates a "simple rule" about power, reads: "those who command space can always control the politics of place even though ... it takes control of some place to command space in the first instance." This was precisely what the Associated Farmers and other factions of organized capital sought to do in California in the 1930s by naming "the local" as the scale of political legitimacy and defining its boundaries so as to include capital but not "outside"

188

workers. By fully controlling "some place" they could better regain command of a space economy transformed through the extensive restructuring of the Depression era. Labor, in its fight against the state Proposition I, understood Harvey's "simple rule" implicitly and fought to ensure that capital's "place" did not jump scales as easily as did capital's organizations and forms of production. In short, labor appealed to a larger-scale notion of justice. It sought to reinforce ideology at the scale of the state and the nation in direct opposition to capital's invocation of the primacy of the local community for determining the nature of social justice in labor relations. Nomenclature is indeed important, and these large-scale notions in turn have to be continually struggled over; they are not just given.

Neither the geography of labor nor labor's geography is ever enacted in a single scale. Rather, these geographies result from and produce both scales themselves and interactions between scales. In turn, scale consists of both materiality (for example, the "levels" at which production or reproduction are, through struggle, organized) and ideology (the "levels" at which legitimacy is, through struggle, organized). Each feeds off and informs the other. And often, as we have seen, ideological investment at one scale makes possible the production of other scales. A labor geography, focused as it ought to be on justice and therefore on the control of space, needs to keep the analysis of scale-production and scale-based ideology at the fore. "Political struggles need to be fought on at least two levels," Blomley (1994, 222) advises. "We must not only fight a traditional politics, resisting the material structures and spatial practices within which we live, such as the 'hyperspatial' circuits of capital investment and disinvestment, we must also bring the representational geographies, constituted and constitutive of such practices, to account." That is why this essay has focused on examining the structure of capital and its invocations of community (if seemingly sometimes at the expense of an analysis of the structure of labor). To rephrase a now hackneyed truism, labor makes its own geographies, but not under conditions of its own choosing. The recognition that, first, scale is produced and not given, and second, that the production of scale is a great deal of work, is important. Such recognition reminds us that neither labor nor capital can make the scales of production and reproduction just as they please and under conditions entirely of *their* own choosing. As long as labor continues to take hold of geographies and continually seeks to transform them in the name of a justice that, while sensitive to "the local," is also universal in outlook, the geography of capitalism will always be contested.

Notes

Thanks to Dick Walker, Ruth Gilmore, and the others who questioned me when this paper was presented at the Association of American Geographers Annual   189

Meeting in Chicago (March 1995). I hope they finally see the answers to their questions in this version. Special thanks to Andrew Herod for organizing the AAG sessions on labor geography, for his suggestions and careful editing, and especially for his inspiration when it comes to issues of labor and geography.

1. In its progressive guise, this ideology prizes "local knowledge" as an important resource, a fund for understanding social and ecological relations. In its regressive guise, it valorizes racism and fascism.

2. For this reason, it seems to me that Duncan and Savage's (1989) discussion of scale and locality, which begins by asserting that "space does not actually exist in the sense of being an object that can have an effect on other objects" (179), is wide of the mark.

3. The La Follette Committee (United States Senate, Subcommittee of the Committee on Education and Labor) was formed with the passage of Senate Resolution 266, 74th Congress, a resolution directing the Senate to investigate "violations of free speech and the rights of labor." From 1936 to 1940, the La Follette Committee investigated abuses of labor throughout the United States, including employer-sponsored campaigns of vigilantism and union busting in the steel, auto, and related industries in the Northeast. Drawn to California by the exceptional violence of agricultural labor relations, the committee held a series of hearings in San Francisco and Los Angeles in late 1939 and early 1940. The transcripts of the committee hearings (some twenty-five thousand pages), together with its detailed reports, provide an impressive archive of information on labor struggles and conditions during the Depression. It has been an invaluable resource for me in dissecting and theorizing labor geographies both in California and in Pennsylvania. On the La Follette Committee, see Auerbach (1966); on its reception in California and the failure of its reports on the state (released in 1942 and 1944) to have the impact they should have had, see McWilliams (1944, 1968, 1982). In what follows, I rely heavily on this public record of the La Follette Committee.

4. I will return to this point. The ability of growers to valorize so effectively the local rested on their ability to mobilize vast armies of labor from other regions, and indeed from around the world, who were, by definition, permanently outsiders.

5. This point too will be examined more fully later in this essay. It is a rather curious recommendation given the ways in which, and the scales at which, growers and shippers in fact were organized.

6. Such language — nationalism defined as localism, and the defense of narrowly defined property rights — is a well-developed and virulent strain in American social relations and politics.

Don Mitchell

7. For a fuller account of racist ideology as it intersected with grower concerns over a "proper" labor supply, see Mitchell (1996a, chapter 4).

8. Blomley's (1994) discussion of the 1984 British coal strike presents a striking example of how "the local" can be reinforced as a means of undermining worker power. See also Griffiths and Johnston (1991); Johnston (1991).

9. This paragraph draws on analysis in Mitchell (1996a).

10. Cotton actually saw increased seasonal demand at this time, masking a greater decline of labor demands in other field crops.

11. As Daniel (1981, 254) points out, the CAWIU was formally killed off at the same time by the Communist Party's decision, made at the behest of the Comintern, to abandon "dual unionism" and return to a policy of "boring from within" more conservative unions.

12. The Wagner Act (National Labor Relations Act) actually excluded agricultural workers from the right to unionize, but growers felt that the general organizational flurry that the act would induce would extend to them.

13. Warren's plans for the Alameda County harvest were geographically quite sensitive and included the removal of labor-supply camps off public roads (so that strikers could not get to them), and the release of local unemployed workers for work in the fields. See Mitchell (1996a).

14. Actually, the ordinances claimed to protect "peaceful picketing" at the expense of violent picketing, but they were based on Supreme Court Chief Justice William Howard Taft's 1921 determination that picketing "cannot be peaceable" (*American Steel Foundries v. Tri-City Central Trades Council*, 257 US [1921], 184, 205). For an analysis of this point, see Mitchell (1996b).

15. I examine the intricacies of, and the legal foundation for, such antipicketing provisions in Mitchell (1996b).

16. In July 1937, activists meeting in Denver created the United Cannery, Agricultural, Packing, and Allied Workers of America (UCAPAWA). Affiliated with the CIO, UCAPAWA drew together numerous independent, ethnic, and left-leaning AFL unions in California, Alabama, Arizona, Colorado, Florida, Michigan, Ohio, Tennessee, and Texas (Majka and Majka 1981, 94).

17. This should not be taken as an absolute statement. The recently successful anti-immigrant initiative campaign in California is proof that the language of community too can transcend scales and be constructed on the bases of an "imagined community" of skin color and, absurdly, white victimization.

Bibliography

Auerbach, J. 1966. *Labor and Liberty: The La Follette Committee and the New Deal.* New York: Bobbs-Merrill.

Bancroft, P. 1962. "Politics, Family and the Progressive Party in California." Oral History Interview by Willa Klug Brown, Regional Cultural History Project. Berkeley: Bancroft Library, University of California.

Blomley, N. 1994. *Law, Space, and the Geographies of Power.* New York: Guilford Press.

Burke, R. 1953. *Olson's New Deal for California.* Berkeley and Los Angeles: University of California Press.

Chambers, C. 1952. *California Farm Organizations.* Berkeley and Los Angeles: University of California Press.

Chan, S. 1986. *This Bitter Sweet Soil: The Chinese in California Agriculture, 1860–1910.* Berkeley and Los Angeles: University of California Press.

CSRA (California State Relief Administration). 1936. *Transients in California.* Sacramento: Mimeo.

Daniel, C. 1981. *Bitter Harvest: A History of California Farmworkers, 1870–1941.* Ithaca, N.Y.: Cornell University Press; Berkeley and Los Angeles: University of California Press.

Daniels, R. 1962. *The Politics of Prejudice: The Anti-Japanese Movement in California and the Struggle for Japanese Exclusion.* Berkeley and Los Angeles: University of California Press.

DIR Records. Department of Industrial Relations, Division of Immigration and Housing, Records, Bancroft Library, University of California, Berkeley.

Dubofsky, M. 1988. *We Shall Be All: A History of the Industrial Workers of the World.* 2d ed. Urbana: University of Illinois Press (originally published in 1969).

Duncan, S., and M. Savage. 1989. "Space, Scale and Locality." *Antipode* 21: 179–206.

Federal Writers Project. 1938. "Labor in the Market Pea Crop." Typescript. Berkeley: Bancroft Library, University of California.

Foner, P. 1964. *The History of the Labor Movement in the United States,* vol. 4, *The Industrial Workers of the World, 1905–1917.* New York: International Publishers.

Fuller, V. 1939. "The Supply of Agricultural Labor as a Factor in the Evolution of Farm Organization in California." In LFC, *Hearings,* Part 54, Exhibit 8762-A, 19777–898.

Griffiths, M., and R. Johnston. 1991. "What's in a Place? An Approach to the Concept of Place, as Illustrated by the British National Union of Mineworkers' Strike, 1984–5." *Antipode* 23: 185–213.

Herod, A. 1991. "The Production of Scale in United States Labour Relations." *Area* 23: 82–88.

Harvey, D. 1989. *The Condition of Postmodernity.* Oxford: Basil Blackwell.

192

Don Mitchell

Johnston, R. 1991. *A Question of Place: Exploring the Practice of Human Geography.* Oxford: Basil Blackwell.

La Peire, R. 1930. *The Armenian Colony in Fresno County.* Stanford, Calif.: Stanford University Press.

Levine, B., S. Brier, D. Brundage, E. Countryman, D. Fennell, M. Rediker, and J. Brown. 1989. *Who Built America? Working People and the Nation's Economy, Politics, Culture and Society,* vol. I, *From Conquest and Colonization through Reconstruction and the Great Uprising of 1877.* New York: Pantheon.

LFC, *Hearings* 1936–40. United States Senate, Subcommittee of the Committee on Education and Labor, *Hearings on S. Res. 266, Violations of Free Speech and the Rights of Labor,* 75 Parts.

LFC, *Report,* Part IV. 1942. *Report of the Committee on Education and Labor Pursuant to S. Res. 266, A Resolution to Investigate Violations of the Right of Free Speech and Assembly and the Interference with the Right of Labor to Organize and Bargain Collectively,* Senate Report 1150, 77th Congress, Part 4.

———. *Report,* Part VIII. 1944. *Report of the Committee on Education and Labor Pursuant to S. Res. 266, A Resolution to Investigate Violations of the Right of Free Speech and Assembly and the Interference with the Right of Labor to Organize and Bargain Collectively,* Senate Report 398, 78th Congress, Part 4.

———. *Report,* Part IX. 1944. *Report of the Committee on Education and Labor Pursuant to S. Res. 266, A Resolution to Investigate Violations of the Right of Free Speech and Assembly and the Interference with the Right of Labor to Organize and Bargain Collectively,* Senate Report 398, Part 5.

Majka, L., and T. Majka. 1981. *Farmworkers, Agribusiness and the State.* Philadelphia: Temple University Press.

McFadden, I. 1934. "The Spring Pea Deal Is On: Imperial Crop Rolling for Twentieth Time to Snowland Markets despite Harvest Difficulties." *Los Angeles Times Farm and Garden Magazine,* March 18, 1934.

McWilliams, C. 1944. *Ill Fares the Land: Migrants and Migratory Labor in the United States.* Boston: Little, Brown.

———. 1968. *California: The Great Exception.* New York: Grossman Publishers.

———. 1971. *Factories in the Field.* Santa Barbara: Peregrine Smith (originally published in 1939).

———. 1982. "Honorable in All Things." UCLA Oral History Program, Typescript.

Military Intelligence Division, U.S. Army. 1984. *Military Intelligence Reports: Surveillance of Radicals in the United States, 1917–1941.* Ann Arbor: University Microfilms.

193

Mitchell, D. 1994. "Landscape and Surplus Value: The Making of the Ordinary in Brentwood, California." *Environment and Planning D: Society and Space* 12: 7–30.

———. 1996a. *The Lie of the Land: Migrant Workers and the California Landscape.* Minneapolis: University of Minnesota Press.

———. 1996b. "Political Violence, Order, and the Legal Construction of Public Space: Power and the Public Forum Doctrine." *Urban Geography* 17: 152–78.

Saxton, A. 1971. *The Indispensable Enemy: Labor and the Anti-Chinese Movement in California.* Berkeley and Los Angeles: University of California Press.

Smith, N. 1990. *Uneven Development: Nature, Capital, and the Production of Space.* 2d ed. Oxford: Basil Blackwell (originally published in 1984).

———. 1992. "Contours of a Spatialized Politics: Homeless Vehicles and the Production of Geographical Scale." *Social Text* 33: 55–81.

Smith, N., and W. Dennis. 1987. "The Restructuring of Geographical Scale: Coalescence and Fragmentation of the Northern Core Region." *Economic Geography* 63: 160–82.

Stein, W. 1971. *California and the Dust Bowl Migration.* Westport, Conn.: Greenwood Press.

Teague, C. C. 1944. *Fifty Years a Rancher.* Self-published.

Wedderburn, R. L. 1985. "The New Politics in Industrial Relations Law." In *Industrial Relations and the Law in the 1980s,* edited by P. Fish and C. Littler, 22–65. Aldershot: Gower.

Don Mitchell

Part III

Political Geographies of Labor Union Organizing

Andrew Herod

Political geographers have long known that geography is crucial to understanding political practice for a number of reasons, not least of which is that political practices differ widely across space. Yet, they have also traditionally had a rather narrow view of the relationship between politics and space, and have tended to see this relationship either in geopolitical terms of the international activities of states and the practice of statecraft, or in terms of electoral geographies in which geographic context is used to throw light on the outcome of elections to public office (see Clark 1990 for a critique of how traditional electoral geography has ignored union elections). It is only recently that, instead of simply seeing how certain political characteristics play out across space, political geographers have begun to examine how social actors actively create and use space in particular ways as an integral part of their political praxis, although relatively little of this work has addressed the ways in which labor unions and workers create and use space (for a critique, see Herod 1994b). And yet, power is clearly expressed through space and spatial relations as, for example, when some social actors are able to exclude others from particular spaces through legal means (e.g., trespass laws, pass laws, immigration controls), through intimidation (e.g., many women avoid certain spaces because of their fear of being raped), or by creating physical barriers to access (e.g., as British police did during the 1984–85 miners' strike by imposing roadblocks to prevent union "flying pickets" from moving about the country [Blomley 1994]). Spatial relations are subject to social contestation, and can be shaped in ways that enable and/or constrain political praxis. As the two essays in part III show, the ability of union organizers and members to think geostrategically, to adopt strategies that were sensitive to the particular geographical conditions in which they found themselves, and to use space in creative ways was an important part of their political practice and suggests a need to pay much closer attention to how unions actively use space and create spatial structures and relations when organizing workers and conducting campaigns.

197

The first essay, by Lee Lucas Berman, examines how activists designed and implemented specifically spatial strategies in a campaign to organize clerical workers at Yale University. Adopting a Foucauldian analysis to power and power relations, Berman shows how the space of the Yale campus had historically been constructed as an exclusionary male space. Drawing on Foucault's (1979) notions of enclosure and partitioning, she shows how the physical built environment of the campus with its imposing stone walls separating the university "community" from the city of New Haven (deemed to be the seventh poorest city in the United States in 1980), together with the campus's plazas and quads physically dividing workers in different parts of the university, had served to reinforce the campus as a "disciplined space," a space of privilege within New Haven, and a partitioned, fragmented, and cellular space in which the Yale administration could limit the possibilities of collective action by workers opposed to the disciplinary regime it exercised over the campus. The university administration was able to make use of the campus's physical layout to encourage the social segregation and insularity of clericals from one another as it created a paternalistic and patriarchal notion that workers were part of the "university family" and should therefore identify their interests with those of the administration. For Berman, a key element in the administration's ability to discipline and control its workforce in this way was its ability to use the geography of the campus to spatially isolate workers through, for example, the creation of a number of semiautonomous "fiefdoms" and through the physical separation of workers in small cubicled offices, or to expose them to the panopticon-like surveillance of supervisors through the use of "open landscape" office designs.

Whether by design or happenstance, then, the geography of the campus's built environment was a central element in the administration's ability to control its workers. As Berman shows, however, when activists began in the early 1980s to organize clerical and technical workers, a key element to their campaign was their ability to turn the campus's spatial layout against the administration, in effect to turn the campus's geography inside out. Organizers for, and members of, Local 34 of the Hotel Employees' and Restaurant Employees' International Union developed organizing strategies that were sensitive to the campus's geography and designed to overcome the spatial, and hence social, barriers that had been used by the administration to divide Yale's workers. Part of this geographical sensitivity involved designing an organizing committee that would overcome the fragmentation among workers imposed by the campus's spatial layout, a strategy that resulted in the creation of a 450-person committee that drew membership from each of the work sites on campus and was integrated into a steering committee structured around the three main areas of the campus (central, science, and

198

medical). Union members and supporters also conducted actions designed to appropriate particular spaces (cafés, buildings, plazas) for short or long periods of time, such that some became known as union "strongholds." They also held lunch meetings at particular cafeterias in each section of the campus and conducted coordinated activities with the local New Haven community designed to breach the enclosing walls of the campus and thereby expose the closed space of Yale to outside political forces. Such activities, Berman argues, were crucial to opening up spaces of resistance on the campus and challenging the administration's ability to control and impose its own disciplinary regime on the campus's space.

Lydia A. Savage continues the theme of the spatial nature of organizing through an examination of the Justice for Janitors campaign organized by the Service Employees' International Union in Los Angeles. This campaign has been a highly successful movement to organize a low-wage, service-sector, minority, and, often, immigrant workforce. Significantly, its success has largely been predicated on an understanding on the part of activists that organizing service-sector workers requires a very different model of organizing than the one that has traditionally served to organize manufacturing workers, a model that is very different in its geographic structure. Traditional models of organizing manufacturing sites have been based on a number of spatial assumptions: they have been designed principally for large, centralized work sites with a few entrance gates and regular shift changes that can be picketed easily by a small number of organizers at minimal expense of time and money in plants where "hot shops" of workers have already identified themselves to organizers as being interested in chartering a local union. Most service-sector work sites are very different in character, however. A larger proportion of service-sector workers work in smaller sites, often in direct contact with customers, are temporary or part-time workers, and, as in the Yale case, work in sites whose physical layout makes it difficult to organize because workers are rarely grouped together on a factory floor with one supervisor but are more often located in an office or counter space right next to their supervisor. On the other hand, service-sector employment (which by its very nature is often customer-oriented) is often more spatially rooted than is manufacturing work and so is less vulnerable to capital flight, whether actual or threatened (cf. Herod 1994a for more on how the rhetoric of capital flight can be used to undermine labor solidarity).

As Savage explains, the nature of the employer-worker relationship in janitorial work has required that the Justice for Janitors campaign adopt quite different tactics than are usually followed by a union conducting an organizing drive in the manufacturing sector. Janitors are rarely employed directly by the owners of the buildings where they work but are, instead, more often employees of a   199

Political Geographies

janitorial firm contracted to clean by the owners. Consequently, the places where janitors work are not usually owned by the employers with whom they have a contractual relationship. Further, many janitors clean several buildings and therefore move from site to site as part of a "route job." The geographic separation of janitors' places of work from the locations of their immediate employers' offices, together with the spatially mobile nature of some janitorial jobs, makes it more difficult for union organizers to identify "hot shops" the way they can with manufacturing workers who usually have a direct contractual relationship with the owners of their work sites. Because of the difficulty of trying to organize the janitorial firms themselves, each one of which may have fifty work sites operating under different conditions scattered throughout a given area, union organizers have adopted a strategy that relies less on undertaking job actions at particular work sites and more on conducting actions in public spaces such as shopping plazas and parks designed to embarrass building owners into pressuring the janitorial companies to whom they subcontract out the cleaning work to recognize the union and improve working conditions. By shifting the geographic terrain of struggle from the private space of the workplace to the public space of the streets, the Justice for Janitors campaign has sought to bring greater public pressure to bear on the industry than the workers directly involved could themselves hope to generate through traditional job-site actions.

A further key aspect of the Los Angeles Justice for Janitors campaign has been the adoption of a model of "geographical unionism" in which activists have broken the city into distinct, geographically defined labor markets based on such characteristics as location, the type of industry found in different parts of the city (the nature of work routines and cleaning in downtown Los Angeles are very different from Century City's entertainment industry and South Bay's aerospace industry, for instance), and the local working-class community from which janitorial staff are drawn (African-American, Mexican, Salvadoran, Honduran, Korean, etc.). Rather than attempting to develop a "one model fits all" strategy, the Justice for Janitors campaign has been sensitive to the geographic variations in the labor markets operating in different parts of Los Angeles, tailoring strategy and tactics to the specific market within which janitors find themselves. Hand in hand with this division of the city into identifiable labor markets, the union has waged an ideological campaign designed to expand the geographic scale of workers' identities and to encourage them to see their individual struggles as part of a wider movement, instead of being simply related to the conditions in "their" particular building. This struggle over the spatial extent of workers' collective identity has been a central part of a broader campaign to develop a new geographic scale of bargaining that will replace the old system of labor contracting, in which conditions of work and remuneration were established more or less on a building-by-building basis, with a new master contract covering fifteen specific areas in the city. Clearly, as the essays by Berman and Savage show, unions often struggle in their organizing either to overcome spatial hindrances and to imbue space with particular meanings, or to use space to bolster their own causes. This suggests that a geographical perspective can add much to our understanding of the politics and practices of labor organizing.

Bibliography

Blomley, N. 1994. *Law, Space, and the Geographies of Power.* New York: Guilford Press.

Clark, G. L. 1990. "Regulating Union Representation Elections: Towards a Third Type of Electoral Geography." In *Developments in Electoral Geography,* edited by R. J. Johnston, F. M. Shelley, and P. J. Taylor, 242–56. New York: Routledge.

Foucault, M. 1979. *Discipline and Punish: The Birth of the Prison.* New York: Vintage Books.

Herod, A. 1994a. "Further Reflections on Organized Labor and Deindustrialization in the United States." *Antipode* 26.1: 77–95.

———. 1994b. "On Workers' Theoretical (In)visibility in the Writing of Critical Urban Geography: A Comradely Critique." *Urban Geography* 15.7: 681–93.

Chapter 6 • In Your Face, in Your Space
Spatial Strategies in Organizing Clerical Workers at Yale

Lee Lucas Berman

I turned around and looked at the place — I saw the long row of
lights in the old Brick Row, and felt as if I had some sort of kinship
with the men who were studying around those lamps, or smoking,
chatting, singing, on those window-seats. The Chapel clock struck the
three-quarters . . . and clanked in the hard air against the walls of
Durfee. But it was the Yale clock striking; it was striking for me as one
of the "Yale men."

From L. S. Welch and W. Camp (1900),
Yale: Her Campus, Class-rooms, and Athletics

Yale's history as a "training ground for the nation's elite" (Gilpin et al. 1988,
12) inspired a reverential awe in the turn-of-the-century undergraduate quoted
above. Even today, this Ivy League school provokes similar sentiments, as it continues to be known as an institution of and for the privileged. Its ivy-covered
walls and massive buildings are symbolic of permanence, tradition, and (I shall
argue) maleness, all of which imply a sense of power. The nation's elite have, of
course, historically been male. Since 1789, Yale men have held approximately 10
percent of the United States' major diplomatic posts, and an average of fifteen
members of Congress each year are Yale graduates (Gilpin et al. 1988). President
George Bush and Supreme Court justice William Howard Taft attended Yale
College, as did John C. Calhoun and William F. Buckley. If we include Yale's
professional schools, the power multiplies. One example in the 1990s is the
pervasive political influence of President Bill Clinton, his wife Hillary, and their
colleagues from the Yale Law School.

The Yale campus itself has traditionally been viewed by many as a male preserve, a place and a space for the exercise of male power. Such imagery has been
at the forefront of Yale's identity for most of its history, as alumni L. S. Welch
and Walter Camp (1900, 168) note:

203

It adds to a man's education to be reminded that the place in which he is studying has become the mother of colleges in America...[as] he thinks of the signers of the Declaration who were Yale men, of those who have labored in the public service in the Senate and in the Congress of the United States...of the many times when Yale has been honored by the choice of one of her sons to a place in the highest court in the Republic.

Jane Lever and Pepper Schwartz (1981, 2) argue that there has been a "pervasive male hegemony" at Yale, one that only recently has been challenged. Chronicling the university's uneasy transition in 1969 to coeducation among undergraduates, these authors (who were themselves graduate students in sociology at the time) write:

It is only after a newcomer is struck with the omnipresence of tradition that he notices a subtler but perhaps more significant characteristic of Yale — its maleness.... It was not just the absence of female faces that made it a man's institution. It was also the wood paneling, the leather library chairs and the fireplace in almost every dorm suite. Yale had, and has, a pipe and slippers atmosphere. Small touches, like four-inch thick doors designed for the male hand, and stark stone hallways, give the buildings a kind of male gender. There are no frills or feminine touches. The overall effect is lush, expensive, and cloistered. (Lever and Schwartz 1981, 14)

The presence of women on the Yale campus — as graduate students since the turn of the century and as undergraduates since 1969 — has done surprisingly little to dilute this overpowering sense of male dominance. Even after 1969, there were still areas on campus that remained off limits to women, including the "library's most comfortable reading room, which, with its overstuffed green chairs and massive fireplace, suggests a hunt club rather than a study area" (Gilpin et al. 1988, 13). In 1983, although almost one-half of its undergraduate students were female, 95 percent of its tenured faculty were male, a percentage that had not improved in six years (Cupo et al. 1984; Ladd-Taylor 1985). Indeed, only within Yale's clerical and technical workforce did men form a numerical minority. Although women composed, and still compose, more than 80 percent of this group, they nevertheless still worked under the direct supervision of mostly male administrators and professors.

It was in this context that Yale's clerical and technical (C&T) employees began forming a union during the early 1980s.[1] Other unions had attempted without

Lee Lucas Berman

success to organize these workers during the 1950s, 1960s, and 1970s (LaBotz 1991).[2] In 1984, fewer than 10 percent of office workers and only 15 percent of female workers were represented by unions (Serrin 1984b). In spite of this, Yale's C&Ts affiliated as Local 34 with the Hotel Employees' and Restaurant Employees' International Union, won a National Labor Relations Board (NLRB) representational election, and successfully negotiated a first contract following the well-publicized strike of September 1984 (Gilpin et al. 1988). Today, Local 34 is known for its innovative organizing techniques (distinguished by an unusual degree of employee involvement) and is considered a significant political force within the Yale and New Haven communities (LaBotz 1991).

Although Local 34 articulated a platform geared toward the general recognition and dissolution of gender- and race-based inequities at work, this essay will concentrate on the imposition of, and organized resistance to, particular gendered roles. It will apply Michel Foucault's conceptualization of the social construction of "docile bodies" to an analysis of this group of mostly female workers, with a focus on the union's strategies during its prolonged organizing drive and strike, which culminated in a first contract signed in January 1985.

Foucault writes that societal institutions restrain and constrict individuals in such a way as to impose a continuous discipline, and thus social control (Foucault 1979). As its clerical workforce expanded over time, Yale University implemented numerous "micro practices of control" that served to subjugate and control the behavior of the group in a variety of subtle ways. These disciplinary practices produced a gendered sexuality among the clerical and technical staff that was characterized by a submission to Yale's mostly white male (and masculinist) managerial and professorial staff. (By *masculinism*, I refer to the existence of a dualism wherein *masculine* represents normalcy and authority, and *feminine* represents an irrationality and lack of control that necessitates discipline [Rose 1993].)

Using data derived from archival exploration and personal interviews with union leaders, I will also examine the spatial strategies used by the union in countering these disciplinary practices, a resistance that has allowed the employees to subvert the physical/geographical and social restrictions imposed on them.[3] I draw in part on my experience as a Yale employee (assistant in research at the Yale Medical School from 1975 to 1985), as a member and rank-and-file organizer of Local 34 from 1981 to 1985, and as a paid union chief steward/organizer from 1985 to 1989 and again from 1995 to 1997. Throughout, I have included the voices of others who were involved in the organizing drive and strike. This reflects one of Local 34's explicit tactics, which was to incorporate such a dialogical practice into its organizing process.

In Your Face, in Your Space

The clerical and technical (C&T) workforce had grown over time at Yale such that in 1983, when the Local 34 bargaining unit was certified, it numbered 2,600 (Gilpin et al. 1988). Yale C&Ts were secretaries, laboratory technicians, library assistants, computer operators, museum attendants, autopsy technicians, and more. In terms of occupational hierarchy, they stood one step above the predominantly male service and maintenance employees (members of Local 35, HERE). With regard to salary, however, they were at the bottom of Yale's structure (Gregg 1993).[4] The bargaining unit was 82 percent female and 14 percent black, and the workers earned an average of $13,372 yearly at a time when the U.S. Bureau of Labor Statistics determined that a New England family of four needed at least $16,402 annually to maintain a *low* standard of living (Gilpin et al. 1988). In 1983, the average pension for C&Ts with eighteen years at Yale was $181 per month (*Report to the Community from the Members of Local 34* 1984). Local 34 members had always understood that their salaries were much lower than those of the members of Local 35, but when C&T bargaining unit salaries were analyzed statistically, a pattern of sex- and race-based salary discrimination appeared even *within* the unit, as indicated in table 6.1.[5] Yale's C&T salary classification system consisted of twelve gradations. Women, especially minority women, were most numerous in the lowest four salary grades, while the top two grades combined contained only one woman and two minorities.

Citing these salary figures, the members of Local 34 contended that the work they did was undervalued because they were mostly female. Women earned approximately $1,000 per year less than their male counterparts, and minorities (mostly African-American) earned about $1,000 per year less than whites. The sexual division of labor in the offices and labs — where men held most of the managerial positions and women filled the majority of low-level C&T jobs — was a division that mirrored the positions held by men and women outside the office. In a male-dominated society, the work of women is not generally held in high esteem — a circumstance that was magnified at a male-dominated institution such as Yale. John Wilhelm, the business manager of Local 35 and architect of Local 34's strategy, described the union's goals: "The union [Local 34] sought to improve the second-class economic status of this predominantly female group, and argued that a university that prides itself on its intellectual and moral leadership had an obligation — and an opportunity — to lead the nation in voluntarily beginning to address economic discrimination against women" (Wilhelm 1985).

206

Table 6.1. Yale University clerical and technical employees:
full-time employees (data by race and sex)

Group	Number	Avg. salary	Avg. yrs. at Yale	Avg. yrs. in grade
All employees	2,236	$13,372	5.7	3.6
White males	328	$14,372	5.3	3.8
White females	1,527	$13,344	5.7	3.5
Black females	250	$12,534	7.0	4.2
Black males	59	$12,170	5.2	3.7

Source: Statistics supplied by Yale University, analyzed by Local 34 (March 25, 1984). Reprinted by permission of Local 34, Federation of University Employees, Hotel Employees' and Restaurant Employees' International Union.

The University as Disciplinarian

Foucault reminds us that our bodies are shaped and impressed with the stamp of normalizing forms of individuality, masculinity, and femininity (Foucault 1978, 1979). This inscription is a form of disciplining the body itself for participation in a more efficient, streamlined society. Emily Martin describes the implementation of such a process in her study of the transition from a "Fordist" to a "post-Fordist" body; she argues that the success of any new production system would depend on "new constructions of sexuality, reproduction, family life, moral ideals, masculinity, femininity" (Martin 1992, 121). For Foucault, this construction of selfhood occurs as bodies become virtually addicted to a discipline that emerges from systems of institutions and practices that sustain patterns of dominance and subordination. Under these circumstances, Foucault writes, bodies enter into a relation of "docility-utility." "Thus discipline produces subjected and practiced bodies, *docile bodies*" (Foucault 1979, 137). In *Discipline and Punish*, Foucault is interested in the role that space plays in the implementation and maintenance of such discipline. In emphasizing the sociospatial nature of these power relations, he rearticulates in a particularly interesting manner two useful geographical concepts — *enclosure* and *partitioning*.

Enclosure

Discipline requires *enclosure*, Foucault writes, "the specification of a place heterogeneous to all others and enclosed in upon itself" (Foucault 1979, 141). Enclosure emphasizes spatial barriers between "inside" and "outside," and is exemplified by such entities as school fences and monastery cloisters. Such barriers

207

serve to allow discipline to be imposed within certain spaces and distinctions to be made between these controlled spaces and those spaces beyond.

The campus space of Yale University itself is set within New Haven, Connecticut, deemed by the 1980 U.S. Census to be the seventh poorest city in the nation (Gilpin et al. 1988). Toni Gilpin (ibid., 14) writes that the Yale campus is "insular and clearly separate from its surroundings," a sentiment echoed by Cupo et al. (1984, 9), who assert that "Yale is a weight in the middle of the city."[6] The wider New Haven community is kept at bay by the stone walls that enclose the much-touted Yale "community." Town-gown relations are somewhat acrimonious and have been since the 1960s, when the poverty of the city's black residents became a problem for many at the university, and people began locking their doors out of fear of burglary or vandalism. Most students rarely stray from the campus space, and few of the city's residents (most of whom are black and Hispanic) mingle with the students. Although the university attempts to integrate itself into the social and political fabric of the city, it is with a profound skepticism borne by centuries of class division that these efforts are received by many city residents. Particularly in light of the university's refusal to make contributions in lieu of taxes to the city, the New Haven community remains ambivalent toward its largest employer (Bass and Bass 1984b).[7]

Several commentators who are longtime residents of the area have characterized Yale's attitude toward New Haven as one of condescension. Still, the university is New Haven's largest employer, and many aspire to a career at Yale. As Carole and Paul Bass write: "university employees in general, and Ivy League workers in particular, tend to think of themselves . . . as professionals, part of a privileged elite. Many workers are proud to work in such a prestigious environment" (Bass and Bass 1984a, 4). Louise Camera-Benson, a research assistant at the medical school, was born and raised in New Haven. She says of her arrival at the Yale campus as a lab technician in 1969: "I was a New Haven kid. Yale was, to me, always behind those walls, inaccessible. I thought it was great to be on the *inside* for a change!" (Camera-Benson 1994; emphasis added).

Yale fostered its prestigious image through a careful cultivation of its enlightened and liberal (read "elitist, Ivy League") reputation.[8] This representation of the university was internalized by many employees, as the following statement by Pam Ossorio, ophthalmic technician, indicates: "I was impressed with myself, to be actually working at Yale University. My mother used to say that I was 'at Yale.' She wouldn't say that I *worked* at Yale. She would say that I was '*at* Yale,' because I don't have a college degree" (Ossorio 1994; emphasis added). To Pam, the memory of her first visit to the university evokes intense sentiments, similar to those described by the undergraduates quoted earlier: "What

208

I remember about it was, in '73, touring Beinecke museum [Beinecke Rare Book Library], and walking in and being so impressed with these marble walls with the sunlight shining through, seeing the Gutenberg Bible, and thinking, 'This is it. This is the day I've arrived. I work at Yale!'" (ibid.).

The spatial distinction between Yale and the surrounding New Haven community was reinforced by the way the campus's built environment was constructed as an almost fortresslike enclosure. The historic center of the campus is Beinecke Plaza (aka Hewitt Quadrangle), which, according to Professor Emeritus Richard B. Sewall, is "Yale's most austere enclosure" (Sewall 1991, 98). Its surrounding buildings were erected at the turn of the century to connect the "heart" of the campus (the Old Campus dormitories) with the Sheffield Science School to the North (Holden 1967). Woodbridge Hall, containing the president's office and the Corporation Room (site of meetings of the board of trustees), serves as the university's "head" (ibid.). During this century, the campus has expanded toward the south with the construction and development of the Yale–New Haven Medical Center. Much of the almost two square miles of campus space lies adjacent to, yet separate from, the sort of blighted neighborhoods that have become characteristic of contemporary urban America.

Partitioning

In addition to enclosure as a means toward discipline, Foucault stresses an accompanying *partitioning*, a compartmentalization of space within the enclosure: "Each individual has his own place; and each place has its individual" (Foucault 1979, 143). For Foucault, partitioning is a means whereby individuals are separated one from the other so that collectivity might be discouraged. The powerful must seek to partition space in such ways as to "avoid distribution [of their opposition] in groups; break up collective dispositions; analyze confused, massive or transient pluralities" (ibid.). Partitioning is thus a means by which discipline may be imposed through control of space, time, and movement. Foucault describes this disciplinary space as essentially cellular. He draws on the examples of monastic cells, schools, hospital wards, prisons, and factory buildings to advance his argument that the partitioning of space serves to manage and control individuals by constricting their activity and ability to communicate.

On the Yale campus, "enclosure" resulted in the university's insularity from the greater (outside) New Haven community. Within the campus, examples of partitioning abound. Indeed, Sewall characterizes Yale as having "no campus at all, just a series of enclosures," which he also calls "moated inwardnesses" (Sewall 1991, 90). These "inwardnesses" are courtyards and squares created on the medieval model of Oxford and Cambridge universities (ibid.). The university is organized into a series of residential colleges, for example, each with its own dining hall, common room, library, and courtyard, and each of which is encircled by a mortared wall with iron gates. Also notable on campus are several other "inwardnesses." The university's freshman dormitories surround an enormous courtyard known as the Old Campus. The main library and several other Gothic-style buildings encircle an area called Cross Campus. Furthermore, the aforementioned Beinecke Plaza, encircled by the impressive rare book library, the Greek colonnade of the Bicentennial Buildings, and Woolsey Hall, is a premier example of the partitioning of campus space.

Whether by design or artifact, the Yale University campus evolved by 1983 into an architectural configuration that segregated the C&T workforce into approximately 250 buildings (Gilpin et al. 1988). The average work site consisted of two to four people, though individual work sites were not uncommon. Laboratories, in which many C&Ts toiled, were often designated "off limits" to all but those who worked within, and labeled with "Biohazard" or "Radiation" signs that reinforced their exclusivity. In those rare instances when an office or lab contained more than ten people (the hospital billing office, the communications center, data processing, clinical labs), it was common for workers to be partitioned off either into cubicles behind video display terminals (VDTs), or in an "open landscape" office design where secretaries or technicians sit at desks or tables in full view of the supervisor at all times. In such settings, communication is discouraged as much by the geography of the office as by the actions of the supervisor (Weisman 1994). The peripheral surveillance characteristic of this work-site geography is reminiscent of Bentham's Panopticon, a medieval prison designed so that prisoners could be viewed without their knowledge and therefore disciplined/controlled (Foucault 1979).

The result of the physical/geographical separation of workers was, of course, a *social segregation*. For example, work units became like "families," and secretaries and technicians became surrogate wives and daughters to the male bosses, who took on the role of the patriarchal father figure. Ellen Lupton characterizes the boss-secretary relationship as "structured by such differences as masculine/ feminine and active/passive" (Lupton 1993, 48). This situation was typical at Yale. The role of "office wife," the woman who took charge of office affairs, became the norm, particularly in those instances where a faculty member had a personal secretary (Tepperman 1976). In the laboratory, the technician often fulfilled this role. "They were the father figure; we were the women," Pam Ossorio says. "We were the workers. We trusted them to take care of us." Former administrative assistant Deborah Chernoff considers that "Yale was a family, and

210

the traditional manager-worker relationships didn't exist here" (*Waterbury Republican* 1984, A8).

Drawing on the geography of Yale's built environment and the social relations it helped mold, Local 34 organizers often characterized the university as being organized into "fiefdoms," each ruled by a powerful male faculty member under whom the mostly female clerical and technical employees worked. One result of this was that many C&Ts lived vicariously through the accomplishments of these male bosses. Ossorio was a typical example. In 1974, after she had worked at Yale for two years, her boss won the Nobel Prize in medicine. She says: "I was real happy — I was working for a Nobel laureate!...And you know, you worked for the 'Father of Cell Biology' and...it rubbed off on us, you know. *It made our work valid.*...Because he was important, our work was important....It was just a *Camelot time!*" (Ossorio 1994; emphasis added).

Another example of discipline through partitioning on the Yale campus is that of a small number of employees who had the distinction of performing as housekeepers in the homes of the inauspiciously labeled residential college "Masters" (faculty chosen to oversee the colleges). These women, mostly immigrant and/or African-American and geographically and socially segregated from the remainder of the community, were expected to perform the duties of maidservant while in the university's employ. They ordinarily cooked and cleaned, but were sometimes required to baby-sit, retrieve dry cleaning, and prepare and serve food at evening events at the home of the "Master" and his wife.[9]

Many of those C&Ts who worked with students tended to identify with the university rather than with other workers, which served to separate them from most of their fellow employees. Lucille Dickess, registrar and former three-term president of Local 34, was "enticed" to join an antiunion committee during a 1970s organizing drive. "I had a good job," she explains. These were honorable people. They're doing the right thing, every time [laughter]. We're talking *Yale* here! This is the best that could possibly be, like the Marine Corps. Light and truth....I felt so lucky to be working at Yale. When the unions came I thought, 'This is not the place for *this!*'" (Dickess 1994; emphasis added).

In partitioning its C&T workforce, therefore, Yale did indeed "break up collective dispositions," as Foucault writes (1979, 143). The university even discouraged interaction overtly, which resulted in a muting of its female workers on particular issues. No one ever talked about salaries, for example. Dickess likens workers' reticence to speak of salaries to the "Mafia code of silence" (*Catering Industry Employee* 1984, 7). "Talk about money?" she asks. "That was tacky, low rent" (LaBotz 1991, 211). Ossorio reiterates: "Salary was a 'no-no.' You never

211

discussed your salary!... What they told us was that other people would be up-set if they found out what you were making. Because, 'I'm giving you a 10 or 20 percent raise, and you should not share this with anybody because I can't give that to everyone' " (Ossorio 1994).

Even when C&Ts did converse, relations were sometimes strained. Linda An-derson, an administrative assistant in women's studies, writes:

> Before the union... many of the other clerical people I dealt with... left me feeling estranged. Another secretary's rudeness or lack of co-operation would leave me screaming..., "What's the matter with her? Why is she taking her anger out on me?" This happened often enough that it became clear many staff people hated their jobs and apparently... felt powerless to change the working conditions.... Horizontal hostil-ity. The system thrives on it. (Anderson 1986, 30)

Women at Yale were thus conditioned to accept proscribed and limited in-volvement at the workplace, seemingly powerless to change their working condi-tions. At the university, a docile, isolated, and feminized workforce was consti-tuted over time through disciplinary practices such as those outlined earlier and others. An informational booklet published during the negotiations reads: "Over the period of many years, many of us felt we were the invisible part of the Yale community, there to do the work without which the University couldn't func-tion, but overlooked, ignored, voiceless" (*Report to the Community from the Members of Local 34* 1984, 6). At Yale University, this "voicelessness" was actively encour-aged by administrators, and C&Ts were complicit with its maintenance until union organization brought them out of the shelter of their offices and labs.

The Insurrection

Susan Bordo, invoking Foucault, observes that power relations are continuously spawning "new forms of culture and subjectivity, new opportunities for trans-formation" (Bordo 1993, 27). Dominant institutions, she writes, "are continu-ally being penetrated and reconstructed by values, styles, and knowledges that have been developing and gathering strength, energy, and distinctiveness 'at the margins' " (ibid.). The organization of Local 34 represents just such an oppor-tunity, as the needs of a marginal portion of the university population (the cler-ical and technical employees) were increasingly brought to the fore both within and beyond the Yale campus. More generally, the fact that women would dare to organize a union on the Yale campus represented a challenge to the administration's ability to control and order the campus's space and to reproduce that space as a disciplined landscape.

212

Lee Lucas Berman

The geographic and social isolation that characterized the life of the average C&T—black or white, male or female—on the Yale campus began to break down in 1980 with the organizing of Local 34. Solidarity within Local 34 and between Locals 34 and 35 was built across lines of gender and race and around the issue of gaining respect for the work done by all Yale employees as being essential to the functioning of the university. Local 35's eleven hundred members had recognized, after four bitter strikes during the late 1960s and the 1970s, that organizing the C&Ts into Local 34 would strengthen the workers' bargaining position with the university. They therefore voted twice to increase their dues in order to finance the C&T organizing drive and donated many hours' time assisting in the contact and recruitment of potential members. When Local 34 struck the university in September 1984, 95 percent of the members of Local 35 honored the picket line for the duration of the ten-week strike.[10] This demonstration of solidarity (which forced the closing of student dining halls and a curtailment of maintenance services on campus) was of inestimable significance to the struggle of the C&Ts.

Dan LaBotz attributes the success of the HERE campaign to "an entirely different approach" (LaBotz 1991, 210), an approach that Rick Hurd calls "bottom-up organizing" (Hurd 1986).[11] "The H.E.R.E. organizers," writes LaBotz, "encouraged the workers to forget any preconceptions about what a union could do, that Local 34 could be whatever they wanted it to be and tackle whatever issues it chose" (LaBotz 1991, 210). The C&Ts thus took charge of their work lives in a manner never before considered feasible at Yale: they "built" a union from the bottom up. Significantly, this process was both sensitive to the geography of the campus and designed to overcome the physical and social barriers that had served to divide workers.

The first step in Local 34's campaign involved the establishment of a 450-person organizing committee whose members were located strategically across the campus so that every work unit was represented. Such diversity of employee experience and opinion and the geographic inclusivity of the committee were important factors in the union's organizing campaign. Indeed, the union's geographic sensitivity in organizing was reflected in the fact that "the structure of the union was based on the layout of Yale" (Ladd-Taylor 1985, 469). From the organizing committee, a steering committee emerged in each of three geographic areas of campus (central, science, and medical). The committee structure (a semblance of which persists today) ensured that communication within the union was facilitated on an ongoing basis and that union members need not feel isolated from one another. It also supported the integration of new activists into the organization and encouraged their involvement at whatever level they chose

213

(Prasad 1991). For the first time on the Yale campus, daily *conversations* took place among hundreds of C&Ts. Yale's women workers began to understand that their individual grievances about salary or job classification were part of a systemic discrimination rather than individual cases of mistreatment.

The level of organization within the union also facilitated a high degree of rank-and-file activism. The campaign was punctuated by a dynamism never before witnessed on campus, and by a level of confrontation to which the Yale community was unaccustomed (Hamm 1984a; Serrin 1984a, 1985). Over the prolonged organizing drive, the year and a half of contract negotiations, and the ten-week strike for a first contract beginning in September 1984, C&Ts joined together to confront Yale administrators, alumni, and parents at every turn and at various venues (Duffy 1984; Hamm 1984a, 1984b; Pirozzolo 1984). The campus was continually challenged by union activity designed to take control of particular spaces, at least temporarily, through silent vigils, mass demonstrations, smaller "actions," informational picket lines, marches, and hundreds of organizational meetings (LaBotz 1991; Stevens 1984b). Furthermore, as a part of a campaign against salary-based discrimination at Yale, Local 34 broke the "Mafia code of silence" — its members began to talk about their salaries, loudly, and in public. Issues previously restricted to the private spaces of employees' individual work sites were now brought into the public spaces of meeting halls, picket lines, and various media outlets.[12]

The 1984 strike itself provoked an even greater militancy among the C&Ts. Although the strike was a financial and emotional strain, many women who had been previously isolated from one another and whose active lives had left them with little time, found the strike liberating. Picket lines were established at strategic sites to impose on the campus the strikers' own calculus of spatial control, a control designed to partition the campus both symbolically and materially in ways that facilitated the collective exercise of political power by the C&Ts. Workers who had been almost invisible within the private spaces of their offices and labs became visible in the public spaces of the picket lines. The strike helped to break down the very physical and social isolation that characterized women's work on the Yale campus. Those administrators, faculty, and students who crossed the picket lines were challenged directly by many strikers, who became bold enough to confront even Yale's top administrators. Anderson, for instance, recalls that "I especially liked pelting [A. Bartlett] Giamatti [president of Yale] with 'Coward!' and 'Shame on You!' " (Anderson 1986, 30).

In addition to this "communal" aspect of Local 34's organizational strategy, the existence of a large and highly visible group of rank-and-file organizers on campus produced and maintained a palpable union presence at the university.

Lee Lucas Berman

Union members and supporters appropriated spaces that became known either as union "strongholds" because of "permanent" occupation (Harkness Cafeteria in the Medical School, Naples Pizza Restaurant, and "The Sterling Spoon," a snack bar in the main library) or as temporary sites of resistance as a result of some union "action" at that place (auditoriums where large union meetings were held). Organizers tended to hold lunch meetings at particular cafeterias in each area of the campus. On specified days, union members would hold "Local 34 days" in the cafeterias, and invite all members to wear Local 34 buttons to lunch as a way of proclaiming the union's strength.

One distinctive place on campus, Beinecke Plaza, holds especially dear memories for Local 34 members, many of whom now think of it as their own. Over time and through its continued use as a gathering spot for union members and students, the significance of the plaza was transformed. A memorable C&T "speak-out against salary discrimination," designed to publicize the inadequacies and inconsistencies in Yale's C&T salary structure, was but one of the many demonstrations and rallies that took place there. "I remember [J. S.] saying that she was a single mother, and that she had been at Yale a number of years, and how she had an eight-year-old son and only made eight thousand dollars" (Ossorio 1994). Of the speak-out, Camera-Benson (1994) says, "I think it was one of the first real, tangible things that we did that made a lot of people realize . . . the reality . . . of working at Yale and what we were fighting for."

The strike enhanced the significance of the space of Beinecke Plaza in the minds of C&Ts, as it functioned as the central rallying point for workers picketing the length of the campus.

> One of my strongest [memories] is having a silent vigil or rally in front of Giamatti's offices, and having two friends of mine hold the banner that said "We Can't Eat Prestige."[13] And they, at twenty-three and twenty-four years old, they still understood the fact that the struggle was not only for ourselves, but for future generations, future employees at Yale. (Ossorio 1994)

Ann Mulvey-Fischer, a former administrative assistant, reminisced about the plaza: "I remember walking from the Medical School to the plaza. That was a powerful, very powerful march. Unbelievable. Stopping traffic, marching and singing and chanting. We took New Haven over! And then ending up at the plaza where there were hundreds of us already there" (Mulvey-Fischer 1994).

Dozens of events brought C&Ts together on Beinecke Plaza, and still more brought other members of the Yale, New Haven, and wider communities to voice support for the workers before and during the strike. Faculty walked a

215

weekly "Faculty Support Picket Line" in front of Woodbridge Hall, and unions from over the Northeast held a support rally (LaBotz 1991). Students demonstrated frequently (Stevens 1984b, 1984c), and more than six hundred union members and supporters submitted to arrest in two massive acts of civil disobedience near the plaza (Stevens 1984a; Hamm 1985b).

All of these events found C&Ts and their supporters occupying the university campus's central control point, effectively laying claim to that space. Beinecke Plaza became known popularly as "People's Plaza," and it remains that in the memories of those who redefined its very meaning. In effect, the plaza was transformed from an elite, white, male-dominated space to a more gender-neutral, proletarian space. As Ossorio (1994) states: "I feel like Beinecke Plaza belongs to the unions. It is *our* space!" (emphasis added). The redefinition of the meaning of spaces such as Beinecke Plaza has been a result of labor struggle characterized by a particular confrontational style of political praxis, one that the Yale administration would certainly consider "in your face." I prefer to call this manner of praxis "in your space," a consummate example of sociospatial resistance to domination.

The voices of Local 34 were heard well beyond the Yale campus as a result of a carefully crafted campaign to organize a broad support network and to encourage widespread media coverage in order to disseminate word of the dispute (LaBotz 1991). The New Haven Board of Aldermen, the region's congressman and senator, local activists, the Association of New Haven [Black] Clergy, and Yale alumni and parents communicated with President Giamatti and the union to recommend settlement. Union members appeared on local radio talk shows, and on the nationally broadcast *MacNeil-Lehrer Report, Donahue,* and *NBC Nightly News* (Hamm 1985b). National figures such as Ralph Abernathy, Lane Kirkland, and Cesar Chavez traveled to New Haven to offer encouragement while simultaneously garnering national media attention (Hamm 1985b; Ladd-Taylor 1985).

Other tactics included a "corporate campaign" waged against members of the Yale Corporation (the university's board of trustees), a predominantly male and white group of mostly businessmen who lived and worked all over the country. This strategy allowed Yale's workers to lay temporary claim to spaces well beyond the university campus, while spreading word of their plight outside their immediate locality. The union sent buses to New York City to leaflet the offices of clerical workers at Brown Brothers-Harriman, whose board chair was on the Yale Corporation; to Boston to picket Eleanor Holmes Norton, former head of the Equal Employment Opportunities Commission; and to Cambridge to confront President Giamatti when he spoke at the Harvard Club (Hochstadt and Wulkan 1985).

216

Lee Lucas Berman

In all senses of the word, the integrity of Yale University became suspect. The "enclosed" nature of the university was breached repeatedly as "insiders" took to the city's streets and "outsiders" entered the space of the campus to offer support or to cover campus events for newspapers, radio stations, and television networks. Yale's employees effectively penetrated not only those barriers that had formerly separated them from one another, but also those boundaries that served to insulate the campus space from the surrounding community. One might say, therefore, that the Yale campus was turned "inside out" through the efforts of Local 34.

Victory

It is Bart who hires the lawyers,
It is Bart who calls the shots,
He treats his women workers like a bunch of timid tots,
It is Bartlett who has tied the university in knots,
But the union makes us strong!
sung to the tune of "Solidarity Forever,"
published in the Local 34 Songbook, *1984*

The first contract between Yale University and its clerical and technical employees was ratified on January 22, 1985, and was hailed as an important victory for the union (Hamm 1985a; Hamm and Stevens 1985; Finley 1985; Gilpin et al. 1988). It represented a significant step toward eliminating economic discrimination against women and minorities at Yale by providing an average wage increase of 35 percent over three and a half years and eliminating the lowest labor grade, which included many older black women (Finley 1985; Hamm 1985a). The wages of some of these poorest workers increased by 80 to 90 percent and the salaries of the more undervalued workers were brought in line with prevailing standards. The contract also guaranteed employees' health and safety and job security, and improved procedures for grievances, promotions, and transfers (Hamm and Stevens 1985). Later contracts (in 1988, 1992, and 1996) have provided even greater job security, an improved pension scheme, a revamping of the job classification system, and even a program to train inner-city New Haven residents to qualify for entry-level bargaining unit positions after the completion of a designated course of study at the local community college (paid for by Yale). Local 34 has been involved in charity drives and political campaigns, and is known to be an influential sociopolitical entity in the community (LaBotz 1991; Bass and Bass 1985).

In addition, Local 34 has been a catalyst for increased awareness of gendered social relations among its predominantly female membership (Mercier 1984). **217**

The class and gender-based consciousness that it has awakened has been the foundation for altered social and spatial relations both at the workplace and at home. Dickess (1994) describes her transformation eloquently: "I've been a daughter; I've been a wife; but it wasn't until I became a [union] sister that I became a woman." Ossorio (1994) sums up her experience as follows:

> I'm so different from how I started.... I'm proud, immensely proud! The best thing I've ever done is my work with Local 34.... The strike was a crossroads for me. My husband didn't support it, my closest friend didn't support it, and I had to find it within myself, or someone or something else, to find my strength. And my strength was that Local 34 became my family.

Changes on the Yale campus involved more than just the C&Ts, however. Since Local 34's first contract, three other unions have organized at Yale. The Human Relations Area Files, the teachers at Yale's Cedarhurst School, and the Yale police have negotiated contracts without strikes. In addition, Yale's graduate teaching assistants have been organizing since the mid-1980s, and discussions have continued concerning the feasibility of unionizing other segments of the Yale community.[14] Beyond the Yale campus, Local 34's victory encouraged successful efforts at Harvard, Cornell, and New York University (Gooding and Reeve 1993; Jackson 1984). In New Haven, a stronger union presence has evolved, and labor activity has risen dramatically.

David Montgomery, renowned labor historian at Yale, characterizes the Local 34 struggle as a "preview and trial run for the strategies and tactics that will be necessary in labor movement struggles in the years to come" (Miller 1987). Male dominance in the Ivy League had enabled the Yale administration over time to shape the campus world in ways that subjugated and regulated the mostly female C&Ts, producing and reproducing a "docile," feminized workforce. This was achieved through the implementation of a subtle discipline characterized by spatial practices such as *enclosure* and *partitioning*, in which the campus community was separated from its surroundings and C&Ts were separated one from the other. With its combination of "in your space" organizing strategies, innovative bargaining, and clever manipulation of the media, Local 34 members managed to subvert those "micropractices of control" to which they had been subjected. In particular, the women at Yale were enabled to overcome the geographic/physical and social barriers that had disciplined them into submission to the powerful, white male-dominated institution. In doing so, the individual women have been transformed, and so has the institution. As one union member states,

218

"There's a whole different sense of being at a place where there's a strong union. We changed the face of the university" (Miller 1987).

Notes

1. I will use C&T throughout this paper to denote an employee belonging to the bargaining unit consisting of all clerical and technical employees at Yale. These workers are represented by Local 34, Federation of University Employees, affiliated with the Hotel Employees' and Restaurant Employees' International Union (HERE), AFL–CIO.

2. In the 1950s, the Distributive, Processing, and Office Workers' Union attempted to organize Yale's C&Ts. This was followed by organizing drives run by the Association of Clericals and Technicals (ACT) in the late 1960s, the Yale Non-Faculty Action Committee (YNFAC) in the early 1970s, the Office and Professional Employees' International Union (OPEIU) in the mid- to late-1970s, and the United Auto Workers (UAW) from 1979 through 1982 (Gilpin et al. 1988; Ladd-Taylor 1985). The earlier organizing drives at Yale originated in the medical school, where employees tended to work under greater stress than in other areas of the campus and where job security was more tenuous because of inconsistencies in grant funding possibilities. In two earlier NLRB elections, the union was defeated, by a 2 to 1 margin in 1971 and by a much smaller margin in 1977 (Wilhelm 1985, 1996).

3. For this study, I interviewed three current and one former union leader, all white females, aged thirty-six to sixty-two. Two are classified as clerical employees — Ann Mulvey-Fischer is a former administrative assistant in the Department of Genetics and Lucille Dickess is a registrar in the Department of Geology and Geophysics. The other two are technical workers in the Medical School — Louise Camera is a research assistant in molecular medicine and Pam Ossorio is an ophthalmic technician (photographer) in the Department of Ophthalmology. The names of the interviewees have been provided with their permission. All quotations are verbatim from audiotapes, with editorial clarifications in brackets.

4. In one union publication, Local 34 cited the comparison between a $13,524 average salary for a senior administrative assistant (requiring an associate's degree and a typing speed of fifty to sixty words per minute) to the $18,470 salary for a truck driver (requiring the ability to read and a valid driver's license) in the Local 35 bargaining unit as an example of gender-based salary discrimination at Yale (*Report to the Community from the Members of Local 34* 1984). The Local 34 bargaining unit was 84 percent female in 1984; the Local 35 bargaining unit was more than 60 percent male.

219

In Your Face, in Your Space

5. When Local 34 first published these figures, the university claimed that they were misleading. Yale Chaplain John Vannorsdall proposed that the university and the union agree on an impartial panel to investigate the claims. The union agreed, but the university refused to submit to such scrutiny. Ultimately, Yale economist Ray Fair performed an independent analysis, which confirmed the union's claims.

6. See Bass and Bass (1984b) for further discussion of town-gown relations in New Haven. In 1996, Locals 34 and 35, while engaged in yet another protracted struggle for contracts, enlisted the aid of civil rights leader Jesse Jackson. On Sunday, April 27, in a sermon delivered at Varick AME Zion Church in New Haven, Jackson proclaimed, "New Haven is Yale's Plantation," echoing the sentiments of Cupo and Gilpin (Cupo et al. 1984; Gilpin et al. 1988).

7. See Woolf (1996) for a recent update on Yale's finances and further discussion of town-gown relations in New Haven, which he terms "the most dangerous Ivy League community today." Of particular interest is Woolf's outline of the university's long-range plan to systematically transform New Haven into a place that caters primarily to the university. This sentiment is echoed by Andrew Ross (1996, 26), who writes: "New Haven's once-proud industrial town will more and more resemble an Ivy League theme park for tourists to gawk at and for upper-income Connecticut to colonize."

8. Local 34 was eminently successful in pointing out the dichotomy between this liberal image and the university's less than beneficent attitude toward its workers. Even today, Barbara Ehrenreich (1996, 3) describes Yale as an institution that "teaches 'the humanities' while ignoring the humanity of its own employees. . . . [At Yale] you learn that ethics and fine ideals belong in seminars and in books, but not in dining halls, laboratories, offices, or other places where people mingle."

9. Rhonda Williams and Peggie Smith (1990), who investigated the incorporation of race and gender privilege in the determination of wages in Local 35, found a pattern similar to that of Local 34, where minorities were relegated to the lower salary grades. In particular, black women were confined to specific occupations, "the dirtiest, most back-breaking, unrewarding, low-paying, menial and insecure jobs" (Williams and Smith 1990, 60). In the Local 34 bargaining unit, the "black women's jobs" were as housekeepers and laboratory aides, both of which offered little remuneration and even less opportunity for advancement.

10. See Wilhelm (1996) for a brief history of Local 35 and its contribution to the success of the Local 34 organizing drive.

Lee Lucas Berman

11. For a discussion of "bottom-up organizing" at Harvard, see Gooding and Reeve (1993) and Hamm (1985b), and for further analysis of the Yale organizing drive, see Bass and Bass (1985). The successful organizing drive at Harvard in 1988 is thought to have been influenced substantially by the earlier drive at Yale (Ladd-Taylor 1985).

12. See the essay by Savage in this volume, which describes how the Justice for Janitors campaign in Los Angeles transgressed the boundaries of private space and brought workplace issues into the wider arena through actions in shopping malls and other public spaces.

13. The slogan "We Can't Eat Prestige" was coined by the C&Ts at Harvard during their organizing drive in the mid-1980s.

14. See Eakin (1996) and Bérubé (1996) for comprehensive discussions of recent graduate student activism at Yale. Yale's Graduate Employees' and Students' Organization (GESO) began organizing in earnest in 1990 with the support of Locals 34 and 35. Despite the setback of a failed grade strike in early 1996 and bolstered by a National Labor Relations Board charge against Yale for using "intimidatory" tactics against grade strikers, GESO has continued to press for unionization. The NLRB also recognized graduate students' right to unionize, which represented a clear change in the agency's historical view of teaching assistants (TAs) as employees (Dilger 1996). On July 27, 1997, a federal court judge acceded to Yale's request to dismiss NLRB charges against the university, ruling that the TAs' withholding of student grades during their grade strike was only a partial strike and therefore illegal (Kita 1997, A1). On this charge, the NLRB is appealing the ruling. Still, the judge's decision did not question the fundamental right of graduate students to organize, and the TAs continue their drive toward unionization. In April 1996, in the midst of another prolonged contract dispute between Yale and its unions, a large group of casual employees petitioned for an NLRB election and voted overwhelmingly (61 to 2) to become members of Local 35.

Bibliography

Anderson, L. 1986. "On Strike against Yale University." *Frontiers* 8.3: 26–32.
Bass, C., and P. Bass. 1984a. "Rewriting Labor History." *New Haven Advocate*, December 5, 33.
———. 1984b. "Union Victory at Yale." *Dollars & Sense* (July–August): 16–18.
———. 1985. "Breaking New Ground for Labor." *Changing Work* (spring): 21–24.
Bérubé, M. 1996. "The Blessed of the Earth." *Social Text* 49 (winter): 75–95.

Bordo, S. 1993. *Unbearable Weight: Feminism, Western Culture, and the Body*. Los Angeles: University of California Press.

Camera-Benson, L. 1994. Interview with Lee Lucas Berman, March 16, New Haven, Conn.

Catering Industry Employee 93.10: 6–7. 1984. "On Strike at Yale: Sex Discrimination, 'Comparable Worth' at Issue." Cincinnati, Ohio: Hotel Employees' and Restaurant Employees' International Union.

Cupo, A., M. Ladd-Taylor, B. Lett, and D. Montgomery. 1984. "Beep, Beep, Yale's Cheap: Looking at the Yale Strike." *Radical America* 18.5: 7–20.

Dickess, L. 1994. Interview (by telephone) with Lee Lucas Berman, December 7, Wallingford, Conn.

Dilger, P. 1996. "Grad Students at Yale Cite Need for Union." *New Haven Register*, November 24, A5.

Duffy, T. 1984. "Union Takes Dispute to Yale Alumni." *New Haven Journal-Courier*, April 25, 21.

Eakin, E. 1996. "Walking the Line: A Report from the Yale Grade Strike." *Lingua Franca* (March–April): 52–60.

Ehrenreich, B. 1996. "What Yale Is Teaching Us." *Social Text* 49 (winter): 1–4.

Finley, L. 1985. "Women's Work at Yale Wins Respect." *Hartford Courant*, January 27, EI.

Foucault, M. 1978. *The History of Sexuality*. Translated by Robert Hurley. New York: Vintage Books.

———. 1979. *Discipline and Punish: The Birth of the Prison*. New York: Vintage Books.

Gilpin, T., G. Isaac, D. Letwin, and J. McKivigan. 1988. *On Strike for Respect: The Clerical & Technical Workers' Strike at Yale University (1984–1985)*. Chicago: Charles H. Kerr.

Gooding, C., and P. Reeve. 1993. "The Fruits of Our Labor: Women in the Labor Movement." *Social Policy* (summer): 56–64.

Gregg, N. 1993. "'Trying to Put First Things First': Negotiating Subjectivities in a Workplace Organizing Campaign." In *Negotiating at the Margins: The Gendered Discourses of Power and Resistance*, edited by S. Fisher and K. Davis. New Brunswick, N.J.: Rutgers University Press.

Hamm, S. 1984a. "Pickets Angry, Resolute." *New Haven Register*, September 26, I.

———. 1984b. "Yale Union, Students Hold Rallies." *New Haven Register*, September 28, I.

———. 1985a. "Euphoria Is Mood of Local 34." *New Haven Register*, January 23, AI.

———. 1985b. "Member Involvement Called Key to Union Resurgence." *New Haven Register*, March 24, FI.

Lee Lucas Berman

Hamm, S., and B. Stevens. 1985. "Exploring the Breakthrough at Yale." *New Haven Register,* January 27, A2.

Hochstadt, J., and F. Wulkan. 1985. "Yale Strikers: Pay Us What We're Worth." *Labor Page,* no. 18 (January–February): 1, 4–5.

Holden, R. A. 1967. *Yale: A Pictorial History.* New Haven and London: Yale University Press.

Hurd, R. 1986. "Bottom-up Organizing: H.E.R.E. in New Haven and Boston." *Labor Research Review* (spring): 4–19.

Jackson, B. 1984. "Local 34 Success Unusual for C&Ts." *Yale Daily News,* April 17, 2.

Kita, W. 1997. "Grad Students Lose Round in Grade Dispute." *New Haven Register,* July 29, 1997, A1.

LaBotz, D. 1991. *A Troublemaker's Handbook: How to Fight Back Where You Work—and Win.* Detroit, Mich.: Labor Notes.

Ladd-Taylor, M. 1985. "Women Workers and the Yale Strike." *Feminist Studies* 11.3: 465–89.

Lever, J., and P. Schwartz. 1981. *Women at Yale: Liberating a College Campus.* New York and Chicago: Bobbs-Merrill.

Lupton, E. 1993. *Mechanical Brides: Women and Machines from Home to Office.* Princeton, N.J.: Architectural Press.

Martin, E. 1992. "The End of the Body?" *American Ethnologist* 19.1: 120–39.

Mercier, M. 1984. "Part of the Larger Picture: For Many Members of Local 34, the Strike Has Been a Catalyst for Personal Change." *New Haven Advocate,* October 24, 6–8.

Miller, A. 1987. "Work Culture and the Formation of Local 34 at Yale University, or Clerical Workers Strike Back." Unpublished manuscript.

Mulvey-Fischer, A. 1994. Interview with Lee Lucas Berman, March 17, Wallingford, Conn.

Ossorio, P. 1994. Interview with Lee Lucas Berman, March 16, New Haven, Conn.

Pirozzolo, L. 1984. "Union Rallies as Corporation Talks Go On." *Yale Daily News,* September 24, 1.

Prasad, P. 1991. "Organization Building in a Yale Union." *Journal of Applied Behavioral Science* 27.3: 337–55.

Report to the Community from the Members of Local 34, Federation of University Employees, AFL–CIO. 1984. Published by Local 34, HERE, September.

Rose, G. 1993. *Feminism and Geography: The Limits of Geographical Knowledge.* Minneapolis: University of Minnesota Press.

Ross, A. 1996. "The Labor behind the Cult of Work." *Social Text* 49 (winter): 25–29.

223

Serrin, W. 1984a. "Union's Struggle Raises Tensions at Yale." *New York Times*, March 24, 26.

———. 1984b. "Union's Success at Yale: New Focus on White-Collar Women." *New York Times*, April 10, B24.

———. 1985. "Labor's Study: Blend of Old and New." *New York Times*, February 23, 8.

Sewall, R. B. 1991. "An Unofficial Tour of Yale." *American Heritage* (April): 88–102.

Stevens, B. 1984a. "Local 34 Marches to Giamatti's Home: 225 Strikers Arrested." *New Haven Register*, October 5, A1.

———. 1984b. "Unions Offer New Plan." *New Haven Register*, October 4, 2.

———. 1984c. "Yale Strikers Backed." *New Haven Register*, September 27, 1.

Tepperman, J. 1976. *Not Servants, Not Machines: Office Workers Speak Out.* Boston: Beacon Press.

Waterbury Republican. 1984. "Showdown Nears on Strike at Yale." March 19, A8.

Weisman, L. K. 1994. *Discrimination by Design: A Feminist Critique of the Man-made Environment.* Urbana and Chicago: University of Illinois Press.

Welch, L. S., and W. Camp. 1900. *Yale: Her Campus, Class-rooms, and Athletics.* Boston: L. C. Page.

Wilhelm, J. W. 1985. "It May Have Been Yale University, but It Was Still the Law of the Jungle." Remarks to the session "The Aftermath of Yale's Strike: The Lessons Learned" at the 34th Annual Conference of the Association of Labor Relations Agencies, Portland, Maine, July 22.

———. 1996. "A Short History of Unionization at Yale." *Social Text* 49 (winter): 13–18.

Williams, R. M., and P. R. Smith. 1990. "What *Else* Do Unions Do? Race and Gender in Local 35." *Review of Black Political Economy* 18.3: 59–77.

Woolf, R. 1996. "Why Provoke This Strike? Yale and the U.S. Economy." *Social Text* 49 (winter): 21–24.

224

Lee Lucas Berman

Chapter 7 • Geographies of Organizing
Justice for Janitors in Los Angeles

Lydia A. Savage

In October 1995, John Sweeney was elected president of the American Federation of Labor and Congress of Industrial Organizations (AFL–CIO). His election signaled a change in organizing models and strategies — he was elected in large part on his promise to organize the service sector, a promise he had pursued during his presidency of the Service Employees' International Union (SEIU). This election was remarkable in labor history: the presidency of the AFL–CIO had never been contested before and has been held by only three men.[1] As a result, the election convention provided an unusually public forum for considerable debate about the future of American unionism. Both candidates (Sweeney and Thomas Donahue) declared that unions needed to organize and promised to increase substantially the resources devoted to organizing new workers (women and people of color) in new sectors (service jobs). Along with the recognition of the need to organize the service sector, both promised to have a more representative board that included more women and people of color.[2] Although they agreed in principle to the changes that needed to be made to revitalize the labor movement, they were decidedly split on strategies and tactics. Each camp proposed strategies that would create different geographies of labor activism and different uses of space — public and private — and would involve different kinds of political and social actions, and different groups of people.

In the convention debate, Donahue stated that unions needed to stop blocking bridges — a reference to a group of workers from Sweeney's union that had blocked the 14th Street bridge in Washington, D.C., and caused a major traffic snarl as part of the national Justice for Janitors campaign. Instead, Donahue argued, unions needed to build bridges to society and avoid signs of militancy. Sweeney responded by saying that building bridges would only happen "when the shelling stops long enough to put up the steel." Until that time, the Justice for Janitors campaign would continue to block bridges. Donahue argued that unions should rely on formal union leadership to represent workers in closed door negotiations, but Sweeney countered that rank-and-file workers should

225

represent their own interests and, if necessary, use large public demonstrations to gain contracts. For the labor movement, this election was not so much a question of goals as of strategies. By choosing Sweeney, the movement chose new strategies and new models of organizing.

Models of organizing used by labor unions in the United States have always been based on certain geographic assumptions and required certain spatial strategies, strategies that reflected the economic, political, and social context from which they emerged. In the late 1800s, craft unions organized skilled occupations within *local* rather than national labor markets, in the 1930s industrial unionism was community-led and community-based, and since the late 1940s business unionism has focused on controlling and standardizing working conditions across entire industries on a *national* scale. Today, labor unions in the United States are faced with the challenge of organizing workers in the context of an increasingly diverse workforce, new employment patterns, and rapidly shifting industrial and economic geographies, particularly in light of the growth of the service sector. As the country moves toward a more service-oriented economy, the traditional ways of organizing manufacturing workers are no longer appropriate and new models are necessary.

New models of organizing assume a different understanding of the importance of space and spatial context. Organizing strategies that were created for the manufacturing sector must change to take account of the different spatial arrangements (i.e., factory floor versus individual offices) and geographies of service workplaces. In addition, beyond merely recognizing the fact that women, people of color, and immigrants are predominantly employed in services, unions must engage in a meaningful way with the identities of workers, identities that are socially constructed in geographically specific ways.[3]

Although geographers have been relatively silent about the role of workers and labor unions as agents of change in economic restructuring, the literature in labor studies and industrial relations is equally inattentive to the role of place and local context in the efforts of unions to organize and represent workers. I argue that labor unions must place organizing drives and worker representation in a local spatial context in order to understand how different groups of workers are being affected by labor market changes, how workers might be successfully organized, and how employers would best be challenged. I also argue that geographers need to recognize the role of workers in structuring local labor markets through union representation. This essay first discusses the spatial assumptions underlying new models of organizing and then uses a case study of Justice for Janitors, a national organizing campaign created by the Service Employees' International Union, to illustrate the importance of local spatial con-

Lydia A. Savage

text in organizing efforts. This latter issue is particularly significant because it raises issues concerning the geographic tensions between developing a *national* campaign designed to address issues that janitors across the country face (low wages, job insecurity, etc.) while at the same time being sensitive to *local* conditions and challenges.

The State of Union Organizing in the United States

It is widely recognized by supporters and detractors alike that the labor movement faces an uncertain future. Union membership has fallen dramatically, resulting in waning political influence and fading hope for labor law reform. Conventional wisdom suggests that the decline in union membership and the resulting consequences are a direct result of economic restructuring. Unions lost members, so this argument goes, because union jobs were lost in the manufacturing sector and because workers in the expanding service sector are assumed to be inherently less interested in unionization than manufacturing workers. The lack of interest in unionization is seen as a result of the fact that service-sector workers are women, people of color, professionals, part-time workers, immigrants, and others with low unionization rates.

At first glance, sectoral change seems a reasonable explanation for the steady decline of union density in the United States. By now, the changes in employment patterns are familiar. The percentage of workers employed in U.S. manufacturing fell from 37 percent in 1965 to about 21 percent in 1990 (U.S. Bureau of the Census 1965, 1990). Between 1970 and 1990, service employment increased by 74 percent (Marshall and Wood 1995, 9). It is estimated that nearly one-third of all jobs in the United States are low-wage service jobs such as retail sales, clerical, food preparation and service, and health care (Wial 1993, 671). Almost simultaneously (between 1951 and 1990), union density fell from 32 percent to 16 percent of the workforce. If only the private sector is examined, union density has dropped to 12 percent (Eaton 1992, 20).

A closer examination, however, suggests that different factors may be at work. Chaison and Rose (1991), for example, suggest that although the structural change theory is attractive because of its simplicity and "nonaccusatory" character (it avoids examining the actions of employers, unions, and organizers), labor market shifts are not a primary determinant of membership change in labor unions. Studies have documented that only one-quarter to one-third of union growth or decline can be explained by structural changes in employment (Farber 1985; Mitchell 1989). The remaining two-thirds of lost unionized production jobs were a result of the labor movement's inability to deal effectively with an antiunion climate. For example, labor unions have bargained concessions, allowed the implementation of two-tier wage systems, and failed to organize new workers (Bluestone and Harrison 1982; Harrison and Bluestone 1988; Storper and Walker 1989).[4] Much of the labor movement's energy and resources have been spent trying to save unionized jobs, and union organizing efforts have, as a result, suffered in both the declining manufacturing sector and the quickly growing service sector. Rose and Chaison (1996) argue that it is not a structural shift in the economy that is to blame but the fact that unions *do not organize.*

Organizing expenditures by unions fell from more than 20 percent of union budgets to about 5 percent between 1950 and 1990 (Eaton 1992; Voos 1984).[5] Organizing became a low priority at approximately the same time that rapid economic restructuring was taking place. Furthermore, since World War II, American unions have favored a model of business unionism. As a result, most unions developed "traditional" organizing strategies that are *uniform over space, workplace-centered, and based on the premise that the typical worker is a white, male, head of household working in the manufacturing sector* (Crain 1991; Green and Tilly 1987). During the 1940s and 1950s, this form of unionism worked so well that by 1956 almost 50 percent of all manufacturing workers were union members.

Sayer and Walker (1992, 189) point out, however, that the "familiar organizational forms [adopted by unions at this time] do not represent a golden age for labor, even if, at their height, labor was stronger than now, for it was a highly selective and ambivalent strength, one which actively reproduced divisions in the workforce, particularly between men and women." For many observers, the decline of U.S. unions lies in their failure to aggressively seek out new members (e.g., women and people of color) in emerging and growing service-sector industries and to bargain for more than "bread-and-butter" issues when they were at their strongest (Chaison and Rose 1991; Hurd and Rouse 1989; Moody 1988).[6]

Chaison and Rose (1990, 1991) argue that it is important to trace the lack of organizing to internal decisions made by union leaders within the context of dwindling income from union dues, increased employer resistance, and legal procedures perceived as unfavorable. Employer resistance is one problem that has been especially significant, particularly since the early 1980s when one of Ronald Reagan's first acts as president was to fire air-traffic controllers during their 1981 strike.[7] Fiorito and Maranto (1987, 12) call employer resistance the "single most powerful explanation for union decline."

Employer resistance ranges from employee intimidation, in-house antiunion campaigns, and captive audience meetings to long, drawn-out legal challenges that few unions have the resources to match. In many cases, these forms of employer resistance are illegal, and if charges are brought against employers, the

228

Lydia A. Savage

National Labor Relations Board rules in favor of the worker or union.[8] Enforcement varies greatly, however, rulings can take years, and penalties are so minimal that the mere fact that many forms of employer resistance are illegal is not a sufficient deterrent. For example, Bronfenbrenner's (1994) research shows that in 30 percent of organizing campaigns, employees were fired for union activity. Forty-three percent of discharged workers were reinstated by the NLRB, but only 40 percent of those were reinstated *before* the union election. Reinstatement after an election is often too late in terms of positively affecting election outcomes and few workers can afford to lose their jobs even if they are reinstated at a later date. Some, then, have suggested that a major impediment to organizing is the fact that the current structure of labor law does not offer protections to workers in an organizing drive.

Proponents of labor law reform argue that if unions are to organize and represent workers successfully, the legal framework within which they operate must be substantially and comprehensively changed to reflect new forms of work relations and new forms of business organization, particularly with regard to the service sector (Cobble 1994; Crain 1991; Rogers 1994; Wial 1994).[9] Rogers (1994, 16) contends that there is an "institutional mismatch" between the legal structure and the economic structure. Labor laws reflect their historical roots in the New Deal era and are premised on "large firms featuring assembly-line production for standardized goods by skilled and semiskilled labor." Cobble (1994) and Wial (1994) agree, and suggest that current labor law hinders the efforts of unions in organizing and representing workers, particularly in the service sector. Indeed, Cobble (1994) maintains that current labor law does not just hinder but in fact completely bans unions from organizing and representing some service workers. She estimates that about 20 million working women are currently denied the right to join a collective bargaining unit under the National Labor Relations Act. Current labor law, Cobble asserts, is premised on two assumptions: "its worksite orientation and its adherence to Taylorist practices" (286). The result is that service occupations that are temporary, subcontracted, at-home, or tied to the household economy (i.e., domestic workers) are excluded. In addition, occupations that have highly collaborative employee-employer relations, such as confidential secretaries, personal assistants, and professional occupations, are typically excluded because of the "managerial" aspects of the jobs (i.e., planning and organization).

Others have suggested that the spatial assumptions implicit in labor law must be addressed if unions are to be more successful in organizing. Wial (1994), for example, favors what he terms geographic unionism, where unions focus on organizing workers who share an occupation within a local labor market rather than on organizing all workers at one work site. He points out that although the current labor law framework technically allows geographic unionism, it actually provides disincentives for organizing workers on that basis because of the bias toward work site-specific unionism. Bargaining units are defined by the NLRB on the notion of a "community of interest" shared by workers. The criteria used to define a "community of interest," Wial contends, are a variety of conditions that individual employers control, and the NLRB "presumes the appropriateness of units that do not extend beyond the boundaries of individual firms" (1994, 309). As a result, it is difficult to organize occupations within a local labor market and to bargain with multiple employers across a geographic area.[10]

Although it is difficult to assess the effect of employer resistance and the legal framework on organizing, empirical evidence belies the theory that the decline in union density results from a structural change and service workers being more difficult to unionize than manufacturing workers. Increasingly, low-waged service-sector workers are voting for union representation even though organizing budgets have been reduced and the few resources devoted to organizing are still being allocated disproportionately to the manufacturing sector. In 1991, 30 percent of all union elections were held in manufacturing and 11 percent in construction. Nine percent of elections were in health care, 22 percent in other services, and less than 2 percent in communications and finance. Only 35 percent of all union elections were in the service sector, despite the fact that two-thirds of all workers are employed in services (Eaton 1992, 22).

Much as spatial assumptions are built into U.S. labor law, certain spatial assumptions underlie models of organizing. Indeed, increasingly, unions are developing new models in their attempts to organize service-sector workers. I now turn to a discussion of how old and new, manufacturing and service, models vary in their geographic structures.

New Models of Organizing

Labor studies and industrial relations literature have recognized both the need for unions to organize workers in the service sector and the growing propensity for service workers to vote for union representation. This small body of literature argues that unions must alter their model of unionism if they are successfully to organize the growing service-sector workforce. Yet, despite the widespread agreement that labor unions must change their institutional forms and strategies, however, remarkably little research has been done on new organizing efforts.

One of the few pieces written in this vein is that by Green and Tilly (1987). They suggest that "traditional" methods of organizing were developed in a man-

230

Lydia A. Savage

ufacturing era that no longer exists and that new models must be created.[11] They have identified six steps followed in a "traditional model" of union organizing drive: (1) the strategy is designed for "hot shops," in which an organizer is contacted by a group of employees who have already decided they want to be unionized; (2) the organizer then appeals to workers on "bread-and-butter" issues such as the potential for better wages and benefits rather than product quality, worker participation, and broader social issues; (3) the organizer appeals to workers solely on the basis of their identity as workers for a specific employer, with little or no attempt to appeal to other identities — women, immigrants, blacks, parents, community members, and so on; (4) the union views organizing as a technical ability and not a shared process; thus, there is no real need to involve various groups of rank-and-file employees, the union needs only to send a skilled organizer, and tactics generally include running a top-down campaign rather than involving rank-and-file members; (5) organizing strategies are based on large, centralized workplaces with a few entrance gates and regular shift changes; (6) traditional models focus on winning an NLRB certification election by gaining 51 percent of the union representation election vote as quickly and as inexpensively as possible and then moving on to the next organizing drive. If an election has already been lost or a quick victory seems unlikely, unions typically do not attempt to organize a workplace. Under this model, organizing efforts are frequently abandoned if they do not develop quickly enough.

Green and Tilly (1987) also outline what are generally considered to be the most significant characteristics of service workers with regard to "traditional" models of organizing. First, they propose that, compared to manufacturing workers, service workers often have little personal experience with unions so service workplaces are seldom "hot shops." Second, service workers often come into contact with the customer, who is receiving a service, and, as a result, may be less concerned about "bread-and-butter" issues and more concerned with product quality. Third, large concentrations of women, people of color, and undocumented workers are found in low-wage service jobs and, despite evidence supporting the greater propensity of these groups to unionize than white men, organizers often view them as "unorganizable." Finally, employment in services is characterized by small businesses with high turnover, contingent, part-time, and temporary workers, whereas traditional models of organizing are predicated on large, stable workforces. Based on these findings, Green and Tilly propose the need for a new approach to organizing service workers that "calls for the adoption of strategies developed in community organizing, for the forging of labor-community coalitions."[12] Bronfenbrenner (1993) agrees with the need for a new model but disagrees with the assumption that such new strategies are

Geographies of Organizing

only appropriate for organizing service workers. She argues instead that, based on statistics for the preceding two decades, traditional models of organizing do not seem to be working well in manufacturing either, because the manufacturing sector has the lowest union election win rates.

Although Green and Tilly prescribe a new model of organizing, they are short on specifics. Building on their call for a new model, Bronfenbrenner (1993) suggests specific tactics required to develop a new model of organizing such as running a grassroots campaign with house calls and intensive personal contact. These suggestions are based on the results of her research, a large-scale survey of union organizers in which she found that "unions are more likely to win certification elections when they run campaigns utilizing a grassroots, rank-and-file intensive organizing strategy including a reliance on person-to-person contact" (1993, 379). She concludes that unions must reexamine their targeting and organizing strategies around changes in the workforce, the economy, and the political and legal environment.

Few would disagree with the call by Green and Tilly for a new model or with the specific tactics suggested by Bronfenbrenner. Little research has been done on new models, however, and few unions are actually implementing new models of unionism on a national scale. As a result of the focus on survey research, several important aspects to organizing service workers have yet to be fully explored. We have little understanding of how the new geographies of service jobs affect organizing, the ways in which the spatial arrangements of service workplaces act as a resource and a constraint on organizing strategies, and how the identities of an increasingly diverse workforce affect organizing. We need, in fact, to understand how these three things affect the process of organizing and the decisions made by workers in order to target, organize, and represent workers more successfully.[13]

The new economic geography of the service sector means that labor unions can no longer concentrate resources on organizing in areas that already have a high union density or have been union strongholds in the past. (This is frequently done because organizing is thought to be quicker and less expensive if a community is already familiar with unions.) Most union members still work in manufacturing, so there can be a mismatch between locations with high union density based on manufacturing and areas with a high concentration of service-sector employment. Daniels and Thrift (1987) argue that, given the diversity of services, we should expect a diversity of locational patterns. For example, public-sector employment is not driven by the same market pressures as private-sector services. Government attempts to create equal access to services or to expand work opportunities in disadvantaged areas often influence locational decisions more than does profit maximization. Retailing is determined in large part by

232

---

the location of customers. Moreover, most service jobs are far more spatially rooted than are manufacturing jobs, and capital mobility does not pose the same threat to those service jobs. Hotels, hospitals, universities, restaurants, child care, and much secretarial work simply must be where the clients and customers are located; unlike assembly jobs, nursing and janitorial jobs cannot be moved offshore. This is not to say that all service work is immobile — some service jobs can be and have been relocated (Bozzotto 1989; Nelson 1986) — but on the whole they are less mobile than are manufacturing jobs and this shapes the possibilities for union organizing.

Simply because many service-sector jobs are less geographically mobile than are most manufacturing jobs, however, does not mean that they are unaffected by other economic changes such as the cycles of investment and disinvestment in the built environment and/or shifts of capital between sectors and geographic areas. Shifting capital between sectors may not result in a plant closure or relocation per se, but it can affect employment patterns and labor relations significantly (Martin, Sunley, and Wills 1994; Herod 1994). Also, the heavily unionized public sector is continually being threatened with privatization (which often brings job loss) and all jobs are subject to subcontracting, speedups, and downsizing.

At a smaller scale, the spatial arrangement — the actual physical layout — of service work sites differs greatly from factory floors and the spatial fragmentation of workers engenders different labor relations and organizing strategies. Hence, whereas a common organizing strategy in the manufacturing sector is to leaflet workers at plant gates during shift changes, leafleting is not a practical tactic at most service workplaces, where shifts are varied and it can be difficult to decipher by sight alone who is an employee and who is a manager. Moreover, leafleting is a tactic based on large workforces, and research shows that the average size of a service workplace is only fourteen employees (Wial 1993, 678).

In addition, the spatial arrangement of the workplace creates more than a physical barrier to organizing. Service workers are not grouped together on a factory floor with one supervisor but are often in an office right next to their supervisor. Their physical isolation from each other, relative to manufacturing, engenders different social relations with coworkers, supervisors, and management (Massey 1993; Spain 1992; Berman in this volume). Workers are often isolated in individual offices and spend more time with their supervisors than with fellow employees, blurring the line between manager and employee on a daily basis (Braverman 1974; Cobble 1991a, 1991b). If unions are portrayed as adversarial, they may not appeal to workers who are happy with their individual supervisor and do not want to feel or appear disloyal.

233

It is easy to see only obstacles posed by the service workplace because service workplaces are spatially fragmented and often small. Is it possible, however, for differences to become advantages in organizing efforts? For example, some service workplaces (e.g., retail stores, educational institutions, health-care facilities) are much more accessible to union organizers because they are customer-oriented. As a result, although in theory management can ban union organizers from the premises, in practice it is often unable to do so (Savage 1996). Also, workers in some service jobs (e.g., secretaries) have access to "inside" information that can prove useful to an organizing drive. The spatial barriers to organizing (scattered offices, small work sites) are frequently mentioned, but the topic has yet to be explored in any depth. To date, we have little understanding of how these barriers can be overcome or used to advantage in organizing.

Finally, service workers have long been seen as resistant to unionization because of their professional image, yet the service sector encompasses a great deal of heterogeneity: janitors, secretaries, salespeople, waitresses, lab technicians, and so on. The service sector is increasingly characterized by the polarization of work—white-collar, upwardly mobile jobs and "sticky floor" jobs with little glamour, few pink collars, and no advancement opportunities (Christopherson 1989; Marshall and Wood 1995; Sassen 1994; Sayer and Walker 1992). Although large contingents of professional and technical workers may or may not be able to reconcile their identity as a "white-collar" worker with unionism, there are also large numbers of workers in the service sector who provide labor-intensive and/or physical labor—custodians, nursing assistants, gardeners, and waitresses. Additionally, many "white-collar" workers recognize the lack of autonomy they have in the workplace even though they are not performing "manual labor."[14]

Aside from occupational differences, union demographics have changed and a white male working in manufacturing is no longer the typical union member. Surprisingly, as total union density has shrunk, it has become more diverse. Despite the growing number of women, people of color, and immigrants joining unions, organizers have generally not paid attention to the characteristics and identities of individual workers. Altering organizing strategies to take account of the changing spatial arrangement and the new economic geographies of the service sector can be accomplished within the current institutional organization of unions. Engaging with the identities of workers in a meaningful way is much more difficult because it requires a deeper, more fundamental change. Union culture(s) cannot just add women, workers of color, and immigrants to their membership. The culture of unionism must change in profound ways.

It seems inevitable that unions will try to organize service-sector workers. It is also clear that unions must alter their organizing strategies. The important

Lydia A. Savage

question is how unions will change strategies to reach out to workers with whom they have had at best ambivalent relationships. Some unions have begun to develop such new strategies. One of the most imaginative and dynamic has been the Justice for Janitors campaign by the Service Employees' International Union. This campaign uses direct actions and tactics reminiscent of the 1930s labor movement with a strategy that addresses the widespread use of subcontracting by employers. The Justice for Janitors campaign has been very successful and is one of the most documented examples of the new service unionism (Howley 1990; Hurd and Rouse 1989; Lerner 1996; Mines and Avina 1992; Waldinger et al. 1997; Wial 1993). This national campaign has been successful largely because it has challenged traditional spatial assumptions concerning the geography of organizing. Although their departure points are slightly different, most observers agree that organizing workers in a local labor market and negotiating master contracts with multiple employers is a necessary form of unionism. Hence Cobble (1991b) addresses the needs of the "new workforce" and draws on lessons from craft unions, particularly waitress unions, to argue that work site-specific unionism is less effective for workers with ties to an occupation but not to individual employers. Piore (1991) argues for some combination of workplace unionism and community-based unionism. Wial (1993) contends that in the face of smaller, scattered work sites, unions should organize in geographically defined areas along "loose occupational lines" (692). All agree, however, that the nature of unions must change so that a union can be both an "economic pressure group and a social movement" (Wial 1993, 692). Justice for Janitors most clearly embodies this new model of unionism.

The Justice for Janitors Campaign:
One Industry, One Union, One Contract

Union organizer Ana Navarette often begins her sales pitch in a company's restroom, free from security cameras. After sneaking past guards, she spends hours hiding in a toilet stall until — around midnight — the roar of the vacuum cleaners in the hallway signals that it is time to spring out and launch her appeal to the janitors she is trying to organize.

Los Angeles Times, August 19, 1993

This opening paragraph of a newspaper article about the Justice for Janitors campaign may seem a bit dramatic, but it illustrates one of the biggest spatial barriers to union organizing in the service sector: How do you gain access to workers who are scattered throughout hundreds of private work sites? Once you

235

gain access to workers, how do you convince multiple employers across a local labor market to recognize the union representation of workers when they seemingly have no incentive to do so? Some answers to these questions have been found by the Justice for Janitors campaign being run by the Service Employees' International Union (SEIU). Begun in 1987, Justice for Janitors (J4J) became one of the most celebrated, creative, and effective organizing efforts in years. The campaign is responsible for the fact that the SEIU now represents one in five of the 1 million janitors in the United States.

Hurd and Rouse (1989) write that the idea for the J4J campaign emerged from a labor dispute between the SEIU and Mellon Bank in Pittsburgh. In 1985, Mellon Bank, after having renewed an SEIU contract, replaced its cleaning company with a nonunion contractor. The new contractor refused to honor the Mellon-SEIU contract and offered to hire only forty of the eighty janitors as part-time workers with reduced pay and the elimination of their benefits. Mellon disavowed all responsibility and claimed that the labor dispute was between the contractor and the union. The SEIU called a strike, rallied community support, and used media exposure in its campaign against Mellon. In addition, it filed unfair labor practice charges with the National Labor Relations Board. In 1987, the NLRB ruled that Mellon was a "coemployer" of the janitors. As a result, Mellon reinstated the janitors under the terms of the previously negotiated contract and paid back wages. In 1987, the SEIU began the Justice for Janitors effort based on the knowledge and new tactics gained from the Mellon campaign. The SEIU committed organizing, legal, and corporate research resources for a national campaign to organize janitors who work in commercial building services and began to target specific cities for organizing.

The goal of J4J is to organize all janitorial workers in a single metropolitan area or a "district" through a highly public campaign. J4J mobilizes workers and community groups to organize and participate in large, public actions that put pressure on contractors and owners to recognize the union via card check rather than a union certification election.[15] Once the union is recognized, it bargains over wages and work conditions with multiple employers and creates a standard wage and benefit package for all members within a district. This approach to organizing and representing workers is called "geographical unionism" by Wial (also referred to as "occupational unionism" by Cobble) and recognizes that work site-specific or employer-specific organizing is not feasible for occupations in which only a small percentage of workers in an occupation are employed at any one work site or by any one employer (janitors, waitresses, etc.) — unionized firms will quickly become noncompetitive and lose contracts unless all of the employers in a geographic area abide by the same wage and

Lydia A. Savage

benefit standard. By organizing all workers and negotiating with employers across a local labor market, unionized firms remain competitive.

The most common element of work shared by building-service janitors everywhere is that they work for a contractor, not the building owner. Most janitors are hired by contract firms to work in scattered, multiple work sites, but the contractors in turn have been hired by the building owners. The potential instability of the relationship between contractor and building owner creates an unstable work situation for the janitor. Contractors can be replaced easily by a building owner if they become more expensive as a result of unionization. The union recognizes that even though it negotiates with contractors, the building owners are critical to determining the rate and situation for workers. J4J holds the building owner accountable through direct actions in public space and in some areas — San Francisco, New York, and Chicago — the union also bargains pieces of the contract with building owners.

J4J begins organizing workers by representing them even before the union has gained official recognition by employers as a collective bargaining unit. Unions can organize workers, represent them in disputes, and file unfair labor practices and lawsuits on their behalf — all without a contract (Howley 1990). These activities mobilize workers and pressure employers to recognize the union through card check, thereby avoiding an NLRB election. Union recognition via card check is a key aspect of the campaign because organizing all workers in a district and bargaining with multiple employers led J4J to recognize the mismatch between current labor law and the way the janitorial labor market operates.[16] Recognition via card check results when a contractor agrees to recognize the union as the representative of the workers and bargain with the union because the union has obtained union authorization cards from a majority of workers. Normally, union authorization cards are collected in order to petition the NLRB for an election, but J4J asks contractors to recognize the union without an election.

Direct action and public attention are usually necessary to win recognition via card check because contractors have no real incentive to recognize the union. To successfully pressure contractors to recognize the union, J4J makes the quality of employment a community interest and bridges the gap between the work site and the community. Campaign themes are chosen by J4J to appeal to a broad range of community groups. Problems such as working conditions, the lack of health insurance, racism, and sexism are concerns that can appeal to the community at large. Organizers not only visit people at work but make home visits and involve community groups and churches. In every city, J4J seeks the cooperation of community groups such as churches, environmental groups, immigrant advocacy groups, and coalitions for the working poor. J4J deliberately takes organizing out of the workplace and into the community by making workers' issues community concerns.

J4J translates the strength generated by community support into large turnouts for public actions. J4J challenges the assumption that organizing should take place in private work space by transgressing into public space. Public actions are encouraged as a way to build a community-wide movement with external as well as internal support and develop rank-and-file leadership. J4J creatively uses public space in direct actions and acts of civil disobedience designed to pressure building owners to take responsibility for how their janitorial contractors operate. For example, in Philadelphia the unionized Philadelphia Electric Company (PECO) hired a nonunion contractor, A-to-Z. After establishing that PECO shared responsibility as a coemployer with A-to-Z, janitors began picketing PECO's offices. A-to-Z soon required that workers clean toilet bowls with toothbrushes, which the janitors had to provide themselves. J4J quickly recognized the opportunity to gain public support and janitors picketed while carrying giant toothbrushes to illustrate their plight. Public sympathy and outrage quickly followed the media coverage and A-to-Z recognized the union (Howley 1990).

Despite the common themes that J4J relies on, each local union is encouraged to develop tactics for its particular labor market and bargaining position (Howley 1990). The development of local tactics is important for several reasons. It encourages the emergence of local rank-and-file leadership and mobilizes the workforce. Local tactics also are more responsive to the diversity of workers, the differing levels of strength that unions have, and the range of employers found in any given local labor market. For example, in Atlanta the janitorial workforce is largely black women who work part-time cleaning the offices of companies such as Coca-Cola, CNN, and Georgia Pacific. The SEIU did not have a membership base in Atlanta, so when the J4J organizing effort began in 1987, J4J had to start by immediately organizing nonunion workers. In Los Angeles, however, the SEIU did have a preexisting membership base and began its J4J campaign by consolidating and mobilizing its membership. In the second phase of its campaign, J4J is organizing the nonunion workforce, primarily Latino men and women, who clean buildings for a variety of industries: entertainment, aerospace, hotels, and downtown office towers.

The Fall and Rise of Local 399 in Los Angeles

SEIU Local 399 in Los Angeles is in many ways, a perfect illustration of what happened to many unions in the 1980s. Between 1983 and 1987, union membership plunged 77 percent and by 1987 only fifteen hundred janitors were

Lydia A. Savage

union members (Nazario 1993, 20). Union janitors receiving wage and benefit packages of $12.53 an hour in 1983 had been replaced by 1985 with nonunion janitors earning $3.35 an hour and no benefits (Mines and Avina 1992, 431, 442). The seemingly sudden change in circumstances for the union and its members was caused by several factors.

As discussed earlier, union avoidance became common practice for L.A. janitorial contractors during the 1980s. This was made easier by the rapid increase in office buildings in Los Angeles, which was accompanied by a geographic shift in the focus of the local real-estate market. Real-estate developers created new office markets in L.A.'s suburbs, where medium-sized nonunion contractors controlled the janitorial services market. Over time, nonunion firms from the suburbs began to make inroads into the heavily unionized city market by undercutting union firms.

In the early 1990s, the commercial real-estate market went from boom to bust and rental revenues fell. Building managers and owners were faced with cutting costs when, in reality, many of their costs (financing, taxes, utilities, and insurance) are fixed. As a result, janitorial services became the target of cost cutting even though they account for less than a nickel of every rent dollar (Howley 1990). Waldinger et al. (1997) point out that along with the building boom of the 1980s and the increase in the number of nonunion firms, the actual numbers of janitors doubled to 28,883 between 1980 and 1990 and the type of workers employed changed. In 1970, 33 percent of L.A. janitors were African-Americans and Latino immigrants accounted for only 7 percent. Waldinger et al. contend that as the union lost power and wages fell, African-Americans moved out of the occupation and were replaced with Latino immigrants. In addition, "the new jobs [mainly in nonunion companies] went to Latino immigrants, whose share of employment rose from 28 to 61 percent [between 1980 and 1990] (Waldinger et al. 1997, 38). When the downturn in the office rental market and the growth of nonunion suburban contractors in the city market were combined with an increase in unskilled immigrant labor, the result was what Howley (1990, 64) calls "a triple whammy."

Local 399 stumbled when confronted with this "triple whammy." In 1982, the union agreed to a two-tier wage structure. Local 399 was not alone. Across the country, many labor unions conceded givebacks during the 1980s. Eventually, the master contract that covered the Los Angeles metropolitan area was undermined by Local 399's cutting deals with individual contractors or clusters of contractors in an effort to save union jobs. In addition, organizing nonunion firms was largely unsuccessful. Some union leaders argue that they were not successful because the lengthy NLRB election process favors the contractor rather   239 than the union. Others, however, argue that had the union launched an all-out effort to organize nonunion firms, it could have been successful. Local 399 watched its membership continue to fall until finally, one union leader says, "the union lost control as the workforce moved from a black to a Latino workforce" (Shaffer 1996–97).

In 1987, the SEIU targeted Los Angeles for the J4J campaign. At that point, there was only a 10 percent union density rate countywide in the commercial office janitor market. Jono Shaffer, the first organizer hired in the J4J campaign in Los Angeles, reports that the J4J campaign completely turned union density numbers around so that by 1996 the SEIU represented 90 percent of the janitors who clean L.A.'s office towers. Organizers focused on reaching undocumented workers as well as legal immigrants and only bilingual or monolingual Spanish-speaking organizers were hired.[17]

The goal of organizers is to organize all the janitorial workers in Los Angeles, but they recognize that the size of the city makes it impossible to organize them all at once. Shaffer remembers that the first thing the J4J organizers did was "choose a geography." He explains that "the way we use geography is by breaking up the immensity of community into manageable, logical pieces." The Los Angeles metropolitan area was broken into districts based on existing office markets (e.g., downtown, Century City, Burbank).

After dividing the Los Angeles area into districts, J4J targeted the downtown district, where the union already had a membership base and union density was about 30 percent for building-service janitors. On a national scale, J4J asks workers to identify with a movement, not just sign a union authorization card. On the scale of downtown Los Angeles, Shaffer (1996–97) reports that the union's message to the membership was "downtown was one big office building." At the time there was very strong work site-specific identification. The union argued that the workers had to see "all of downtown as their place, not just their building" before they could identify with a movement. In essence, such a strategy was designed to expand the geographic scale at which workers identified themselves (see Mitchell in this volume for more on the ideological aspects of identity and scale construction).

The first phase of organizing was aided by the ability of the union to mobilize workers who were already union members and could then, in turn, help organize nonunion workers in the building next door. By building on an existing membership base, the union was able to gain momentum fairly quickly and successfully use direct-action tactics such as marches and demonstrations. By 1989, more than 50 percent of the downtown janitors were union members and this gave the union more power when the new master contract was renegotiated.

Lydia A. Savage

In the master agreement that resulted from the 1989 negotiations, organizers and employers created fifteen specific areas that were defined as districts. The union's goal is to achieve union representation in the majority of the total square footage of buildings in each district and then standardize wages and benefits across each of the districts. In order to gain majority representation, J4J can organize nonunion companies to sign the master agreement and/or pressure building owners to sign contracts with union firms. By organizing workers at a nonunion firm, J4J can get an employer to recognize the union and sign the master agreement. When a contractor signs the master, all employees of the firm in all districts are then represented by the union. The other method is to pressure a building owner to cancel a contract with a nonunion firm and sign a contract with a union firm. For example, one Wilshire district building owner opted to cancel a contract with a nonunion firm and sign up with International Service Systems (ISS), a company that J4J organized in 1990. Both methods involve knowing how the contractor and the building owner operate, and this often varies by district.

Shaffer observes that each district has different characteristics because of the industry. For example, the entertainment industry is located in Century City and the aerospace industry is in the South Bay. The union has to figure out how the employment situations work in such different markets and how that matters to its organizing effort. Types of cleaning vary by industry and affect work routines, schedules, and standards. Client-contractor relationships also vary — the aerospace industry handles contractors through purchasing departments while entertainment offices usually rely on a building management company. In addition, districts differ by how many contractors are present. The downtown district has a number of contractors hiring janitors, whereas most of the janitors in Century Center (250 out of 400) worked for one company, ISS. As a result, if the SEIU could get ISS to recognize the union, it would have control of most of the district.

Districts also have different reactions to the public actions used by J4J. In 1989, J4J began organizing the district of Century City — home to many entertainment companies and very different from downtown L.A. Eventually, on May 29, 1990, the janitors went on strike and mounted a series of daily public actions, which included marching through every building in Century Center. The union won the fight in Century City in 1990 but not before there was a dramatic conflict on June 15 between workers and community members, including children, who were marching in a public demonstration and the L.A. Police Department (LAPD). In full view of the media, "the cops beat them up in a march," remembers Shaffer (1996–97) (the LAPD later settled a lawsuit filed by the union).[18] Century City proved to be a district where the union could quickly provoke a reaction and gain attention. Shaffer speculates that the downtown district is an area where "urban life concentrates" and outlandish behavior such as blocking streets and massive protests are annoying but not shocking to most people. In Century City, on the other hand, "a much smaller thing drew much bigger reaction.... Five people at a building would get five police cars, but two hundred people marching through downtown would get a traffic cop" (ibid.).

Within each district, J4J organizers targeted individual contractors and tried to get management to agree to abide by the prevailing wage and benefit standards in that district if enough workers signed union authorization cards. As Shaffer explains, organizers called the company and said "we can do it easy or we can do it hard" (ibid.). Easy is when a company decides to avoid a confrontational organizing campaign and gives the union the names and addresses of employees, grants the union access to the workplace, and remains neutral. Hard is when the company decides to fight an organizing effort and the union proceeds to organize workers, hold public actions, represent workers in unfair labor practices, and wage a corporate campaign that is targeted at the contractor and the building owner. As one observer noted, "They pick a target and beat them into submission by whatever methods are necessary" (Nazario 1993, 20). In one case, organizers contacted a company that agreed to cooperate without having to be pressured publicly after learning that it was being targeted as part of the J4J campaign.

J4J works with community organizations and community leaders to strengthen the organizing effort by connecting work to the workforce's community. The union's message in the community is that J4J is about "social justice in our community for these workers. They are us and we are them." The union's biggest challenge, according to Shaffer (1996–97), is to "engage with community and political work that advances economic and social justice" and to contribute to the community so that it is not a "one-way street of solidarity." Mobilizing workers and community members to participate in public demonstrations is made much easier by the union's effort to connect the workplace to the community. Organizing the workers themselves also takes place at the work site, in the community, and at workers' homes — again transgressing ideological spatial boundaries separating private home space from public work space.

Contact with workers initially begins at the work site, but organizers quickly turn to home visits and one-on-one contact with workers. The logistics of maneuvering through a sprawling city like Los Angeles could make home visits unfeasible. Yet despite a long journey to work for most janitors, they are clustered in neighborhoods such as Westlake, Koreatown, and Hollywood, largely as a re-

Lydia A. Savage

sult of residential segregation. Shaffer recalls that organizers contacted a janitor at work and he gave them his home address. Upon arriving at his apartment building to visit him, organizers discovered that about fifteen other janitors lived in the same building. Not surprisingly, personal networks are often responsible for job and housing information and can become powerful tools for organizers in the J4J campaign.

Shaffer acknowledges that organizing workers and community members is facilitated by a shared identity in two respects: most workers share an occupational identity as janitor and an ethnic or cultural identity as a member of the Latino community. In addition, he observes that the direct actions favored by the J4J campaign work much better and more quickly with the Latino workforce. To some extent, he thinks that this was related to their previous union experience, but he also speculates that there is a higher level of class consciousness among the Latino community and thus the union was able to use a "heavier working-class message that resonated with the community" (Shaffer 1996–97). Others agree that the Latino immigrant community had a much higher level of class consciousness than did other workers (Waldinger et al. 1997). The issue of identity, however, needs to be more fully explored in order to understand its relationship to organizing. Does identity matter in Los Angeles because it connected workers politically or because it made contacting workers easier as they all lived in the same neighborhoods? It should also be noted that the term *Latino* covers a wide range of cultural groups and is not a referent to a homogeneous group of people. Thus, it is important to assess the differences within the Latino community. Laura Pulido (1996), who has explored the differences within the Latino community of workers, contends that although there are varying degrees of class consciousness within the larger Latino community, Central Americans generally are more politicized than are Mexican immigrants. She speculates that the higher level of class consciousness found among Central Americans is often a result of their experiences in their country of origin.

Although the Latino workforce in Los Angeles responded more quickly to the public actions used by J4J than did other groups, direct actions have been successful with a variety of workforces ranging from Polish workers in Chicago to African-Americans in Atlanta. Shaffer (1996–97) argues that the actions work with any group, but one has to know one's workers because "it takes different approaches to move a workforce." J4J has also helped train other unions in the Los Angeles area to adopt direct actions.

As successful as J4J has been in organizing the workforce around a shared identity as Latinos, Shaffer cautions that the union must struggle to balance the workers' identification as janitors with their racial or ethnic identity because the   243 workforce is going to change. The union was unable to deal effectively with the change from a U.S.-born black workforce to a Latino workforce without experiencing a loss in membership and power. While recognizing that the racial and ethnic identity of the workforce is important and not coincidental, Shaffer argues that unions should not "identify too strongly with one identity" or they risk "failing to deal effectively, incorporate, and grow with the new workforce" (ibid.). In the same way that U.S.-born black workers were replaced with Latinos, the industry will strategically target a new workforce to exploit. Even while keeping an eye toward the future, the union continues to build the movement and plans to continually organize so that new workers replacing old workers keep the union alive.

Conclusion

In 1995, J4J mounted its most aggressive organizing effort in Los Angeles. The union broke Los Angeles into regions with teams organizing in each region. Direct-action tactics were used with public demonstrations and acts of civil disobedience ended with well-publicized arrests. The contract the union won was worth the effort: wages and benefits will become standardized throughout Los Angeles county by the year 2000 for building-service janitors. In order to maintain its gains, J4J cannot stop organizing. To stay strong, it must remain a campaign that organizes rather than a union that services its members.

The success of the J4J campaign has often been credited to the grassroots efforts of rank-and-file workers and community members; J4J is very much a model of bottom-up organizing rather than the "traditional" top-down model. Waldinger et al. (1997) point out, however, that the campaign has had one important top-down component: financial resources. J4J is a labor- and time-intensive campaign and requires a large commitment of money and personnel by the national headquarters of the SEIU. The SEIU has also committed research resources so that local campaigns have information on building owners, contractors, and their relationships and corporate structures.

As a national campaign, J4J challenges the geographic assumptions of "traditional" organizing models in several ways. The campaign challenges the notions that only workers in one specific work site should be organized (J4J targets workers across a local labor market) and that union organizing campaigns must end in a union certification election (it seeks to gain recognition via card check). To gain card-check recognition and build an active, strong union, J4J challenges the narrow focus on the work site and workplace issues of "traditional" models by taking the organizing into the wider community. Finally, J4J challenges the long-held belief that women, workers of color, and immigrants are "unorganizable."

244

As a local campaign, specific tactics devised by the J4J campaign may not readily transfer to other organizing campaigns — they sometimes do not even transfer from one part of a city to another. The attention that J4J pays to the local geographies of a city such as Los Angeles results in a variety of approaches and demonstrates that an aspatial analysis of labor unions and organizing strategies cannot fully explain their successes and failures. In fact, it is only by being aware of the spatial context in which women and men live and work that labor unions can successfully organize a changing workforce. Labor union activists must not only be aware of events in the larger political economy in which they operate but must also be attuned to the social relations that are created in place and, in turn, create place. The meaning of work, gender, identity, skill, community, and family varies over time and place, and to be successful unions must recognize and organize around these spatial differences.

Although geography as a discipline has been relatively silent about the role of workers and their institutions in creating and transforming geographic landscapes, it has much to contribute to a more complete study of labor activism. Current debates in the labor movement focus on the effects of economic restructuring on employment patterns, labor market changes, and the possibilities for change. Geographers are particularly well positioned to contribute to the labor movement's understanding of how large-scale processes are articulating at a local level and how the local spatial context affects efforts to resist or challenge certain aspects of economic change. A more fully developed understanding of the geography of labor needs to emerge if we are to understand current economic restructuring and the possibilities for progressive change.

Notes

I would like to thank Andrew Herod, Jono Shaffer, and an anonymous reviewer for their comments.

1. Only two men have been officially elected president since the merger of the AFL and the CIO in 1955: George Meaney and Lane Kirkland. When it became clear that Kirkland could not win the 1995 election, he stepped down two months before the convention, allowing his vice president, Thomas Donahue, to be named president and to run against John Sweeney as the incumbent.

2. The day after Sweeney's election, the executive board of the AFL–CIO was expanded from thirty-three to fifty-one seats. Twenty-nine members of the thirty-three-member council had been white men. The new board includes six women, nine African-Americans, one Latino, and one Asian-American.

3. Even while acknowledging differences between the service sector and the manufacturing sector, I recognize the inherent danger of defining these sec-

tors too rigidly. Some industries share many of the same characteristics regardless of their sector (or SIC code), and many of the innovative strategies emerging from service-sector organizing drives would work in manufacturing. Nevertheless, there are significant differences between organizing service-sector workers and manufacturing workers. More important, it is with respect to perceived sectoral differences that organizing is being discussed within the labor movement.

4. Examples of concession bargaining include wage and pension freezes or reductions, increased employee contributions to health and welfare benefits, loss of paid holidays, and the elimination of cost-of-living increases. Two-tiered wage systems are also an example of concession bargaining but affect future employees who are hired at a reduced wage.

5. Current estimates are that only 5 percent of union budgets are dedicated to funding organizing efforts, but the SEIU, under John Sweeney's leadership, allocated about 25 percent of its budget to organizing (Waldinger et al. 1997). Since Sweeney's election to the AFL–CIO presidency, organizing has been a focus of the new leadership. The centerpiece of this focus is the newly established AFL–CIO Organizing Department with a $30 million budget. In addition, new programs have been created such as the 1996 "Union Summer," which was aimed at involving young people in the labor movement, and the new "Union Cities," which is designed to transform Central Labor Councils into local organizing centers. It is important to note, however, that the AFL–CIO has no real authority to organize — organizing is the responsibility of the individual unions that make up the AFL–CIO. Nevertheless, it can play an important leadership role in organizing efforts and providing incentives. For example, as a way to encourage local unions to organize, it created the "Changing to Organize" program, which rewards unions that shift 30 percent of local resources away from servicing current union members to organizing new members. Central Labor Councils will receive staff support and resources as part of the "Union Cities" program if half of their locals adopt the "Changing to Organize" program.

6. Increasingly, both academic and activist commentators have come to argue that unions need to reach out and organize groups of workers that have traditionally been ignored and/or excluded by unions — especially women and minorities — particularly since such workers are making up an ever larger proportion of the U.S. working class (see Cobble 1991b, 1993; Crain 1991; Eaton 1992; Lerner 1996; Macdonald and Sirianni 1996; Savage 1996; Wial 1993; Berman in this volume). The new leadership of the AFL–CIO has made organizing these "new workers" a focus of its efforts, as demonstrated by both its financial commitment to organizing programs and its efforts to diversify union

Lydia A. Savage

leadership, beginning with the election of Linda Chavez-Thompson as executive vice president and the expansion of the executive board.

7. Not only did Reagan fire the air-traffic controllers for going on strike but he took the unprecedented, and some would say punitive, step of banning them from working as air-traffic controllers for the rest of their careers.

8. The National Labor Relations Board is made up of presidential appointees and oversees the designation of bargaining units, union certification elections, unfair labor practice complaints, and so on.

9. Current labor law is not comprehensive in terms of being standardized and uniform across space. Federal labor law is the basic framework but states, counties, and cities are allowed to pass their own labor laws within the federal framework. As a result, laws regarding aspects of unionism such as closed and open union shops and prevailing wages are highly variable geographically. The public-sector workforce, in particular, is subject to state and local regulation.

10. "Geographic unionism" is the approach favored by the Justice for Janitors campaign.

11. The process of union organizing generally follows several basic steps. Union organizers first contact workers and collect signed "union cards" in support of unionization. Once a sufficient number of cards have been gathered (usually from 30 percent of the workers), the union can request a certification election from the National Labor Relations Board or, in the case of public-sector workers, a state labor board. A union certification election is then held in which the union must receive 51 percent of the vote in order to be recognized. Although this is the basic framework of organizing, many things can slow down the process considerably, such as disagreements over which workers are included in the bargaining unit or the presence of more than one union.

12. This represents a dramatic change in focus for U.S. unions, which, unlike their European counterparts, have traditionally emphasized workplace issues in isolation from broader community issues (see Jonas in this volume). Labor-community coalitions are not without precedent in the United States, however. The 1930s were a time of community-led and community-based unionism. Labor historians have argued that it is only after the enforcement of the 1935 Wagner Act, granting workers the right to organize, that unions and capital formalized labor relations at a national level and placed them firmly in the public arena. The separation of unionism from the private arena devalued community-based participation in general and marginalized the role of women in particular (Cohen 1990; Faue 1991a, 1991b).

13. In a larger study, I examine these three specific issues through a comparative case study of two organizing drives of clerical and technical workers at   **247**

Harvard University and the University of Massachusetts Medical Center. Both campaigns involved female-dominated workforces and union organizers were predominantly female (Savage 1996).

14. In 1997, a group of physicians employed by a health maintenance organization (HMO) in Tucson, Arizona, voted 93 to 32 to join a union. The doctors argued that the HMO had effectively eliminated their control of the work process by imposing gag orders, increasing patient loads, and restricting diagnosis, referral, and treatment options. Some physicians in the public sector are unionized, but this union is thought to be the first formed by doctors at a for-profit managed-care company (Adelson 1997).

15. An employer can voluntarily opt to recognize a union based on the number of union authorization cards collected by organizers. Employers do not have to agree to card check recognition, however, which obliges the union then to petition the NLRB for a certification election. Card-check recognition is much quicker and less expensive for unions because elections can be delayed through challenges by employers to the NLRB. Not surprisingly, most employers will not recognize a union via card check.

16. As discussed earlier, labor law is generally considered to be work site-specific and NLRB elections are not suitable for the employment relations shared by most building-service janitors. Howley (1990) explains that a contractor may have a thousand employees in fifty work sites scattered throughout a city working under different arrangements—a hundred employees at one site and "route jobs" where employees go from one small account's site to another. The NLRB could define a bargaining unit as a single account, a group of accounts, or the whole operation. A union could begin to organize all the workers only to have an employer challenge the composition of the bargaining unit. In addition, even if an NLRB election is held and won by the union—a lengthy process under the best of circumstances—the contractor can simply walk away and set up new companies that are not legally bound to honor the election results. Wial (1993), in fact, argues that petitioning for an NLRB election would create almost insurmountable delays for the union as challenges over the appropriate bargaining unit would be raised. In addition, it is doubtful that the NLRB would support "geographical unionism" and would probably support work site- or employer-specific units, which would weaken the union's ability to standardize working conditions across a local labor market.

17. Janitorial work is one of the "safer" forms of work for illegal immigrants as janitors typically work in small groups in buildings scattered throughout the city. Immigration and Naturalization Service (INS) raids usually target larger groups of workers found in more centralized workplaces such as factories.

Lydia A. Savage

18. One pregnant woman was beaten so badly that she later suffered a miscarriage.

Bibliography

Adelson, A. 1997. "Physician, Unionize Thyself." *New York Times*, April 5, 27–28.

Bluestone, B., and B. Harrison. 1982. *The Deindustrialization of America.* New York: Basic Books.

Bozzotto, D. 1989. The Shifting Gears Conference on The Changing Meaning of Work in Massachusetts. Videotape available from the Massachusetts Foundation for the Humanities and Public Policy.

Braverman, H. 1974. *Labor and Monopoly Capital: The Degradation of Work in the Twentieth Century.* New York: Monthly Review Press.

Bronfenbrenner, K. L. 1993. "Seeds of Resurgence: Successful Union Strategies for Winning Certification Elections and First Contracts in the 1980's and Beyond." Ph.D. diss., Cornell University.

———. 1994. "Employer Behavior in Certification Elections and First-Contract Campaigns: Implications for Labor Law Reform." In *Restoring the Promise of American Labor Law,* edited by S. Friedman, R. W. Hurd, R. A. Oswald, and R. L. Seeber, 75–89. Ithaca, N.Y.: ILR Press.

Chaison, G., and J. Rose. 1990. "Continental Divide: The Direction and Fate of North American Unions." In *Advances in Industrial and Labor Relations,* edited by D. Lewin, D. Lipsky, and D. Sockwell, 169–205. Greenwich, Conn.: JAI Press.

———. 1991. "The Macrodeterminants of Union Growth and Decline." In *The State of the Unions,* edited by G. Strauss, D. Gallagher, and J. Fiorito, 3–45. Madison, Wis.: Industrial Relations Research Association Series.

Christopherson, S. 1989. "Flexibility in the U.S. Service Economy and the Emerging Spatial Division of Labour." *Transactions of the Institute of British Geographers,* n.s., 14: 131–43.

Cobble, D. S. 1991a. *Dishing It Out: Waitresses and Their Unions in the Twentieth Century.* Urbana: University of Illinois Press.

———. 1991b. "Organizing the Postindustrial Work Force: Lessons from the History of Waitress Unionism." *Industrial and Labor Relations Review* 44 (April): 419–36.

———. 1994. "Making Postindustrial Unionism Possible." In *Restoring the Promise of American Labor Law,* edited by S. Friedman, R. W. Hurd, R. A. Oswald, and R. L. Seeber, 285–302. Ithaca, N.Y.: ILR Press.

———, ed. 1993. *Women and Unions: Forging a Partnership.* Ithaca, N.Y.: ILR Press.

Cohen, L. 1990. *Making a New Deal: Industrial Workers in Chicago, 1919–1939.* Cambridge: Cambridge University Press.

Crain, M. 1991. "Feminizing Unions: Challenging the Gendered Structure of Wage Labor." *Michigan Law Review* 89: 1155–1221.

Daniels, P. W., and N. Thrift. 1987. *The Geographies of the U.K. Service Sector: A Survey.* Working Paper on Producer Services, no. 6. Department of Geography, Portsmouth Polytechnic and University of Bristol.

Eaton, S. C. 1992. *Women Workers, Unions and Industrial Sectors in North America.* Geneva: International Labour Organisation.

Farber, H. S. 1985. "The Extent of Unionization in the United States." In *Challenges and Choices Facing American Labor,* edited by T. A. Kochan, 15–43. Cambridge: MIT Press.

Faue, E. 1991a. *Community of Suffering and Struggle.* Chapel Hill: University of North Carolina Press.

———. 1991b. "Paths of Unionization: Community, Bureaucracy, and Gender in the Minneapolis Labor Movement of the 1930's." In *Work Engendered: Toward a New History of American Labor,* edited by A. Baron, 296–319. Ithaca, N.Y.: Cornell University Press.

Fiorito, J., and C. L. Maranto. 1987. "The Contemporary Decline of Union Strength." *Contemporary Policy Issues* 5: 12–27.

Green, J., and C. Tilly. 1987. "Service Unionism: Directions for Organizing." *Labor Law Journal* 38 (August): 486–95.

Harrison, B., and B. Bluestone. 1988. *The Great U-Turn.* New York: Basic Books.

Herod, A. 1994. "Further Reflections on Organized Labor and Deindustrialization in the United States." *Antipode* 26: 77–95.

Howley, J. 1990. "Justice for Janitors: The Challenge of Organizing in Contract Services." *Labor Research Review* 15: 61–72.

Hurd, R., and W. Rouse. 1989. "Progressive Union Organizing: The SEIU Justice for Janitors Campaign." *Review of Radical Political Economics* 21: 70–75.

Lerner, S. 1996. "Reviving Unions." *Boston Review* (April–May): 3–8.

Macdonald, C. L., and C. Sirianni. 1996. *Working in the Service Economy.* Philadelphia: Temple University Press.

Marshall, N., and P. Wood. 1995. *Services and Space: Key Aspects of Urban and Regional Development.* Essex, England: Longman Scientific and Technical.

Martin, R., P. Sunley, and J. Wills. 1994. "Unions and the Politics of Deindustrialization: Some Comments on How Geography Complicates Class Analysis." *Antipode* 26: 59–76.

250

Lydia A. Savage

Massey, D. 1993. "Power Geometry and a Progressive Sense of Place." In *Mapping the Futures: Local Cultures, Global Change*, edited by J. Bird et al., 59–69. New York: Routledge.

Mines, R., and J. Avina. 1992. "Immigrants and Labor Standards: The Case of California Janitors." In *U.S.-Mexico Relations: Labor Market Independence*, edited by J. Bustamante, C. Reynolds, and R. Hinojosa Ojeda, 429–48. Stanford, Calif.: Stanford University Press.

Mitchell, D. 1989. "Will Collective Bargaining Outcomes in the 1990s Look like Those of the 1980s?" In *Proceedings of the Spring Meeting of the Industrial Relations Research Association*, edited by Barbara Dennis, 490–96. Madison, Wis.: Industrial Relations Research Association Series.

Moody, K. 1988. *An Injury to All: The Decline of American Unionism*. London: Verso.

Nazario, S. 1993. "For This Union, It's War." *Los Angeles Times*, August 19, 1993, I.

Nelson, K. 1986. "Labor Demand, Labor Supply and the Suburbanization of Low-Wage Office Work." In *Production, Work and Territory*, edited by A. Scott and M. Storper, 149–71. Winchester, Mass.: Allen and Unwin.

Piore, M. 1991. "The Future of Unions." In *The State of the Union*, edited by G. Strauss, D. Gallagher, and J. Fiorito, 387–410. Madison, Wis.: Industrial Relations Research Association Series.

Pulido, L. 1996. "The Creation of 'Whiteness' in Oppositional Struggles." Unpublished paper presented at the American Association of Geographers Annual Meeting, April, Charlotte, North Carolina.

Rogers, J. 1994. "Reforming U.S. Labor Relations." In *Restoring the Promise of American Labor Law*, edited by S. Friedman, R. W. Hurd, R. A. Oswald, and R. L. Seeber, 15–28. Ithaca, N.Y.: ILR Press.

Rose, J. B., and G. Chaison. 1996. "Linking Union Density and Union Effectiveness: The North American Experience." *Industrial Relations* 35.1: 78–105.

Sassen, S. 1994. *Cities in a World Economy*. Thousand Oaks, Calif.: Pine Forge Press.

Savage, L. 1996. "Negotiating Common Ground: Labor Unions and the Geography of Organizing Women Workers in the Service Sector." Ph.D. diss., Clark University.

Sayer, A., and R. Walker. 1992. *The New Social Economy: Reworking the Division of Labor*. Cambridge, Mass.: Blackwell Publishers.

Shaffer, J. 1996–97. Organizing Coordinator, Service Employees' International Union. Telephone interview by the author, August 21, 1996, and March 15, 1997.

251

Geographies of Organizing

Spain, D. 1992. *Gendered Spaces.* Chapel Hill: University of North Carolina Press.

Storper, M., and R. Walker. 1989. *The Capitalist Imperative: Territory, Technology, and Industrial Growth.* Cambridge, Mass.: Basil Blackwell.

U.S. Bureau of the Census. 1965. *County Business Patterns, United States.* Washington, D.C.: U.S. Government Printing Office.

————. 1990. *County Business Patterns, United States.* Washington, D.C.: U.S. Government Printing Office.

Voos, P. 1984. "Trends in Union Organizing Expenditures, 1953–1977." *Industrial and Labor Relations Review* 38.1: 52–63.

Waldinger, R., C. Erickson, R. Milkman, D. J. B. Mitchell, A. Valenzuela, K. Wong, and M. Zeitlin. 1997. "Justice for Janitors." *Dissent* 44.1 (winter): 37–44.

Wial, H. 1993. "The Emerging Organizational Structure of Unionism in Low-Wage Services." *Rutgers Law Review* 45: 671–738.

————. 1994. "New Bargaining Structures for New Forms of Business Organization." In *Restoring the Promise of American Labor Law,* edited by S. Friedman, R. W. Hurd, R. A. Oswald, and R. L. Seeber, 303–13. Ithaca, N.Y.: ILR Press.

252

Lydia A. Savage

Part IV

Labor Unions and the Making of Economic Geographies

Andrew Herod

Economic geographers historically have not paid much attention to the activities of labor unions, despite the fact that unions can play significant roles in shaping economic geographies, both passively and actively. Whether it is in terms of how organizing in particular places can affect local labor markets and living conditions, or how unions' strength in certain regions may encourage capital to relocate elsewhere (as in the Snowbelt–Sunbelt shift familiar to students of postwar U.S. economic history and geography; see Peet 1983), or through unions' efforts to actively shape social and spatial economic relations in particular ways, unions can be powerful molders of the economic geographies of particular localities, regions, nations, and even (as we saw in part IV) of the international space-economy (Herod 1997). The impact of unions' activities on local and regional economic geographies is the theme of part 4. The essays address such issues as how unions' different geographies of organization can set the environment for capital's subsequent actions, how through their activities unions can fundamentally restructure the geography of local labor markets, and how unions can draw on the local resources of place to shape the space-economy in ways they perceive to be advantageous.

Brian Page's essay concerns the historical and spatial evolution of the meatpacking industry in the Midwest and shows how understanding the geography of unionism in the industry is crucial to understanding its spatial evolution. The industry underwent a dramatic geographic reorganization in the 1950s as many of the great slaughterhouses in Chicago, Saint Louis, Omaha, Kansas City, and elsewhere were closed down and production shifted to smaller towns in the livestock-producing areas of the Great Plains. Traditionally, analysts of the industry have drawn on the ideas of Alfred Weber (1929) to explain this geographic reorganization. Weber argued that industries that are weight- or bulk-gaining tend to locate near to their final customers, whereas those that are weight- or bulk-losing tend to locate closer to the sources of their raw materials. This way, industries can reduce their production costs by not having to transport materi-

255

---

als unnecessarily. Although in the case of the meatpacking industry approximately a third of the weight of livestock is dropped during the slaughter and processing phase, traditionally firms had been forced to locate in large cities in order to be close to their labor supply. With new labor-saving and transportation technologies that became available during the immediate postwar period, however, combined with the building of the Eisenhower interstate highway system, both the need to be close to the major urban areas and relative distances between the agricultural regions of the Great Plains and the packers' major urban customer bases were dramatically reduced in the 1940s and 1950s. As a result — so the Weberian argument goes — firms were able to decentralize and locate slaughtering operations closer to their livestock supply. They were able thereby both to reduce transport costs and to avoid organized labor in the plants of Chicago and elsewhere.

Such a Weberian cost-minimization explanation is problematic, however, for several reasons, not least of which is that it fails to take into account the role of the geography of unionization in the spatial reorganization of the industry. As Page demonstrates, a distinctive geography of labor organization in the industry has been crucial to shaping the industry's historical development. In the early twentieth century, many packinghouses in the large urban areas were organized by the craft-based Amalgamated Meat Cutters and Butcher Workmen, affiliated with the American Federation of Labor (AFL). The Amalgamated union historically pursued a policy of avoiding direct confrontation with the employers where possible. In the 1930s, however, the rise of the Congress of Industrial Organizations (CIO) brought a more militant industrial-based unionism to the industry as the Packinghouse Workers' Organizing Committee (later the United Packinghouse Workers of America [UPWA]) began to organize plants throughout the Midwest. This set off a period of intense rivalry between the new CIO meatpacking local unions and those of the older Amalgamated Meat Cutters and Butcher Workmen, a rivalry that was reflected in the different geographic strategies pursued by the two unions. Whereas the UPWA sought to organize the large plants of the industry leaders in the traditional urban centers of the industry, the Amalgamated increasingly focused instead on the plants of the smaller independent firms located in the isolated small industrial towns of the Midwest.

This geography of rival unionism played a crucial role in the geographic restructuring of the industry. When the packers attempted to introduce mechanization to their meat-slaughtering and processing operations in the large, urban centers, they were fought by the UPWA. Labor's opposition to technological innovation and work rationalization during the 1950s and 1960s was perceived

Andrew Herod

by the packers as an impediment to competition in the large urban meatpacking centers such as Chicago. As opposition from the UPWA grew, packers increasingly began to relocate to new places where they could avoid the pockets of militant union culture that had emerged in the 1930s and introduce new work practices in areas "uncontaminated" by the UPWA and its brand of radical unionism. By dispersing production facilities throughout the Midwest, often relocating to small towns with no previous experience of meatpacking, the firms sought to drive a geographic wedge between workers that would limit their collective power, particularly that derived from the demonstration effects present in the larger urban areas where union locals were located near each other. Unlike the relocation of Chicago steel producers to Gary, Indiana, earlier in the century (see Gordon 1978), this strategy was not designed to avoid unions altogether, for most of the new plants were in fact organized and tied in with national agreements. Rather, it was designed to avoid the areas where the more militant UPWA had drawn strength, and instead to build up production in those decentralized small towns where the less radical, more accommodationist Amalgamated union dominated. Page shows how traditional explanations of the industry's spatial reorganization that have relied on Weberian principles fall short of the mark. Only by understanding the geography of dual unionism in the industry can its postwar geography of technological innovation and restructuring be understood.

Whereas Page's essay shows how the geography of unionism and the rise of the CIO were crucial to shaping the locational decision making of the meatpackers in the Midwest, Meghan Cope examines how the process of unionization itself impacted work rules and the geography of local labor markets in Lawrence, Massachusetts, during the 1930s and 1940s. As was the case in meatpacking, so too in textiles the creation of the CIO fundamentally transformed the nature of work and labor markets. Historically, work in the mills had been characterized by a reliance on casual labor, piece rates, and a highly stratified ethnic and gendered division of labor. With the coming of the Textile Workers' Union of America in 1937, however, a rapid transformation took place in the ways in which local labor markets operated. Most importantly, the union brought with it a greatly increased regularization of work through the standardization of tasks, hiring processes, and work relations, and a stabilization of employment resulting from the securing of contracts containing provisions for uniform wages, seniority rights, and guaranteed hours. Such regularization was a key union goal as organizers and officials sought to eliminate the casualization of the labor market that had kept workers reliant on the favoritism of particular hiring bosses for their livelihood, a favoritism that the hiring bosses often used to enrich themselves (see Kimeldorf 1988 for an example of how similar hiring practices in casual labor markets bred a system of kickbacks and corruption in the longshoring industry).

What was an ostensibly aspatial union policy designed to encourage regularization of work, however, had significantly different impacts on different groups of workers precisely because of the spatial contexts within which they lived their lives. As Cope shows, the gendered division of labor and spatial realms in Lawrence meant that men and women lived very different social and spatial lives, particularly with regard to the geographic separation of home and paid employment. The social construction of womanhood placed the bulk of domestic responsibilities in the hands of women. Indeed, Barrett (1980) has argued that the geographic separation of home and wage-earning work during the early industrial revolution was necessary for the creation of the nuclear family and the subsequent real subsumption of labor to capital through the spread of the factory system. Nevertheless, many women had often bridged, socially and spatially, the two realms of home and the mills by working sporadically in textiles when domestic responsibilities such as child rearing allowed (cf. Kessler-Harris 1982). In fact, for many women, the casual nature of employment in textiles actually facilitated their ability to combine paid work outside the home with the domestic sphere. For men, on the other hand, the spatial separation of home and work had historically been much more geographically entrenched and so the regularization of work that came with unionization was seen as a way of increasing (male) earning power through the union's ability to negotiate seniority clauses, to eliminate casual work, and to secure higher wages and full-time hours of work. As regularization of work proceeded, Cope argues, the cultural expectation that women's primary social role was that of guardians of the home and raisers of children increasingly confined women both socially and spatially to the domestic arena through the limits placed on their ability to pick up odd work in the mills.

Not only did the union policy of regularization reshape the gendered geographic and social relationships between home and the mills, but it also helped to restructure Lawrence's ethnic geography. By helping to eliminate ethnic favoritism in mill hiring, regularization reduced the hold on particular types of jobs that certain ethnic groups had historically enjoyed. The old ethnic division of labor that had dominated the industry began to erode, helping to produce an increasingly "Americanized" workforce that interacted socially to a much greater extent than previously, a process that in turn led to a gradual breakdown of the spatially defined ethnic neighborhoods that once characterized the residential geography of the city. The breakdown of ethnically defined neighborhoods and

258

the improvement in real wages brought about by more regular work (at least for men) helped to facilitate the growing postwar suburbanization of Lawrence's mill workers by expanding the spatial scale of the local labor market. Workers could now afford to live farther from the mills if they had a regular full-time job to go to every day and higher incomes to help defray the increased costs of commuting longer distances to work (cf. Walker 1981, who argues that the ability of workers to secure increases in real wages was central to the process of suburbanization in the United States). In sum, Cope shows how a policy that was not consciously designed (as far as we know) with any particular spatial goals in mind nevertheless had distinct geographic implications and consequences in the local labor market as a result of the unevenly developed underlying ethnic and gendered geography of Lawrence within which it was implemented.

Andrew E. G. Jonas pursues the influence of local context on union practices by examining how a union campaign to prevent the shutdown of the Stewart-Warner manufacturing plant in Chicago was shaped by the local context within which workers found themselves. Three elements relating to the local context of the dispute were important in shaping the union's political praxis. First, the union involved (the United Electrical Workers) had long had a history of allowing great autonomy to its local unions. Such autonomy, Jonas suggests, was crucial in allowing those officials closest to the situation in Chicago to develop strategies that were sensitive to local conditions, rather than seeking to impose a strategy developed at national headquarters that perhaps reflected national union concerns. Local union officials were free to develop a campaign that could take into account the complexities and subtleties of the local context in which they were working.

Second, the union was able to develop close links with a number of local community groups and thus was able to expand its political base. In contrast to Europe, where the labor movement is often seen as a broad social movement, in the United States unions have tended to be more narrowly focused on workplace issues (Katznelson 1981). In the case of the Stewart-Warner campaign, however, the local union was successfully able to bridge, both politically and geographically, the workplace-neighborhood divide to develop an anticlosure campaign with a considerable social and spatial base that involved many different community groups.

Third, the union was able to exploit the locality dependence of the local state and enlist the help of city of Chicago and state of Illinois officials in the campaign to save the plant. As Cox and Mair (1988) have pointed out, the immobility of certain social actors relative to more spatially mobile capital often makes them especially interested in developing ways to continue local invest- 259 ment in their areas. Mortgage companies, utility companies, and other local service providers all have investments in the local built environment that cannot readily be relocated elsewhere. More particularly, the local state itself, together with the politicians who occupy positions within the local state apparatus, are jurisdictionally tied to certain geographic locations, a fact that makes them particularly dependent on the continued vitality of the local economy as a provider of jobs and as a tax base. Consequently, such actors are frequently prominent participants in coalitions designed to encourage continued investment into their particular locality (Molotch 1976; Humphrey, Erickson, and Ottensmeyer 1989). The union was able to make use of such spatial dependence on the part of city politicians to elicit the help of several powerful groups within the local state, including the mayor's office.

Through a detailed examination of the anticlosure activities surrounding the Stewart-Warner plant, Jonas shows how the union was able to creatively use the resources of place in a campaign that was highly sensitive to the local geography in which workers found themselves. His example highlights what some have come to call the "local-global paradox" or, relatedly, "glocalization," by which is meant that despite the increasing globalization of economic processes and relations, many social actors are adopting responses that are highly sensitive to local conditions. Although this term has often been used to refer to the activities of transnational corporations who are able to play off workers and places against each other on the basis of almost imperceptible economic differences, Jonas's essay shows how it can also appropriately be used to describe the activities of labor unions. As he suggests, the local context and conditions within which political praxis originates may often provide significant resources for challenging forces that operate on regional, national, or even global scales.

In addition to showing how the union articulated a strategy to oppose closure that relied on the particularities of local geography, Jonas illustrates how the union and its community supporters sought to impose a distinctly geographical solution to their problems by quite literally carving out within the local built environment both a space and a scale of opposition to deindustrialization through their effort to have the Stewart-Warner plant included in a Planned Manufacturing District (PMD) in which special tax and other incentives would be available to corporations who invested in it. (Cf. Herod 1991, which examines how the garment workers' union in New York City adopted a similar strategy in response to the conversion of manufacturing lofts to office space by pressuring the local state to implement a special [and spatial] garment preservation district in which office conversions would be limited.) Although the union's approach ultimately was unsuccessful, through such activities workers managed to put forward local economic development plans that challenged the dominant corporate discourses about the need for capital relocation. They were able to show that the company's poor performance was not so much the result of international competition and high business costs in Chicago as it was the outcome of a failure to invest in situ and to modernize production facilities. Clearly, in attempting to manipulate space (in the form of the PMD) as part of their strategy to reshape local economic conditions and, hence, the geography of local capital investment and production, union members saw their ability to refashion the local geography of state regulation over the built environment as an integral part of their political practice and effort to secure their own livelihoods and future social reproduction (cf. Herod 1994).

Bibliography

Barrett, M. 1980. *Women's Oppression Today: Problems in Marxist Feminist Analysis.* London: Verso.

Cox, K., and A. Mair. 1988. "Locality and Community in the Politics of Local Economic Development." *Annals of the Association of American Geographers* 78: 307–25.

Gordon, D. M. 1978. "Capitalist Development and the History of American Cities." In *Marxism and the Metropolis: New Perspectives in Urban Political Economy,* edited by W. K. Tabb and L. Sawers, 25–63. New York: Oxford University Press.

Herod, A. 1991. "From Rag Trade to Real Estate in New York's Garment Center: Remaking the Labor Landscape in a Global City." *Urban Geography* 12.4: 324–38.

———. 1994. "On Workers' Theoretical (In)visibility in the Writing of Critical Urban Geography: A Comradely Critique." *Urban Geography* 15.7: 681–93.

———. 1997. Labor as an Agent of Globalization and as a Global Agent. In *Spaces of Globalization: Reasserting the Power of the Local,* edited by K. Cox, 167–200. New York: Guilford Press.

Humphrey, C. R., R. A. Erickson, and E. J. Ottensmeyer. 1989. "Industrial Development Organizations and the Local Dependence Hypothesis." *Policy Studies Journal* 17: 624–42.

Katznelson, I. 1981. *City Trenches: Urban Politics and the Patterning of Class in the U.S.* New York: Pantheon.

Kessler-Harris, A. 1982. *Out to Work: A History of Wage-Earning Women in the United States.* New York: Oxford University Press.

Kimeldorf, H. 1988. *Reds or Rackets? The Making of Radical and Conservative Unions on the Waterfront.* Los Angeles: University of California Press.

261

Making of Economic Geographies

Molotch, H. 1976. "The City as Growth Machine: Toward a Political Economy of Place." *American Journal of Sociology* 82: 309–32.

Peet, R. 1983. "Relations of Production and the Relocation of United States Manufacturing Industry since 1960." *Economic Geography* 59: 112–43.

Walker, R. A. 1981. "A Theory of Suburbanization: Capitalism and the Construction of Urban Space in the United States." In *Urbanization and Urban Planning in Capitalist Society,* edited by M. Dear and A. Scott, 383–429. New York: Methuen.

Weber, A. 1929. *Theory of the Location of Industries.* Chicago: University of Chicago Press (originally published in German in 1909).

262

Andrew Herod

Chapter 8 • Rival Unionism and the Geography of the Meatpacking Industry

Brian Page

Halstead Street Car

Come you, cartoonists,
Hang on a strap with me here
At seven o'clock in the morning
On a Halstead street car.

Take your pencils
And draw these faces.

Try with your pencils for these crooked faces,
That pig sticker in one corner—his mouth—
That overall factory girl—her loose cheeks.

Find for your pencils
A way to mark your memory
Of tired empty faces.

After their night's sleep,
In the moist dawn
And cool daybreak,
   Faces
Tired of wishes,
Empty of dreams.
                    Carl Sandberg 1946 (1916)

For most of the twentieth century, Chicago—more than any other American city—symbolized brute strength and raw productive power; and more than any other arena of work and industry, meatpacking symbolized Chicago. These themes were immortalized eight decades ago by Carl Sandberg, whose poem "Chicago" presented the city as "a bolder, more magnetic, more titanic force than the 'soft little cities' of the nation." When the collection *Chicago Poems* was published in   263

1916, it was this "he-man slugging" poem that garnered most of the attention.[1] It rattled the cages of established American literature, to be sure, but more importantly it projected a proud and defiant identity that Chicagoans and outsiders alike embraced wholeheartedly. Yet, published alongside "Chicago" were more than a hundred other poems, including "Halstead Street Car," which represent the working city in very different ways. Here, Sandberg's unflinching eye and keen ear uncover a city of great human depth and reveal the enormous personal cost of Chicago's success. The composite is a city of stark and brutal contradictions: at once triumphant "hog butcher for the world" and home to the weary, hopeless "pig sticker."

It should come as no surprise, then, that the emblematic industry of the city most closely associated with the accomplishments of labor was the site of some of the worst working conditions in the history of American manufacturing. Chicago's great slaughterhouses sucked in animals and spewed out meat and offal at a scale never before imagined. Inside, packinghouse workers encountered uncertain hours, low wages, arduous labor, dangerous working conditions, and the arbitrary exercise of management power on the shop floor. Under these circumstances, the spark of unionism was certain to appear. The AFL-chartered Amalgamated Meat Cutters and Butcher Workmen led major organizing drives in 1904, 1919, and 1933, but each time these efforts were crushed by the packing firms.[2] Finally, during the late 1930s and the 1940s, the industry was organized, but only under the umbrella of state guarantees that thwarted packer resistance. Although New Deal labor legislation allowed workers unprecedented freedom and opportunity to organize, however, it was not the established Amalgamated that took advantage of the new institutional environment. Instead, it was the newly formed and upstart Packinghouse Workers' Organizing Committee (PWOC) of the CIO that successfully organized the industry's labor force — giving rise to a situation of rival unionism that would last well beyond the AFL–CIO merger of 1955.

It is one of the sad ironies of history that meatpacking workers in Chicago would enjoy the fruits of their victory for only a few years. After waging a fifty-year fight for unionization, the power of organized labor in the city's packing plants was finally consolidated during the late 1940s. Soon after they had organized the plants, employment in meatpacking began to contract and plants began to close. By 1960, all of Chicago 's great slaughterhouses stood silent and tens of thousands had lost their jobs, part of a pervasive geographic reorganization of the industry in which plants were relocated from Chicago and other urban packing centers to small cities and towns in livestock-producing areas. In explaining this reorganization, students of industrial development — without

264

Brian Page

exception — have attributed this process of decentralization to classic Weberian dynamics (Weber 1929): the development of truck transport and all-weather roads is held to have allowed significant cost advantages to packers located nearer to livestock supply — given the fact that meatpacking is a weight-losing activity in which a third of the weight of livestock is dropped during slaughter (e.g., Brody 1964; Aududdell and Cain 1973; Williams 1979; Skaggs 1986). In this view, transport-induced shifts in factor costs after 1950 led directly to the closing of rail-based plants in the urban packing centers.

This kind of cost-minimization approach to industrial location has many problems, however.[3] Chief among them is the failure to adequately conceptualize the role of labor. In such explanations of industrial and geographic restructuring, labor is treated as just another factor of production that influences locational decisions, invariably as a result of spatial gradients in its price, with little consideration given to differences within or between groups of workers and no consideration given to the actions of workers themselves or of their organizations. Weberian interpretations have been contested by new approaches to industrial geography that replace the traditional focus on allocative market functions with an emphasis on the propulsive force of capitalist production (Harvey 1982; Massey 1984; Scott and Storper 1986; Storper and Walker 1989). This "new industrial geography" contains a greatly enriched view of the role of labor and highlights significant differences between place-specific labor forces in terms of age, gender, skill, levels of organization, conditions of reproduction, and so on. Yet, even here, workers too often remain on the outside looking in at industrial changes driven by technological dynamism, shifting state policy and competition among firms.

In this essay, I want to challenge such conceptualizations of labor within the economic geography literature by revisiting the restructuring of meatpacking in the postwar era from the point of view of workers. I contend that workers in the slaughterhouses were not simply passive recipients of a process of industrial change initiated and carried out by firms. Instead, their actions — particularly their efforts at unionization and the evolution of distinctive practices within their unions — actively shaped the geography of production. In making such a claim, let me be clear from the outset that I do not intend to replace a reductionism based on transport costs with one based on labor. On the contrary, by raising the question of labor I am attempting to enrich the interpretation of industrial restructuring, not to simplify it. The story of restructuring in meatpacking is a complicated one involving the interplay of meatpacking firms, workers, communities, and the state in an environment of technological dynamism, organizational upheaval, and intensified competition occurring within and be-

Rival Unionism

tween various stages of the broader meat production-consumption chain (Page 1993). This story is made all the more complicated by the existence in the industry of rival unionism. Labor organization in meatpacking pitted not only company against union, but also union against union. This is not a case in which workers unite and shape the progress of industry through a clear collective voice. Rather, it is a case in which rupture and competition within the union movement play the key roles. In what follows, I discuss the evolution of rival unionism in meatpacking and then go on to assess the impacts of workers' organizing activities on the structure and geography of the industry.

The Problematic Course of Unionism in Meatpacking

The Amalgamated was chartered by the AFL in 1897 and given the enormous task of organizing the nation's meatpacking plants. The new union was up against a group of mostly Chicago-based firms known collectively as the "Big Five" or the "Beef Trust" — one of America's first and most powerful industrial oligopolies.[4] During the 1880s and 1890s, these firms came to dominate the meatpacking industry through a series of related innovations. The first of these was the advent of refrigerated rail transport, a response to the severe problems of circulation in the fresh meat business associated with perishability. Because beef was sold mainly as fresh meat, beef packing was a small-scale and highly localized industry up to this point. But the refrigerated boxcar changed this structure. It unlocked the potential of cattle slaughter for Chicago meat packers by allowing them to sell fresh beef in distant markets. The second innovation, which evolved simultaneously, was the creation of a new product, fresh or "dressed" beef in the form of half-beef carcasses. The third change was the development of a national branch house system, which allowed Chicago packers to distribute both fresh and processed meat products throughout the country. The fourth innovation concerned the development of new production facilities and new work practices. As sales of dressed beef and processed pork skyrocketed in the late 1880s and 1890s, the Big Five built enormous new plants that slaughtered cattle, hogs, and sheep and made more efficient use of by-products. Inside these plants, gravity was put to work and mechanical systems were expanded beyond conveyance to include aspects of disassembly such as scalding and de-hairing (Clemen 1923).[5] Finally, a fifth innovation involved changes in management structure that evolved in an environment of rapid expansion in both production and markets.[6]

On the basis of these innovations in product, process, and marketing, the Big Five put an ironclad grip on the industry that would last for fifty years.[7] Capital requirements in the industry escalated as a result of the increasing scale

Brian Page

of operations. Barriers to entry rose steeply and, at virtually the same time, conditions of economic crisis drove many smaller packing firms out of business (Yeager 1981). The Big Five dominated their competition but also controlled wider relations within the overall meat-producing commodity chain. On one end, they purchased livestock in the stockyards from thousands of widely scattered, mostly small-scale farmers and ranchers via a network of commission agents. The Big Five effectively controlled the infrastructure of livestock marketing through their ownership of stockyards, exchange buildings, and terminal railroads and also attempted to control input costs through the manipulation of pricing information. On the other end, they sold their products to small-scale neighborhood-based retailers through a centralized distribution system. These packers controlled meat distribution through their ownership of meat storage facilities, transport equipment, and retail outlets and colluded to set meat prices through the use of marketing pools and joint ventures (Yeager 1981).

The geography of meat production that emerged at this time consisted of urban manufacturing centers set within an extensive farming landscape — a spatial division of labor in which rural agrarian production and capitalist factory production were fundamentally intertwined. Chicago became the unquestioned center of the industry, but growth peripheries of the Big Five were established in Saint Louis, Omaha, Kansas City, Saint Joseph, Sioux City, and elsewhere. The urban location of meatpacking was not, however, solely a product of a transportation system that funneled livestock into centralized stockyards. Rather, it was also linked to the industry's distinctive labor requirements, which in turn derived from the fact that the industry's material input was a biological product of a land-based agricultural system.

An agricultural integument governed labor requirements in two ways. First, because of the tenacity of biological architecture, meatpacking was difficult to mechanize and thus extremely labor-intensive. Impressive advancements in the mechanization of killing and disassembling animals had been made by Cincinnati packers in the 1830s, and Chicago packers later extended and refined these techniques. Although mechanization proceeded in a way that maximized the ability to handle the irregularity of animal carcasses, it nevertheless met with strict limitations. Movement of the carcass through the plant could be mechanized, but killing the animal and cutting it apart could not. The exacting and difficult work of separating muscle from skin, bone, tendon, and viscera remained the purview of human skill. A consequence of such great dependence on labor in the context of a "commodity" industry characterized by very low profit levels per unit of product sold was that packing firms had a strong incentive to keep overall labor costs low. This was accomplished by locating in areas of plentiful labor and by pursuing a classic strategy of de-skilling through a refinement of the detail division of labor. Simultaneously, firms attempted to increase the productivity of labor through intensification. Work in meatpacking plants of the turn of the century was fast-paced, physically demanding, dangerous, and unhealthy (Herbst 1930).

Second, because of cycles of animal reproduction as well as the social form of agricultural production, the supply of livestock was variable and thus meat production was uneven and work scheduling unpredictable. Livestock inputs flowed into Chicago in a largely uncoordinated and seasonal fashion from geographically dispersed small-scale family-labor farms that were tied to the natural rhythms of animal gestation, birth, and development. Despite the regularizing effects of the Union Stockyards, this flow remained uneven and caused problems with labor utilization not only seasonally but also daily. Plants could only operate when there were animals to kill and work often had irregular hours owing to a late start because of late-arriving trains or a late stop owing to the need to kill all available livestock before they lost weight in the stressful stockyards environment. Meat packers responded to this situation by attempting to maintain a stable core of mostly skilled workers undergirded by a larger labor force that could work flexible hours and could be expanded or contracted quickly according to the capricious dictates of input supply (Herbst 1930). As the industry expanded at the turn of the century, the Big Five found their ideal labor force — destitute immigrants who poured into the packinghouses to work long hours for little pay.[8]

When it began to attempt to organize the industry in the 1890s, then, the Amalgamated was attempting to bring unions to firms that had an absolute imperative to maintain control over labor in production. Focusing on the plants of the Big Five, the new union immediately began to organize workers into craft-based locals. The Amalgamated grew rapidly and took action quickly. By 1903, it had organized the majority of packinghouse workers in the major urban centers and in 1904 they went on strike at the Big Five plants seeking higher wages, union recognition, and collective bargaining. The strike was an unmitigated disaster. Nowhere did the Big Five cooperate so fully as in their opposition to unionization. Aided by municipal police and state militia, the packing firms brought in strikebreakers by the thousands and continued to operate their plants, gradually wearing down the union's resistance. But internal problems also contributed greatly to the Amalgamated's defeat. Because the strike lacked any strong centralized leadership, there was little consensus on strike issues and demands. In particular, union leaders could not bridge the widening gap between skilled and

268

unskilled workers and, after two months, this gap became an uncrossable gulf when several skilled locals came back into the plants (Barrett 1992; Brody 1964).

After the 1904 strike, the issue of unionization lay dormant until the First World War. Due to conscription, enlistment, and an abrupt decrease in immigration from Eastern Europe, the packing firms faced a severe labor shortage just as wartime demand for their product began to increase rapidly. In response to problems in the local labor market, meat packers started to tap new sources of labor by recruiting black workers from the rural South. Black workers not only allowed Chicago's packing firms to continue to operate at capacity but also to grow and to profit handsomely. During the war years, total employment in Chicago's packinghouses nearly doubled while the number of black workers increased from just 3 percent of the workforce to 25 percent (Herbst 1930). At the same time, the profits of the four largest packing firms more than tripled (Barrett 1992). Yet, the war also presented new opportunities for organizing. As workers became aware of labor shortages, spontaneous and uncoordinated work stoppages spread through the industry. In many instances, employers capitulated to these work stoppages, granting slight increases in wages and making some minor changes in working conditions in the plants and departments where action was taken. Nonetheless, scattered and isolated actions did not lead to more generalized improvements in the terms of employment for the mass of packinghouse workers (Halpern 1992b).

Attempts to mold this newfound aggressiveness into a union movement were not spearheaded by the Amalgamated, which was slow to respond to wartime organizing opportunities because of internal factionalism and a great reluctance on the part of union leadership to return to the sites of the union's bitter 1904 defeat (Brody 1964). Instead, it was the socialist-led Stockyards Labor Council (SLC), established by the Chicago Federation of Labor, that took the lead. Between 1917 and 1919, the SLC conducted a massive organizing drive in Chicago that brought together the disparate and often hostile elements of the packinghouse workforces. Using unskilled and semiskilled Slavic workers as its base, the SLC organized the mostly native-born German and Irish skilled butchers, as well as significant numbers of black workers. The fact that many blacks were brought into the union (albeit through a black-only local) was no small accomplishment. Overall, black workers were the largest group of union holdouts in this period. These workers either had little prior experience with industrial work and little knowledge of the concept of unionism, or were wary of white-run unions and their history of racial exclusion. Moreover, black antipathy toward unions was cultivated by the packing firms through the use of paternalistic poli-

269

cies and via the active cultivation of racial discord in the plants (Barrett 1992; Halpern 1992b).

The SLC-led union movement soon revived many Amalgamated locals and the two organizations joined forces in an organizing partnership characterized as much by mistrust as by cooperation. Facing the prospect of a massive labor action, and under intense pressure from the federal government to continue and expand production for the war effort, meat packers entered into a federally mediated arbitration agreement with their unions in 1918. This agreement granted workers the eight-hour workday and significant wage increases, while also prohibiting strikes and lockouts. It did not require union recognition or grant the right to collective bargaining, however (Brody 1964). At war's end, the Amalgamated turned on its rival: it extended the agreement with the packers without consulting its rank and file or the SLC—a move calculated to prevent a likely SLC-led strike. Nonetheless, the SLC pushed forward with its organizing drive, focusing particularly on promoting racial unity and understanding in an environment characterized by intensified racial polarization.[9] Despite some success, the entire movement soon fell apart in the wake of the Chicago race riot of July 1919. The Amalgamated quickly set up a rival body to oversee union activity in the stockyards and demanded that all of its locals withdraw their association with the SLC. The skilled butchers locals complied immediately, but the unskilled locals stayed with the SLC. Ultimately, most of these locals also came over to the Amalgamated, but only after the leader of the Slavic unionists defected from the SLC (Barrett 1992). Such was the magnitude of the defections that by 1920 the SLC had evaporated as a force in the packinghouses.

Fundamentally, the split between the Amalgamated and the SLC had been one over organizing strategy. The SLC's strategy was aggressive: gain 100 percent representation in the plants and then press for union recognition via a strike. In contrast, the Amalgamated pursued a more conservative strategy that was aimed at consolidating the gains achieved through wartime arbitration and was committed to avoiding direct confrontation with the packers (Barrett 1992). Although it seemed that the Amalgamated's strategy had paid off, the union would pay dearly for its victory over the SLC, both in terms of membership and in terms of solidarity. The attack on the SLC greatly exacerbated conflict between craft and unskilled locals. The union also lost thirty thousand members when it expelled fourteen locals that remained loyal to the SLC, locals made up mostly of unskilled Slavic workers. But most important, the Amalgamated virtually abandoned any attempt to bring black workers into the union—a product of the strong antiblack bias that prevailed within its ranks—and in this way deepened racial hostilities among packinghouse workers (Halpern 1992b).

In 1921, the folly of the Amalgamated's strategy of conciliation was revealed for all to see. When the last of the extensions of the wartime agreement expired, the packers announced sharp, uniform wage cuts and a return to the ten-hour day. In response, the Amalgamated called for an industry-wide strike, but it was not in a strong position. Many workers, some of whom had joined the new company unions, ignored the strike and stayed in the plants. Again, the packers successfully brought in strikebreakers and kept the plants running. And, once again, the Amalgamated could not keep many of its skilled butcher locals from returning to work. After two long winter months of hardship for most of the strikers and their families, the strike was called off in February 1922.

In the wake of the 1921–22 strike, labor organization in meatpacking collapsed. During the next decade, wages in the industry actually dropped in real terms and labor activists were systematically purged from the plants (Halpern 1992b). Moreover, the packing firms acted to blunt any remaining union edge through the establishment of employee representation programs (company unions). Although there was great variation in the scope and sincerity of these programs from firm to firm, overall the practice of welfare capitalism during the 1920s was quite effective in keeping true unionism at bay.

Rival Unionism

Further efforts to organize the meatpacking industry did not occur until the early 1930s and the coming of the Roosevelt administration's New Deal program. Of particular importance was the National Industrial Recovery Act of 1933, which established the right of workers to bargain collectively and to hold representational elections. In this new institutional environment, the Amalgamated's membership once again expanded. The union organized many of the industry's major plants and pushed for recognition, but the packing firms refused to recognize the union or to allow elections. The packers maintained that they already had unions — the nominally independent company unions. The Amalgamated appealed to the newly formed National Labor Relations Board, but the NLRB proved unable to enforce the law. After a series of failed local strikes in 1934, union membership once again contracted dramatically.

The Wagner Act of 1935, and particularly the upholding of the act by the Supreme Court in 1937, put an effective end to the packing industry's resistance to unionization. Under the act, companies were no longer permitted to operate company unions, were forced to allow free union elections at their plants, and were obligated to recognize and bargain with the victorious labor organization. This was the keystone of an institutional arch within which unions could take hold and flourish. But just as labor organizing gained renewed vigor, a rift de-

271

veloped within the AFL as a group of unions, calling themselves the Committee for Industrial Organization (CIO), advocated a switch from the traditional craft unionism to industrial unionism. Led by John L. Lewis of the United Mine Workers, the CIO strategy met with considerable success in the auto and steel industries, fueling the internal struggle. In late 1936, the CIO unions were suspended from the AFL (Raybeck 1966).

The split in the labor movement had important consequences for packinghouse workers. The Amalgamated leadership had supported the CIO position but eventually turned down Lewis's offer to join the new federation.[10] In response, the CIO formed the Packinghouse Workers' Organizing Committee (PWOC) in 1937, setting into motion a heated rivalry for the hearts and minds of packinghouse workers. The Amalgamated leadership viewed the CIO union as an intruder on its territory. Over the next five years, the Amalgamated tried to undercut its competitor at every step as part of the AFL's broader self-destructive "fratricidal mania" (Davis 1986). It attempted to discredit the PWOC through the use of red-baiting tactics during organizing drives. It made use of company unions in order to better compete in representational elections. It undermined the PWOC's bargaining position with the packing firms. And it tried to halt its rival's progress toward negotiating the industry's first national agreements. Nevertheless, the PWOC succeeded in organizing most of the Big Four plants in the major packing center cities. By 1943, it represented more than 60 percent of the nation's packinghouse workers. The Amalgamated's efforts met with more limited success: in 1943, the union represented only 20 percent of the industry's workforce (Brody 1964).

Despite the fact that their plants were organized during the war, the packing firms resisted union power at every step, refusing to bargain in good faith, refusing to sign contracts, and steadfastly refusing to enter into national agreements covering all of their plants. Broader institutional forces created the context in which national bargaining was established in the meatpacking industry. During World War II, the National War Labor Board (NWLB) pressured the major packing firms to enter into collective bargaining agreements with their unions in order to keep meat supplies flowing smoothly without work stoppages or other labor problems. Beginning with Armour, national agreement contracts were signed by all of the major packing firms before the end of the war. As part of this bargaining process, terms of employment in meatpacking improved. The NWLB kept a lid on wages, but the unions were able to negotiate stable interplant and interregional wage rates, industry-wide overtime pay after an eight-hour day or forty-hour week, and other benefits. Thus, the meatpacking industry approached the end of World War II with unionism firmly established, but

Brian Page

with two rival labor organizations competing for membership. To understand this rivalry, and to grasp the ways in which it influenced the course of sectoral development in meatpacking, it is necessary to explore a set of important differences between the two unions. Indeed, the PWOC and the Amalgamated followed remarkably divergent paths — and stayed apart until 1968 despite the broader AFL–CIO merger of 1955.

The first difference was momentum. By the late 1930s, the Amalgamated's long history in meatpacking had become an enormous liability among packinghouse workers. The union was steeped in failure — an impression that was reenforced by its recent 1934 collapse. The PWOC, meanwhile, basked in the glow of CIO victories in automobiles, steel, and other sectors. CIO affiliation tied packinghouse workers together under the umbrella of a popular and successful national entity and gave them great hopefulness and confidence in their organizing efforts.

A second difference was the source of the union impulse. For the Amalgamated, this source came from the top of the organization as part of a careful decision-making process that weighed the costs and benefits to the union's core retail meat trade. As always, the Amalgamated was cautious in meatpacking. In 1917, it had followed the lead of the SLC and again, in 1938, had waited until the PWOC had demonstrated the viability of a concerted organizing campaign. Once established in meatpacking, the Amalgamated followed an organizational path characterized by strong centralized planning and control. This model of "one-party rule" carried out by a stable and powerful national cadre was forged when the union successfully organized the retail meat cutters during the 1930s, a campaign characterized by open conflict between the national leadership and powerful local unions over who would control strikes and other localized job actions. Ultimately, the Amalgamated's leadership gained full control over organizing and bargaining strategy, and dissident meat-cutter locals were suppressed and punished (Brody 1964).

The PWOC, on the other hand, was characterized by a remarkable degree of rank-and-file participation and control born of its localized and often radical origins. The CIO did not so much organize meatpacking as respond to and connect preexisting pockets of labor activism scattered throughout the industry. The rise of the PWOC in Chicago, for example, was based on multiple sources, including the remnants of the short-lived "second" SLC as well as the Communist-affiliated Packinghouse Workers' Industrial Union (Street 1986). In the smaller packing centers of the upper Midwest, several anti-AFL industrial unions — including the Independent Union of All Workers (IUAW) in Austin and the Midwest Union of All Packinghouse Workers (MUAPW) in Cedar Rapids —   **273** formed the basis of the PWOC's organizing efforts. Thus, the PWOC emerged as a collection of powerful, highly participatory local unions that retained considerable autonomy, and for this reason exhibited an immediate concern for broad-based involvement in union affairs.

This "rank-and-file unionism" (Horowitz 1986) operated at two linked scales. First, on the shop floor, PWOC organizing was almost always based on pro-union activists in the plant. From this indigenous base of leadership emerged a system of elected department chief and co-stewards (numbering one hundred in the larger plants) and a host of other elected union representatives including grievance committee members, divisional representatives, and local officers. In this way, responsibility was spread throughout the membership, creating both a democratic union structure and a network of individuals capable of breaking the grip of management authority through coordinated "job actions," including work slowdowns and stoppages (Brody 1964). Second, at the level of union policy, strategy and direction also emerged from the bottom up. Unlike the Amalgamated, the PWOC leadership was never able to dictate union policy to the locals. This continued to be the case even after wartime national agreements with the major packing firms were signed. In other industries, national agreements acted to increase the authority of the national union leadership at the expense of local unions. But in the PWOC, locals were centrally involved in the contract negotiation process. Representatives of local unions from plants of the same company met in separate "chain" conferences to discuss contract negotiation strategy and each local also participated in the national bargaining sessions.

The force of local autonomy was also at work when the CIO—under pressure from several locals—granted an international union charter to packinghouse workers in 1943, transforming the PWOC into the United Packinghouse Workers of America (UPWA). In other CIO unions where comparable changes took place, the international office dominated the new organizations and a wide gap developed between union leadership and the rank and file. But in the UPWA, the power of the locals was codified within a new organizational structure that allowed individuals to hold powerful positions without being appointed or supported by the international cadre. The union was divided into nine districts, each of which elected regional officers who served on the executive board of the international union along with four international officers. As the new union lacked any established ruling group able to enforce its will, union policy could only emerge through a process of consensus building in which the districts (representing collections of locals) played the key roles (Brody 1964; Horowitz 1986).

A third difference between the Amalgamated and its CIO rival was the approach that each union took in its dealings with the packing firms. The PWOC,

Brian Page

and later the UPWA, was the much more aggressive and confrontational of the two, an attitude that had everything to do with the autonomy and militancy of its locals. PWOC locals used job actions to settle grievances at their plants concerning the pace and distribution of work, violations of the seniority system, and abuse of authority by management — reflecting the fact that workers were concerned not only with improved wages and benefits, but also with control over how the work was done (Horowitz 1986). Such shows of shop-floor power often emerged from the rank and file in response to problems in particular departments without the knowledge of local officers. And, even when resistance was coordinated by the local leadership, the national office could not keep the locals from pursuing job actions in support of their demands. Locals followed this strategy for a simple reason: it worked. During the early organizing period and through World War II, the packing firms capitulated to the pressure brought on by work stoppages. The fact that such tactics were used often and with a high rate of success set into motion a self-reinforcing cycle that solidified the union's democratic character: rank-and-file militancy created results, which instilled a sense of authorship in the union's activities, which led to greater levels of rank-and-file participation, more local action, and so on.

Such militancy carried upward to the national level as well. During the late 1930s, PWOC national officials understood the power of "action at the base" (Street 1986) and used it to hasten the changes in management behavior brought on by government intervention. Later, once unionism was entrenched, the UPWA took a hard line in contract negotiations, using random work stoppages to achieve its desired ends. For its part, the Amalgamated followed a much more conservative approach. The AFL union considered the UPWA to be rudderless and much too militant. Its own members were more controllable and less confrontational. Following the strategy that they had developed in the retail meat trade, the Amalgamated leaders preferred a more cooperative approach based on establishing a solid working relationship with management that avoided any embarrassing breaches of trust brought on by localized militancy. In this way, the Amalgamated sought to methodically consolidate and protect the gains that it achieved (Brody 1964).

Differences in bargaining strategy were particularly evident in the years immediately following World War II. In 1946, the Amalgamated reluctantly joined the UPWA in a joint strike designed to protect and expand wartime gains. This was a troubled alliance, however, as the Amalgamated attempted to settle with the packers without the knowledge of the UPWA (and on terms less favorable than stated in the original bargaining position). So, too, when the plants were seized by the federal government under the War Labor Disputes Act and workers   275 were ordered back into the plants, the Amalgamated complied and the UPWA refused. In the end, the Federal Wage Stabilization Board granted the unions most of the wage increase that they sought, although the packers did not object too strenuously as all of the 16 cent per hour increase they were forced to concede was compensated for by increases in federal meat price ceilings (Brody 1964).

In 1948, in the absence of wartime institutional governance, the UPWA pressed for a sizable 29 cent per hour wage increase. But this time its position was undercut by the Amalgamated, which settled for only a 9 cent per hour gain. Buoyed by the union split, the packing firms did not give in to the UPWA's demands and the union went out on strike. The UPWA was undermined by both the lack of interunion unity and the erosion of public support and ended the strike after ten weeks, standing idly by as hundreds of striking workers were fired. Yet, unlike times past, losing the strike did not destroy the union. In the aftermath of the strike, Amalgamated raids yielded nothing. In fact, the UPWA was able to win every one of the more than twenty representational elections that occurred in the following year, a testament to the bottom-up strength of the organization. Moreover, the UPWA managed to get nearly all of its discharged members restored to their jobs.

A fourth difference between the unions concerned organizing strategy and capability. The Amalgamated officially abandoned its craft-based approach in 1937 but had great trouble finding organizers who could operate effectively in a mass-production industry because the union's standing pool of retail-trade organizers and business agents simply could not match the experience in industrial unionism brought to the PWOC by veteran CIO organizers (Brody 1964). More important, the Amalgamated's history of divisiveness along skill, and especially race, lines prevented it from carrying out successful plant-based organizing drives in many locations. In contrast, the ability to bridge the gulfs that separated packinghouse workers — gulfs that had crippled union efforts in the past — was the hallmark of the PWOC. Here, once again, the CIO was building on an existing foundation. In Chicago, for example, the labor activism that provided the basis of the PWOC during the 1930s was multiracial in character, a situation that reflected a keen awareness among early organizers of the imperative of interracial cooperation (Street 1986).

Blacks were an essential component of organizing efforts in the major packing centers not only because of their considerable numbers, but also because they composed the great majority of workers on the strategically important kill floor, which was the department that controlled the pace and flow of work for the rest of the plant. Work in the hog and beef kill departments was skilled work, but also difficult, wet, and bloody. The fact that blacks were concentrated

276

there reflected a wider pattern of racial segregation in the plants in which blacks were assigned to the least desirable departments, including fertilizer, rendering, glue, and the freezer rooms. This racial division of labor worked to the packers' advantage for a number of years. In particular, because of the historical animosity between black workers and the Amalgamated, the kill departments remained strongly antiunion throughout the 1920s. But by the mid-1930s, this strategy of divide and conquer began to backfire. Blacks and whites worked alongside one another in many departments, and over the years a degree of shared experience and mutual dependence — the necessary conditions of interracial unionism — emerged among these workers.[11] Added to this was the fact that Depression-era layoffs severely undermined pro-company attitudes among black workers who had come to view the packing firms as reliable bastions of black employment in the cities (Halpern 1992).

The fact that large numbers of black workers joined the PWOC during the late 1930s was the key to the union's success in the large urban packing centers. Indeed, the development of the union's shop-floor power discussed earlier rested on a foundation of interracial cooperation. Growth in black membership reflected a genuine commitment to racial equality on the part of the PWOC. The organization took an early and aggressive stand on race issues in the plants, it had disproportionately high numbers of black local officers, and it had strong representation of blacks among organizers and national officers (Helstein 1957; Street 1986). The PWOC's stand was entirely in keeping with the progressive social unionism espoused by the early CIO. Yet, in most CIO unions, the promise of interracial unionism faded after World War II as blacks were systematically discriminated against. The chief exception to this was the UPWA, which forged ahead with progressive racial policies (Hill 1993). In 1949, the union conducted a survey of both its leadership and its rank and file that led to the initiation of a far-reaching antidiscrimination (A-D) program in 1950 aimed at eliminating discrimination and segregation in all of its plants. A national A-D office and district A-D committees were established to oversee progress toward this goal. During the 1950s, the unwavering and aggressive support of the national office kept this issue in front of the membership and, as a result, significant progress toward racial equality was made, including increased participation in leadership by minorities, the elimination of discriminatory hiring practices and departmental segregation, the elimination of segregated dressing and eating facilities in plants throughout the nation, and the narrowing of the wage differential between Northern and Southern plants (Hope 1957).

A fifth difference between the rival unions had to do with the relationship between union and community. Historically, this had been a trouble spot for the Amalgamated. Craft-based labor organization had actively reinforced social divisions within the labor market and the community, while past failures made local leaders hesitant to support the union's cause. Understandably, the path taken by the Amalgamated leadership after 1938 did not depend heavily on strong ties to local groups or organizations, nor did the union concern itself centrally with social issues in the broader community.[12]

In contrast, the success of the PWOC was based on a reciprocal entanglement with the community. On the one hand, early organizing progress in Chicago and elsewhere depended on outreach to community leaders. In particular, support from both black and white clergy, often in the form of public statements, lent the union much-needed credibility and gave its membership drive a major boost (Street 1986; Horowitz 1990). On the other hand, the distinctive brand of industrial unionism pioneered by the PWOC itself fostered the breakdown of social divisions within surrounding communities. The most notable example of this was the participation of the PWOC in the creation of the "Back of the Yards Neighborhood Council" in Chicago. Led by sociologist Saul Alinsky, the Back of the Yards Council became a model of community self-determination based on social cooperation across ethnic and race lines (Jablonsky 1993). This union-community linkage was a key part of the overall success of the PWOC and later the UPWA: a strong neighborhood base reflected the development of a shared place-bound identity among packinghouse workers, which in turn translated into heightened shop-floor coordination.[13] The focus on wider social issues lived on in the UPWA during the 1950s, particularly with respect to civil rights, when the union engaged in a wide range of efforts aimed at eliminating discriminatory practices within the communities where union members resided (Hope 1957; Hill 1993).[14]

A sixth difference between the UPWA and the Amalgamated lay in the political sphere. The UPWA's tradition of social unionism reflected a commitment to the CIO's original political agenda—an ambitious plan to elevate the entire working class through labor's central involvement in national economic planning (Lichtenstein 1989). This overall vision was influenced by the participation of communist trade unionists, and this was certainly true of the UPWA. However, the fate of the UPWA differed from that of other left-led unions. After the war, as conservative business forces began to curtail labor's gains by reshaping the New Deal state, a political split tore the CIO apart. Whereas the CIO leadership lined up squarely behind the Democratic Party and the emergent postwar growth model based on the twin pillars of international expansion and anti-communism, many left-led CIO unions (some blindly following the fervently pro-Soviet American Communist Party line) vehemently opposed both the Mar-

278

shall Plan and the delegitimation of a Communist voice in national politics. This conflict erupted during the 1948 presidential election when the wayward unions did not follow the official CIO position in support of Truman but instead supported the third-party candidacy of Henry Wallace. In the aftermath, eleven left-led unions were first expelled from the CIO and then raided ruthlessly, while the remaining unions began to purge Communist Party members and independent leftists from their ranks (Davis 1986; Rosswurm 1992).

The UPWA remained in the CIO by walking this political line adroitly. It complied with the anticommunist requirements of the Taft-Hartley Act and officially backed Truman, but it did not make this support binding on its officials, district organizations, or locals — a position that both derived from and strengthened the organization's tradition of local autonomy. In this way, the UPWA continued to house a broad spectrum of political positions at the height of the Cold War (Horowitz 1986). Indeed, the left survived a right-wing bid for power in 1948 and maintained control of the union at both the national and the local levels (Brody 1964). For this reason, the UPWA continued to cling to its own expansive vision of social unionism long after the CIO had abandoned such aims in favor of a more narrowly defined interest-group politics designed to provide economic security for the existing membership alone.

Meanwhile, the Amalgamated's political outlook remained solidly in line with the AFL's traditional conservatism rooted in its mostly skilled, native-born, white Protestant membership. Like most AFL unions, the Amalgamated did not share the CIO's broader social vision. Rather, it was a model of the narrow, tightly controlled economism that would flower into a bureaucratic unionism allied with business. Nor did the AFL share the CIO's commitment to "tripartite" governance of the economy during or after World War II, in part because its base of membership lay outside of the core oligopolistic manufacturing sectors where such involvement had yielded the greatest benefits to labor (Lichtenstein 1989). Instead, its strength lay in the decentralized construction, transport, and service trades, where employers had less power. For this reason, the AFL pushed for less restrictive forms of collective bargaining that would allow it to continue to pursue "collusive contract making," even going so far as to join with business in an attempt to amend the Wagner Act to allow employers to express a union preference (Davis 1986). The Amalgamated was very active in this effort, given that its chief approach to the organization of the retail meat trade was to deal directly with the upper management of retail chains — a strategy that was hampered by the inconvenience of union competition and fair representational elections at the local level. So, too, the AFL threw its considerable weight behind the Marshall Plan and the ferreting out of domestic communists. The Amalga-   279 mated, in the appreciative words of historian David Brody, was "impeccably non-Communist" and from this unassailable position continually pointed out the specter of the red menace within the belly of its meatpacking rival.[15]

A seventh, and final, difference related to organizational structure and strategy. The UPWA, a product of the concept of industrial unionism, was a single-industry organization. It emerged from the period of intense rival unionism as the victor, but had no base of membership outside of the confines of meatpacking until well into the 1950s. In contrast to the UPWA's specialization, the Amalgamated had a wider scope born of its historical focus on the meat trade broadly defined and the fact that in the postwar years it continued to diversify away from meatpacking by expanding its role in retailing and extending its organizational horizons (often via the absorption of other unions) into seafood, poultry, eggs, canning, fur, leather, livestock shearing, and livestock handling (Brody 1964).

Given these differences, the two unions pursued decidedly different *spatial strategies* in meatpacking. The UPWA concentrated on the heart of the industry: the plants of the Big Four in the major urban packing centers where thousands of workers were clustered into the districts surrounding the terminal stockyards. It was in this multiplant environment that its unique brand of unionism — consisting of rank-and-file militancy, interracial solidarity, and strong community linkages — emerged, took hold, and flourished. So, too, the demonstration effects (see Wills in this volume), direct aid, and communication that developed between nearby locals gave the union movement great strength and resilience. In this case, one can make the argument that space was much more than simply the terrain of contest. Rather, it was itself constitutive of union experience, the essential medium through which these new social relations were produced. Lacking the tools that would allow it to organize as effectively in the urban centers, the Amalgamated took a different tack. Drawing on its tradition of organizing decentralized work sites, the union targeted the scattered, smaller plants of the independent firms located outside of the Big Four-dominated packing centers and focused on the smaller industrial towns of the Midwest.

The contentious drive to organize the industry, then, had culminated in the solidification of unionization. Between them, the two unions had the bases covered and by the late 1940s the meatpacking industry was almost entirely organized. Even though the packing firms won the 1948 strike, the strike itself forced them to accept the lasting presence of unions and to seek labor stability. Industry master agreements, arrived at through national pattern bargaining, became the norm. In addition to higher wages and benefits, the new master agreements stipulated guaranteed work hours and instituted new shop-floor work

Brian Page

rules. The 1948 strike also was a watershed for the rival unions, however. From that point on, the two acknowledged their dependence on one another and entered an era of greater cooperation marked by a no-raid pact in 1953 and the initiation of merger talks in 1955. But, as the preceding discussion makes clear, these were two remarkably different labor organizations, with quite different geographies of support, and whose differences effectively prevented a combination.

Labor, Rival Unionism, and Industrial Restructuring

The postwar capital-labor accord in meatpacking took shape in the context of rapid technological changes occurring not only in transport methods, but inside the packinghouses themselves. During the late nineteenth century, meatpacking had been a pioneer of modern production techniques, but during the first half of the twentieth century, technological development in meatpacking languished: labor productivity increased by only 0.5 percent per year, as compared to the 2.2 percent average for all manufacturing industries (Brody 1964). But just as the new landscape of unionism emerged in the 1940s, an abrupt burst of innovation occurred in the industry. Mechanization was extended beyond the overhead chain via the introduction of waist-high conveyors while mechanical power augmented muscle in the form of hand-operated mechanical stunners, knives, hide skinners, and saws. The most dramatic innovations, however, came in the curing and processing of pork products. Sausage, bacon, and frankfurter operations were automated via the development of electronic slicing, weighing, stuffing, and smoking machines, new packaging materials were developed, and improvements were made in wrapping and packaging machinery (Ives 1966). Between 1947 and 1954, total labor hours in meatpacking decreased by 6 percent while total liveweight of animals slaughtered increased by 17 percent. As a result, productivity rose 24 percent through this period—an annual increase of more than 3 percent per year—and continued at this pace through the late 1950s (U.S. House of Representatives 1958).

How do we explain this spurt of technological innovation? Three considerations stand out: product focus, competition, and labor. In the years following World War II, the Big Four's market orientation began to shift as each firm pursued growth strategies based on the expanded output of high-value-added processed products. Indeed, these firms devoted most of their research and development money to the creation of patented meat products and patented processes for packaging, freezing, and canning meats, which in turn led to the continual introduction of new machinery and new ways of working. This strategy dovetailed with the proliferation of sales of prepackaged "convenience" foods of all kinds during the postwar era and was linked to rising national incomes as well 281 as to the increasing participation of women in the labor force and the associated shifts in patterns of household food purchases and consumption. Given the fact that most of the meat from cattle is marketed fresh, whereas most of the meat from hogs is marketed in processed form, this new direction also brought with it a gradual shift away from beef and toward pork within the Big Four firms.[16]

Product and process innovations in pork packing were also spurred by competition. Pork had traditionally been a more competitive business than beef because of the presence of a number of established "independent" companies such as Morrell, Hormel, Oscar Mayer, and Rath. In fact, competition among and between the Big Four and the independents intensified in the postwar era as each firm attempted to create a more differentiated family of branded meat products. Despite the fact that several of the independents were innovative, profitable, and aggressive firms, the Big Four held their own and increased their share of total hog slaughter in the first decade following the war (U.S. NCFM 1966).

Competition was also the key to technological changes in beef packing. Here, the Big Four's once insurmountable position began to fade because of shifting power relations within the overall meat-producing chain. Downstream of meatpacking, large-scale food retailing firms bypassed the meat packers' warehouses and developed their own meat distribution systems that purchased directly from the slaughtering plants. In addition, retailers replaced the existing system of packer-defined grades of fresh beef with new buying practices based on USDA grades while encouraging competitive bidding among packing firms. Together, these changes removed barriers to entry into beef packing associated with the Big Four's traditional control over distribution and retail methods and so allowed small, specialized beef packers to emerge and compete effectively during the 1950s.

Upstream of meatpacking, the industrialization of cattle feeding brought with it radical shifts in both the social organization and the geography of cattle production as large-scale specialized feedlots emerged in the Great Plains.[17] The rapid expansion of fed-cattle production undercut the Big Four's dominance over livestock markets. In essence, the new beef-packing firms inserted themselves into an emerging fed-beef chain between feedlots and the supermarkets by locating in rural areas near the source of livestock supply. As this happened, long-distance, rail-based stockyard marketing gave way to local truck-based auction and direct marketing. Thus, the Big Four found themselves operating with increasingly outdated livestock procurement and meat marketing practices and began to lose their grip on the beef-packing industry. Between 1947 and 1964, the Big Four's share of both beef sales and total cattle slaughter declined dramatically (U.S. NCFM 1966). Meanwhile, the fact that the new specialized beef firms were pioneering new slaughtering and butchering techniques (many of which had been developed initially by the Big Four) put pressure on the older firms to follow suit.[18]

The third consideration is labor. The correlation between technological changes and the solidification of unionization in meatpacking is exact. It is my contention that the wave of innovations that swept through the industry in the immediate postwar period goes beyond shifting competitive conditions and new marketing strategies. It was also a response to the increasing cost and power of labor. Through a pervasive rationalization of production, meat packers began to reduce their dependence on an increasingly expensive and problematic labor force. Mechanization had the greatest impact on employment in processing, but other departments were also affected. New work practices on the kill floor were particularly important because they began to eliminate the need for skilled butchers, the group that played perhaps the key role in establishing and maintaining the union's presence in plants. Thus, although meat packers may have accepted the new reality of organized labor in the context of higher meat prices and expanding sales of high-value-added processed meats, they moved quickly to undermine the base of union power by further mechanizing and de-skilling packinghouse work. The motive for technological change is debatable, but the effect of such change is not. In a five-year period during the mid-1950s, total labor hours in meatpacking dropped by 13 percent (Brody 1964).

Rationalization, however, was only one component of a broader process of restructuring that would soon engulf packinghouse workers. Beginning in 1954, with the closing of four large Cudahy plants, the Big Four relocated their manufacturing facilities en masse. Once under way, locational change proceeded with amazing speed. By 1960, all of Chicago's famed slaughterhouses were shut down and, four years later, virtually every plant in every major packing center city stood silent. As the old urban multispecies plants were closed, the Big Four purchased or constructed specialized plants for their beef and pork operations in the livestock-producing regions, solidifying the new pattern of species specialization in the industry.[19] Between 1952 and 1962, the total number of Big Four employees dropped by 37 percent as more than sixty-seven thousand workers lost their jobs. At Armour and Cudahy, employment was cut in half (Danton 1968). In each of the major meatpacking cities, the communities that surrounded the plants and stockyards were devastated.

The abandonment of the packing centers was undoubtedly a response to new technological and organizational conditions in the industry. While other firms became increasingly specialized and modernized, the Big Four were still operating aging, oversize, and inefficient multispecies plants. And, while the competition pioneered new truck-based methods of livestock procurement and meat distribution, the Big Four remained tied to the rail-based stockyards and branch warehouses. But the story does not end there. In many instances — specifically at those plants that were already located in the livestock-producing regions (e.g., Sioux City, Saint Joseph, Kansas City) — the packers could have rebuilt or remodeled in place while adapting to the new transport mode. Again, the role of labor must be considered. It is my contention that the packers' choice to relocate was also influenced by the new labor conditions in the urban packinghouses, a point that has been largely overlooked in the analyses of packing industry locational shifts. Traditionally, when labor has been considered in explanations of restructuring in the industry, it has been in terms of a "pull" factor wherein cheaper wage rates in rural areas acted to entice packing firms to set up operations (e.g., Skaggs 1986). This interpretation, however, ignores crucial "push" factors having to do with changes in the labor process. Rationalization greatly reduced the number of employees required to operate a meatpacking plant and thus lessened the ties that bound meat packers to a large urban workforce and enabled them to operate in smaller labor markets.

More important than this, though, was labor's resistance to technological innovation and work rationalization. This was an extremely contentious issue in the industry throughout the 1950s and 1960s. Organized labor was widely perceived as an impediment to industrial progress because of its resistance (both actual and feared) to the adoption of labor-saving technology (U.S. House of Representatives 1958). New technologies changed the labor process by introducing new tasks and responsibilities, eliminating others, rearranging job loads, or changing the speed of the production line. Workers' objections to changes in existing practices were filtered through the rules of work established by collective bargaining, specifically the channels and procedures for handling grievances that were set out in the contract. In and of itself, the constant repetition of grievance filing/committee meeting/arbitration was distracting for the packers, and certain situations could become much more of a problem if workers decided to exercise their right to strike in support of their position while the contract was in effect. But the biggest problem for the packers was the UPWA's ability to exercise power on the shop floor. It was the uncoordinated and often spontaneous action of cohesive, informal work groups in various departments throughout the factory that exerted the strongest pressure on packers to slow down or change course in their efforts to reorganize the workplace. Using their capacity to mount sudden and seemingly random work stoppages, slowdowns, and other job actions in the context of perishable product manufacturing, union members could influence the outcome of grievance procedures and sometimes reach an agreement with managers or supervisors completely outside of the grievance system.

In reviewing the problem of resistance to work reorganization in meatpacking, a congressional subcommittee recommended that firms attempt to balance technical change with higher wages (U.S. House of Representatives 1958, 6): "Local workers may resist the introduction of labor-saving machinery and labor saving techniques which reduce labor requirements. Opposition to technological progress can be lessened by fair and equitable arrangements with the employees during the transitionary periods and by assurances of higher wage levels as a result of the economies achieved." In the end, however, the Big Four found a more effective way to deal with their recalcitrant workforce: they sought out new laborers in new places where the implementation of new work practices could move forward unobstructed. Let me be clear: relocation did *not* avoid unions or the union wage. The new plants of the Big Four were organized and they continued to be tied to national agreement contracts that contained provisions for stable interregional wage rates. Nor was this an easy or painless process for the packers — adjustment involved high costs for severance pay, early retirement, and transfer programs associated with plant closures (Schultz and Weber 1966). But, relocation *did* allow packers to escape the pockets of union culture that had emerged during the struggles of the 1930s and 1940s. Plant closures eliminated thousands of experienced and often militant workers from the industry and undercut the legacy of union solidarity that had evolved in the packing centers. Packinghouse workers hired at the new locations, having little knowledge of the industry's past working conditions and no sense of past struggles, were far less likely to resist the new technologies via strikes, slowdowns, or industrial sabotage. In addition, the relocation strategy pursued by the packing firms scattered the new plants over several states and separated the workers at one plant from others in the industry, a fragmentation of production that avoided the powerfully contagious effects of resistance that had developed among various locals in the multiplant environment of the packing centers.

In this sense, the massive locational shift in meatpacking must be viewed not just as a response to market cues, but as a strategic counterattack against organized labor, a spatial response to the spatially concentrated power of the UPWA. Here is where unionism's effect on geographic development is most apparent. Unionism defined the terrain on which the relocation of firms was played out. As the packers set out to construct a new manufacturing landscape, they were reacting to a distinctive geography of labor created by the two rival unions. In turn, the actions of the packing firms were not neutral with respect to the dynamics of rival unionism. Indeed, the abandonment of the packing centers ex-

285

ploited the lasting split in the labor movement and precipitated a major upheaval in the balance of power between the two unions that led to the virtual
annihilation of the UPWA.

Relocation struck at the core of the UPWA. Suddenly, the union's most important advantages were lost. Its traditional strongholds—the Big Four plants
in the urban packing centers—were decimated and membership was lost irrev-
ocably. True, some workers were able to find work at the new plants via interplant transfer programs at Armour and Cudahy (both Swift and Wilson refused
to give their displaced employees any such option), but these programs were not
even initiated until 1961, well after the period of greatest labor displacement.[20]
Moreover, because of the drastic job cuts that preceded actual plant closings,
the pool of workers eligible for these programs was a fraction of what the
workforce had been a few years earlier. For this reason, and because many workers chose not to leave their communities, relatively few union members transferred to new locations (Schultz and Weber 1966). Transfers may have allowed
the union to survive as long as it did (each new plant had to undergo a recertifi-
cation election), but it did not establish the basis for future success and expansion. Likewise, the UPWA's single-industry strategy, a key to its earlier success,
became an important limiting factor. The union had diversified little outside of
the packing industry and so lacked a broader base of membership from which
to rebuild in the wake of relocation.

In contrast, relocation played to the Amalgamated's strength. The union's
base of membership in meatpacking lay in that segment of the industry that
was growing—the widely scattered plants of the independent firms and the
Big Four plants outside of the packing centers. Its organizers excelled in the decentralized environment. The Amalgamated could also better absorb some loss
of membership in meatpacking given the growth and diversification that had allowed it nearly to double its overall membership between 1950 and 1960—one
of the few labor unions to expand during that decade (U.S. Department of Labor
1969). Additionally, the Amalgamated followed organizational procedures that
facilitated expansion. Unlike the UPWA, Amalgamated locals were self-financing,
thus allowing their international office to invest much more in the work of organizing (Brody 1964).

Capital's mobility "checked" the UPWA. Having lost the old plants, the
union was forced onto the terrain of its rival and into a mimetic strategy of diversification. It did not survive for very long. By 1968, with its membership
down to sixty-eight thousand, the UPWA was folded into the Amalgamated via
a formal merger of the two organizations. Of course, the UPWA spirit was not
totally eradicated. Within the packinghouse section of the combined organiza-

Brian Page

tion, former UPWA locals were assigned the prefix "P" and many clung fiercely to this identity. Moreover, some former UPWA officials were retained. Nevertheless, the organization and its distinctive practices ceased to exist. Happy coincidence or self-conscious strategy, the packing firms had rid themselves of the aggressive pattern-setting labor union. And the patient, persistent Amalgamated had finally vanquished its rival.

Conclusion

Just as industrial geographers are now beginning to recognize the need to differentiate within the realm of capital (exploring important differences between industries and between firms within industries across a whole range of issues) and within the realm of the state (probing the regional and sectoral regulation of economic activity, for example), so too we need to be attentive to differences within the realm of labor and the ways in which such differences can shape sectoral development. In meatpacking, the distinctive course of rival unionism exerted a powerful influence on the overall process of geographical industrialization during the 1950s and 1960s. In particular, the ongoing competition between the Amalgamated and the UPWA allowed the packing firms to manipulate the course of union politics. The strategy of spatial decentralization, in essence, enabled the employers to choose their union. Had the two unions combined into a single labor organization during the 1950s when the UPWA was still strong, this spatial strategy would not have been open to the packers.

Thus, the failure to merge—and the subsequent collapse of the UPWA— had lasting consequences for the labor movement in meatpacking. In hindsight, relocation from the packing centers was only the opening salvo in a thirty-year assault by capital on organized labor that culminated in the brutal union-busting episodes of the late 1970s and 1980s. In particular, the Amalgamated, and later the United Food and Commercial Workers (UFCW)—which was formed via a merger of the Amalgamated and the Retail Clerks' International Association in 1979)—could not withstand the force of new, vehemently antiunion firms such as Iowa Beef Processors (IBP) and Missouri Beef Packers (MBPXL).[21] These packers expanded dramatically after 1970 on the basis of a powerful product, process, and marketing innovation—boxed beef.[22] The boxed beef firms rolled like competitive juggernauts through the industry, unleashing a flurry of mid-contract wage and benefit concession demands, plant closings, and relocations as older firms attempted to both survive and follow suit. By the early 1980s, union representation in beef packing had plummeted and wages had been cut nearly in half. Soon thereafter, IBP, using the same strategy that had been so successful in beef, brought boxed fresh meat production and nonunion 287 labor to pork packing. The entrance of IBP into pork packing increased slaughtering capacity in the Midwest and thus put severe competitive pressure on established firms in terms of both livestock and labor costs. The result was a cascading attack on union labor similar to what had occurred earlier in beef.

Through all of this, the gains made by unions in meatpacking over the past fifty years have been steadily eroded. Whereas union representation was nearly complete in the mid-1950s, today fewer than half of packinghouse employees work under union contracts. In 1971, wages in meatpacking were 117 percent of the average for all manufacturing. Today, they are less than 80 percent of that average. Workplace health and safety have also deteriorated; more than forty-three of every one hundred workers are now seriously injured on the job each year. A strong, surviving UPWA might not have prevented this fate, but organized labor in meatpacking was certainly weakened by its absence. The UPWA had been a last bastion of early CIO social unionism and its defeat marked the narrowing of the union project in meatpacking and the ascendance of a more self-interested unionism that was distanced from social issues and resigned to a segmented working-class structure. Lacking any established or extensive linkage to broader social movements or to particular communities, the Amalgamated had fewer ways to reach out and mobilize public opinion in support of its struggles.[23]

Organized labor in meatpacking has also missed the UPWA's industrial focus. Meatpacking had always been somewhat of a secondary concern for the Amalgamated and when the UFCW was created, packinghouse workers became even smaller fish in a rapidly expanding organizational pond dominated by retail workers. Given the traditional bargaining practices in the retail field and the fact that packinghouse workers account for only a small fraction of the UFCW's total membership, the union's leadership has not always taken an aggressive stance in the meatpacking industry. In fact, in 1987 the UFCW leadership chose to abandon its yearlong organizing drive at IBP plants—over the objections of its packinghouse division chief—as part of a backdoor "sweetheart" agreement with IBP that kept some plants unorganized while allowing the union into other plants, although under terms quite favorable to the company.[24] This is not to say that good union people have not fought valiantly under the banner of the Amalgamated or the UFCW, or to deny the existence of remnant pockets of UPWA-style rank-and-file aggressiveness within the UFCW. But these are altogether different issues than whether or not union members have had the benefit of focused, aggressive leadership.

Perhaps more than anything else, however, the union movement in meatpacking was hurt by the loss of the UPWA's tradition of shop-floor militancy. By the mid-1970s, an entire generation of activist union members—a cohesive

288

group of men and women born of an aggressive union instinct and schooled in the art of successful collective action—had been lost. Had the UPWA survived intact, had there been better continuity in the packinghouse labor force, it is possible that the ongoing use of shop-floor pressure tactics might have afforded additional avenues of resistance to the onslaught of the packing firms.

The legacy of rival unionism also continues to shape the locational dynamics of meatpacking today. Clearly, this case illustrates the vulnerability of place-bound collective consciousness and the very unequal power relations over space between labor and capital. Indeed, packinghouse workers are subject to a "politically induced historical amnesia" (Rosswurm 1992), but meatpacking firms have not forgotten the era of powerful unionism. Now, meat packers follow locational strategies that have at their core the imperative to avoid the very conditions that allowed the UPWA to take root fifty years ago. These firms prefer rural locations that have little or no history of meatpacking. They prefer to hire individuals without prior experience in the industry who do not live in the area, and have instead developed systematic labor recruitment systems that funnel potential employees to their plants from around the country and internationally. They prefer to hire people from a variety of nonnative English-speaking immigrant groups. With an eye toward history, today's dominant meat packers attempt to construct and maintain social and spatial barriers to communication and mutual understanding among workers and to isolate them from other workers in the industry and from the communities in which they live and work. Sadly, this strategy works as well in the 1990s as it did a century ago. Without the benefit of knowledge of past practices and accomplishments that might allow contemporary workers to translate the powerful urban experience of the UPWA to the industry's new rural locations, union organizing—let alone strong union cultures—will be painfully slow to appear in America's small, isolated packing towns.

Notes

1. These quotes are from Lloyd Lewis's introduction to *Poems of the Midwest* (Sandberg 1946), a republication of Carl Sandberg's first two volumes of poetry, *Chicago Poems* (originally published in 1916) and *Cornhuskers* (originally published in 1918).

2. Hereafter, I will refer to the Amalgamated Meat Cutters and Butcher Workmen as the Amalgamated.

3. Despite the fact that the veracity of traditional locational principles remains virtually unquestioned in this case, cost-minimization interpretations of meatpacking have the same static and mechanistic character that has been iden-

289

tified for the approach more generally (Chapman and Walker 1987; Dicken and Lloyd 1990). Allocation models of this type simply cannot account for the rise of large firms, variations in firm strategy or competitive behavior, the process of technological change, or abrupt and radical changes in the geography of industry.

4. These five firms were Armour, Swift, Cudahy, Morris, and Swartschild and Sulzberger (later Wilson). In 1920, Armour acquired Morris, so the Big Five became the Big Four.

5. The movement of carcasses through the plant on mechanical overhead rails had been part of the industry since the 1830s (Gidieon 1948).

6. Armour and Swift, taking their cue from the railroads, initiated the development of the modern departmentalized manufacturing corporation (Chandler 1977).

7. In 1887, the Big Five had just 7 plants and a handful of branch houses between them. By 1897, they had 20 large plants and 600 branch houses. By 1917, at their peak, they had 91 plants and 1,120 branch houses. In 1917, the Big Five killed 82 percent of the cattle, 77 percent of the sheep, and 61 percent of the hogs that entered interstate trade. In 1916, Swift and Armour alone slaughtered more than 50 percent of interstate trade totals for every type of livestock except hogs, of which they accounted for 43 percent (Arnould 1971).

8. In 1909, immigrants from Eastern Europe alone accounted for 43 percent of the workers in the nation's four largest centers of meatpacking employment (Brody 1964).

9. After World War I, black and white workers were increasingly pitted against one another and race relations in the packing industry worsened. This occurred for several reasons: many black workers lost their jobs to white workers returning from military service; overall, there was much greater competition for jobs given the sudden labor surplus; and black workers constituted the largest block of laborers opposed to unionization.

10. The Amalgamated chose not to join the CIO for several reasons. First, it would have had to drop its focus on meat retailing in order to follow the industrial focus of the CIO, which wanted it to focus exclusively on meatpacking. Second, abandoning the retail meat trade would have been extremely difficult to do given the Amalgamated leadership's strong ties to the Teamsters, the heart of the AFL. Third, the Amalgamated leadership feared that it would lose some degree of control with CIO affiliation. In particular, they did not want to have to share power with the more radical elements in the industry (Brody 1964).

11. One of the unanticipated outcomes of the packing firms' company unions was an increase in contact and communication between black and white employees (Street 1986; Halpern 1992a). This fits with Cohen's (1990) broader

Brian Page

contention that welfare capitalism, in perverse fashion, provided the basis of 1930s industrial unionism by encouraging the development of a collective identity among workers.

12. This began to change somewhat in the middle and late 1950s as the Amalgamated expanded into canneries, seafood plants, poultry plants, and egg production. The organization of these new manufacturing activities brought many more blacks, Hispanics, and women into the union and as a result the union became increasingly progressive, engaging, for instance, issues of race in the community and problems of migrant labor.

13. This was true not only of Chicago and other large packing centers where the workforce was multiracial, but also of CIO packing plants in Iowa and Minnesota where the workforce was mostly white. At the Morrell plant in Ottumwa, Iowa, for example, a powerful community unionism emerged based on a shared cultural identity among white ethnic workers, as well as a shared animosity toward Morrell's English managers and owners (Warren 1992).

14. The UPWA's record is not as strong concerning women's rights. The union resisted compliance with Title VII of the 1964 Civil Rights Act banning gender discrimination in the workplace. The indifference and sometimes hostility toward women's rights displayed by many UPWA locals reflected the lasting ideological power of conceptions of the family based on a single male wage earner, particularly in the context of rapid mechanization and widespread job loss. Ironically, the UPWA tradition of local autonomy allowed individual locals to shape the international's gender policy and thereby hold back the equitable treatment of women (Deslippe 1993; Fehn 1993).

15. The Amalgamated was criticized within the AFL when it absorbed the International Fur and Leather Workers' Union (IFLWU) in the late 1950s. The IFLWU was one of the eleven left-led unions that had been expelled from the CIO and was still communist-influenced when merger talks began in 1954. AFL fears were misplaced, however. In reality, the Amalgamated-crafted merger was the vehicle that ultimately stamped out the left in the IFLWU. Going far beyond the Taft-Hartley provisions, it required every official down to the local level to sign noncommunist affidavits, and prominent communist leaders were forever barred from union participation (Brody 1964).

16. Some observers have interpreted the fresh meat/processed meat split as a voluntary abandonment of beef production and a retreat into processed pork production by the Big Four and other established firms (Aududdell and Cain 1981). These firms did shift their focus based on differential returns on investment, but to characterize this as an abandonment is off the mark. In fact, the established firms responded to their competition (albeit belatedly) and pushed

forward with their beef operations. Two of the Big Four firms (Armour and Swift), as well as another established firm (Morrell), remained among the top five beef packers until the early 1980s.

17. This process of expansion was fundamentally tied in with broader trends. On the one hand, beef consumption—and particularly consumption of high-quality grain-fed beef—had been rising steadily since the end of the war, thanks to generally rising incomes and the aggressive sales efforts of supermarkets. On the other hand, feed-grain agriculture was being transformed through the appropriation of farming by the oil, chemical, machinery, and seed industries in the form of integrated input-intensive practices. Together with an institutional framework aimed at disseminating technological advances, expanding output, and developing new markets, these changes led to unparalleled increases in total output and yield of feed grains (Goodman and Redclift 1990; Friedmann 1993). In turn, cheap feed grains combined with industrial advances in cattle feeding, hog raising, and dairying to keep the price of meat and dairy products low, thereby fueling further increases in consumption.

18. Although new firms emerged in beef packing, few opportunities existed for new firms in pork. Barriers to entry remained in place for three reasons. First, because of the focus on processing, pork packing required much higher levels of capital investment in plant and equipment than beef packing. Second, while distribution channels for pork products were transformed, the way in which processed meat was sold at retail remained unchanged. Packaged pork products such as ham, sausage, and bacon continued to be sold under the familiar brand names of the major packers. Third, the impact of changes in livestock marketing were not as pronounced in pork packing. This had much to do with the existence of the established independents located in the smaller cities of the corn belt. The increasing importance of these firms in the pork-packing industry after 1920 led to a gradual shift away from the terminal stockyards toward country auction hog marketing. When the huge multispecies plants of the Big Four were closed, they relocated their new specialized pork-packing operations to the corn belt, where auction and direct marketing practices were firmly established.

19. Between 1950 and 1962, the number of plants slaughtering only cattle increased from 34 to 127; the number of plants slaughtering only hogs increased from 37 to 60 (U.S. NCFM 1966).

20. For instance, the UPWA's membership dropped from 158,000 to 103,000 between 1958 and 1960 alone—a 35 percent decline (U.S. Department of Labor 1969).

21. In 1979, MBPXL was acquired by Cargill and renamed Excel Corporation.

292

22. Boxed beef production involved an extension of mechanized disassembly within the plant in which the beef carcass is broken down into primal and subprimal cuts of meat that are then vacuum-sealed and loaded into boxes. The new techniques of boning, wrapping, and packaging were incorporated into huge and efficient state-of-the-art slaughtering/processing plants that yielded significant economies of size based, in part, on improved by-product recovery and sales. Vacuum packaging added weeks to the normal shelf life of fresh beef. These boxes of smaller cuts could also be shipped directly to the retail store where the final retail cuts were performed. Thus, boxed beef production revolutionized the distribution system by eliminating the need for a separate "fabrication" stage in between the packinghouse and the retail store. It also revolutionized retail butchering by effectively transferring the work of thousands of skilled, union butchers from the fabrication warehouse to the packinghouse, where the tasks were de-skilled and performed by low-wage, nonunion laborers.

23. More generally, as Lichtenstein (1989) has observed, the kind of business unionism allied with pro-growth politics represented by the Amalgamated had long ago withdrawn from serious efforts to shape national economic policy and thus unions were without any "effective voice" in the broader political debates and decisions concerning technological change and the reorganization of work.

24. This information was provided to me by Lewie Anderson, former head of the packinghouse division of the UFCW, during a personal interview conducted in Chicago on August 26, 1990.

Bibliography

Arnould, R. 1971. "Changing Patterns of Concentration in American Meat Packing, 1860–1963." *Business History Review* 45: 18–34.

Aududdell, R. M., and L. P. Cain. 1973. "Location and Collusion in the Meat Packing Industry." In *Business Enterprise and Economic Change*, edited by L. P. Cain and P. J. Uselding, 85–117. Kent, Ohio: Kent State University Press.

———. 1981. "The Consent Decree in the Meatpacking Industry, 1920–1956." *Business History Review* 40: 359–78.

Barrett, J. R. 1992. *Work and Community in the Jungle: Chicago's Packinghouse Workers, 1894–1922.* Champaign: University of Illinois Press.

Brody, D. 1964. *The Butcher Workmen: A Study of Unionization.* Cambridge: Harvard University Press.

Chandler, A. D. 1977. *The Visible Hand: The Managerial Revolution in American Business.* Cambridge: Belknap Press.

293

Chapman, K., and D. Walker. 1987. *Industrial Location*. Oxford: Basil Blackwell.

Clemen, R. A. 1923. *The American Livestock and Meat Industry*. New York: Ronald Press.

Cohen, L. 1990. *Making a New Deal: Industrial Workers in Chicago, 1919–1939*. New York: Cambridge University Press.

Danton, L. A. 1968. "The Decline of an Oligopoly: Changes in the Meat Packing Industrial Structure." *Rocky Mountain Social Science Journal* 5: 35–45.

Davis, M. 1986. *Prisoners of the American Dream*. London: Verso.

Deslippe, D. A. 1993. "'We Had an Awful Time with Our Women': Iowa's United Packinghouse Workers of America, 1945–75." *Journal of Women's History* 5.1: 10–32.

Dicken, P., and P. Lloyd. 1990. *Location in Space*. New York: HarperCollins.

Fehn, B. 1993. "Chickens Come Home to Roost: Industrial Reorganization, Seniority and Gender Conflict in the United Packinghouse Workers of America, 1956–1966." *Labor History* (spring): 324–41.

Friedmann, H. 1993. "The Political Economy of Food: A Global Crisis." *New Left Review* 197: 29–57.

Gidieon, S. 1948. *Mechanization Takes Command: A Contribution to Anonymous History*. New York: Oxford University Press.

Goodman, D., and M. Redclift. 1990. "The Farm Crisis and the Food System: Some Reflections on the New Agenda." In *Political, Social, and Economic Perspectives on the International Food System*, edited by T. Marsden and J. Little, 19–35. Aldershot, England: Avebury.

Halpern R. 1992a. "The Iron Fist and the Velvet Glove: Welfare Capitalism in the Chicago's Packinghouses, 1921–1933." *Journal of American Studies* 26: 159–83.

———. 1992b. "Race, Ethnicity, and Union in the Chicago Stockyards, 1917–1922." *International Review of Social History* 37: 25–58.

Harvey, D. 1982. *The Limits to Capital*. Oxford: Basil Blackwell.

Helstein, R. 1957. "The Packinghouse Workers." *AFL–CIO American Federationist* 64 (December): 33–36.

Herbst, A. 1930. *The Negro in the Slaughtering and Meat Packing Industry in Chicago*. Boston and New York: Houghton Mifflin.

Hill, H. 1993. "Black Workers, Organized Labor, and Title VII of the 1964 Civil Rights Act: Legislative History and Litigative Record." In *Race in America: The Struggle for Equality*, edited by H. Hill and J. E. Jones Jr., 263–341. Madison: University of Wisconsin Press.

Hope, J., II. 1957. "Equal Employment Opportunity: A Process Analysis of Union Initiative." *Phylon Quarterly* 18 (July): 140–54.

Brian Page

Horowitz, R. 1986. "It's Harder to Struggle Than to Surrender: The Rank and File Unionism of the United Packinghouse Workers of America, 1933–1948." *Studies in History and Politics* 5: 83–96.

———. 1990. "It Wasn't a Time to Compromise: The Unionization of Sioux City Packinghouses, 1937–1942." *Annals of Iowa* 50: 241–68.

Ives, R. I. 1966. *The Livestock and Meat Economy of the United States.* Washington, D.C.: American Meat Institute.

Jablonsky, T. J. 1993. *Pride in the Jungle: Community and Everyday Life in Back of the Yards Chicago.* Baltimore: Johns Hopkins University Press.

Lichtenstein, N. 1989. "From Corporatism to Collective Bargaining: Organized Labor and the Eclipse of Social Democracy in the Postwar Era." In *The Rise and Fall of the New Deal Order, 1930–1980,* edited by S. Fraser and G. Gerstle, 122–52. Princeton, N.J.: Princeton University Press.

Massey, D. 1984. *Spatial Divisions of Labor: Social Structures and the Geography of Production.* New York: Methuen.

Page, B. 1993. "Agro-Industrialization and Regional Transformation: The Restructuring of Midwestern Meat Production." Ph.D. diss., Department of Geography, University of California, Berkeley.

Raybeck, J. G. 1966. *A History of American Labor.* New York: Free Press.

Rosswurm, S. 1992. "An Overview and Preliminary Assessment of the CIO's Expelled Unions." In *The CIO's Left-Led Unions,* edited by S. Rosswurm, 1–17. New Brunswick, N.J.: Rutgers University Press.

Sandberg, C. 1946. *Poems of the Midwest.* Cleveland: World Publishing.

Schultz, G., and A. Weber. 1966. *Strategies for the Displaced Worker.* New York: Harper and Row.

Scott, A., and M. Storper. 1986. *Production, Work, Territory: The Geographical Anatomy of Industrial Capitalism.* Boston: Allen and Unwin.

Skaggs, J. M. 1986. *Prime Cut: Livestock Raising and Meatpacking in the United States, 1607–1983.* College Station: Texas A&M University Press.

Storper, M., and R. Walker. 1989. *The Capitalist Imperative: Territory, Technology and Industrial Growth.* Oxford: Basil Blackwell.

Street, P. 1986. "Breaking Up Old Hatreds and Breaking through the Fear: The Emergence of the Packinghouse Workers Organizing Committee in Chicago, 1933–1940." *Studies in History and Politics* 5: 63–82.

U.S. Department of Labor, Bureau of Labor Statistics. 1969. "Directory of National and International Labor Unions in the United States." *Bulletin* no. 1665. Washington, D.C.: U.S. Government Printing Office.

U.S. House of Representatives, Committee on Agriculture, Consumers Study Subcommittee. 1958. *Trends in Efficiency in Meat Processing and Distribution.* Washington, D.C.: U.S. Government Printing Office.

U.S. NCFM (National Commission on Food Marketing). 1966. "Organization and Competition in the Livestock and Meat Industry." *Technical Study No. 1.* Washington, D.C.: U.S. Government Printing Office.

Warren, W. J. 1992. "The Heyday of the CIO in Iowa: Ottumwa's Meat Packing Workers, 1937–1954." *Annals of Iowa* 51: 363–72.

Weber, A. 1929. *Theory of the Location of Industries.* Chicago: University of Chicago Press (originally published in German in 1909).

Williams, W. F. 1979. *The Changing Structure of the Beef Packing Industry.* Lubbuck, Tex.: TARA.

Yeager, M. 1981. *Competition and Regulation: The Development of Oligopoly in the Meat Packing Industry.* Greenwich, Conn.: JAI Press.

Brian Page

Chapter 9 • "Working Steady"
Gender, Ethnicity, and Change in Households, Communities, and Labor Markets in Lawrence, Massachusetts, 1930–1940

Meghan Cope

The decision of Congress in 1935 to lend the support of the law to the right of collective bargaining [by passing the National Labor Relations Act] has brought into employment relationships a new element.... Some modes of action long looked upon as permissible are definitely under the ban of the law. New ways of dealing between employer and employee are being built up. New attitudes are required.

> Primer of Labor Relations,
> *Bureau of National Affairs, Washington, D.C., 1940*

Although the textile industry has in the past always been a low-wage industry, it need not necessarily remain a low-wage industry in the future. Like the workers in coal, steel, oil, automobile, and other important industries, textile workers want to share the riches of our country, enjoy the opportunities of our industrial system, and exercise freely the rights of industrial citizenship. To translate into reality these desires and aspirations of American textile labor is the primary aim of the Textile Workers' Union of America.

> *Emil Rieve, president, TWUA-CIO, 1941*

When you organize into a union, favoritism and abuse from the foreman go out the window.

> *Textile Workers' Union of America advertisement,*
> Fitchburg Textile Labor, *May 1942*

The union got you this stuff. The mill owners didn't give it to you out of the goodness of their hearts, it was more or less forced. That's my opinion, but like I say, I've been union all my life and I like unions. I think the union has done a lot of good for the people. The old-timers built up what the young people are reaping now.

> *Frank Costello, former woolen mill worker, Lawrence, Massachusetts*

297

The postwar accord between "Big Labor" and "Big Business" in the United States that facilitated an unprecedented period of industrial stability, productivity, and profits, as well as social-economic gains in incomes, education levels, home ownership, and financial security, was clearly buttressed by the growth of a Keynesian welfare state and a Pax Americana. What is less often recognized is that the accord could not have developed without the significant changes in labor policy and practice that were implemented during the 1930s (Milton 1982). Legislation emerging out of the New Deal, which put new regulations on industries in the areas of employment policies and relations, in combination with the growth of strong national unions (made feasible in part by the newly granted right to bargain collectively), made the decade of the 1930s one of the most vital in U.S. labor history and geography. Indeed, the contrasts between working conditions and the terms of employment at the beginning of the 1930s and after World War II are staggering. While there are many excellent reviews of these changes and their impacts at the national and regional levels (e.g., Foner 1980; Milton 1982), fewer analyses focus on the impacts such shifts had on individual workers and their households, on neighborhoods and communities, or on local labor markets.

Attention to the smaller-scale effects of policy changes and unionization is a crucial part of understanding how diverse workers (rather than an undifferentiated "labor") in the context of specific industries and cities experienced these changes as members of different social groups, as members of households, and as member of communities, and, conversely, how social relations, households, and communities were modified by labor developments. Further, by looking at the effects of these developments within their local geographic context, we can begin to see how spatially defined labor markets were constructed and reconstructed as the rules, the definitions, and the very nature of work changed. This essay, which focuses on the unionization of textile workers in Lawrence, Massachusetts, suggests that the *regularization* of employment that was gradually brought about by New Deal labor policies and union agreements fundamentally influenced the geographic relationships between work and home and between work and community, and, consequently, restructured the local labor market.

When a permanent union was finally established among the woolen and worsted textile workers of Lawrence in 1937, it came after ninety years of woolen manufacturing in the city, numerous strikes, and countless unsuccessful attempts at achieving full unionization. Two national-level changes served as important catalysts for the organization of Lawrence's woolen and worsted textile workers. First, in 1935 the National Labor Relations Act (also known as the Wagner Act) was passed by Congress and signed by President Roosevelt, providing for

Meghan Cope

the first time the federally guaranteed right of workers to form unions and bargain collectively. Second, in 1936 and 1937 massive unionization campaigns were instigated by John L. Lewis and the newly independent Congress of Industrial Organizations (CIO) in an attempt to organize the millions of unskilled and semiskilled industrial workers who had traditionally been shunned by the elitist, craft-oriented American Federation of Labor.

In the woolen and worsted mills of Lawrence in 1937, these two national-level developments precipitated the rapid achievement of nearly 100 percent unionization in the Textile Workers' Union of America (TWUA) without even the threat of a strike. The American Woolen Company — a multinational corporation whose production was centered in Lawrence — conceded to worker and union demands with little resistance. Although larger-scale changes enabled and prompted the unionization of Lawrence's textile workers, the local situation, the character of the city's working population, and the organization of production in the mills deeply influenced the form of the changes that the unions brought to the mills. In Lawrence, as elsewhere, these changes were seen primarily in the *standardization* of jobs, hiring processes, and work relations, and in the *stabilization* of employment attained through signed contracts for guaranteed hours, negotiated wage rates that were uniformly applied, unemployment relief, and seniority rights. These two forces — standardization and stabilization — combine to form what is referred to here as the *regularization* of labor.

The effects of union-led regularization were not evenly distributed across Lawrence's workforce, however, and in fact, union-led changes in the labor process spurred a dramatic transformation of the labor landscape. Although unionization was generally popular among workers and the imposition of standardized employment relations did reduce perceived unfair practices (favoritism, sporadic layoffs, lack of seniority rights), the regularization of labor also had the potential to squeeze some contingent workers out of the workforce and to eliminate the advantages of subjective hiring that some groups had experienced. I show specifically how the union's efforts to make "working steady" the norm caused gender- and ethnicity-based changes in labor relations in three important arenas of social/spatial relations: households, neighborhood-based ethnic communities, and, consequently, the local labor market.

This essay is organized as follows. First, impacts of the union's regularization processes on the links between home and work are examined. I outline the organization of production, divisions of labor, and the terms of employment before unionization to demonstrate how the standardization and stabilization of labor in the mills subsequently affected workers' households and families and changed their employment strategies. This examination highlights the asser- 299 tion that the regularization of terms of employment brought by the union lessened the ability of some individuals and households to negotiate for optimal work situations. For example, many women in Lawrence had frequently moved in and out of the textile labor force as household and child-care obligations had allowed or necessitated. With the coming of unionization, however, the formalization of hiring, seniority, wages, and work times threatened the employment of women who needed such flexible arrangements, or prohibited them altogether from participating in the waged textile labor force. Similarly, the diverse household income-generating activities and time-management strategies that had evolved as adaptive responses to fluctuating economic and employment demands in the city during the 1920s and 1930s underwent significant changes as the nature of the labor process shifted.

The second section examines the impact of unionization on ethnic neighborhoods in the city. Because there was a fairly clear ethnic residential pattern in Lawrence during the 1930s (see figures 9.1 and 9.2), changes in the structure of work and the relations between workers and employers also impacted neighborhood-level ethnic community relations. Ethnic divisions of labor and traditional hiring networks constructed along ethnic lines were ostensibly eliminated with the advent of the unions, because regularization influenced the ability of ethnic groups to obtain and keep jobs: some groups were affected negatively, others positively. Local ethnic communities had varying degrees of strength and influence in the city, which were tied intrinsically to the patterns of mill employment through long-standing ethnic divisions of labor. Therefore, the standardization processes of the union had the potential not only to erode the numerous mill-based ethnic associations and social relationships, but, by extension, to influence the ability of some local communities to "take care of their own" by blocking ethnic inroads to employment.

The third section examines how these trends together reshaped the geography of the local labor market. While union changes at least outwardly minimized preferential hiring, sporadic employment, and flexible or contingent working terms, they also fundamentally reconstructed the labor market. For example, hiring workers for the day (or even part of the day) had been a central pillar of support for the woolen companies' profit margins. This was, of necessity, an inherently local process that depended on a set of workers living near enough to afford to come to the mills every day and desperate enough to accept short-term work for low wages. When we consider the end of day hiring in combination with greater job security for individual workers and higher wages, we can see the shift toward a labor market that was less contingent and encompassed a larger area from which to draw workers (who could afford a longer commute if they

300

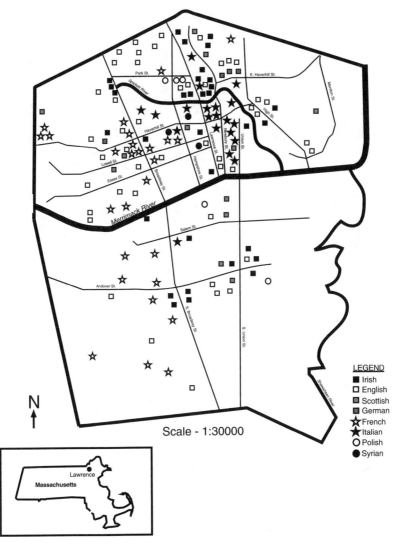

Figure 9.1. Ethnic backgrounds of sampled households in Lawrence, Massachusetts, 1930. "English" includes "Yankees" and English Canadians, as well as British; "French" includes French Canadians and Franco-Belgians, as well as French.

Source: Author sample, Lawrence City Directory

301

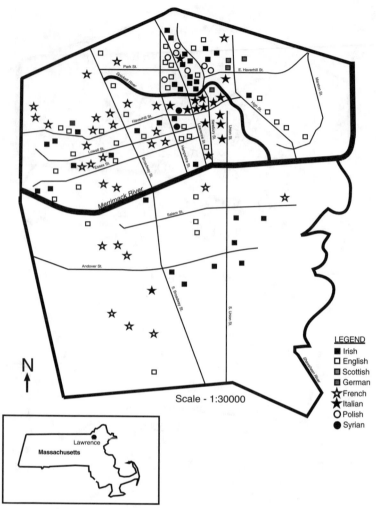

Figure 9.2. Ethnic backgrounds of sampled households in Lawrence,
Massachusetts, 1939. "English" includes "Yankees" and English Canadians,
as well as British; "Frnech" includes French Canadians and Franco-Belgians, as
well as French.
Source: Author sample, Lawrence City Directory

knew they had a job to go to). Overall, the labor market of the preunion years
during the Depression was one in which flexibility, personal and household circumstances, community relationships, and cultural associations were intertwined in the construction of a localized labor process. After unionization, reg-
ularity, stability, uniformity, and predictability were increasingly written into the

302

Meghan Cope

construction of labor markets. With steadier terms of employment and guaranteed wages, the labor market could grow spatially larger, suburbanization could accelerate, and breadwinning could become an increasingly male domain, particularly after World War II.

My argument, then, is that despite workers' desires for "fairness" and for eliminating the abuses of power on the part of employers, unionization had varying impacts on social groups, on households, on neighborhoods and communities, and on the local labor market. The spatial-scale implications of this cannot be ignored. Successful unionization was made possible by national and regional developments, but it was significantly conditioned by local context. In this case, the changes brought about by the Textile Workers' Union of America in the areas of standardization and stabilization were felt not only at the national and regional levels, but also at smaller scales in the restructuring of urban labor markets, of ethnic communities and neighborhoods, and of households.

It is important to stress that the regularization of employment did not occur in the absence of real people. Rather, workers, families, and ethnic communities played important roles in actively forming and re-creating ethnic and gender relations, the social relations of production, and Lawrence's social and spatial divisions of labor through everyday practices. Although these actions were clearly constrained by existing social structures, individuals were not merely passive recipients of their fates. Clearly, the state, institutions, union organizers, firms, and local elites played critical roles in the unionization process (for an excellent account of the roles played by some of these actors in the context of Ontario, Canada, see Parr 1990). The focus of this essay, however, is on workers, families, and social groups within the context of a particular labor structure. Here, I take the viewpoint that these social actors contributed in part to the *structuration* of local political and economic geographies, which in turn shaped the effects of unionization on the labor landscape.

Home-Work Links and Gender Relations

According to Hanson and Pratt (1992, 375), "the home-work link is crucial in suggesting the scale at which the expectations, standards, and preferences of employers and employees are shaped in a dynamic interactive process." The standardization of jobs and the stabilization of employment that came with unionization in Lawrence fundamentally influenced the nature of the links between home and work for many of the city's working families, which in turn influenced the larger arenas of the community and the local labor market. These changes resulted in greater financial and job security for many mill employees' households but also influenced the finely tuned mesh between divisions of labor 303 in households and at work that had been developed over years of accommodation and negotiation between workers and employers. In particular, gender-based changes resulting from unionization and New Deal legislation affected the ways households responded to and managed the challenges of mill work. In this section, I examine home-work links of the 1930s and suggest ways in which regularization affected the relations between households and employers. Social and economic relations revolving around gender are the primary focus of the examination of home-work links because the household was greatly affected by gender-based changes in mill employment.

Oral history accounts of workers recalling the 1920s and 1930s and wage-rate data from Lawrence's mills suggest that women were more likely than men to be employed on a contingent basis, making them more susceptible to changes brought by the regularizing forces of standardization and stabilization. The contingency of many women's employment involved various forms of flexibility. First, because of the gendered division of labor in woolen production, most women were paid on the basis of piecework, while most men worked for hourly wages or "day pay." Historically, and across industrial sectors, those workers on piecework have always been more vulnerable to fluctuations in take-home pay, variations in production requirements, and increasing quotas coupled with decreasing piece rates than have those on hourly wages or day pay. Many residents of Lawrence recalled the effort, tedium, and uncertainty that went into piecework labor. One French-Canadian woman, for instance, recalled of her mill work in the 1930s:

> I was on piecework and I found my work very tedious and hard and you had to keep running and working all the time. . . . See, the difference between my husband's salary and mine was that he was a day worker, like he got paid by the day. . . . And I didn't. I got paid piecework for the amount of work I could produce in a day. So, at the end of the week I was never sure if my pay would be larger or smaller according to the amount of work I did. (Luciene Adams)

Although many women disliked the difficulty, they frequently were able to make more money on piecework by pushing themselves harder for greater production, something they could no longer do after wage stabilization. Workers recall piecework becoming less common after unionization, which meant that women's work was restructured and, despite the comfort of a guaranteed wage, individuals often earned less than they had prior to standardization as wage rates were reduced and work hours shortened. This is one case in which the union saw piecework as a system designed to drain workers of all possible production effi-

Meghan Cope

ciency, whereas in terms of everyday household survival, many individual workers (particularly women) saw piecework in terms of its (arduous) potential for higher earnings.

Although data documenting this shift are not available for the union period, the ironic result of efforts at standardization—that is, women's net loss of work and wages—certainly was not without precedent and would undoubtedly have been the case in Lawrence. A clear example of how women's work and wages (and therefore their roles and contributions in households) in the woolen and worsted industry were influenced negatively by regulation even before unionization is shown by the effects of the earlier National Recovery Administration (NRA) textile codes. These codes became effective August 14, 1933, establishing a minimum wage of thirty-five cents per hour for woolen workers in the northern United States (the majority of whom were centered in Lawrence). The Bureau of Labor Statistics (BLS) published the data in table 9.1 in June 1935 for the woolen and worsted industry. From these data, the BLS determined that, indeed, the enforcement of a minimum wage had caused a rapid rise of hourly wage rates among all woolen workers, a rise that was particularly concentrated among "low-paid, and especially female employees" (Bureau of Labor Statistics 1935, 1) because they were overwhelmingly the ones who had worked for less than the minimum before the codes came in. When the BLS looked at average

Table 9.1. Wage changes in the U.S. woolen and worsted industry, 1932–34

Occupation	Sex	Avg. hourly ¢ Jan.–March 1932	Avg. hourly ¢ August 1933	Avg. hourly ¢ August 1934
Percher	M	46.0	53.2	52.4
Weaver	F	44.0	49.2	51.5
Drawer-in	F	42.3	49.7	53.0
Mender	F	37.1	47.9	53.0
Picker tender	M	35.9	41.3	40.1
Trucker	M	35.1	41.1	42.0
Gillbox tender	M	34.8	39.7	38.9
Spinner, frame	F	34.0	41.6	41.2
Winder	F	31.0	39.9	40.5
Drawing-in frame tender	F	30.8	37.5	37.8
Spooler tender	F	30.4	38.9	40.2
Burler	F	29.4	39.8	41.6
Gillbox tender	F	28.8	37.1	37.5
Doffer	F	24.8	36.0	36.3

Source: Bureau of Labor Statistics, Serial no. 253, June 1935.

305

"Working Steady"

weekly incomes, however, it found that a precipitous drop in wages between 1932 and 1934 was the result of a shrinking of available work hours, and, most significantly, that "female workers lost more time than male workers—28% and 14% respectively—and consequently their weekly earnings showed a greater decline—18.5% and 11.8% respectively" (ibid., 9). This trend suggests that although some women (with higher skills) were able to earn approximately the same hourly rates as men (with lower skills), the overall opportunity structure for women concentrated them in the lower-paying jobs, paid them less in the same jobs (compare male and female gillbox tenders in table 9.1), and men were given preference when there were a limited number of hours available for work. These data suggest that the regularization of work and wages did not necessarily lead to uniform improvements in employment conditions or terms across genders.

The second element of contingency that influenced the home-work link and had gender implications was subjective hiring that took into account personal and household circumstances. Although favoritism was generally disliked, preferential hiring was sometimes used to assist needy families, a practice that was also found in Parr's (1990) study of male furniture workers in Ontario. A French-Canadian woman recounts her experience of favoritism in Lawrence during the 1930s:

> I had problems working steady. My father and mother had died and I was left to support my younger brothers and sisters. We would work two weekdays, 6 A.M. to 2:30 P.M., then alternate two weeknights, 2:30 P.M. to 11 P.M. At the start of the shift, the women would gather at one end of the room so the section hand could pick out the amount of workers he needed for his section. They would always pick out the married women with families first and the rest were sent home. Since I was not married I was always sent home. At first I was too shy to talk up and was sent home on a regular basis. I finally got up enough nerve and went to the boss, Mr. Whitehead. I explained to him that being parentless and supporting six brothers and sisters, I needed a job. He sent me down to the section hand and put me to work on a steady basis. (Lucy Mele)

It is impossible to know how common this practice was because, although it was mentioned by several oral history respondents, there are no existing records indicating a policy or measuring numbers of such incidents. Knowing that preferences for needy families were used at all, however, is valuable evidence of the subjective nature of hiring. "Working steady" was clearly a goal for Lawrence

Meghan Cope

mill workers, and the potential of the union for making this a reality was highly attractive at the time. Ironically, however, with the union-directed policies of formalized hiring procedures, Lucy Mele and others like her may in fact have suffered unfortunate consequences of the ending of subjective preferences for those workers supporting families.

The final element of contingency examined here concerns the fact that, for many employees of both genders, work in Lawrence's woolen mills during the 1930s was sporadic. Workers from this time recall frequent "slack periods." The French-Canadian woman quoted earlier, who started mill work in 1931, experienced slack times and indicates that there was some use of part-time schedules, particularly after NRA legislation that mandated minimum work hours:

> If they didn't have a lot of work for the day they had to guarantee you four hours of work. And then they could send you home. . . . You went back the next day. The next day they might have more work. And there were times you worked steady all the time. . . . Unless there was a big slack period. By slack I mean where they knew they wouldn't have much work. Then you had a sort of seniority, which meant that the longer you had been working there you were the last one to be let go.[1] They could tell you you're laid off for a while but they would call you back when they needed you. That could be for weeks or months. (Luciene Adams)

Seasonal shutdowns of entire mills, periodic layoffs, and daily hiring episodes constituted the normal state of affairs at this time, though not everyone experienced these fluctuations in the same ways. In particular, less-skilled and younger workers, as well as those on piecework (the majority of whom were women), were more vulnerable to these erratic schedules of production, which again influenced the home-work link. For example, women often exited and reentered the labor force during the course of a year as household demands allowed or necessitated. The American Woolen Company's *Employees Booster,* a magazine published by the corporation in Lawrence for its workers, frequently noted individual women's passage in and out of mill work with the explanation only that they were "attending household duties."[2] This type of sporadic labor was of a more voluntary character than layoffs, and women did not necessarily have control over the scheduling of either their waged labor or their "household duties," but the very nature of mill work as erratic and seasonal also made it more feasible for women to come and go in order to accommodate their families' needs and to lace together household divisions of labor with industrial production schedules. Further, although both men and women were subject to periodic layoffs, 307 the gender division of labor in the mills was such that the most stable salaried jobs (e.g., loom fixers, foremen, supervisors) were entirely male occupations. This is one example of the interdependence of the divisions of labor at home and in the mills. In the household, women were seen as responsible for the maintenance of their homes and child rearing, whereas in the mills the more contingent nature of many women's jobs meant that it was in some cases possible to use production flexibility to complement obligations to home and family (though rarely on the women's own terms). Taken together, these factors suggest that the eradication of sporadic employment, although generally seen as a positive development, also meant that fewer women could take advantage of flexible household schedules to work for wages and, conversely, had more difficulty taking advantage of flexible mill schedules to work at home. Perhaps even more significantly, the stabilization of mill employment, the formalization of seniority rights, and the later requirements of "continuous service" for fringe benefits (O'Connell 1993) penalized women who tried to continue to pass in and out of the workforce.

I have argued that there was a strong potential for unionization to change the nature of work through the erosion of flexible terms, which, because of the gender division of labor in the mills, affected women more. This shift, however, did not immediately result in a net decline of women's employment in the mills. Tables 9.2 and 9.3 show that the initial period of unionization in the late 1930s saw a slight decline in women's participation in textiles in Lawrence, while men's proportion increased slightly. However, a combination of factors — the lingering influence of wartime production practices, the shift to white-collar and service jobs among men after the war (see table 9.3), the continued stagnation of women's wages, and the imminent permanent shutdown of the Lawrence mills — resulted in a slight rebound for women's employment in textiles by 1950.

Women clearly were not being shut out of mill employment in Lawrence in the union period — in fact, the proportion of women in the mills of all employed women was nearly as high in 1950 as in 1930. It is also true that the

Table 9.2. Textile workers as percentage of all employed males and females, Lawrence, Massachusetts

	1930	1940	1950
Male	42.3	43.2	37.4
Female	54.0	48.8	50.5

Source: United States Bureau of the Census 1930, 1940, 1950.

Meghan Cope

Table 9.3. Top five industries or industry groups in employment, percentage change, Lawrence, Massachusetts

Industry or group	1930–40		1940–50	
	M	F	M	F
Textiles	(8)[a]	(5)	(19)	8
Other manufacturing industries	(28)	1.2	19	(11)
Personal, professional, public services	(8)	(2.7)	39	20
Wholesale & retail trade	(6.7)	1.2	13	45
Transport, communications, utilities, construction	(42)	[b]	24	[b]

[a]Numbers in parenthesis indicate decreases.
[b]Numbers too small for comparison.
Source: United States Bureau of the Census 1930, 1940.

changes brought by the union were undoubtedly implemented very slowly and may have affected some operations sooner than others. To the extent that contingency and flexibility were being eliminated, however, some workers were affected in positive ways (their earnings increased and uncertainty decreased) while others were affected in negative ways (to the extent that for some, full-time, standardized work was not feasible). In general, then, unionization could be seen as creating a "fairer" set of work rules, but these were not necessarily to everyone's benefit.

The impacts of increasingly standardized working conditions on the household-work link during the 1940s are difficult to ascertain, but the war effort may have assisted women in absorbing the changes in the terms of textile labor during this time. Because the textile industry had largely abandoned Lawrence by 1954, it is impossible to know whether, in this particular urban context, unionization would have continued to influence women's employment in peaceful times. It is quite likely, however, that even if the elimination of contingency did not actually result in fewer women employees, the *nature* and *terms* of many women's mill work were significantly transformed.

Ultimately, the erratic schedules of mill employment not only affected the ways that individual women worked, but also affected *households'* abilities to cope with uncertainty and therefore played a major role in shaping the nature of the home-work relationship. Seasonal shutdowns and slack periods, which were some of the most debilitating features of mill work in the 1930s, led households to develop strategies to ensure some minimum level of income—such as diversi-

309

fying the workplaces and industries that different members worked in, putting as many members as possible into the waged workforce (particularly teenage children and women not engaged in child rearing), and staggering householders' shift work to accommodate family needs.

First, there was a perceived value in having a household that was not entirely dependent on the mills. One woman commented:

> The wives would work, and push their husbands into a better job, like a trade. I told some of our friends, "Don't let your husband work in the mills. There's no future in it." What I mean is that he's better off with a trade. They're better off to have the man in the trade and the woman in the mills. (Alice Burke)

By diversifying the types of jobs held by household members, the household would be less susceptible to layoffs and more resilient during slack times, therefore protecting a base level of income.

Second, achieving a diverse range of employment was complemented in many households by simply increasing the *numbers* of employed members. One man remembered having little choice in going to work when he turned fourteen, the legal minimum working age: "It was Friday night. We were around the supper table and [my father] just, well, he says, 'Well, you won't be going to school Monday, you'll be going into the Wood Mill'" (Frederick Arold). Examining the composition of the labor force of Lawrence's mills at this time also indicates a gender component to this numerical household strategy. Women accounted for 50 percent of the woolen mills' workers, yet the age profile of this labor force shows high participation rates for women in their teens and early twenties, a dip during child-rearing years, and another rise among women over age forty-five. The age profile for male workers in Lawrence's mills shows a steadier rise with a peak at ages forty to fifty and a slow decline among older men (United States Bureau of the Census 1930, 1940; author's compilations). This suggests that there was indeed a social preference for mothers to avoid waged labor, but the practical necessities of Depression-era working families meant that women without young children were very likely to be employed, along with a large share of those who were raising children.

Third, daily household schedules and responsibilities were manipulated to accommodate the demands of mill work through strategies such as staggering wage earners' shifts to allow children to be cared for by their parents. As Frederick Arold, an ethnically German mill worker in Lawrence, recalls, however, this strategy wore on the parents themselves:

310

Meghan Cope

When I was first married, and when my kids were born in 1936 and
'37 — they were only fifteen months apart — my wife worked the 6 to
2 shift and I worked the 3 to 11 shift and we used to meet on Union
Street. There was a fish market there, Atlantic Fish Market, and we always met there and I would tell her what went on. I was taking care of
the kids in the morning, you know, and on my way to work I'd drop
the kids off at my mother's house and she'd go there and pick them up
and take them home. So we compared notes under the fish market and
the only time we spent together was at night from, say, I'd be going to
bed about midnight and she had to get up at about 4:30 in the morning. (Frederick Arold)

In the Arolds' case, we see that the home-work relationship was one of sacrifice
and accommodation to the financial and emotional demands of family and the
production demands of industry.

The relatively large proportion of women employed in Lawrence's mills, the
practice of taking teenagers out of school and placing them in waged labor, and
staggered shift work among family members demonstrate tactics that were the
results of both gender- and age-based social relations. In turn, we can see that
these social relations permeated both working-class households and the local
labor market. The home-work link was one in which mill workers' households
depended on all of their members for support and, conversely, the costs of uncertainty in the production process were absorbed by the flexibility of workers'
households. Lawrence's local labor market had been structured around the employment of multiple family members in the mills for generations: for employers, such arrangements cut down on hiring costs, kept workers more dependent
and possibly more cooperative, family members were most likely already social-
ized for mill work and schedules, and, by hiring women and teens as well as
grown men, took advantage of a source of workers who were spatially constrained
by the location of the head of the family in traditionally patriarchal households.
The strategies of households for maximizing income by placing as many members as possible in the waged labor force thus created a flexible pool of locally
dependent, knowledgeable labor for the mills.

The regularization of mill employment, on the other hand, disrupted patterns
of household adaptation that had been developed over the previous decades, in
turn reorganizing the relationships between home and work and thus impacting
the operation of the local labor markets. Although we often consider the effects
of unions and New Deal legislation as having generally *improved* the lot of work-

311

"Working Steady"

ers (through more secure rights and steadier work, wages, and terms of employment), we cannot ignore the small-scale changes these caused in the everyday lives of workers and their families and cannot assume that they were applied uniformly for the better. Unions generally did not perceive male and female workers as having any different interests or needs. Yet, the restructuring of jobs was potentially detrimental to women's wages or work conditions, and technological changes meant that the gender division of labor was being reorganized—a process that affected both men and women. The *standardization* of jobs meant that fewer operations were structured as piecework, hiring and task allocation were formalized through written procedures and personnel offices, and contracts specified the terms and conditions of work. The *stabilization* of employment meant that continuous work was more likely to be available but also was more likely to be expected of workers, regardless of personal or household obligations.

Community-Work Links and Ethnic Relations

Although the preceding discussion suggests that the regularization of work brought by unionization and New Deal legislation affected the nature of women's work to a greater degree than that of men and so transformed the home-work link, evidence exists to suggest that the standardization of employment helped level the playing field in mill employment for Lawrence's ethnic groups. This again demonstrates that the effects of regularization were not evenly distributed across the workforce. The historical advantages experienced by some ethnic groups as they were employed in the woolen mills came about through an interlocking system of ethnic hiring networks, ethnic favoritism, and preferential treatment. The ostensible elimination of this system should have equalized the opportunity structures for workers of all backgrounds. Again, quantified data that would show this conclusively are scarce, but oral history accounts demonstrate that unions were effective in minimizing favoritism, and therefore in changing the links between ethnic communities and mill employment. These changes had important influences on the divisions of labor in the mills and, by extension, influenced the local labor market as well.

To understand the impact of regularization, particularly in the forms of standardization of hiring and task allocation that resulted from unionization, we must first examine the local context in which ethnicity played a role as important as gender in determining the occupational options open to an individual. Favoritism in hiring and task allocation, ethnic discrimination, and the resulting wage differences contributed to a quite highly differentiated labor force. A deeply entrenched ethnic division of labor in Lawrence's mills was created and perpetuated by this favoritism and these hiring networks. For example, loom fixers were

312

generally French-Canadian men, weavers tended to be German men or Irish women, and spinners were overwhelmingly Italian women. These divisions of labor were mirrored in the social geography of the city. Lawrence did not have neat, discrete ethnic neighborhoods (it was common for individual tenements to house families of many different ethnic backgrounds), but the city's ethnic communities had spheres of influence indicated by spatial concentrations of ethnic residences (though these were permeable) and anchored by clusters of churches, club buildings, entertainment facilities, and food markets (see figures 9.1 and 9.2). In terms of the links between community and work, these nodes served as the social, economic, and political sites for communications regarding working conditions, job openings, and the further development of ethnic bonds between workers.

A bit of cultural context is useful here. In broad terms, in Lawrence during the 1930s, the English and old "Yankees" were the most powerful groups: they owned the mills, banks, and much of the real estate. The Irish had risen from early persecution in the 1860s to dominate the political structures of the city and the supervision of the mills by the early twentieth century. Germans and Belgians had come later as skilled craft workers and maintained a high position in the city, in businesses, and in the mills' most highly regarded strata. By the 1930s, the Italians had done fairly well at raising themselves to a wide range of positions in the mills and were a strong force politically in the city because of their large population. Similarly, the French Canadians had started to overcome initial discrimination and were rising in the ranks of the mills, as well as the city. The poorest and least powerful groups in Lawrence during the 1930s were the latest arrivals, those who arrived just before the doors shut in the mid-1920s with the implementation of immigration quotas. These immigrants had come from Eastern Europe — Poland, Lithuania, Russia — and from Syria and Armenia, and occupied the cheapest housing and the lowest-paying jobs in the mills (for more on Lawrence's ethnic background, see Cole 1963; Goldberg 1989; Dorgan 1924).

The role of ethnicity in Lawrence's mills was significantly developed by the 1930s. The city had been built and prospered on the labors of generations of newcomers and had earned the moniker "Immigrant City." The vast majority of Lawrence's population even at this time was either foreign-born or first-generation American (United States Bureau of the Census 1930, 1940), which was reflected in close ethnic communities bound together through church, language, specialty food shops, clubs, and newspapers. Through these, as well as family connections, job opportunities could be accessed quite simply. Later-arriving groups with smaller numbers and members who were less well established were 313 at a disadvantage for scarce work and had more difficulty penetrating the system. Before the implementation of legislative reforms and union policies, working conditions and the terms of employment involved sporadic work and subjective hiring. As shown in the preceding section, preferential hiring was advantageous to some, but favoritism was also a sore point of contention for many workers. One Italian woman remembered of the preunion period: Before the union came, "you had to look for work in the morning, then go back home, then go back in the afternoon, and then [the bosses would] go 'You, You, You.' They'd pick out the same ones all the time. They didn't pick out who was good or who did their jobs or anything" (Filomena Parolisi). A Lithuanian man recalls that ethnicity also played a role in who got which work and under what conditions:

> When I was working in the winding room in the wool mill . . . I always noticed the section hand was Italian. It was always the Italian women that got the best yarn, they would sit there asleep and that yarn would run whereas just three girls away, she couldn't make a dollar if she tried all week. The yarn would break and break and break — that was favoritism. (J. Milauskas)

In addition to ethnic-based hiring, tasks were also allocated along the lines of the social construction of what counted as a "skilled" job. Jobs classified as "skilled" tend to evolve through a cycle of who performs them and a building of "mystery" around the operations involved (Gaskell 1987). For instance, loom fixers were overwhelmingly French-Canadian men, paid on day rates. Loom fixing was a "skilled" operation that required unpaid instruction by a relative or friend, as well as the personal collection of proper tools, in order for a new worker to be hired — requirements that clearly limited the scope of ethnic (and gender) groups who gained entry into this position. Thus, the construction of loom fixing as skilled, the passing on of those skills, and the hiring of new workers all depended on the ethnicity and gender of those already involved in the job.

The preunion combination of favoritism, flexible employment, and uncertainty was devastating to many Lawrence residents, and undoubtedly caused many workers to feel that they had little control over their work situation and no recourse in cases of abuse of power by foremen, supervisors, and employers. On the other hand, these ethnic divisions had been actively forged over the years by the ethnic groups that were able, through privilege or struggle, to carve out advantages for their members. In effect, for some people, ethnic divisions of labor and preferential hiring created outstanding opportunities as they were perpetuated by favors, the passing on of skills, and through connections formed by networks of family and friends. As one man explained: "You see, when you're Italian, you can get a job if you know an Italian that's got influence with some other guy, whether he's Irish or not, they can get you a job. That's the way it was in them days. You know, we took care of ourselves, our people" (Casparino Robito). Therefore, the development of ethnic hiring networks and preferences over decades of mill employment helped some groups, such as the Italians, to combat the uncertain and erratic nature of mill work. In this way, we can see the active (though not necessarily empowered) roles that ethnic communities played in the creation and re-creation of both the divisions of labor in the mill, and, more broadly, the nature of the local labor process. Community-work links were deeply sedimented social processes by the 1930s and had emerged after years of struggle, negotiation, and accommodation; that is, ethnic communities were active agents in the development of favorable labor relations and practices, even within the larger constraints of social structures such as prejudice, profit motives, and exploitation. Thus, while union-led standardization benefited many individuals by eliminating ethnic favor through seniority and other formalized means, the power of some communities to "take care of themselves" was also increasingly challenged.

The combination of favoritism, divisions of labor, and notions of skill created a situation in which workers were often unable to move beyond the opportunities shaped for them by their gender, their ethnicity, and their community-based connections in the mill. For workers who perceived their employment as limited by factors out of their control, the union was clearly an attractive equalizing force in Lawrence's woolen mills. Workers hoped that, in addition to stabilizing the availability of work, the union would make the conditions of hiring and firing more fair — indeed, as one man commented, "Some of the outrageous things that they had been doing were stopped" (Jack DiLavore) — although some preferential hiring continued after the union came, but in less explicit forms. Therefore, although personal social networks continue to be important in finding work today (see, for example, Hanson and Pratt 1995), the increased formalization of personnel offices, recruiting policies, work contracts, seniority rights, and specific rules for hiring and promotion that were slowly being implemented under the unions served as a challenge to the favoritism that went hand in hand with close-knit ties to a community.

It is impossible to know the full effect on favoritism of changes brought by the union's regularization, but many workers recall improvements in opportunity and some level of recourse against abuses after the New Deal legislation was implemented and the TWUA was established in Lawrence's mills in 1937. Comparing the early days to the situation after the adoption of the union, workers articulated the connection between unions, legislation, and fair working conditions. One Russian woman observed:

> People used to bring the section hand—at the end of the week—fresh eggs, vegetables, fruits, just to keep their job, to be on the right side of them.... He was the one that lorded over you. And if he decided he didn't want you there, he'd say, "Out!" That would be the end, you were fired.... Well, I didn't bring him anything. But the thing was, he used to go by...and give me a pat on the behind, which I didn't particularly think was necessary. Then the next step, he asked if I'd like to go out. I thought to myself, "I'm only seventeen, you're an old man. You're asking me to go out!" I was shocked, but that's the way it was. I didn't show up, of course.... See, when you don't have unions, you don't have anybody to run to, you're afraid [to lose your job] in your own way. (Sandra Cashman)

And a man working in one of the largest mills recalled:

> [During the Depression] I was working in the combing room, but they weren't steady jobs. You went in there every morning and the boss picked out how many he needed for the day, you know: "You, You, You, You," and you went to work for the day, and then you had to come in the next day and maybe you'd get a day's work. And you never got a full week. I'm talking about before the union came in, and the NRA. You never got a full week in the mill unless you fit good with the boss.... But then the unemployment insurance came in when Roosevelt came in, you know, and the union after that.... [Then] you got your share, *according to seniority.*

He continued:

> [Some people] used to bring the boss fruit and vegetables and wine. That went on. But see that was before the union, you know, because when the union came in they wouldn't stand for that. They might still have done it on the sly, but the union would never stand for anything like that. (Harold Adams)

The standardization of the hiring and job allocation processes did serve to minimize (though not completely eradicate) the favoritism and abuses of power that had abounded in the mills. As qualifications and abilities of an individual became the formalized criteria for hiring (at least superficially), ethnic background and "who you knew" were somewhat less significant in shaping oppor-

316

Meghan Cope

tunities. This suggests that when favoritism was gradually eliminated, the effects of ethnic discrimination on employment were minimized, and the ethnic division of labor in the mills was slowly eroded. In this case, a lessening of the favoritism and contingent employment that were disliked by many workers was seen as one of the most important results of these changes, in part because it affected the way that people lived their everyday lives and appealed to a sense of fairness and opportunity that was highly valued by many of Lawrence's workers. Overall, then, there is a sense that standardization of employment helped minimize the effects of ethnic biases in Lawrence's woolen mills.

Indeed, by the time World War II began, the strength of the city's ethnic communities was weakening across the board as the effects of immigration limits were seen in the paucity of newcomers, young people spoke English and longed for "American" lifestyles, intermarriage between groups increased, and early suburbanization dispersed a formerly spatially concentrated population. It is possible to say, then, that the equalizing effects of the union contributed in part to a blurring of ethnic boundaries and the increasing "Americanization" of the working people of Lawrence's mills. Ethnicity-based inroads into employment had run their course and were, along with languages and traditional cultural practices, losing their centrality in individuals' ethnic identities and the communities' struggles for success.

The Local Labor Market

This essay began with the argument that the regularization of work brought by New Deal legislation and the adoption of unions did not affect workers in all social groups equally. The variation in who was affected and how led in turn to shifts in home-work links of mill employees (particularly through gender-specific changes) and in community-work links (particularly through ethnicity-specific changes). Consequently, the changes experienced in the social/spatial arenas of households and neighborhood-based ethnic communities led to a variety of shifts in both the social composition and the spatial extent of the local labor market.

In the preunion period, various forms of flexibility developed by manufacturers involved constantly tailoring production to demand, resulting in hiring by the day (or even by the hour), frequent layoffs, wage cuts, speeding up machines and "stretching out" workers, the use of piecework, and, perhaps most significantly, shutting down a mill entirely for weeks or months at a time. This flexibility of production maintained a high level of profit for the owners and stockholders but resulted in a high degree of uncertainty among workers, who wondered on a daily and weekly basis how hard they would have to work, how

317

much they would be paid, and, in fact, whether they would work at all. I have argued that the union's drive to eliminate such contingent work conditions and terms of employment—through the dual forces of stabilization and standardization—fundamentally restructured the home-work link by rewriting the rules of work and revising the household strategies needed to maximize income within the constraints of family demands. Further, I suggested that these had particularly salient effects on gender relations, both within the workplace and within households.

The gender-specific implications of these forces of regularization on the relationships between home and work affected the labor market in several ways. First, the combined effects of formalized hiring and expectations of continuous work created a situation for households in which it was increasingly advantageous to commit one spouse entirely to waged work and the other entirely to household responsibilities. Here we see the continued construction of the male "breadwinner" (Parr 1990) in Lawrence woolen mills. Although this had long been held as an ideal among Lawrence's working families, it had simply not been feasible within a context of low wages, unpredictable hours, and sporadic work. Similarly, although the construction of the male "breadwinner" was by no means new at this time, the union's activities were intrinsically tied to such conceptions and thus played a role in reinscribing them on the labor process. Thus, regularization had a strong potential to cause shifts in gender relations and divisions of labor both at home and at work.[3]

Second, the social transformations brought by the regularization of mill work were expressed spatially in the labor landscape. As suggested earlier, employment that was constructed on a contingent basis was inherently more locally entrenched because of the costs involved in traveling longer distances for a job that may not be there from day to day, and for wages that were minimal (for a comparison with clock work, see Larrowe 1955). When the terms of labor became more stabilized, and when a contract was signed for employment, longer-distance journeys to work became possible. When these two trends are considered with the forces of suburbanization and rising home ownership (which were nascent during the late 1930s but rampant after the war), we can see that the spatial extent of the mills' workforce was able to expand rapidly; that is, the labor market was able to shift from a focus on the highly concentrated urban population of Lawrence to one that was increasingly dispersed. Census figures confirm that, even during the 1930s, adjoining small towns such as Methuen and the Andovers were growing rapidly while Lawrence's population declined slightly (see table 9.4). The stabilizing effects of "steadier" work, formalized training and hiring, and the eventual development of a predictable "family wage"

318

Table 9.4. Population shifts in Lawrence and contiguous towns, 1930–40

City/town	1930 population	1940 population	Percentage change
Lawrence	85,068	84,323	(.9)
Andover	9,969	11,122	11.6
Methuen	21,069	21,880	3.8
North Andover	6,961	7,524	8.1

Source: United States Bureau of the Census 1930, 1940.

played significant roles in changing both the social composition of the local labor market by favoring male breadwinners, and the spatial extent of the local labor market by enabling residential suburbanization.

In the period before unions and New Deal legislative reforms of industrial employment, ethnicity also played a central role in the woolen mills of Lawrence, influencing the spread of information about jobs and working conditions, the passing on of skills, and the favor of the "bosses," ultimately resulting in a distinct ethnic division of labor in the mills that created a differentiation in prestige and wages. The standardizing efforts of the union to eliminate favor and subjectivity in the processes of hiring and task allocation caused some groups to lose their long-sought advantage within the mills while it allowed others to gain greater access to jobs and levels of employment previously closed to them. Particularly for the formerly powerful groups, these changes impacted the community-work links that had been established over the decades and practiced in churches and clubs, and in the markets and on the doorsteps of the ethnic community's neighborhood areas. These shifts, together with the lessening of contingent employment through stabilization policies, caused a restructuring of the community-work relationship by slowly eroding the social role of ethnicity and leading to the spatial dispersion of younger generations of workers away from the "old neighborhood." These forces, again, encouraged suburbanization and therefore a more spatially extensive market from which workers were drawn. In terms of the social composition of the labor market, these results of standardizing policies tended to foster a more ethnically diverse set of potential workers.

First, and most obviously, the standardization of the hiring process shifted preferences toward competence and employability and away from ethnic identifiers. Similarly, the allocation of work (e.g., who got the good yarn) and the broader establishment of the division of labor were less directed by ethnicity as standardized labor relations policies took hold. Ethnicity-based networks could

319

still spread information, but they could no longer ensure that a word spoken on one's behalf would result in a job.

Second, the stabilization of employment — the development of "steadier" work, wages, and conditions — meant that ethnic networks were probably less necessary in obtaining access to work on an everyday basis. Longer-term job security led workers to be less dependent on the ethnic community to provide entrance to mill employment, though they undoubtedly continued that role in some capacity. Similarly, predictable work conditions and wage rates meant that favors and subjective practices were no longer the only means through which to ensure adequate incomes.

Third, the transformation of the community-work link, through the weakening of ethnic ties and the blurring of cultural boundaries, resulted in a shift in the spatial construction of the local labor market of Lawrence. As the more predictable nature of work and wages allowed for suburbanization and longer commutes, it had the effect of gradually eroding the old spatially concentrated, ethnic neighborhoods as young working people increasingly married outside of their ethnic groups, spoke only English, and physically moved out of their parents' areas of the city and out of their ethnic groups' cultural domains. Walker (1981, 398) points out: "There is no question that, however different it is from that of the middle class, working-class life in the suburbs is quite different from that of the traditional ethnic districts of the inner city. This difference can be seen clearly in the interfamilial tensions between parents in the inner city and children moving to the suburbs." Suburbanization and the decline in importance of the old ethnic community ties went hand in hand and both were, in part, facilitated by the changes in the organization of work brought by the effects of the union's regularization. These factors taken together created a more spatially dispersed labor market and at the same time contributed to the waning of ethnic divisions of labor within the mills.

Therefore, the effects of regularization on the local labor market were mixed. Both the restructuring of home-work links and of community-work relationships tended to enhance the spatial extent of the labor market, broadening it out into the outlying areas of the city and the growing suburban towns surrounding Lawrence (table 9.4). When we consider the changes that regularization brought to the social composition of the labor market, we see, on the one hand, the potential for fewer ethnically based impediments as diverse cultural groups gained access into new jobs and strata of employment, but, on the other hand, potentially more gender-based limitations as "steadier" work conditions and wages encouraged heightened household reliance on male breadwinners.

320

Meghan Cope

Conclusion

Much labor-related social-science research has had a tendency to focus on "labor" as a monolithic group and on unions as universally beneficent. By opening up the discussion through a geographic perspective on the small-scale arenas of households, neighborhoods, and labor markets, this analysis has attempted to capture a greater sense of the diversity of experiences of the changes brought about by unionization. Home, work, and community are the primary arenas of everyday life and must also be central to small-scale analyses. I used the rubrics of the home-work link and the community-work link to demonstrate that these arenas cannot be logically separated or considered in isolation because the changes that affect one area of local, everyday relations inevitably have repercussions in all areas.

Further, by examining the multiple processes involved in social, economic, and power-political interactions, the complexity of urban daily life in a textile town during the Depression is acknowledged and perhaps more easily grasped. By taking gender and ethnicity as sets of dynamic relations that shaped people's lives at home, in their communities, and at work, we can more readily recognize the diversity of experiences caused by the regularization of work. Finally, analyses focusing on the small-scale and everyday level of industrial labor allow a glimpse of the active role individuals played in shaping home, community, and work relations. Clearly, there were significant constraints on Lawrence's workers, but within those they managed to accommodate the multiple demands of family and bosses through household strategies to minimize uncertainty and maximize income, and, through ethnic networks of assistance, to "take care of themselves."

Notes

I wish to thank Immigrant City Archives of Lawrence, Massachusetts; the Museum of American Textile History of Lowell, Massachusetts; and the Center for Lowell History, Lowell, Massachusetts, for kind assistance in sharing their oral history transcripts from workers in Lawrence. Thanks also to Patrick Haight for cartography assistance, and to Andrew Herod and Lynn Staeheli for comments on earlier versions.

1. Although Mrs. Adams mentions "a sort of seniority" here, it was a very informal affair, and not documented as it was after the unions came in.

2. The American Woolen Company's *Employees Booster* ceased publication in the mid-1920s, but oral history accounts suggest that this trend continued into the 1930s as well.

3. I say "potential" here because Lawrence had lost the last of its woolen mills by 1952 and the longer-term results cannot be known. It is clear that

321

many women were still working in Lawrence's mills after World War II, but by then the industry was on such a clear downward spiral, and so many mills had already shut down or relocated to the South, that it is difficult to know what the situation might have been if production had continued.

Bibliography

Bureau of Labor Statistics. 1935. Serial no. 253, June.

Cole, D. B. 1963. *Immigrant City: Lawrence, Massachusetts, 1845–1921.* Chapel Hill: University of North Carolina Press.

Dorgan, M. 1924. *History of Lawrence, Massachusetts.* Lawrence, Mass.: By the author.

Foner, P. S. 1980. *Women and the American Labor Movement: From World War I to the Present.* New York: Free Press Macmillan.

Gaskell, J. 1987. "Conceptions of Skill and the Work of Women: Some Historical and Political Issues." In *The Politics of Diversity: Feminism, Marxism and Nationalism,* edited by R. Hamilton and M. Barrett, 361–80. Montreal: Book Center.

Goldberg, D. 1989. *A Tale of Three Cities: Labor Organization and Protest in Patterson, Passaic, and Lawrence, 1916–1921.* New Brunswick, N.J.: Rutgers University Press.

Hanson, S., and G. Pratt. 1992. "Dynamic Dependencies: A Geographic Investigation of Local Labor Markets." *Economic Geography* 68.4: 373–405.

————. 1995. *Gender, Work, and Space.* New York: Routledge.

Larrowe, C. P. 1955. *Shape-Up and Hiring Hall.* Berkeley: University of California Press.

Milton, D. 1982. *The Politics of U.S. Labor: From the Great Depression to the New Deal.* New York: Monthly Review Press.

O'Connell, M. E. 1993. "Coming Unfringed: The Unraveling of Job-Based Entitlements." *American Prospect* 13: 55–63.

Parr, J. 1990. *The Gender of Breadwinners: Women, Men, and Change in Two Industrial Towns, 1880–1950.* Toronto: University of Toronto Press.

Primer of Labor Relations. 1940. Washington, D.C.: Bureau of National Affairs.

Rieve, E. 1941. "Textile Workers Union of America." *Labor Information Bulletin,* U.S. Department of Labor 8.7: 7–10.

United States Bureau of the Census. 1930. *Census of Population and Housing: 1930; A Report of the Fifteenth Decennial Census of the United States.* Washington, D.C.: U.S. Government Printing Office.

United States Bureau of the Census. 1940. *Census of Population and Housing: 1940; A Report of the Sixteenth Decennial Census of the United States.* Washington, D.C.: U.S. Government Printing Office.

Meghan Cope

United States Bureau of the Census. 1950. *Census of Population; 1950; A Report of the Seventeenth Decennial Census of the United States.* Washington, D.C.: U.S. Government Printing Office.

Walker, R. 1981. "A Theory of Suburbanization: Capitalism and the Construction of Urban Space in the United States." In *Urbanization and Urban Planning in Capitalist Society,* edited by M. Dear and A. Scott, 383–429. London: Methuen.

"Working Steady"

Chapter 10 • Investigating the Local-Global Paradox
Corporate Strategy, Union Local Autonomy, and Community Action in Chicago
Andrew E. G. Jonas

Arguably, the most puzzling paradox to confront contemporary researchers of the politics of economic restructuring is what I call the "local-global paradox." Edmund Preteceille (1990) has captured the essence of this paradox. He argues that, while economic relationships have become ever more *global* in scope and nature, political responses to economic globalization are becoming more *localized*. His argument has a particular bearing on the politics of deindustrialization. Because many of the economic problems facing localities once heavily dependent on manufacturing employment seem to be the result of events and decisions framed at the global scale, it seems somewhat paradoxical that in many cases political responses have emphasized local solutions, such as plant-by-plant negotiating, decentralization of responsibility for economic development to local authorities, local regulation of labor markets, and so forth (cf. Peck 1996).

The local-global paradox has profound implications for unions involved in contesting plant closures and turning back the tide of deindustrialization. Certainly, a number of changes are under way that have undermined the political capacity of unions to respond effectively at the national and international levels to deindustrialization. The decentralization of wage bargaining, the shift to a more flexible labor market, and growing pressures on localities to compete for inward investment mark attempts by national governments to break out of the institutional rigidities of postwar class accords. Decentralization is buttressed by politically and ideologically motivated assaults on unions by proponents of neoliberal economic policy, and it composes one element of a "solution" to the crisis of mass production/Keynesian welfarism. It is a solution, moreover, that seems to involve a deliberate policy of "localizing labor" (Peck 1996; Tickell and Peck 1995). Political decentralization has fragmented the labor movement and encouraged "union retreat" into old industrial heartlands where last-ditch political campaigns have been conducted by the remnants of once-powerful industrial organizations (Griffiths and Johnston 1991; Martin, Sunley, and Wills 1993).

325

For a variety of reasons, then, the national-level presence of labor, and its political organization through "top-down" union structures, have been seriously weakened. Consequently, labor is limited in its responses to more local levels, and by so limiting itself is placed in a position where resistance is difficult. This "new political localism" for labor has played into the hands of national and multinational corporations that increasingly divide workers in different localities against each other in the competition to maintain high profit levels (Hudson and Sadler 1983). Faced with the threat of plant closures, redundancies, and membership losses, labor is more likely than ever before to acquiesce to the needs of mobile industry. Indeed, unions have been known to co-opt local opposition movements in the fear that future inward investment opportunities might by jeopardized by organized political action (Herod 1991). Michael Burawoy (1985) points to the growing political acquiescence of labor as evidence of a currently dominant "global labor control regime" characterized as "hegemonic despotism" (cf. Peck 1996, 234–48). Under this regime, capital's bargaining power is enhanced "by virtue of collective labor's vulnerability to [capital's] national and international mobility" (Burawoy 1985, 127). Such conclusions are supported by numerous case studies of local antiplant closure campaigns, which document how locally dependent actors, including workers, unions, public officials, and community organizations, have often been powerless in the face of more mobile capital (Bluestone and Harrison 1982; Clark 1989; Haughton 1989; Herod 1991; Lauria 1994; Lynd 1982; Metzger 1980).

It seems, then, that labor has embraced the discourse of capital mobility and interlocality competition and in so doing has limited its responses to the local scale. Capital, too, has its local agents eager to lend credence to the discourse of mobility. These locally dependent businesses — participants in local "growth coalitions" (Logan and Molotch 1987) — conjoin with local governments to promote fiscal and land-use policies that make their localities more attractive to inward investment. It may be extremely difficult for labor to promote local economic strategies and discourses that are inconsistent with, or even pose a direct threat to, the projects of the growth coalition, legitimated as they often are by the hegemonic discourse of capital mobility and place competition (Cox and Mair 1988).

Unions, too, are confronted with the local-global paradox. At a time when globalization is breaking down old regional or national boundaries and differences between places are becoming increasingly significant in the calculus of corporate location — what some have termed the "glocalization of capital" — some researchers and activists argue that unions should develop local responses that are sensitive to the particularities of place (Martin, Sunley, and Wills 1996).

326

Andrew E. G. Jonas

Such commentators are cautiously optimistic about the opportunity for union empowerment through "local" or community-based action (McDermott 1980). Union-community collaboration in local economic policy making offers a means by which unions can proactively influence the direction of economic restructuring in their locality and channel investment and resources to needy sectors and workers (Brecher and Costello 1990; Fisher and Kling 1993; Fitzgerald 1991; Fitzgerald and Simmons 1991; Jonas 1995). In this context, local dependence becomes a condition for political empowerment such that workers, unions, community organizers, and local politicians are able to harness the powers and resources of the local state to rebuild the local social fabric and develop alternative economic strategies (Brown 1995; Fitzgerald and Simmons 1991; Jonas 1992). This involves, among other considerations, propagating a discourse on local economic development that challenges the hegemony of discourses referring to capital mobility and interlocality competition. Such place-based movements are among a rapidly diminishing range of options for rebuilding national and international structures of union representation and organization (Martin, Sunley, and Wills 1996).

"Union retreat" cannot, therefore, be directly attributed to capital mobility and the relentless process of globalization. To do so imparts a greater degree of rationality and uniformity to union response than is in fact the case. Rather, local modes of organizing and place-based opposition by unions can make a difference. But whether these can provide the basis for an effective counterhegemonic discourse depends on the presence of enabling organizational and political capacities at the local level. In this essay, I focus on three local capacities: the capacity for locally autonomous action within national union structures; the presence of community-based networks in local economic policy making (and accessible to unions); and the extent of integration of such networks into the local political establishment (i.e., the local state). My investigation of these local capacities is based on a case study of a union-community campaign to prevent plant closings in Chicago.

In 1985, the United Workers' Association-United Electrical Workers (UWA-UE) Local 1154 organized a union-community coalition and began a six-year campaign to prevent plant closures at Stewart-Warner Corporation, a manufacturer of automobile instruments and air-powered tools based on the North Side of Chicago. At least twenty-five hundred production jobs were at stake. The union's campaign to save Stewart-Warner was built on a long legacy of locally autonomous action within the United Electrical, Radio and Machine Workers (UE), a union that had traditionally targeted low-skilled and low-paid workers in medium and small electrical components companies. Although the union

327

Investigating the Local-Global Paradox

was ultimately unable to save the threatened facilities, it did succeed in publicly exposing the company's investment policies and gained considerable support for a modernization plan that would have led to local reinvestment. The plan was eventually rejected by management after Stewart-Warner's acquisition by a British conglomerate in 1987.

The coalition to save Stewart-Warner developed a strategy that not only challenged the prevailing discourse of capital mobility and place competition but also linked into a community-based initiative to prevent further deindustrialization of the Chicago economy. This initiative itself had only limited success, in part because community-based organizations failed to become fully integrated into the local state apparatus. The untimely death of Mayor Harold Washington and the fragmentation of the political coalition he was in the process of building created a political space for the downtown business-political establishment to promote the commercial and residential redevelopment of older manufacturing districts, thus hastening the closure of local facilities, including those operated by Stewart-Warner.

Stewart-Warner Corporation

For some seventy years, Stewart-Warner Corporation was one of the largest private manufacturing corporations located on the North Side of Chicago. It was incorporated in December 1912, following a consolidation of small manufacturers of automobile parts and instruments. The next two decades saw steady growth in the company's Chicago operations in response to increasing demand in the automobile aftermarket. The company diversified and by 1929 had become one of the largest manufacturers of automobile accessories, radios, and electronic equipment and components in the United States (Archambault 1963). During World War II, Stewart-Warner converted its plants to military production. The workforce was expanded to seven thousand, the highest level in the company's history. After the war, employment returned to the prewar level of five thousand and the company discontinued its production of radios and television sets, but maintained its business with the military. During the Korean War, 45 percent of the company's annual sales were to the federal government and defense contractors (ibid.).

In the early 1950s, the company relocated its main electronics division to a modern facility on North Kostner Avenue and appointed Bennett Archambault president and chairman. Archambault, who had close ties to the military, ran the company authoritatively from its headquarters on Diversey Avenue (figure 10.1). By the early 1980s, Stewart-Warner operated seventeen facilities worldwide, five of which were located in Chicago. The company employed three thou-

Andrew E. G. Jonas

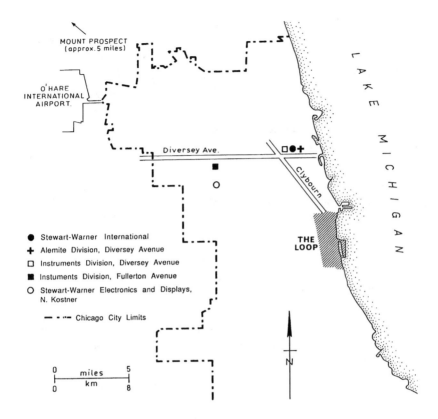

Figure 10.1. Stewart-Warner facilities in Chicago.

sand workers making a wide range of products, mainly for the automobile after-market, including air-powered tools, casters, pumps, spray equipment, power brakes, speedometers, and electromechanical equipment.

But in the 1980s, Stewart-Warner experienced difficulties. The 1982–83 recession exposed weaknesses in the company's financial policies, and annual sales fell by 8 percent (Stewart-Warner 1983). The company's problems were such that facilities were operating well below capacity. In 1986, Stewart-Warner began transferring operations out of Chicago and, by 1991, all but one of its five major operations in the city had been closed, with a loss of more than twenty-five hundred jobs. Most of its commercial production was relocated to the Southwest and abroad; the one remaining facility on North Kostner Avenue continued to supply the military.

It would be tempting to attribute this dramatic change in Stewart-Warner's fortunes to the "crisis of Fordism" (Lipietz 1987). During the 1970s and 1980s, **329**

U.S. corporations involved in manufacturing components for the mass-production sector responded to growing international competition by adjusting production strategies and relocating parts of operations to low-cost and low-skilled labor locations. As a company operating in the components sector of automobile production and employing a low-skilled and unionized workforce, Stewart-Warner was clearly vulnerable to growing capital mobility and interlocality competition, and this vulnerability could have shaped the workers' response. But instead of bowing to management prerogatives and accepting contract concessions to save their jobs, the workers and their union took a different approach. Their strategy involved negotiating for improved wage and working conditions, putting pressure on management to modernize Stewart-Warner's outmoded operations, and forcing the company to adjust in situ rather than relocate in response to growing competition in its sectors and markets.

An instrumental force in the development of this strategy was the United Electrical, Radio and Machine Workers of America (UE). The UE had a long history of militant industrial organizing that stretched back to the 1930s and the founding of the Congress of Industrial Organizations (CIO). The fact that workers turned to the UE is significant for understanding developments at Stewart-Warner in the 1980s because the UE has historically operated with a decentralized structure in which greater autonomy of action has been given to union locals and districts. Also significant is the union's deliberate policy of targeting electronic components companies employing low-skilled, minority, and female workers, a policy it pursued to great effect in the turbulent decades of the 1930s and 1940s.

The UE: A Legacy of Local Autonomy and Action

Like other small but expanding electronics manufacturers, Stewart-Warner became a target of labor organizing in the Great Depression. After a decade of struggle, in 1943 Chicago-based employees at Stewart-Warner elected UE Local 1154 to represent them. The UE had an active left-wing leadership, although the locals spanned the political spectrum. Red-baiting by rightist union organizations divided the union. Nevertheless, despite internecine struggles the UE emerged from the Depression as the third-largest industrial union in the United States and the CIO's largest affiliate (Filippelli and McColloch 1995).

Because of its alleged ties to the U.S. Communist Party, the UE was the first union to be expelled from the CIO in the McCarthyite purges that took place at the eleventh constitutional convention of the CIO in 1949. The left-wing leadership of the UE, which did not attend the convention, was criticized for its opposition to the Marshall Plan. At the convention, rightist factions in the

Andrew E. G. Jonas

union organized the International Union of Electrical, Radio and Machine Workers (IUE), creating dual unionism in the electronics industry (ibid.). Thereafter, the UE struggled to hold its own in the face of raids on UE-held plants by other unions, including the CIO's IUE and the International Brotherhood of Electrical Workers (IBEW), which was affiliated to the American Federation of Labor (AFL).

The UE's organizational structure and strategy contrasted markedly with those of other industrial unions, such as the United Auto Workers (UAW) and the United Steelworkers (USW). Whereas these industrial unions operated as patriarchal "top-down" organizations that strove to protect the privileged status of (male) American-born workers in the international economy, the UE allowed for broad participation of its membership, supported the integration of women, minority, and foreign-born workers into the American workforce, and encouraged the districts and the locals to shape policy at the national level.

Filippelli and McColloch (1995, 187) suggest that "much of the story of the UE can be explained by the high degree of local autonomy that characterized the union from the beginning." UE locals held pragmatic views on wages and contracts, were more inclined to challenge than to support management prerogatives in the workplace, and sought to improve working conditions for unskilled and semiskilled workers rather than to defend privileges based on craft or skill.

Local autonomy also meant that the views and strategies of UE locals tended to be shaped by the local contexts in which they operated. During the union's formative years, UE locals organized workers across localities that varied greatly in terms of underlying economic conditions, social institutions, and political traditions and attitudes. As a result, the union met with varying levels of resistance to its activities. The UE's decentralized structures often made it difficult for general officers to control rightist elements within the union, and there were numerous occasions when UE locals became influenced by anticommunist attacks from rival unions, plant managers, owners, and local political organizations.

The UE's approach also reflected conditions in the sectors in which it organized. The electronics industry was composed of a few large-scale enterprises employing mass-production methods and numerous small but growing motor and appliance shops. The employment practices of the small enterprises were vastly different from the paternalistic and welfarist operations of large-scale appliance manufacturers like Westinghouse and General Electric. Workers in electrical components firms were semiskilled, lacked a tradition of trade unionism, and held little or no autonomy in the workplace; many were women whose grievances about pay and working conditions were often not shared by their skilled male coworkers (Filippelli and McColloch 1995). Because the large as- 331 sembly firms were held by the more conservative AFL affiliates, the UE targeted smaller operations that were unorganized and whose workforces were segmented by race, gender, and ethnicity. Consequently, the union built a large constituency of active members among unskilled and semiskilled minority and female electronics workers. Throughout the 1940s, the UE made substantial inroads into plants held by rival unions, until the UE itself became internally fractured by red-baiting.

Ideological attacks on the union eventually undermined UE control at Stewart-Warner. In 1949, the company unilaterally canceled its contract with the UE and announced that it would request an election for the IBEW. The UE local was not put on the ballot because local officers refused to sign affidavits stating that they were not Communists. After the election, the UE was forced to rescind its charter, and Stewart-Warner entered into a sweetheart deal with IBEW Local 1031, a craft union representing skilled (male) workers. Under IBEW jurisdiction, Stewart-Warner introduced collective bargaining and a Fordist-style management-labor compact. By restricting strike action and allowing management control over production, the compact became a centerpiece of Archambault's overall production strategy. Tellingly, Archambault makes no mention of labor unrest or unions in his "official" account of the origins, growth, and development of the Stewart-Warner Corporation, an account that is largely a financial history of the company (Archambault 1963).

Under Archambault, the management maintained strict control over production and the workforce. Archambault organized the corporation into separate divisions, which operated as quasi-autonomous businesses. This production strategy not only prevented the development of interplant ties among the production workers but also consolidated the influence of the IBEW. Membership in the IBEW was dominated by skilled white male workers, who were mainly interested in protecting their privileged workplace status. The union was regarded by production workers as being in complicity with management and its strict production regime.

Although the geographic concentration of the company's plants in Chicago could potentially have been a source of worker solidarity as it had been in the meatpacking industry (see Page in this volume), it turned out that such close proximity of the plants was not in fact conducive to building unity among the workforce. Employees commuted from neighborhoods throughout Chicago, including the South Side. This frustrated the development of strong ties between the factories, surrounding neighborhoods, and local community organizations. The social and territorial basis of workplace-community solidarity was poorly developed, accentuated by the strict segmentation of the workforce on the basis

332

of skill, ethnicity, race, and gender. As was typical of electrical components manufacturers, Stewart-Warner recruited minorities and women for unskilled and semiskilled assembly positions, whereas white men occupied skilled assembly and supervisory positions. In the early 1980s, the workforce was 60 percent female, 40 percent African-American, 38 percent white, and 22 percent Hispanic and "other" (Howard 1987).

Under Archambault's authoritarian management regime, workers' grievances about pay, benefits, working conditions, and discrimination accumulated. By the 1970s, wage levels for production workers had demonstrably fallen below the industry average. Moreover, machinery and equipment had become outmoded for want of investment and modernization—a fact that would play into the discussion later concerning the plans to close the plants. Led by the UE, union activists began to organize the workforce against the IBEW. Production workers formed an independent union, the United Workers' Association (UWA). In 1979, the UWA won a decertification drive against the IBEW and a year later voted two to one to affiliate with the UE. The two locals merged to form the United Workers' Association-United Electrical Workers (UWA-UE) Local 1154, which represented twenty-five hundred employees at the five Chicago facilities of Stewart-Warner Corporation.

The IBEW tried to regain the plants in 1980 but was heavily defeated by the UWA-UE. The UAW tried to intervene on behalf of the IBEW but lost to the UE in a runoff election by a margin of 1,372 to 936 (*UE News*, July 21, 1980, 6; December 8, 1980, 8). UAW intervention was attributed to its declining membership in the troubled auto industry and to the fact that it represented two other Stewart-Warner plants in Illinois (*Chicago Tribune*, March 18, 1981, 1, 4). In January 1981, the UWA-UE led production workers out on a strike after contract negotiations between management and the union had broken down. The UWA-UE rejected management's offer of an 8 percent wage increase and pressed for an 11 percent raise. The UE assisted the local in further negotiations during the strike. After eight weeks out, the union voted 786 to 694 to accept a new contract offer of a 9 percent pay increase plus additional benefits (*Chicago Tribune*, March 25, 1981, sec. 4, 3).

Deindustrialization and the Rise of Community-Based Economic Development Initiatives in Chicago

The early 1980s marked a turning point in Chicago's industrial history. In 1982, the number of workers employed in manufacturing in Chicago was at its lowest level since the turn of the century. Deindustrialization wreaked havoc throughout Chicago's older industrial districts, but the impact was especially devastat-   333 ing on the South Side, as symbolized by the fate of U.S. Steel Corporation's South Side Steel Works. During World War II, the works had employed eighteen thousand workers. By 1982, the workforce had been reduced to 1,150, and U.S. Steel was threatening outright closure (Serrin 1983).

The discourse of capital mobility and interlocality competition increasingly came to have a bearing on the response of Chicago-based unions to deindustrialization. Unions fought U.S. Steel's proposal to build a new $225 million high-technology mill in Chicago in exchange for new work rules and reduced wages. Unwilling to make wage concessions, the steelworkers instead agreed to change work rules. U.S. Steel's response was to abandon its modernization program and close down its Chicago operations as part of a broader diversification strategy (Smith 1988). The consequences of the closure for the social fabric of South Side communities were devastating: "On the South Side is the detritus of de-industrialization: truck drivers whose terminals have closed, steelworkers living on government cheese, old men sipping Cokes in the bars at noon, young men drifting back from Houston to enroll in community colleges, disciples of Saul Alinsky [a prominent Chicago community activist in the 1960s] picketing chemical dumps" (Geoghegan 1985, 20).

The experiences of South Side communities had a significant impact on the activities of community-based organizations across the city, but especially in North Side neighborhoods. In the past, these organizations had focused on living place issues such as affordable housing and education. But with industrial displacement threatening the entire social fabric of neighborhoods, they now began to mobilize around the broader issue of manufacturing disinvestment (Finn and McCormick 1985). Their goal was to prevent manufacturing displacement, job loss, and community decline by using local powers such as zoning. Consultations with local employers revealed that manufacturers preferred central-city locations to build up a customer and supplier base but were often encouraged to relocate outside the city to avoid high property taxes. On the North Side, for example, industrial districts were losing manufacturing jobs at roughly the city-wide rate of 26 percent between 1977 and 1986 (Ducharme, Giloth, and McCormick 1986). Community organizers put forward the idea of "protected" or Planned Manufacturing Districts (PMDs) in which certain tax abatements and other incentives would be made available for firms as a means of preventing industrial displacements in inner-city manufacturing districts (Ducharme 1991).

The longer-term goal of such a strategy was to integrate community-based organizations more effectively into the city's decision-making structures with a view to challenging existing structures of political patronage and economic power, and hence to shape the city's economic development policies "from below" (Clavel

334

and Wiewel 1991; Mier and Moe 1991). This goal depended, however, on the mobilization of a broad-based electoral coalition increasingly oriented to job issues and, in particular, to the issue of the loss of secure, well-paid union jobs. And such a coalition would need to build support among Chicago's powerful black electorate, which in the mid-1980s had brought Harold Washington into the mayor's office.

But it was also a goal that increasingly brought community-based organizations into conflict with real-estate interests, city planners, and the downtown political establishment (Ducharme, Giloth, and McCormick 1986). These latter groups did not view manufacturing displacement as a problem, and preferred to see "obsolete" manufacturing districts converted into new residential and commercial development as part of a broader strategy to capitalize on Chicago's burgeoning service-sector economy. Throughout the 1980s, inner neighborhoods in Chicago experienced a property boom as redevelopment in and around the Loop significantly boosted rents and property values. Property owners, including manufacturing companies, could make a sizable profit from the sale of sites for redevelopment. The city itself benefited from the increase in tax revenues that came from redevelopment activity. Consequently, those groups that had staked their future on the promotion of Chicago as postindustrial center of financial and commercial employment put up considerable resistance to the idea of PMDs.

Mayor Washington worked hard to overcome the growing conflict between these groups and community-based organizations (Ducharme 1991). Attempting to consolidate his electoral coalition, Washington strove to incorporate community-based organizations into the city's decision-making structures even as his administration continued to encourage fiscally lucrative inner-city redevelopment. The Washington administration lent its support to the concept of PMDs, and viewed such districts as integral to stabilizing the employment base of poorer neighborhoods. Eventually, in 1988, the establishment of PMDs in industrial areas threatened by displacement officially became incorporated into the city of Chicago's economic development policies.

Following Washington's death in 1987, the rift between community-based organizations and supporters of inner-city redevelopment became wider than ever, a rift that Richard J. Daley was able to exploit in his successful mayoral campaign. The priorities of the new administration became apparent in 1990 when the mayor's office and the city's Department of Economic Development expressed opposition to a proposed city ordinance that would have allowed manufacturing companies acquired by outside investors and subsequently threatened with closure to be purchased by local investment consortia. The proposed ordi-

335

nance was never put before the city council for a vote. Meanwhile, the council continued to approve rezonings that put pressure on local manufacturers to abandon the inner city, selling former manufacturing sites for commercial and residential redevelopment.

Mobilizing the Community: The UWA-UE and the Coalition to Keep Stewart-Warner Open

Union involvement in community-based economic development initiatives in Chicago during the 1980s was somewhat limited. The perception was that, if anything, the big industrial unions were in some respects "to blame" for the fate of Chicago's manufacturing districts, and that the concerns of organized labor were not the same as those of the city's diverse but threatened communities (cf. Katznelson 1981). Such views gained some credence in the antiunion political climate cultivated under the Reagan administration and in a city having a torrid history of racial bigotry, political corruption, and brutal repression of workers.

The UE, however, was better equipped than many other unions to bridge the labor-community divide. Its long history of allowing locally autonomous action and its policy of targeting low-skilled minority and female workers in low-paid employment provided greater capacity for place-based resistance. What was unique about the UWA-UE's strategy for Stewart-Warner, then, was the ability of the union to mobilize a labor-community coalition around a modernization plan, and to link into a citywide movement to protect industrial districts from further displacement of manufacturing companies.[1]

When Stewart-Warner began to experience financial difficulties in 1981, the company attributed its sluggish performance to the strike and to competition between the unions for control of the plants. Yet it continued to pay unusually high dividends to its shareholders. Despite the attempt to shift the blame onto the unions, workers had long been concerned about the company's future plans for its Alemite Division located on Diversey Avenue. In 1978, Stewart-Warner had embarked on plans to develop a new production facility in Johnson City, Tennessee, with a view eventually to transferring the Alemite Division from Chicago. The UWA-UE put pressure on management to reveal its intentions and, in particular, to say whether it had plans to close down any or all of the Chicago facilities. Archambault responded by claiming that the Johnson City facility had been built for expansion rather than relocation, but in a newspaper report he cryptically suggested that: "We don't expect to give up any *skilled* personnel in the metropolitan areas [*sic*]" (*Chicago Tribune*, March 18, 1981, sec. 4, 4; emphasis added). Reading between the lines, the UWA-UE began to prepare its members for the possibility of plant closures.

336

Andrew E. G. Jonas

The UWA-UE decided to turn to community-based organizations for support. In December 1985, the union organized the Coalition to Keep Stewart-Warner Open (CKSWO). Members of the coalition included the UWA-UE, labor activists, church groups, the University of Illinois at Chicago, Center for Urban Economic Development (UICCUED), the Midwest Center for Labor Research (MCLR), and aldermen from the Chicago city council. Given their dependence on the multiplier effects to the local economy of Stewart-Warner, the coalition also received limited support from businesses and community-based organizations located in the immediate vicinity of the production facilities (cf. Cox and Mair 1988).

After several months of meetings and discussions, the coalition came up with a strategy to apply public pressure on Stewart-Warner to modernize its facilities and protect jobs in Chicago. This involved organizing a media campaign, staging public events, and producing a videotape of the coalition's activities and plans (see Jonas 1995). The CKSWO also met with representatives at the city, state, and federal levels to seek government assistance, secure new contracts and sales, and identify resources that could be used as incentives for modernization and training. The union further encouraged coalition members to conduct studies of the company's financial standing. Finally, direct negotiations were held with corporate management. In response to demands made by the CKSWO for a resolution on the future of the plants, however, Archambault barred eight out of ten coalition members and the press from attending one of the meetings (*Chicago Tribune*, May 14, 1987, sec. 3, 1).

In January 1986, Stewart-Warner announced its intention to transfer parts of the Alemite Division to Johnson City. Although the company claimed that it would transfer only 150 jobs, the UWA-UE was able to show that in the longer term some twenty-five hundred jobs were at stake (Howard 1987). Studies conducted by CKSWO members revealed underlying weaknesses in the company's wage and financial policies. The union showed that production workers were paid $2 to $4 less per hour than workers with equivalent jobs in firms operating in the same sectors. A study conducted by the MCLR revealed that the company spent about half as much as its competitors on research and development, and that it was not well positioned to compete in technologically dynamic markets. Perhaps the most telling study of Stewart-Warner was conducted by UICCUED (Howard 1987). It showed that from a competitive standpoint the company's investment policies were unsound. The corporation had depreciated 70 percent of its plant and equipment, a rate of depreciation that was higher than that of comparison companies. It had not issued new debt to update machinery and equipment with the result that its operating assets were significantly   337 older than those deployed by comparison companies. Moreover, it paid unusually high dividends to shareholders. In short, Stewart-Warner was not in a strong position to compete in its main markets because it had failed to modernize, was operating with outdated machinery and equipment, and was not reinvesting profits in its core businesses.

Challenging Discourses of Capital Mobility and Globalization

The union's strategy of publicly embarrassing Stewart-Warner was successful.[2] The UICCUED study revealed serious weaknesses in the company's financial and investment policies and was given considerable coverage in the local media. It challenged the company's claims that its poor performance was the direct result of the strike and union demands for higher wages. And it called into question the motives for relocating production outside of Chicago. The company was forced to make some concessions. These included management cooperation in identifying areas where modernization and retraining were required; thirty-day advance notification of any decision to close or relocate product lines or plants; and extended benefit coverage and retraining for any worker who lost a job after a closing or relocation.

But it was also clear that financially Stewart-Warner was in a vulnerable situation. In an attempt to resolve the company's problems, management began to seek an external buyer. In August 1987, the giant London-based conglomerate, British Thermoplastics and Rubber (BTR) Plc. made a $33 per share bid to acquire Stewart-Warner, a deal amounting to $177 million. BTR described the bid as friendly, although, with its large assets and weak operating performance, Stewart-Warner was a recognized takeover target (*Chicago Tribune*, August 4, 1987, sec. 3, 1, 7). With a worldwide workforce of 85,400, sales amounting to $6.72 billion, and more than six hundred subsidiaries, BTR ranked among the top ten companies in the United Kingdom. Ten years earlier, BTR had commenced an aggressive expansion program in the United States which was coordinated from the offices of its U.S. subsidiary based in Stamford, Connecticut. Stewart-Warner was one in a growing list of U.S. companies that BTR had targeted for acquisition.

Upon learning of the bid, members of the CKSWO immediately contacted the offices of the Transport and General Workers' Union (TGWU) in London and the Congress of South African Trades Unions (COSATU) to find out about BTR's investment policies and labor practices in Europe and Africa. BTR, it was discovered, had a reputation for acquiring cash-rich companies and breaking them up into smaller units for resale or relocation to low-wage locations. The coalition was also informed that BTR management was adamantly

338

antiunion. The conglomerate's labor practices in South Africa were considered so exploitative that BTR had been officially condemned by the Parliamentary Court of the European Community in Brussels.

Meanwhile, Stewart-Warner agreed to a merger with BTR. The merger agreement was signed on September 8, 1987. It stated BTR's intentions to maintain a Stewart-Warner office in Chicago and to offer workers benefits "reasonably comparable in the aggregate" to existing arrangements (*Chicago Tribune*, September 9, 1987, sec. 3, 9). The coalition approached BTR management to find out about the conglomerate's plans for the future of the Chicago facilities. Based on comments made by the president of BTR's U.S. operations, coalition members expected BTR to transfer the remaining Alemite operations to Tennessee (*Chicago Tribune*, December 17, 1987, sec. 2, 3). The CKSWO was informed at a shareholders' meeting in London in the spring of 1988 that BTR had no plans to close the electronics division. BTR would not make any promises about the other Chicago facilities, however, including the instruments division located on Diversey Avenue.

Soon after the takeover, Archambault stepped down as president of Stewart-Warner and BTR replaced him with Wesley J. Kiley. In June 1989, Kiley announced plans to open a new research and engineering center in Chicago, where BTR intended to develop instrument panels for heavy vehicles used by the military (*Chicago Tribune*, June 28, 1989, sec. 3, 1, 5). The plant would employ fifty skilled engineers and designers, marking a shift toward small-scale specialized manufacturing. Although welcoming BTR's efforts to make Stewart-Warner more competitive, a member of the MCLR argued that the new research and engineering center was long overdue and expressed concerns for the future of 1,225 employees at the instruments division (ibid., 5). These concerns were prompted by BTR's decision a year earlier to close a Stewart-Warner plant in Spring Valley, Illinois, and the transfer of senior personnel and staff to a new office facility in Mount Prospect, a suburb of Chicago close to O'Hare International Airport (see figure 10.1). Moreover, Kiley had hinted that under BTR Stewart-Warner would subcontract more of its businesses.

The CKSWO stepped up its campaign to put public pressure on Stewart-Warner, now under the new BTR management, to modernize and retrain workers. The coalition organized a rally in December 1987 at which presidential candidate Jesse Jackson spoke in support of the workers and the union. Jackson called for a shift in emphasis in national economic policy "from merging corporations and purging workers to reinvesting in America, retraining workers and reindustrializing our nation" (*Chicago Tribune*, December 8, 1987, sec. 2, 10). His words, however, were targeted as much at the downtown political establishment in

Chicago as at economic policy makers in Washington, D.C., and it was at the local rather than the national level that the union chose to focus its activities. The UWA-UE felt that a community-based strategy was the most effective means of attracting the attention and support of local politicians and policy makers. The coalition decided to attempt to link up with a community economic development initiative already under way on the North Side, with a view to directing public resources toward its campaign to save Stewart-Warner.

Linking up with Community-Based Organizations and the Local State

In 1986, a study conducted jointly by the New City YMCA Economic Development Unit, the City of Chicago Department of Economic Development, and the UICCUED had identified the Goose Island/Clybourn Corridor area as one of the districts where manufacturing displacement was a serious problem. Clybourn Corridor, which included 350 manufacturers and twenty-thousand workers, was bounded to the north by Diversey Avenue (figure 10.2). The study found that the district was undergoing piecemeal conversion to residential and commercial uses, and manufacturers were under pressure to relocate because of rising property taxes and rents. The joint report recommended several measures to prevent further industrial displacement, suggesting that the "corridor could be protected and upgraded for continuing manufacturing use and provide an in-city location for firms displaced from other districts. A protected manufacturing district combined with appropriate tax and financial incentives could strengthen Chicago's industrial and blue collar employment base" (Ducharme, Giloth, and McCormick 1986, 1). The recommendation, then, was that Clybourn Corridor be designated one of Chicago's first Planned Manufacturing Districts.

The CKSWO requested that Stewart-Warner, whose Diversey Avenue facilities bordered the Clybourn Corridor district, be included in the PMD. The coalition hoped that inclusion would qualify Stewart-Warner for special tax and financial incentives. These incentives would then become part of a modernization package to be put forward to BTR management as an alternative to plant closings and relocations. Mayor Washington, who supported the PMD concept, spoke at one of the public meetings held by the CKSWO and pledged the city's support. The Department of Economic Development offered three thousand dollars toward the completion of a modernization study and plan. The Clybourn Corridor PMD was eventually established in 1988, a year after Mayor Washington's death.

The district, however, covered a much smaller area than the original proposal (figure 10.2). It protected thirty-one manufacturers and seventeen hundred

Andrew E. G. Jonas

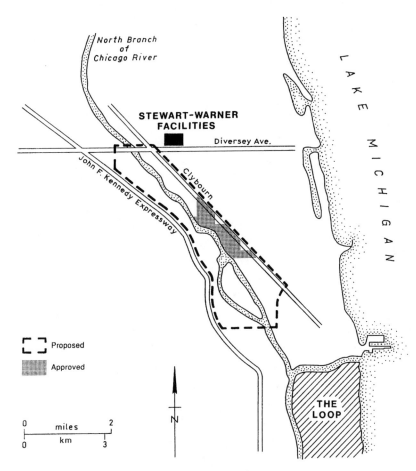

Figure 10.2. Clybourn Corridor Planned Manufacturing District.

workers. Stewart-Warner was not among those manufacturers included, and therefore did not qualify for tax and other incentives. The reason for its exclusion related to ongoing pressures to redevelop abandoned sites proximate to Diversey Avenue, a major thoroughfare linking the Clybourn Corridor and the Lake Michigan waterfront. This part of Chicago had already seen considerable redevelopment activity and rezonings had been approved for residential and commercial development in close proximity to Stewart-Warner's facilities.

Meanwhile, BTR had allowed the number of employees at its Stewart-Warner facilities to dwindle from two thousand in 1987 to about seven hundred in 1990. With support from the Illinois Department of Commerce and Community Affairs and the Chicago Department of Economic Development, the UWA-UE urged BTR management to conduct a study to assess the savings resulting from 341 relocating operations to a modern facility in Chicago. BTR informed the union that its own study showed that the corporation could save $17 million by subcontracting parts' fabrication and relocating assembly operations to the Southwest and Mexico. These savings included revenue from the sale of Stewart-Warner property for redevelopment.

The union severely criticized BTR's assessment of costs and savings. It argued that the BTR study was restricted to a real-estate analysis and failed to address savings resulting from modernization. The study did not take into account labor costs and yet BTR was citing such costs as its reasons for relocating Stewart-Warner operations out of Chicago (*Chicago Tribune*, September 12, 1989, sec. 3, 1; November 4, 1989, sec. 2, 9). The union's own assessment was that $20 million could be saved by relocating within Chicago. The union agreed to accept a 10 percent pay cut if BTR agreed to the modernization plan (*Chicago Tribune*, November 2, 1989, sec. 3, 1, 2).

BTR decided against the union's plan and went ahead with relocation and sale of Stewart-Warner property. It shut down the instruments division on Diversey Avenue in 1991 and laid off the remaining workers. In 1994, contractors began to demolish the factory and former headquarters to make way for new townhouses and condominiums. BTR relocated production to Texas and Mexico and kept one Stewart-Warner facility, employing fifty-five workers, operating in Chicago.

Unions and the Shaping of the Local Economic and Political Landscape

There is nothing very surprising in the *outcome* of the UWA-UE's campaign to save Stewart-Warner. In that respect, it could serve to exemplify the failure of unions to develop a political response to challenge the hegemonic discourse of capital mobility and interlocality competition. It would also highlight the ongoing "union retreat" into old industrial heartlands (cf. Martin, Sunley, and Wills 1996). To focus solely on the outcome, however, would imply that the union's chosen strategy was irrational and that, under the circumstances, plant closings were inevitable. Such a conclusion would be difficult to accept without some qualification. If, for example, the IBEW rather than the UE had represented the workforce at Stewart-Warner, it is quite possible that the closures would have happened much sooner than they did and conceivably with little regard to the future of low-skilled and low-paid workers. In addition, although it is difficult to determine how much difference BTR made to the outcome, its actions nevertheless gave added legitimacy to the discourse of capital mobility and globalization. If the UWA-UE had some success in challenging Stewart-Warner's in-

342

vestment policies, it proved that much harder to convince BTR of the viability of the plants when its intention all along was to sell them off and pocket the cash. The fact is, then, the union's strategy of place-based resistance took full advantage of the available organizational capacities in the locality. These capacities were the high degree of local autonomy within the UE, the presence of a network of community-based organizations, and the increasing integration of those organizations into the local state apparatus.

The UWA-UE's strategy owed much to the high level of local autonomy allowed by its "parent," the UE. The UE not only held "radical" views on issues such as collective bargaining and investment, but it also allowed the full participation of local and district organizations in its national structure (Filippelli and McColloch 1995). The UE had a long tradition of mobilizing low-skilled minority and female workers employed in small electronic plants. Working conditions in such plants were very different from those of workers in larger corporations operating in the mass-production sector and having welfarist labor practices. Stewart-Warner's authoritarian labor control practices were no exception in this regard.

In seeking to address workers' concerns, the UWA-UE fought the IBEW and the UAW for control of the Stewart-Warner plants. The IBEW had been unwilling to challenge management's wage and investment policies, creating an opportunity for the UWA-UE to mobilize the workers around the issues of modernization and retraining. The union demonstrated that Stewart-Warner's weakening performance was not so much the result of unreasonable union demands in the face of growing international competition as it was of a failure to reinvest, modernize, and remunerate workers at levels in line with U.S. companies operating in similar markets.

The union's choice of a community-based strategy reflected its sensitivity to local economic conditions and awareness of local political opportunities. The union attempted to develop strategic links with community-based organizations as a basis for securing political support and resources from local and state government agencies. A network of such organizations already existed and was involved in protecting manufacturing districts on Chicago's North Side from displacements resulting from rising property values, rezonings, and redevelopment pressures. Underlying these pressures were the activities of corporatist interests attempting to convert Chicago into a postindustrial city.

But Chicago's emerging "corporatist regime" (cf. Stone 1989) did not command universal support among the electorate. In particular, there was a growing political constituency in favor of protecting well-paid manufacturing jobs and the social fabric of neighborhoods and communities threatened by deindustrial- 343

Investigating the Local-Global Paradox

ization. This constituency was represented by community-based organizations that, in pushing forward the concept of Planned Manufacturing Districts, were becoming more integrated into the city's decision-making structures. Under the leadership of Mayor Washington, the Department of Economic Development lent its support to the idea of PMDs, which duly became part of an official economic development policy of the city (Ducharme 1991). Working through the PMD initiative, the UWA-UE saw an opportunity to obtain political support and resources from the city and the state. These resources were included in the modernization package that was put to Stewart-Warner management.

The UWA-UE's community-based approach was successful in exposing Stewart-Warner's wage and investment policies to critical public scrutiny, forcing management to seriously consider alternatives to plant relocations and closures, and transforming the local political discourse about deindustrialization. In these respects, it presented rational alternatives to the hegemonic discourse of capital mobility and globalization, a discourse promulgated by promoters of a postindustrial Chicago. The union's approach encountered difficulties, however, when the electoral coalition mobilized by Mayor Washington unraveled. Washington's death marked the end of attempts by the city administration to integrate community-based organizations into its decision-making structures, and public support for the establishment of PMDs dwindled. Those that were established were much smaller than originally planned, effectively releasing more abandoned industrial sites for commercial and residential redevelopment. Moreover, a proposal in 1990 to protect Chicago-based manufacturers from external takeovers was never brought before city council for a vote.

BTR acquired Stewart-Warner in 1987 and shortly after conducted a study to evaluate the future of the company's Chicago operations. Among the options it considered were closure and sale of Stewart-Warner facilities, subcontracting of operations, relocation, and plant modernization. Given BTR's record, its threats to relocate and subcontract production were treated seriously by the union, which responded by offering wage concessions to encourage BTR to modernize. Although BTR promised to invest in a new facility in Chicago, it ran down the remaining Stewart-Warner plants. The closure of the Diversey Avenue facilities effectively brought an end to the UWA-UE's six-year community-based campaign.

In addressing the complex issues currently facing organized labor, academics and activists have suggested that unions should spend more time and effort building political support at the local level. In their extensive study of unions in Great Britain, for example, Martin, Sunley, and Wills (1996, 206) conclude that "there is a strong case for arguing that unions would benefit from adopting

344

Andrew E. G. Jonas

representational strategies which make more use of the local dynamics and networks of political, economic and community affairs." Although strategically it makes sense that unions should devote future energies to (re)building local "modes of representation," it begs the more practical question as to what kinds of "local dynamics and networks" exist that unions can mobilize to their strategic advantage, especially when their members are faced with the more immediate threat of plant closures and capital mobility. This case study has provided some clues about the nature of union-community networks in localities confronted with deindustrialization, and about the opportunities for exploiting those networks for political leverage.

The campaign to save Stewart-Warner was built around a well-organized community base and was linked to a wider political movement to transform economic policy making in Chicago. In this respect, the CKSWO's concerns and goals fed into a broader program of action to protect inner-city neighborhoods from manufacturing displacements, a program that unraveled following a change in the local governing coalition (cf. Lauria 1994). Opportunities to link with political movements beyond the city limits also came up during the course of the struggle, but these were not integral to the union's political campaign. The CKSWO obtained support from Jesse Jackson's Rainbow Coalition and consulted with overseas unions (the TGWU and the COSATU) about the investment record and employment practices of BTR in other countries. These linkages were important in helping the union understand the changing wider context for its local campaign and fed into a wider political debate in America about the social and economic costs of deindustrialization, but they did not alter the substantive goals of the campaign itself. These goals remained focused on plant modernization, reinvestment, and retraining in Chicago.

The experience of the UWA-UE's campaign to save Stewart-Warner suggests, then, that there is some potential for empowering unions and workers (as well as the unemployed) at the local, national, and even international levels through the development of stronger ties between workers, unions, public officials, and community organizations already involved at the local level in alternative programs of economic development (Brecher and Costello 1990; Fitzgerald and Simmons 1991). In this context, workers and residents in localities become politicized through their actual participation in local community economic development problems and goals (Fitzgerald 1991). Because local participation often exposes workers and residents to wider economic and political processes, the experiences of community-based campaigns and strategies can feed into political movements directed at the national and international levels. In this respect, local action should not be viewed as an alternative to political action at wider geographic scales. Rather, it is an important part of the context in which workers and their unions become aware of, and develop political responses to, events and processes that transcend the territorial limits of their localities.

This perspective on community-based action challenges the somewhat negative view of labor's "political localism" that currently pervades the literature on unions and the politics of deindustrialization. It highlights the capacity inherent in locality-based social relations for unions to shape the political and economic landscape of production. It demonstrates that the details of geography and place are central to unraveling the local-global paradox of contemporary economic restructuring processes, and to developing counterhegemonic discourses and practices to those of globalizing capital.

Conclusion: Beyond the Local-Global Paradox

Researchers have begun to grapple with complex changes under way in the global-local nexus of after-Fordist production (Tickell and Peck 1995). A great deal of theoretical emphasis has been placed on the process of economic globalization, which in turn has fed into discussions about the appropriate level of political response by unions, workers, and residents alike. Confronting the apparent paradox of economic globalization and political localization, researchers have emphasized the virtues of political action on the national and even the international level. In comparison, labor's "political localism" is seen as playing into the hands of mobile capital, forcing workers, unions, public officials, and community organizers to retreat into their respective regions or localities. At a time of intensifying international competition, political decentralization, and ideologically motivated political assaults on unions, an emphasis on locally based political action seems to be dangerously misplaced.

These concerns are to some extent justified by the ongoing economic and social devastation of industrial localities throughout the globe, but it is too easy to downplay the potential for political empowerment through community-based action. This is not to idealize the local as the *only* terrain of political action. Rather, it is to recognize that political consciousness is deeply embedded in social relations that are in a number of respects locality-specific (Massey 1984). In the same way that every union has a different history and organizational structure, so every place exhibits differences with every other place in its traditions of union organization and opportunities for local political action (Hanson and Pratt 1995; Jonas 1996). These differences not only shape the way in which economic globalization is experienced within a locality but also establish the conditions for political action at even wider spatial scales.

Andrew E. G. Jonas

The point is not to treat place-based movements as a historical anachronism (cf. Fainstein 1987), but rather to demonstrate how the history and geography of a place — its institutions, actors, and struggles — actively shape political responses to economic globalization. As this case study of the UWA-UE in Chicago has tried to demonstrate, by building on community-based networks and linkages, and by challenging hegemonic discourses of capital mobility and inter-locality competition, unions have an important and influential part to play in molding and transforming political and economic landscapes of production at all scales, from the very local to the global.

Notes

I am grateful to the Academic Senate of the University of California for travel support. Joan Fitzgerald was a great help in conducting some of the background research and interviews on the UWA-UE and its campaign to keep Stewart-Warner open. Bill Howard improved my understanding of the issues involved in the campaign. Ralph Armbruster drew my attention to an excellent new book on the UE. David Wilson was a fine host during one of my visits to Illinois. Graham Haughton, Andrew Herod, and an anonymous reviewer made useful comments on an earlier draft of the essay that was presented at the 91st Annual Meeting of the Association of American Geographers in Chicago. Linda Bobbitt and Keith Scurr produced the maps for this version, and Dave Gibbs and Suzy Reimer offered helpful suggestions for changes in the text. The usual disclaimers apply.

1. This point is developed further in a comparative analysis of labor-community coalitions in two Rust Belt cities (Jonas 1995).

2. For a discussion of changing union campaigns and actions aimed at publicly embarrassing corporations see Jarley and Maranto (1990).

Bibliography

Archambault, B. 1963. *The Origins, Growth and Development of Stewart-Warner Corporation.* Chicago: Stewart-Warner Corporation.

Bluestone, B., and B. Harrison. 1982. *The Deindustrialization of America: Plant Closings, Community Abandonment, and the Dismantling of Basic Industry.* New York: Basic Books.

Brecher, J., and T. Costello, eds. 1990. *Building Bridges.* New York: Monthly Review Press.

Brown, M. 1995. "Sex, Scale and the 'New Urban Politics': HIV-Prevention Strategies from Yaletown, Vancouver." In *Mapping Desire,* edited by D. Bell and G. Valentine, 245–63. London: Routledge.

347

Burawoy, M. 1985. *The Politics of Production: Factory Regimes under Capitalism and Socialism.* London: Verso.

City of Chicago. Department of Economic Development, and Department of Planning. 1988. *Clybourn Corridor Planned Manufacturing District.* Chicago: By the authors.

Clark, G. L. 1989. *Unions and Communities under Siege: American Communities and the Crisis of Organized Labor.* Cambridge: Cambridge University Press.

Clavel, P., and W. Wiewel, eds. 1991. *Harold Washington and the Neighborhoods.* New Brunswick, N.J.: Rutgers University Press.

Cox, K. R., and A. J. Mair. 1988. "Locality and Community in the Politics of Local Economic Development." *Annals of the Association of American Geographers* 78: 307–25.

Ducharme, D. 1991. "Planned Manufacturing Districts: How a Community Initiative Became a City Policy." In *Harold Washington and the Neighborhoods,* edited by P. Clavel and W. Wiewel, 221–37. New Brunswick, N.J.: Rutgers University Press.

Ducharme, D., R. Giloth, and L. McCormick. 1986. *Business Loss or Balanced Growth: Industrial Displacement in Chicago.* Chicago: City of Chicago Working Paper.

Fainstein, S. S. 1987. "Local Mobilization and Economic Discontent." In *Global Restructuring and Community Politics,* edited by M. P. Smith and J. R. Faegin, 323–42. Oxford: Basil Blackwell.

Filippelli, R. L., and M. D. McColloch. 1995. *Cold War in the Working Class: The Rise and Decline of the United Electrical Workers.* Albany: State University of New York Press.

Finn, P., and L. McCormick. 1985. *Industrial Displacement in Major American Cities and Related Policy Options.* Chicago: University of Illinois at Chicago, Center for Urban Economic Development.

Fisher, R., and J. Kling, eds. 1993. *Mobilizing the Community: Local Politics in the Era of the Global City.* Vol. 41, Urban Affairs Annual Reviews. Thousand Oaks, Calif.: Sage.

Fitzgerald, J. 1991. "Class as Community: The New Dynamics of Social Change." *Environment and Planning D: Society and Space* 9: 117–28.

Fitzgerald, J., and L. Simmons. 1991. "From Consumption to Production: Labor Participation in Grass-roots Movements in Pittsburgh and Hartford." *Urban Affairs Quarterly* 4: 512–31.

Geoghegan, T. 1985. "Chicago, Pride of the Rustbelt." *New Republic,* March 25: 18–23.

Griffiths, M. J., and R. J. Johnston. 1991. "What's in a Place? An Approach to the Concept of Place as Illustrated by the British National Union of Mineworkers' Strike, 1984–85." *Antipode* 23: 185–213.

348

Andrew E. G. Jonas

Hanson, S., and G. Pratt. 1995. *Gender, Work, and Space.* New York: Routledge.

Haughton, G. 1989. "Community and Industrial Restructuring: Responses to the Recession and Its Aftermath in the Illawarra Region of Australia." *Environment and Planning A* 21: 233–47.

Herod, A. J. 1991. "Local Political Practice in Response to a Manufacturing Plant Closure: How Geography Complicates Class Analysis." *Antipode* 23: 385–402.

———. 1994. "Further Reflections on Organized Labor and Deindustrialization in the United States." *Antipode* 26: 77–95.

Howard, W. D. 1987. *The Stewart-Warner Corporation: A Financial Analysis.* Chicago: University of Illinois at Chicago, Center for Urban Economic Development.

Hudson, R., and D. Sadler. 1983. "Region, Class and the Politics of Steel Closures in the European Community." *Environment and Planning D: Society and Space* 1: 405–28.

Jarley, P., and C. L. Maranto. 1990. "Union Corporate Campaigns: An Assessment." *Industrial and Labor Relations Review* 43: 505–24.

Jonas, A. E. G. 1992. "Corporate Takeover and Community Politics: The Case of Norton Company in Worcester." *Economic Geography* 68: 348–72.

———. 1995. "Labor and Community in the Deindustrialization of Urban America." *Journal of Urban Affairs* 17: 183–99.

———. 1996. "Local Labour Control Regimes: Uneven Development and the Social Regulation of Production." *Regional Studies* 30: 323–38.

Katznelson, I. 1981. *City Trenches: Urban Politics and the Patterning of Class in the U.S.* New York: Pantheon.

Lauria, M. 1994. "The Transformation of Local Politics: Manufacturing Plant Closures and Governing Coalition Fragmentation." *Political Geography* 13: 515–39.

Lipietz, A. 1987. *Mirages and Miracles: The Crises of Global Fordism.* London: New Left Books.

Logan, J. R., and H. L. Molotch. 1987. *Urban Fortunes: The Political Economy of Place.* Berkeley and Los Angeles: University of California Press.

Lynd, S. 1982. *The Fight against Shutdowns.* San Pedro, Calif.: Singlejack Books.

Martin, R., P. Sunley, and J. Wills. 1993. "The Geography of Trade Union Decline: Spatial Dispersal or Regional Resilience?" *Transactions of the Institute of British Geographers,* n.s. 18.1: 36–62.

———. 1996. *Union Retreat and the Regions: The Shrinking Landscape of Organised Labour.* London: Regional Studies Association, Jessica Kingsley.

Massey, D. 1984. *Spatial Divisions of Labor: Social Structures and the Geography of Production.* New York: Methuen.

Investigating the Local-Global Paradox

McDermott, J. 1980. *The Crisis in the Working Class and Some Arguments for a New Labor Movement.* Boston: South End Press.

Metzger, J. 1980. "Plant Shutdowns and Worker Response: The Case of Johnstown." *Socialist Review* 10: 9–49.

Mier, R., and K. Moe. 1991. "Decentralized Development: From Theory to Practice." In *Harold Washington and the Neighborhoods,* edited by P. Clavel and W. Wiewel, 64–99. New Brunswick, N.J.: Rutgers University Press.

Peck, J. A. 1996. *Work-Place: The Social Regulation of Labor Markets.* New York: Guilford Press.

Preteceille, E. 1990. "Political Paradoxes of Urban Restructuring: Globalization of the Economy and Localization of Politics?" In *Beyond the City Limits,* edited by J. Logan and T. Swanstrom, 237–42. Philadelphia: Temple University Press.

Serrin, W. 1983. "Union's Stand Clouding U.S. Steel Mill's Future." *New York Times,* December 22, 9.

Smith, M. P. 1988. *City, State and Market: The Political Economy of Urban Society.* Oxford: Basil Blackwell.

Stewart-Warner. 1983. *Annual Report to Shareholders.* Chicago: Stewart-Warner.

Stone, C. N. 1989. *Regime Politics: Governing Atlanta, 1946–1988.* Lawrence: University Press of Kansas.

Tickell, A., and J. A. Peck. 1995. "Social Regulation after Fordism: Regulation Theory, Neo-liberalism and the Global-Local Nexus." *Economy and Society* 24: 357–86.

350

Andrew E. G. Jonas

Contributors

Shawn Banasick is a doctoral student in geography at West Virginia University. His research interests are in global and regional economic restructuring, uneven development, and Japan and the Pacific Rim. He lived and worked in Japan for several years.

Lee Lucas Berman received her M.A. in geography with a graduate certificate in women's studies from the University of Kentucky. While on leave from her studies, she served as an organizer for the Hotel Employees' and Restaurant Employees' International Union, Local 34, at Yale University, before assuming her current position as adjunct faculty in geography at Southern Connecticut State University. The author's academic and activist interests combine to inform her research interests.

Meghan Cope received her Ph.D. in geography from the University of Colorado at Boulder and is assistant professor of geography at the State University of New York at Buffalo. The intersection of labor issues, social relations, and a geographic perspective continues to shape her research interests.

Altha J. Cravey earned a doctorate in geography from the University of Iowa, where she was a recipient of the Iowa Fellowship. She is a former active member of the International Brotherhood of Electrical Workers. Her publications and research center around globalization, labor, and gender issues in contemporary Mexico. She is assistant professor of geography at the University of North Carolina at Chapel Hill.

Robert Q. Hanham is associate professor of geography at West Virginia University. His research interests are in global and regional economic restructuring, uneven development, political economy, and labor geography.

351

Andrew Herod received his Ph.D. from Rutgers University and is associate professor of geography at the University of Georgia. His research focuses on the political economy of capitalist development, specifically the spatiality of labor unionism and the role played by unions in shaping the geography of capitalism. He is coeditor (with Gearóid Ó Tuathail and Susan Roberts) of *An Unruly World? Globalization, Governance, and Geography.*

Andrew E. G. Jonas is lecturer in the Department of Geography, University of Hull, United Kingdom. He received a Ph.D. from Ohio State University. His research interests are U.S. urban policy and politics, labor and community responses to deindustrialization, and conservation policy in California. He has published articles in *Economic Geography, Regional Studies, Society and Space, Journal of Urban Affairs, Transactions of the Institute of British Geographers, Urban Geography, Political Geography, Antipode,* and *Area.* He recently completed a two-year National Science Foundation project on habitat conservation planning and urban development in Southern California and is coediting a book on critical perspectives on the city as a growth machine.

Don Mitchell is associate professor of geography at Syracuse University. He is the author of *The Lie of the Land: Migrant Workers and the California Landscape* (Minnesota, 1996). In addition to issues of labor, Mitchell conducts research on the political use of public space by marginalized groups. He is the North American editor of *Ecumene: A Journal of Environment, Culture, and Meaning.*

Brian Page is assistant professor of geography at the University of Colorado at Denver. His major research interests are economic geography, historical geography, and political economy. He has written articles on the meatpacking industry, historical regional development in the Midwest, and the restructuring of U.S. agriculture.

Lydia A. Savage is assistant professor of geography in the Department of Geography-Anthropology at the University of Southern Maine. She received her doctorate in geography from Clark University. Her research focuses on women workers and labor-union organizing in the service sector, particularly the health-care industry.

Richard A. Walker is professor and chair of geography at the University of California, Berkeley. He received a B.A. in economics from Stanford University and a doctorate in geography and environmental engineering at Johns Hopkins

Contributors

University. He has written on a diverse range of topics in economic and urban geography, as well as environmental policy, philosophy, and California studies. He is coauthor, with Michael Storper, of *The Capitalist Imperative: Territory, Technology, and Industrial Growth* (1989) and, with Andrew Sayer, of *The New Social Economy: Reworking the Division of Labor* (1992). He is now at work on a book on the economic, political, and cultural geography of the San Francisco Bay Area. Walker is editor of *Antipode: A Radical Journal of Geography* and a longtime activist in public affairs and on campus.

Jane Wills is lecturer in human geography at the University of Southampton, England. Her research interests include trade unionism, European industrial relations, and the changing world of work. She is coauthor (with Ron Martin and Peter Sunley) of *Union Retreat and the Regions: The Shrinking Landscape of Organised Labour* (1996) and coeditor (with Roger Lee) of *Geographies of Economies* (1997).

353

Contributors

Index

Note: The word *union* does not appear as a subject category, given the prevalence of this subject throughout the book. I have attempted to use more specific categories that would be more useful. A.H.

ABB company, 60
Abernathy, Ralph, 216
ACLU. *See* American Civil Liberties Union
Adams, Harold, 316, 321 n. 1
Adams, Luciene, 304, 307
Adelson, A., 248
AEEU. *See* Amalgamated Engineering and Electrical Union
AEF. *See* Amalgamated Engineering and Foundry Union
AEU. *See* Amalgamated Engineering Union
AF. *See* Associated Farmers
AFL. *See* American Federation of Labor
AFL–CIO. *See* American Federation of Labor and Congress of Industrial Organizations
African-Americans: Justice for Janitors campaign and, 238–44; workers in California agriculture, 200; workers in meatpacking industry, 269
Agnew, J., 45
Agricultural Workers' Industrial League (AWIL), 159
AIRCO company (Mexico), 88–90
Alameda Plan, 179
Alexander, R., 92, 93
Alinsky, Saul, 278, 334
Amalgamated Engineering and Electrical Union (AEEU), 145, 149 n. 8, 150 nn.

9, 10; 153 n. 24. *See also* Amalgamated Engineering Union
Amalgamated Engineering and Foundry Union (AEF), 150 n. 10 *See also* Amalgamated Engineering Union
Amalgamated Engineering Union (AEU), 137, 144, 150 n. 10. *See also* Engineering industry, unionism in
Amalgamated Meat Cutters and Butcher Workmen (AMCBW), 256, 257, 264, 266, 268–70, 272–80, 286–89, 290 n. 10, 291 n. 12, 293 n. 15, 293 n. 23
Amalgamated Society of Engineers (ASE), 150 n. 10. *See also* Amalgamated Engineering Union
Amalgamated Union of Engineering Workers (AUEW), 138, 150 nn. 10, 12. *See also* Amalgamated Engineering Union
AMCBW. *See* Amalgamated Meat Cutters and Butcher Workmen
America, Central: solidarity with by U.S. workers, 22
America, Latin: U.S. labor movement's links with, 16, 43
American Civil Liberties Union (ACLU), 163, 164, 168, 169
American Federation of Labor (AFL), 9, 16, 20, 29, 159, 187, 191 n. 16, 245 n. 1, 256, 264, 266, 272, 273, 275, 279, 290 n. 10, 291 n. 15, 299, 331, 332. *See also* American Federation of Labor and Congress of Industrial Organizations; *and* Congress of Industrial Organizations

355

Index

Index

Index

359

Index

362

Index

364

Index

Index

Index

Piore, M., 235
Pirozzolo, L., 214
Pittston Coal Company (United States), 151–52 n. 17
place: political economy of, xvi; politics of, 186, 188; sense of, 2, 5, 14, 114. *See also* competition between places
place-based activities, 99, 126, 129, 132, 146–47, 183, 245, 255, 265, 278, 289, 336, 340, 343, 345, 346–47
Planned Manufacturing District (PMD), 260–61, 334–35, 340, 341, 344
Plaza Accord, 108
Podkrepa (Bulgaria), 62, 69 n. 4
Poland: foreign investment in, 59, 60; membership in NATO, 46; privatization in, 49, 50; Solidarity union, 18, 64, 69 n. 4; unions in, 53, 58, 61, 64
Popke, E., 45
Portelli, A., 149 n. 5
Porter, Michael, xvii
post–Cold War. *See* Cold War
post-Fordism, 8, 23, 207, 346. *See also* Fordism
postindustrialism, 343–44. *See also* deindustrialization; *and* industrialization
postmodernism, xv
Prasad, P., 214
Pratt, G., 303, 315, 346
Pravda, A., 52
Preteceille, Edmund, 325
PRI. *See* Partido Revolucionario Institucional
Private Ownership Funds, 50. *See also* Romania
privatization: in Eastern Europe, 40, 48–58; in Mexico, 80–88; union responses to in Britain, 23
PRM. *See* Partido Revolucionario Mexicano
product cycle theory, xiii
PRONASOL (Mexico), 84, 96 n. 6
Proposition 1 (California), 184–87, 189
Pulido, Laura, 243
Putnam, Robert, xvii
PWIU. *See* Packinghouse Workers' Industrial Union
PWOC. *See* Packinghouse Workers' Organizing Committee

RAC. *See* Ravenswood Aluminum Corporation
race: and division of labor, 258, 270, 276–77, 290 n. 9, 299, 300, 303, 312–17, 319–20, 321, 333; and union organizing in the United States, 225–49, 263–93, 316; ideologies of, 168, 172
Radosh, R., 39, 46
Railroad Labor Act (RLA), 11
Rainbow Coalition. *See* Jackson, Jesse
Ramírez, J., 87, 88, 89
Ranger, T., 125
Ravenswood Aluminum Corporation (RAC) (West Virginia), 16, 18, 152 n. 19
Raybeck, J., 272
Reagan, Ronald, xi, xii, 228, 247 n. 7, 336
Redclift, M., 292 n. 17
Rediker, M., 161
Rees, J., 23, 24, 130, 131, 148 n. 2
Reeve, P., 218, 221 n. 11
regulation (of labor). *See* labor: regulation of
Reich, M., 105
relations (industrial). *See* labor: relations, after Communism; relations, in Britain; relations system, in Japan; relations, under Communism
Rengo (Japan), 43, 109, 111–12, 114
Retail Clerks' International Association, 287. *See also* United Food and Commercial Workers
Reynosa (Mexico), 82
Rieve, Emil, 297
Rigby, David, xiii
right-to-work (RTW) laws, 12, 29 n. 4, 123
RLA. *See* Railroad Labor Act
RMALC (Mexico), 93
Roberts, Susan, xiii
Robito, Casparino, 315
Rodríguez, J., 80
Rogers, J., 229
Romania: foreign investment in, 59; privatization in, 49–50; unions in, 52, 54, 58, 61, 64
Roosevelt, Franklin, 6, 298
Rose, G., 205
Rose, J., 227, 228

367

Ross, Andrew, 220 n. 7
Rosswurm, S., 279, 289
Rouse, W., 228, 235, 236
Roxborough, I., 78
Rozenblatt, P., 27
Ruble, B., 52
Rusonik, S., 16, 17, 21
Russia: privatization in, 49; unions in, 66.
   See also Union of Soviet Socialist
   Republics

Sadler, D., 14, 39, 123, 326
Said, E., 149 n. 4
Salinas de Gortari, Carlos, 96 n. 6
Samuel, R., 149 n. 6
Sanbetsu (Japan), 104–5, 109
Sandberg, Carl, 263–64, 289 n. 1
Sanpo (Japan), 103–4
Šarčevi;aac, P., 50
Sassen, S., 234
Saturn Motors, 8
Saunders, P., 148 n. 1
Savage, Lydia A., 199, 201, 234, 246 n. 6,
   248 n. 13
Savage, M., 148 nn. 1, 2, 190 n. 2
Saxenian, Annalee, xiii
Saxton, A., 183
Sayer, Andrew, xiii, 105, 106, 148 n. 3,
   228, 234
scale: conflicts over, 19, 23, 83, 100, 103,
   107, 127, 134, 138, 160–62, 167;
   geographic, and political organization,
   19, 20, 24, 27, 40, 42–43, 67, 94, 135,
   140, 169, 178, 180, 183, 186, 188–89,
   200, 240, 259, 303, 346; of analysis, xvi,
   27; theories of, 18, 178. *See also* solidarity:
   practice of
SCAP. *See* Supreme Command for Allied
   Powers
Schoenberger, Erica, xiv
Schultz, G., 285, 286
Schwartz, Pepper, 204
Scott, Allen, xiii, 265
Scott, J., 43
Screpanti, E., 134
SEIU. *See* Service Employees' International
   Union
368   Seiyama, T., 101

Seniority (systems of), 275, 308, 321 n. 1
Serbia: unions in, 62
Serrin, W., 205, 214, 334
Service Employees' International Union,
   199, 225, 235–45, 246 n. 5
Sewell, Richard B., 209
Shaffer, J., 240, 241, 242, 243, 244
Shaiken, Harley, xii
Shapiro, D., 148 n. 1
Shirai, T., 110
Shorter, E., 4, 137, 149 n. 7
Shuhoku Bus case (1968), 103
Shunto (Japan), 107
Sidaway, J., 45
Siemens company, 60
Simmons, L., 327, 345
Singapore: unions in, 111
Sirianni, C., 246 n. 6
Skaggs, J. M., 265, 284
SLC. *See* Stockyards Labor Council
Slovak Republic: unions in, 54, 58, 61,
   63–64
Slovakia. *See* Slovak Republic
Slovenia: foreign investment in, 59;
   privatization in, 50; unions in, 61, 64
Smith, A., 47, 50
Smith, D., 131
Smith, J., 149 n. 7
Smith, M., 334
Smith, N., 147, 153 n. 25, 161, 178, 183,
   188
Smith, Peggie, 220 n. 9
Snowbelt–Sunbelt shift, 12, 255
SNTOAC (Mexico), 92
social unionism, 279, 288
Socialist Workers Party (Britain), 151 n. 14
Sohyo (Japan), 109–11
Soja, Ed, 3, 132
Sokal, Alan, xv
Solidarity (Polish union), 18, 64, 69 n. 4.
   See also Poland
solidarity: "accommodatory," 22; and
   geographic scale, 18; and space, 21, 123,
   133–35, 332; demonstration effect of,
   125, 127, 133–34, 257, 280, 285;
   international, 19, 90–93, 95, 112–15,
   338; practice of, 138, 140, 143–44, 146,
   199, 213, 270; "transformatory," 22

Solidarity Network Asia, 115
Sony Corporation, 92–93
South Korea: as source of investments in
  Eastern Europe, 60; Japanese investment
  in; 43, 113; unions in, 110, 111; workers
  from in California agriculture, 200
South Wales: coal industry unions in, 15,
  131; popular socialism in, 131
South Wales Miners' Industrial Union, 131
Southall, H., 18, 19, 39
Soviet Union. *See* Union of Soviet Socialist
  Republics
space: "spatial fix," 16, 99, 104, 106, 109,
  115; theorized as container, 5; transmittal
  of ideas across, 18, 19, 20, 67, 125, 129,
  131, 133, 140, 145–47; used politically,
  82, 83, 93, 115, 133, 188, 198–200,
  205, 209, 214, 218, 221 n. 12, 225,
  237–38, 242, 280. *See also* class: and space
Spain, D., 233
Sparke, Matt, xi
"spatial fix." *See* space: "spatial fix"
Spencerism, 25, 131
Spivak, Gayatri, xv
state, the: and geopolitics, 45; and ownership of enterprises, 48–51; and industrialization (*see* industrialization); attack
  on unions by, 83; union relationship with,
  259, 327, 328
Stedman-Jones, G., 131
steel industry. *See* metal industry
Stein, W., 183
Steven, R., 106
Stevens, B., 214, 216, 217
Stevens, M., 13, 27
Stewart-Warner Corporation, 259, 260,
  327–30
Stockyards Labor Council (SLC) (Chicago),
  269–70, 273
Stone, C., 343
Stone, R., 49
Storper, Michael, xiii, 228, 265
Street, P., 275, 276, 277, 278, 290 n. 11
strikes, 14, 20, 52, 58, 88, 89, 101, 104,
  134–35, 137–45, 147, 151 n. 14, 159,
  163, 164, 178, 180, 181, 183, 185, 205,
  213–17, 236, 240, 268, 270–71, 273,
  275–76, 280, 284, 285, 298, 332, 333,

336, 338; and strikebreaking, 173, 271;
  British miners' strike (1984–85), 11, 19,
  23–25, 124, 130, 148 n. 2, 169, 191 n.
  8, 197
subcontracting: by firms, 105–7; of labor
  (*see* labor)
suburbanization, 259, 303, 317, 318, 319,
  320; role of unions in, 13; to avoid
  unions, 13. *See also* urbanization
Sumida Electric Company, 113
Sumiya, T., 105, 106, 108
Sunkist, 170
Sunley, P., 24, 26, 27, 39, 130, 148 n. 1,
  233, 325, 326, 327, 342, 344
Sun-Maid Raisin Growers' Association, 171
Supreme Command for Allied Powers
  (SCAP), 104–5
Suzuki company, 64
Sweden: as migration destination, 56
Sweeney, John, 225, 226, 245 nn. 1, 2; 246
  n. 5

Taft, William Howard, 191 n. 14, 203
Taft-Hartley Act, 29 n. 4, 279, 291 n. 15
Taira, K., 105
Taiwan: unions in, 111
Takeda System Company case (1983), 103
Tamaulipas (Mexico), 82, 92
Taylorism, 229
Teague, C., 170
Teamsters. *See* International Brotherhood of
  Teamsters
technological change, 281–87. *See also*
  mechanization: problems of in
  meatpacking
Tepperman, J., 210
textile industry, 10, 257, 260
Textile Workers' Union of America
  (TWUA), 257, 297, 299, 303, 315, 345
TGWU. *See* Transport and General Workers'
  Union
Thailand: Japanese investment in, 43, 113
Thatcher, Margaret, xi, xii, 11. *See also*
  Conservative Party (Britain)
Thelen, K., 55, 70 n. 11
Thompson, E. P., xii, 124, 132, 149 n. 5
Thrift, Nigel, xiii, 129, 232
Tickell, A., 325, 346

Tijuana (Mexico), 82
Tilly, C., 4, 20, 134, 137, 149 n. 7, 228, 230, 231, 232
Tilly, N., 149 n. 6
time-space compression, 132
Timex company, 144
Tocher, John, 138, 151 n. 15
Toyota motor company, 106, 107–8, 111
Trade Union Law of 1947 (Japan), 101–2
traditions. *See* labor: cultures of
transnational corporations (TNCs) 77, 111–13, 115
Transport and General Workers' Union (TGWU), 338
Truman, Harry S., 279
Tsuru, S., 101, 105
turnover: of union officials in Eastern Europe, problems of, 63

UAW. *See* United Auto Workers
UE. *See* United Electrical, Radio and Machine Workers of America
UFCW. *See* United Food and Commercial Workers
Uhlíř, Jan, 55, 60
UICCUED. *See* University of Illinois at Chicago, Center for Urban Economic Development
UMWA. *See* United Mine Workers of America
Uniform Commercial Code (United States), 9
"Union Cities" campaign, 246 n. 5
Union of Democratic Miners, 25. *See also* National Union of Mineworkers
Union of Soviet Socialist Republics: foreign investment in successor states of, 58–61; privatization in successor states of, 49; unions in successor states of, 41, 46, 62, 66
"Union Summer" campaign, 246 n. 5
unionism: business, 293 n. 23; community-based, 235, 327, 340, 345; company, 290 n. 11; dual, 256, 257, 266, 280, 287, 289; enterprise (Japan), 103–5, 108, 115; "geographic," 200, 229–30, 236, 247 n. 10, 248 n. 16; industrial, 278,

280, 291 n. 11; "occupational," 236; problems of in Eastern Europe, 53–58; "social," 279, 288; Soviet model of, 52–53
United Auto Workers (UAW), 8, 16, 21, 219 n. 2, 331, 333, 343; split of U.S. and Canadian segments, 16, 17
United Cannery, Agricultural, Packing, and Allied Workers of America (UCAPAWA), 187, 191 n. 16
United Electrical, Radio and Machine Workers of America (UE), 92, 259, 327, 330–33, 336, 342–44. *See also* International Union of Electrical, Radio, and Machine Workers
United Food and Commercial Workers (UFCW), 287, 288, 293 n. 24
United Mine Workers of America (UMWA), 272. *See also* Lewis, John L.
United Nations, 59
United Packinghouse Workers of America (UPWA), 256–57, 274–80, 284–89, 291 n. 14, 292 n. 20
United States: as migration destination, 56; as source of foreign investment in Eastern Europe, 60; auto production in, 17; Chamber of Commerce, 87; geopolitical concerns of during Cold War, 109; government support for Japanese labor, 101; National Administrative Office, 92; relations with Mexico, 41–42; union organizing in, 18, 20, 22; unions from operating in Eastern Europe, 54
United States Department of Agriculture (USDA), 282
United States Steel Corporation, 334
United Steelworkers of America (USW), 16, 21, 331
United Workers' Association-United Electrical Workers, 327, 333, 336–37, 340, 341–45, 347. *See also* United Electrical, Radio and Machine Workers of America
University of Illinois at Chicago, Center for Urban Economic Development (UICCUED), 340, 357. *See also* Chicago
Upham, F., 106

370

Index

UPWA. *See* United Packinghouse Workers of America

urbanization: historical geography of, 13. *See also* suburbanization

Urry, J., 130, 148 n. 1

USDA. *See* United States Department of Agriculture

USWA. *See* United Steelworkers of America

UWA-UE. *See* United Workers' Association-United Electrical Workers

Utada, T., 104, 107, 108

vagrancy: efforts to control in California, 126, 165

Valenzuela, A., 239, 243, 244, 246 n. 5

van der Linden, M., 39, 46, 133, 134

van Holthoon, F., 39, 46, 133, 134

Vannorsdall, John, 220 n. 5

Velázquez, Fidel, 96 n. 5

Visegrad (countries), 64

Volkswagen motor company, 60

Voos, P., 228

Wagner Act. *See* National Labor Relations Act

Walby, S., 148 n. 1

Waldinger, R., 235, 239, 243, 244, 246 n. 5

Walker, D., 290

Walker, R., xiii, 105, 106, 228, 234, 259, 320

Wallace, Henry, 279

Walnut Growers' Association (California), 170

War Labor Disputes Act (United States), 275

Warde, A., 148 n. 2

Warf, Barney, xiii

Warren, Earl, 160, 179, 180, 181, 182, 191 n. 13

Warren, W., 291 n. 13

Warrington (England), 25, 125

Washington, Harold, 328, 335, 340, 344

Webber, Michael, xiii

Weber, A., 285, 286

Weber, Alfred, xiii, 4, 6, 255, 265. *See also* locational analysis: Weberian tradition of

Wedderburn, Lord, 169

Weisman, L., 210

Welch, L. S., 203

Welwyn Garden City (England), 25

West Virginia (United States), 16

Western Growers' Protective Association (WGPA), 171, 172–73

Westinghouse company, 331

WFTU. *See* World Federation of Trade Unions

WGPA. *See* Western Growers' Protective Association

Wial, H., 227, 229, 230, 233, 235, 236, 246 n. 6, 248 n. 16

Wiewel, W., 335

Wilhelm, John, 206, 219 n. 2, 220 n. 10

Williams, Chester, 169

Williams, E., 82

Williams, P., 129

Williams, Raymond, 131, 148 n. 4, 149 n. 6

Williams, Rhonda, 220 n. 9

Williams, W., 265

Williamson, H., 104, 105, 110, 111, 112, 113, 114, 115

Wills, Jane, xi, 20, 25, 26, 27, 39, 124, 125, 126, 127, 134, 148 n. 1, 149 n. 6, 233, 325, 326, 327, 342, 344

Windmuller, J., 39, 65

Wirin, A., 164, 168

Wobblies. *See* Industrial Workers of the World

Wong, K., 239, 243, 244, 246 n. 5

Wood, P., 227, 234

Woodiwiss, A., 101, 102

Woolf, R., 220 n. 7

work: regularization of, 257, 298–99, 306–7, 311–12, 315, 317–18, 320, 321; rules, 10, 15, 102–3, 257, 298. *See also* labor

Works Councils, 55; European Union directive on, 70 n. 11

World Bank: activities of in Mexico, 76; union pressure on in Eastern Europe, 65

World Federation of Trade Unions (WFTU), 68 n. 2, 109

371

Index

World Industry Councils, 22
Wright, Melissa, xi
Wulkan, F., 216

Yale Non-Faculty Action Committee
   (YNFAC), 219 n. 2
Yale University, 198, 199, 203–21
Yazaki company, 113

Yeager, M., 267
Yugoslavia, 62

zaibatsu, 42, 100, 105
Zeitlin, M., 239, 243, 244, 246 n. 5
Zenro (Japan), 110. *See also* Domei
Zenrokyo (Japan), 111
Zenroren (Japan), 111, 114

Index